CW00420383

Portrait of a Dalai Lama

Portrait of a Dalai Lama
The Life and Times of the Great Thirteenth

Sir Charles Bell

Wisdom Publications London

First published in 1946 by Wm. Collins, London.

This edition published in 1987.
Wisdom Publications, 23 Dering Street, London W1, England.

British Library Cataloguing in Publication Data
Bell, *Sir* Charles
    Portrait of a Dalai Lama: the life and times of the Great
    Thirteenth.
    1. Thub-bstan-rgya-mtsho, *Dalai Lama XIII*
    2. Dalai Lamas – Biography
    I. Title
    951.5'0924   BQ7935.T484

ISBN 0 86171 055 X

Set in Garamond 10½ on 13 point, and printed and bound by
Eurasia Press of Singapore on 60 gsm cream Sunningdale
Opaque paper supplied by Link Publishing Papers of West
Byfleet, Surrey.

Contents

Preface

The value of a biography is based mainly on the personal knowledge of his subject by the writer. The motive of the present volume is to set forth impartially, yet sympathetically, the character and career of the Thirteenth Dalai Lama. The reader will appreciate the significance of the close friendship with which he honoured me. That in a country generally hostile to the foreigner the Dalai Lama could form an abiding friendship with a European, was a feature in his character, and should be made clear in his biography.

My thanks are due to Sir Robert Holland, K.C.I.E., C.S.I., for reading my typescript and making some useful suggestions; to the Rev. Canon Stannage Boyle, D.D., for reading it, and going through it with me carefully and in detail; and to the London *Times* for permission to reproduce the account of my being asked to pray in the temple at Samye. My chief indebtedness, that to my Tibetan friends, has, I hope, been made clear in the text.

Chronological Table

1391 First Dalai Lama, Gedun Drub, born.
1475 Second Dalai Lama, Gedun Gyatso, born.
1543 Third Dalai Lama, Sonam Gyatso, born.
1588 Fourth Dalai Lama, Yonten Gyatso, born.
1617 Fifth Dalai Lama, Ngawang Lobsang Gyatso, born.
1683 Sixth Dalai Lama, Tsanyang Gyatso, born.
1708 Seventh Dalai Lama, Kelsang Gyatso, born.
1758 Eighth Dalai Lama, Jampal Gyatso, born.
17th and 18th centuries, Christian missionaries in Lhasa.
1806 Ninth Dalai Lama, Lungtog Gyatso, born.
1816 Tenth Dalai Lama, Tsultrim Gyatso, born.
1838 Eleventh Dalai Lama, Khedrup Gyatso, born.
1856 Twelfth Dalai Lama, Trinlay Gyatso, born.
1876 Thirteenth Dalai Lama, Thubten Gyatso, born.
1895 Dalai Lama takes up full spiritual and secular power.
1904 British politico-military expedition to Lhasa.
1904 Dalai Lama flees to Mongolia.
1908 Dalai Lama in religious exercises at Wutaishan.
1908 Dalai Lama in Peking.
1909 Dalai Lama returns to Lhasa.
1910 Treaty between Britain and Bhutan.
1910 Dalai Lama flees from Chinese invasion and arrives in India.
1911 Chinese Revolution.
1912 Dalai Lama returns to Tibet.
1912 Dalai Lama repudiates Chinese over-lordship.
1913-14 Simla Conference.

1914-18 First World War.

1920-21 My discussions with the Dalai Lama in Lhasa.

1921 I leave Tibet, and retire from government service.

1923 Panchen Lama flees from Tibet.

1927 and after, Chinese missions come to Lhasa.

1927 A party from the U.S.S.R. comes to Lhasa.

1932 Dalai Lama publishes his Political Testament.

1933 Thirteenth Dalai Lama dies.

1935 Fourteenth Dalai Lama, Tenzin Gyatso, born.

1937 Panchen Lama dies.

1940 Fourteenth Dalai Lama enthroned.

Part One
The Stage

I A Unique Figure in World History

The Dalai Lamas of Tibet are unique. There has been nobody like them throughout the history of the world. During the last three hundred years they have been the rulers of the country on the religious side; and when they so desire, on the secular side as well. But the power does not descend from father to son. Each is discovered by curious methods that will be explained later. The manner of finding them is unprecedented; the nature of the power that they exercise is unparalleled.

Yet again, the Thirteenth Dalai Lama, who passed away in December, 1933, was unique among all the Dalai Lamas, for he was the only one among them to exercise the worldly, as well as the spiritual, power throughout the whole of his adult life, that is to say, for thirty-seven years.

Lastly, there is not likely to be another Dalai Lama exercising the secular power as he did, because other nations are endeavouring to gain influence in Tibet. China and Britain have already done so; Russia and Japan may push in later on, if they are able. Any or all of these will directly or indirectly lessen the Dalai Lama's authority, both religious and secular.

Thus the Thirteenth Dalai Lama played a part which, through out the whole course of world history, none had played before, and – as it seems – none will play again. The first and probably the last. His biography ought to be written.

Though I did not meet him face to face till he was thirty-four years old, I knew him far better than any other European did; indeed better than any Chinese or other Asiatic, except his own Tibetans and a few Mongols. I have therefore, however inadequately, written this biography.

Charles Bell with the Dalai Lama (seated) with Maharaj-Kumar Sidkeong of Sikkim in Calcutta, 1910.

My knowledge of him was derived mainly from numerous meetings and conversations. Usually he and I were alone in his room together. I therefore have to bring myself frequently into the story. Who that knew him intimately could ever forget him? There was a strong personality inside that small body, and he struggled manfully against mighty odds.

A biography of the late Dalai Lama was compiled under the orders of the Tibetan Government. It was completed in February, 1940, between six and seven years after the Dalai Lama's death in December, 1933, and is entitled *The Wonderful Rosary of Jewels*. The Regent of Tibet was so good as to give me a copy of it, printed from the wooden blocks made in the Tibetan style. Sir Basil Gould, the Representative of the Government of India in Tibet since 1935, kindly arranged for the translation of the relevant parts. This translation was supervised by my old friends Raja and Rani S. T. Dorji.

This biography, which reached me after I had completed mine, deals with the Dalai Lama's life on typically Oriental lines. In it he does not figure just as a human being, but mainly as an Incarnation of Tibet's patron deity, Chenrezig, and therefore free from human errors, all-knowing, all-powerful. It is on the lines of former Tibetan biographies – after the usual Oriental style – in which the person, whose life is described, does everything right, nothing wrong. In short, it does not portray the Dalai Lama's character as a human being, and would not appeal to many Western readers.

At the same time it contains many authentic and interesting facts, some of which are suitable for a biography on Western lines. I have found room therefore for a selection of these.

To attempt to delineate the Dalai Lama without his background would be futile. Let me therefore commence by explaining some of the main characteristics of this country and people, and let me explain how I was able to enter the land, and to gain an intimate contact with this Thirteenth Dalai Lama. I call him the Thirteenth Dalai Lama, and other Dalai Lamas also by their numbers in the succession, for Tibetans do the same. But strictly speaking, there have not been fourteen Dalai Lamas, but one

Dalai Lama, and one only, returning for thirteen successive lives.

In Tibet, the loftiest land on earth, even valleys run higher than the summit of any mountain in Europe, Canada or the United States. Wide plains, often bare; it is usually too cold for trees to grow; for hundreds of miles you will see no plant more than six inches high. The greater part of Tibet is icebound during seven or eight months in the year; even the inhabited areas can be cultivated for a few months only. But there is not much snow; it is almost too dry for snow to form. Sunshine is the rule, though less so during the rain months of July and August. But the strong cold wind, which often attains to the force of a gale, sweeps the land; it is especially violent during winter and spring.

The rain clouds come from the south-west, storming over the Indian Ocean and across India herself, and beat against the gigantic mountains of the Himalaya[1] that separate India from Tibet; two hundred inches, and more, of rain fall each year on the Indian side of the eastern Himalaya, but only seven inches fall in Tibet. To such an extent is the rarefied Tibetan climate dry and cold, that meat keeps good for three years, grain certainly for five hundred, and possibly for five thousand.

So clear is the air that those grey-brown rocks you think three miles away are in fact thirteen. A lake – or is it just another of those mirages? – shimmers in the distance. Over vast areas in the more elevated districts you can ride for days without meeting a human being. In other parts of the country you will find them spread out along broad valleys and level plains cultivating their crops, chiefly of barley, peas and mustard, but also in a lesser degree, of turnips and radishes, wheat and buckwheat.

The people belong to what is loosely termed the Tartar branch of the human race. The majority is related in physical type to the peoples of the steppes and deserts farther to the north. They are not closely related to the Chinese of China proper. They are still in the feudal age. By occupation they are mainly farmers, and, in a lesser degree, shepherds. Many take to trade. One man in every three is a monk, one woman in every fifteen or thereabouts is a nun. Monasteries are everywhere, and some of them are huge; most families send at least one of the sons as a monk.

There they are, farmers and shepherds, noblemen and beggars, monks and nuns, traders, hermits, pilgrims and all. The women hold a strong position; they work and laugh and sing with the men; they are not shut behind curtains and veils, as in India, nor have their feet been crushed into an unnatural smallness, as in China.

The staple foods are yak's meat, mutton, barley-flour, cheese, salt and tea. With the tea is mixed butter and a kind of soda which is found as a white powder on the margins of lakes, and mainly on the highlands of northern and western Tibet. The people drink from twenty to fifty cups a day of ordinary tea-cup size. Europeans dislike it intensely, but it is not unwholesome.

The climate and food have produced a race exceptionally robust and hardy, though not particularly long-lived. But they are handicapped by venereal diseases, due to their laxity in sexual relations. This has caused the population, so sorely needed, to grow less and less. The huge number of monks, who are celibate, leads to the same result. Pneumonia, goitre, influenza and smallpox are also prevalent, the last being greatly dreaded. There is no malaria, or cholera, or typhoid fever. Children have to rough it in food and other ways, and many die young.

The main outer garment of a Tibetan, man or woman, is known as the chuba. It is very roomy and has long sleeves which are usually tucked back, so as to allow free play to the hands, but when pulled forward may project far beyond the finger-tips. When you pull them out, you indicate that you are one who has no need to work with his hands; and you will do this especially if you adopt Western ways so far as to have your photograph taken. The chuba is long enough to fall to the ankles, but is caught up at the waist by a cloth girdle, so that it pouches out, providing a capacious pocket, in which is carried a cup for eating and drinking, as well as other odds and ends, perhaps even a small dog. Laymen wear this gown down to the knees; women to the ankles. The ordinary chuba is made of cloth which is woven in Tibet, and is far more durable than the machine-made foreign cloth.

In winter sheepskin chubas are much worn, especially by

those shepherds and herdsmen that encamp on the higher altitudes. The wealthier classes wear gowns of silk in summer and winter. Monks and nuns have their heads close-shaved, and wear robes of a dull red colour with a wide skirt.

Boots are of cloth, felt or leather of various colours, usually including red. They rise to the knee with a slit behind, and are tied with gay-coloured woollen garters, three of four feet long. The soles are of yak hide and have no heels.

Hats are of felt or cloth, and are usually trimmed with fur in winter. Of late years there has been a growing influx of Homburg felt hats imported from Europe, and especially, at very cheap prices, from Japan.

The women wear head-dresses of red cloth on a wooden frame, sewn with corals, seed pearls and turquoises. Their aprons are woven in varied colours, and often so broad that they nearly meet at the back.

Variation indeed there is within moderate limits, but the above kinds of dress are typical over the larger part of Tibet.

What a marvellous spectacle it is to see a cavalcade of high Tibetan officials in their beautiful Chinese brocades, golden and blue, mounted on their shaggy ponies and mules, coming over the crest of a pass and descending towards you, lit by the brilliant Tibetan sunshine in a cloudless sky. The women ride astride like the men, in their red head-dress frames, silk robes, striped aprons and high black velvet top-boots, and numerous ornaments. It is a riot of colour, but all in harmony.

As a rule Tibetans grow old rapidly after fifty years of age. They possess strong bodies and courage. They are not cleanly in their persons, perhaps even less than the British and other European nations were during the feudal age, in which the Tibetans are now. But it must be remembered that the climate is Arctic, the winds are violent, and the houses have no heating arrangements, nor even glass in their windows, but only thin cloth.

They adhere closely to their traditions. You ask them why they do this or that. They reply "It is the custom," and the ordinary Tibetan will give no further reason. They are intensely devoted to Buddhism. I could hardly talk to a Tibetan for fifteen minutes on any subject whatever, without the conversation coming round in some way or other to the all-embracing religion.

The people are orderly and yet independent; a scanty population of mountaineers, inhabiting a country one-third the size of the United States, cannot be governed on narrow lines. The rulers themselves recognise their own and their people's obstinacy, and so it comes that a fair measure of democracy is mixed with their feudalism.

They are industrious, and will not shrink from heavy work when necessary. During the harvest in September the crops must be reaped before they are struck by the inevitable frost; then the men and women, boys and girls, work for eighteen hours out of each twenty-four. When working in groups they sing, especially the women, for Tibetans are a merry race, and many indeed hold that unless a woman sings she must be doing her work badly. They are by nature artistic, and love colour, dress, ceremonial and pageantry, and are expert at them. In making calculations they are weak, but nevertheless they are venturesome in business. A trader will buy a good pony, a striking saddle-cloth, with a first-rate saddle, in order to impress clients with the idea that he is wealthy and therefore dependable. He gets into debt for this purpose but hopes to make good later on.

A love of hospitality lies deep in their nature. They like to entertain and to be entertained, to give as well as to receive presents. Heavy drinkers they are, but mainly of their barley beer, which makes them merry and fuddled, but not quarrelsome. Being inveterate gamblers, they may often be seen sitting on the ground in small circles, each thumping down the solitary die from the palm of his hand on a pad, with an exulting grunt, as though to raise thereby the value of the throw. Such is the favourite gambling of the ordinary people; those who are educated and more wealthy will prefer gambling with dominoes, a game which was introduced from China, and carries heavier gains and losses.

Foreigners may call Tibetans callous and even cruel, but it should be remembered that their physical toughness prevents them from feeling pain as the Westerner feels it. A sense of comradeship is strong among them; they will readily befriend others who are in trouble. Indeed they have a marked capacity for friendship, but jealousy is strong also, especially among officials struggling for place and power. Certainly they are inquisitive, especially the less studious monks, who have a good deal of time to spare. When I have been in places where few or no Europeans have been before, the monks, young and old, would lie on the flat roofs of the houses, staring fixedly into my window. Anything new to them is an object of suspicion; they want to know the reason. On the whole Tibetans are quick to appraise the motives that underlie actions; they study keenly the character of others. Of Chinese or British officials stationed among them you will hear the remark about one that he is working for the purposes of his government; about another, that he is working for his own purposes.

From duke to peasant they have courteous manners, especially among the laity, and are charmingly free from self-consciousness. The great mass of the monks will easily become hostile to foreigners, for they feel instinctively that, being of a different religion, they will directly or indirectly harm their religion and lessen their influence. The laity are tolerant both in religious and social matters, but not the monkhood.

On the whole Tibetans are remarkably honest. During a residence of twenty years among them only twice was any of my property stolen, firstly a pair of razors, and secondly a tube of toothpaste; these removals being caused no doubt by their inquisitiveness about all things new and strange. They have a high standard of truthfulness; such at any rate was my experience.

In any subject under discussion they like to apply proverbs and old sayings. For instance, when discussing why Tibetan officials are apt to deal more severely with their own countrymen than with others, a Tibetan may say:

> If the fox be made king,
> He will above all be hard on foxes.

Shut away by her huge mountain masses from other nations,

Tibet through the ages has lived a life of her own. From India she has received Buddhism, which she has modified to suit her own instincts thereby evolving a strong national religion, the most precious of all her possessions. From China she has received many arts of material civilisation. Indians and Chinese, especially the latter, have come and gone; but even with the Chinese there has been on the whole no close relationship. With Mongolia the contact is more intimate; there is the sense of kinship here. Yet even Genghis-Khan, the great Mongol world-conqueror and his successors, though they subdued so many nations, never conquered Tibet. The mountain barriers keep out foreigners; the inhabitants are in sympathy with their mountains and do all they can to keep the stranger out.

When you come from Europe or America to Tibet, you are carried back several hundred years. You see a nation still in the feudal age. Great is the power of the nobles and squires over their tenants, who are either farmers tilling the more fertile plains and valleys, or shepherds, clad in their sheepskins, roaming over the mountains. With the shepherds are goats as well as sheep, and the highland cattle, known as yaks, with coats far thicker than the cattle of the Scottish Highlands. Those on the border-line between farmers and graziers usually combine both occupations.

There is no strong middle class. It is the monks who exercise the check on the feudal lords. For the Tibetans believe devoutly in their form of Buddhism, and the powerful influence of the monasteries embraces all. Even Buddha himself can do but little without the monks. The Buddha, the Law (i.e. the sacred books) and the Spiritual Community form one of the chief Trinities – perhaps the chief Trinity – of Tibetan Buddhism. And the monks are deeply rooted in their distrust of the foreigner, for they look on the Western nations as essentially irreligious, and likely to injure the Tibetan religion. Thus it comes that this people, simple but intelligent, independent yet orderly, hospitable yet suspicious, fear foreign intrusion as they fear very little else.

2   How I Came to Work in Tibet

Until recent years Europeans and Americans who went to Tibet had great difficulty in travelling even through the deserts and other out-of-the-way regions. Those who came nearer to the centres of interest were stopped by the people, who are quick to detect intruders. The natives would refuse to sell food or transport, and thus the travellers became helpless. Some official, escorted by wild-looking horsemen with swords, daggers and antiquated guns, might arrive and stop further movement into the country. This usually sufficed; it was only when the traveller tried even then to break away, and perhaps also wounded Tibetan religious feeling in a tactless manner, that he disappeared and was not heard of again. As a rule no violence was done, for the Tibetan Government feared subsequent complications with foreign powers. But the fact remains that until the British expedition of 1904, numbering some thousands of soldiers and armed with modern weapons of warfare, fought its way to Lhasa against untrained levies, many of whom were armed only with antiquated muzzle-loaders, no European had succeeded in penetrating to Lhasa for more than fifty years.

To me the fates were kind. I arrived in the Tibetan borderland on the north-eastern frontier of India in 1900. I was then nearly thirty years of age, and after working for nine years on the hot plains of Bengal, Bihar, and Orissa, as an Indian Civil Servant, was a physical wreck from malaria, typhoid fever and other ills. I could not take sick leave; my store of that had been exhausted in earlier attacks of illness. But the authorities posted me to Darjeeling in the eastern Himalaya, so that I might have a chance of recovery in the cool mountain air.

As soon as I was able to leave the hospital, I set about learning Tibetan in the hope of employment and better health in the cooler regions of Tibet or the borderland. As my teacher I engaged at first a gifted monk, who was born in Tibet and had worked for many years in a monastery not far from Gyangtse. He understood Hindustani, though not English, and in Hindustani he interpreted to me, until I could speak a little Tibetan. There was always in Darjeeling a large population of Tibetans of the labouring class, and so when I could understand and speak a little, I used to talk with one of these for an hour before breakfast each morning. It entailed early rising and extra work in addition to the daily work of the office, and many of my friends were satirical; but it was the only thing to do, and in the end I was rewarded.

This teacher was able to remain with me for only a month or two, as I was transferred to one of the outposts. I then engaged a tailor from Lhasa. He spoke the true Lhasan dialect, which is recognised by all Tibetans as the most correct form of Tibetan speech. My first teacher spoke a dialect nearly but not quite that of Lhasa. After a year in Darjeeling I passed the government examination in Tibetan.

About this time I was posted for two years to Kalimpong, to make a land settlement of that district. Kalimpong was a mountainous semi-Tibetan tract, which the British Government had annexed after a war with Bhutan thirty-six years before.

I found a little time to continue my Tibetan studies, and started to write a grammar of colloquial Tibetan and a small English-Tibetan colloquial dictionary. It should be mentioned that the written language differs widely from the colloquial, and is useless for conversational purposes. The language is a difficult one, and the best way to learn it seemed to be to write a colloquial grammar and small dictionary, because one has to make quite certain which are the words used in Lhasa and what are the rules for arranging them, inflecting them, and so on, before one can venture to publish a Tibetan grammar and dictionary. As one instance of the difficulties, different words must be used when addressing the higher classes; e.g. for "come," three words, *yong, peb* and *chip-gyu-nang,* indicate the different social grades in ascending order. The greatest difficulty of all is the spelling; e.g. the Tibetan word for Sikkim is *Den-jong,* which means "The Rice District," for rice grows there plentifully, but hardly at all in Tibet proper. This name, pronounced *Den-jong,* is spelt *Hpras-lchongs.* There is also a variety of tones, as in Chinese. *La* in a low tone means *a pass* over a mountain range; in a higher tone it means the *wages* of a labourer.

Seven years later, when it first fell to my lot to hold long conversations with the Dalai Lama, I noticed that he, when speaking to me, always observed me narrowly to make sure whether I took in his full meaning. He was always ready to explain a word I did not fully understand.

Kalimpong was profitable in this also, that I met Tibetan farmers, pilgrims and traders, and widened my Tibetan horizon.

In Kalimpong I first met Palhese (pronounced Pah-lay-say), What a treasure he was! The Tibetans who live in Indian territory, even those on the Tibetan frontier in Darjeeling and Kalimpong, gain only a partial knowledge of Tibet and Tibetan life, religious, domestic or political, for they are heavily infuenced by Western ideas. So I had asked these Tibetans to keep a look-out for any educated Tibetan, and especially one of good birth from Lhasa, for there, at the heart, life pulsates at its fullest.

After a few months by a happy chance Palhese arrived. A member of the Palha family, one of the twenty-five or thirty families of noble rank in central Tibet, he was a veritable encyclopaedia of things Tibetan, high and low, especially on the secular side. The Tibetan nobility of central Tibet – together with some of the higher lamas – are the leaders of Tibet. The nobility are almost all related to each other, and thus the members of these families are behind the scenes in all the chief happenings of social and political life. Palhese knew not only what leading men were doing, but what they were saying, and even what they were thinking, this last being often quite different from their words and actions. Tibetan politics are indeed a close preserve. My friend's circle of acquaintances was enormous among high-born and low-born, monks and laypeople. He was a shrewd judge of character. If he ever made a mistake, he could refer to the stripes of the tiger, and remind me of the Tibetan proverb:

> The tiger's picture is outside;
> The man's picture is inside.

Again and again I was congratulated by Tibetans on the possession of this incomparable friend, who remained with me as long as I was in or near Tibet. During all the years that I spent in those parts Palhese was the only one of his kind who came to live on the Indian side of the Indo-Tibetan frontier.

When he had been with me for a year and a half, my work in Kalimpong was completed, and I was transferred to the ordinary work of an Indian district. He walked with me down the road from Kalimpong, and in due coure we parted sadly, near a bend in the road. After walking fifty or sixty yards further, expecting him to have passed behind the bend, I looked back to see how empty the place looked without him. But he was still there, sitting on a rock on the hillside, weeping bitterly.

When the government sent me to Tibetan work a few months later, he rejoined me immediately. But at this time I used to be posted to Tibet for fairly short periods and then revert to work in India, and so he impressed on me that he would not work for anybody else, though he was then less than thirty years old. Later on, when posted permanently to Tibet, I gave him a post in the government service. But from time to time he would tell me, "If you leave the government service to-day, I leave to-morrow." And nothing would alter his decision. When I left, he retired to his small estate in central Tibet, though only forty-eight years of age.

Early in 1904, while the armed British mission to Tibet under Colonel (later) Sir Francis Younghusband was halted, through Tibetan opposition, at the head of the Chumbi Valley, I was given the leadership of a small pioneering party. Our duty was to cross Western Bhutan from south to north, looking for an alignment, along which might be constructed a road from India to Tibet, one that would avoid high passes and therefore never be blocked by snow.

The present tracks, rising to an altitude of over 14,000 feet, are impassable during the winter. With me were Stevens, a young engineer, and Bennett, a contractor, who hoped to obtain a contract for the whole or part of the work.

The Governor of Western Bhutan was hostile. Through a trustworthy agent I ascertained that he wrote to his frontier officer, "If the Sahibs come with but few soldiers, you must beat them, and turn them out, and do whatever is necessary. If they come with many soldiers, I will send a high officer from here with soldiers to oppose them." I took nine Gurkha[2] soldiers with me. The Eastern Governor, who was the most powerful of all the governors, had given permission, but the Western Governor, who was the latter's father-in-law, was semi-independent and opposed us actively, until smoothed down a bit by the Eastern Governor's agent, who met us near the foot of the mountain range.

But the agent, Kazi Ugyen (Kazi being a Nepalese title applied to him by the Nepalese and the British), would go with us no further. "You cannot go," he said; "even in summer there is only a goat track, and now it is all under deep snow." It was my first experience of marching through trackless forests, deep in snow, and often so closely shrouded in mist that you could not see fifteen yards ahead. Bhutan refused transport, but I brought over a number of Gurkha peasants from the Kalimpong district as porters, and most nobly they toiled up the snow-covered ridges and passes, though they lived themselves in a warm part of the country. I had worked among them for two years during the land settlement, and we had learned to know and trust each other.

I had sent to the authorities in Cawnpore – I think the military authorities – an indent for boots. Men cannot be asked to walk bare-footed through snow. Gurkhas having very small feet, I had asked for sizes five, six, and seven, so many of each. On reachiing the snow-line we waited for this treasure, and in due course the boots arrived; but alas! the sizes the authorities sent us were nine, ten and eleven. We could not wait in the snow with dwindling food for the ten or twelve days necessary to obtain a second consignment, and, quite conceivably, it would be no better than the first. So we continued through the snow, following a track used by goats and sheep in the summer, but in the snow used by nobody. For seven days we saw neither human being nor beast. We travelled mainly along the crest of the ridge. Thus from time to time when the mist lifted, we obtained fair views of possible routes along and above the valleys below.

The Governor had admitted several thousands of Gurkha families to farm the lands in his lower valleys, obtaining from them a large sum in rents and taxes. The headman of one of these Gurkha settlements I engaged as a guide; this service he was very ready to perform, not being in sympathy with his Bhutanese overlords.

My porters suffered great hardship. As we go on, and on, a man calls out, "I am dead, I am dead." Another, giving that kind of whistle that they emit when short of breath on an uphill march, proclaims, "I have finished dying." The cheery voice of the guide comes back, "Why die at the time of arriving?" I knew then that we were about half-way through the day's march.

Presently one of the porters calls out to the guide, "Ho, elder brother, can we see the place where we halt to-night?"

The guide, "We cannot quite see. Do you see that ridge over there?"

"That so distant one? We see it."

"It is not very far, my brothers. Our halting-place is a little on the other side."

"The other side! There is no hope of arriving. We are completely dead."

Another grunts, "Not even will our corpses be recovered." "It is like that; it is like that," from the others. And the small column of porters plods on doggedly.

Also, there were some places of extra difficulty and danger, as when we had to clamber over an immense slippery rock, lined with snow and ice, almost precipitous, and ending in a very real precipice below.

At length we rounded the shoulder of the mountain, Gyemo Chen, "The Great Queen" (Gipmochi of the maps), where

Tibet, Bhutan and Sikkim meet. From there we soon reached the pass, known as Senchu La, still in deep snow, and scrambled down through fir and tangled rhododendron into the Chumbi Valley, that wedge of Tibet that pushes down between Bhutan and Sikkim. I do not think any European had ever crossed the pass before.

Later on, I was sent to hold charge of Sikkim as well as the Chumbi Valley. In this valley I could see the Tibetans in their own country living their own lives. Much of my spare time I utilised to improve my knowledge of both spoken and written Tibetan.

Another of my Tibetan studies was to ascertain how the Tibetan Government from the Dalai Lama downwards was organised in Lhasa and in the provinces, the lay officials and the powerful ecclesiastics, the nobility and the lesser folk, and the principles, so different from our own, underlying the whole structure. Till then, no information was available on this important subject, except an account, scanty and greatly distorted, from Chinese sources.

In 1905 I was sent back to India. However, after nine months I was again recalled to Tibetan work for four months, and in 1908 I was summoned once more, and placed in charge of the Agency that controls British relations with Tibet, Bhutan and Sikkim. There I stayed for the remainder of my service, i.e. from 1908 to 1921.

During my last twenty-one years of service I spent only seven months in England and one in Canada, with occasional absences in India, China and Japan. Except for these periods I lived in Tibet and its borderland. So I became in large measure Tibetanised. During my last year as the British Diplomatic Agent in Tibet, Palhese was shown a letter, which the chief administrative officer of Reting, a large Tibetan monastery, wrote to the Dalai Lama. In it were the words, "When a European is with us Tibetans, I feel that he is a European and we are Tibetans; but when Lönchen[3] Bell is with us, I feel that we are all Tibetans together."

Again, when bidding farewell to the Dalai Lama in Lhasa,

after a stay of eleven months there, his last words to me were, "We have known each other for a long time, and I have complete confidence in you, for we two are men of like mind."

Truly I had come into a close affinity with this aloof, mysterious Dalai Lama.

At the end of 1933 I returned to Tibet on a private visit and stayed for more than a year in that country and on its southern frontier. A sum total of twenty years in Tibet and its borderland; and all too short.

Part Two
How He Came

3 What is a Dalai Lama?

If one is to attempt any account of the life of the late Dalai Lama, the thirteenth in the order of succession, one should begin by explaining what a Dalai Lama is. How did he come into existence?

The Tibetan religion is Buddhism, modified to suit Tibetan needs. Therefore like other Buddhists and all Hindus, they believe in the transmigration of the minds of humans and animals in rebirth after rebirth on what is called "The Wheel of Life," or more accurately, "The Cycle of Transmigratory Existence." The magistrate of this district was only a pony in his last existence, but he was faithful, and even died to save his master's life. Accordingly in the present existence he has gained great advancement. That sickly sheep, lying on the plain there – probably a wolf will get him to-night – was the magistrate of a district in his last life, but he used his power unjustly, reducing innocent people to beggary; his punishment fits his crime. Indeed had he not died young, before he had committed further sins, he might have been consigned to one of the hells, and remained there for five hundred years or more, until his sins were expiated. This is *karma*, the doctrine of cause and effect; it governs all, pervades all; from it there is no escape. "Whatsoever a man soweth, that shall he also reap."

Thus all beings, i.e. humans, animals etc., go up or down, experiencing the effects, good or bad, of past actions. Then ultimate aim is to transcend this cyclic, limited existence altogether. This can be done only by leading life after life in conformity with the high principles of the Buddhist religion. Then such a one can attain liberation or nirvana, or, as Tibetans

The Dalai Lama on the throne he used on important occasions, in the Norbu Lingka.

call it, "a state beyond sorrow," and eventually achieve the final goal of Buddhahood. Then, there is no need to be reborn, but as a Buddha one chooses to be reborn again and again for the welfare of others.

Buddhism came to Tibet mainly between the seventh and eleventh centuries of the Christian era. It had come from India, Nepal, and Kashmir, at a late state of its evolution, decadent and debased in the land of its birth. When it crossed into Tibet, it became strongly permeated by the animistic religion, called *Bön*, that Tibet had known from time immemorial, the worship of good spirits, the propitiation of demons, the killing and sacrificing of animals for these two ends. The combination of Buddhism and *Bön* formed a strong national faith, suited to Tibetan needs.[4]

It came to a country essentially warlike, which had overrun large parts of Turkistan and India, and of China also, where it had captured the Chinese capital, and exacted tribute from that country for several years. At this time Tibet was one of the chief military powers of Asia. Then Buddhism came to it; this was more than a thousand years ago. Since that time the Tibetans have abandoned their military conquests; they have never attacked any nation; indeed, they have been unable to defend their own. They experienced a real change of heart, which in Britain and Europe has been so often on the lips of men and women, but has not penetrated within. Buddhism has done for Tibet what Christianity, in spite of its high moral code, has failed to do for the nations of Europe. It may be said that the European nations have always been too aggressive and warlike. But so were the Tibetans until they were converted to Buddhism.

Tibet gave up conquest and wordly power, not – as happens with most empires – for economic reasons or lack of military strength; but for religion, and religion only.

According to tradition, Gautama was offered the choice of being a World Conqueror or a religious mendicant evolving into the Buddha. He chose religious poverty rather than great wealth and worldly sovereignty. So did Christ. But here a whole nation did so – Tibet. Has any other nation stood on this high level?

The middle of the fourteenth century saw the birth of a great religious reformer in north-eastern Tibet. His name was Tsong-Khapa, i.e. "The Man from the Land of Onions." He revived the religion in a purer form, preaching the observance of the laws of discipline, insisting on the celibacy of monks and nuns and forbidding the consumption of alcoholic liquors. To lessen the multitude of lower gods and devils from the Tibetan religion was indeed beyond his power, but in a marked degree he curtailed the attention paid to them by this magic-loving people. His followers became known as *Gelugpas*, "Those on the Way of Virtue." Often, too, they are called "The Yellow Hats," because he prescribed yellow hats for his monks, to distinguish them from the red hats of the previous sects. He founded the great monastery, Ganden, "The Joyous," some twenty-six miles outside Lhasa. During the last three hundred years the *Gelugpas* have constituted the most powerful sect in Tibet.

So strong is the stamp which Tsong-Khapa has imprinted on Tibetan Buddhism, that by many he is called "The Second Buddha."

The line of Dalai Lamas started from a humble beginning. In the desolate highlands of western Tibet, cold as few countries in the world are cold, there lived towards the end of the fourteenth century a herdsman, named Protecting Vajra, with his wife, Sky Happiness. To share their life they had five children, four boys and one girl. The third son, Lotus Vajra, was born in the enclosure where the cattle were driven for the night. That very night robbers came and raided their home. His mother hid Lotus between a few stones and fled with the others. Great was her surprise, when she came back next morning, to find her baby still alive, and a crow guarding him. All felt that he was destined to great things. We are told in his biography that in his boyhood he was strong and healthy and of a frisky disposition, with a broad forehead and a prominent nose. His father died while Lotus was still but a boy. He was certainly precocious, for, in spite of his sister's protests, he compiled a religious book for the remission of his father's sins.

When still quite young, he became a monk. He wrote books,

for which he claimed that they were "free from the three faults of excesses, omissions and mistakes." He visited Tsong-Khapa, and from him obtained not only instruction, but – somewhat after the manner of Elisha – one of his skirts as an omen and a weapon of spiritual force. By reason of his great industry and driving power he became known as "The Perfecter of the Monkhood," a leading lama with a host of disciples. Two of the chief monasteries in Tibet were founded by him; one of them, Drepung, "The Rice Heap," has grown into the largest monastery in the world today. The other was named Tashi Lhünpo, "The Mount of Blessing," which has since become the magnificent residence of the Panchen or Tashi Lama, who is as great a spiritual force as the Dalai Lama, though much smaller on the secular side. The Tibetans themselves call him Panchen Rinpoche, "The Precious Great Pandit." Europeans generally call him "Tashi Lama," but Tibetans never do. They have the designation "Tashi Lama," but apply it to lamas of inferior position, who attend weddings and furnish the material for jokes. It is therefore preferable to use the term "Panchen Lama."

The Perfecter of the Monkhood himself became the Abbot of Drepung. In due course he passed from life in a blaze of glory, and was recognised as having attained Buddhahood. His body was entombed in his own monastery Tashi Lhünpo.

After his death, not immediately but some years afterwards, it was recognised that his consciousness had passed into another monk who accordingly became his successor in this monastery. And thus into the Tibetan religion came the germ of a great change. People were accustomed to go up and down in the scale according to the merits or demerits of past lives; they were accustomed to hear of the rare cases when others, through their holiness, passed into Buddhahood returning to mundane existence no more. But here was one who returned to earth to help others. What Tibetan Buddhist could stand against that? His spiritual elevation towered over others. But as yet there was little secular authority.

A number of leading Mongols were converted to Tibetan Buddhism by the third incarnation, and it is to him that the effective conversion of Mongolia is due. He received from them the Mongolian title of "Dalai Lama," i.e. "All Embracing Lama," a title enjoyed by all his successors, and extended to his predecessors.

Tibetans, however, are more inclined to use their own titles, e.g. "The Precious Protector," "The Precious Sovereign," "The Monk Officer," "The Presence," and "The Inmost One."

The Dalai Lama is also regarded as an incarnation or emanation of Chenrezig, the patron deity of Tibet, himself one who has attained enlightenment but remains in order to alleviate the sufferings of the world. Such a one is known as a bodhisattva.

It is unnecessary to explore the many ramifications of Tibetan Buddhism. Even if I could do so, it would only over-lengthen and over-weight this book with ideas that are difficult to understand, and are not essential to this biography.

The monks in Drepung were Yellow Hats, i.e. of the reformed sect. The Red Hats, the unreformed sect, were in opposition to them, and the chief power in the land rested with the king of the Tsang province – west of Lhasa – a Red Hat devotee. The fifth in the line of Dalai Lamas was a remarkable and forceful personality. A young incarnation of high spiritual standing but devoid of power, he succeeded in prevailing upon a powerful Mongol chief to espouse his cause. The Mongol accordingly invaded Tibet, defeated the king of Tsang, and gave the sovereignty of all Tibet to this young high lama of Drepung. This was in 1641.

The latter was now in a unique position. His spiritual status was higher than that of anybody else, and Mongol arms had endowed him also with the highest secular power. He used this power to crush all opposition. John Grueber, a Jesuit priest from Austria, who came to Lhasa during his reign – the first European to enter Lhasa – describes him as the "devilish God-the-Father who puts to death such as refuse to adore him." He established himself as a sovereign, able to help or punish his subjects in this life, and to help or punish them in the life beyond. The Dalai Lama system was now completely established. Any Dalai Lama desiring the position, and possessing great strength of character, could become an irresistible autocrat.

From the time of his ancestor, Lotus Vajra, he had been a monk. Later, he was recognised as an incarnation of Chenrezig. And now he had become the secular ruler, the King of Tibet. He was monk, deity and king. And as this story unfolds, it will be seen that the Thirteenth Dalai Lama, whose life is portrayed in this biography, also filled this triple role of monk, deity and king, even more fully than did the Fifth.

There are indeed others, who, like the Dalai Lama, have set aside the achievement of "passing beyond sorrow," and have consented to be born again in order to help on the upward path all beings, men and women, birds, beasts, fishes and insects, in fact every kind of sentient being. Such a one is known as *Tülku*, i.e. "Emanation Body." These are lamas, in whom the emanation from some deity or bygone saint is present in an esoteric manner. But the high spiritual essence and the overwhelming secular power which the Dalai Lama has inherited, render him supreme.

The young Fifth Dalai Lama made his old teacher, named "The Banner of Religion's Victory," who was abbot first at Tashi Lhünpo and then at Ganden, to be the second Incarnate Lama of Tibet. He gave him Tashi Lhünpo, founded by the first Dalai Lama, as his monastery, and named him "The Precious Great Sage" (Panchen Rinpoche), and declared him to be an incarnation of the celestial Buddha, "Boundless Light," whose spiritual son, Chenrezig was incarnate in the Dalai Lama himself.[5]

This generous action of the young Dalai Lama may perhaps have been the result of that respect for one's teacher, which is a marked characteristic of Tibetans, as it is of Indians.

To the modern Tibetan the Fifth is a national hero. While other Dalai Lamas are known by their numbers, the Eighth, the Eleventh, and so on, you hear the Fifth spoken of as "The Great Fifth." The Seventh also is occasionally called "The Great Seventh." The lines on which The Great Fifth and his Chief Minister fashioned the Tibetan administration are followed to this day.

It has always been one of the cardinal rules that the Dalai Lama should be brought up entirely by the male sex. Celibacy in the strictest sense is their road, and they tread it from the first. So far as we know, they have never strayed from that road except in one instance, the Sixth in the line.

Not only from having obtained the sovereignty of Tibet, but also on account of his strong character, the Fifth had great prestige. However, after a few years he handed over the temporal power to his Chief Minister, who was a man of exceptional ability. The Potala Palace, one of the most wonderful buildings in Asia, was then being rebuilt on a magnificent scale up the sides of, and on the summit of, "The Peak," a small hill half a mile outside the town of Lhasa. The Dalai Lama did not die till 1680, over thirty years later. When he did, the Chief Minister, wishing to keep the power and to use the Dalai Lama's authority to complete the massive pile, concealed his death for nine years, telling the people that he was in spiritual seclusion and none must attempt to interrupt him. The Potala is a very high building, and the Dalai Lama had to live at the top. It would be considered disrespectful, even sacrilegious, for anybody to live over the head of the highest in the land. It was thus possible for the story of his retirement to be maintained for so long that the new Emanation Body, the Sixth Dalai Lama, when publicly announced, was already in his teens. Till then he had lived with his parents, and received a normal upbringing.

The result was calamitous. He had become acquainted with wordly pleasures, and not only acquired a fondness for them, but carried this to excess. He beautified the monastic precincts of the Potala; he adorned his own person, drank wine, and sought the company of girls. Withal, one must admit he had intelligence and taste. He built a beautiful little temple to the Serpent Gods in the picturesque pond that lies at the foot of the massive northern escarpment of the palace. A lovely retreat, held by Chinese and Tibetans to be one of the five beauty spots of Lhasa.

"Melodious Purity" – for this was his Tibetan name – composed songs. Such as I have translated are love songs; this young man was certainly frank; he did not conceal his feelings.

Here are three verses:

> A woodland spreads in a valley,
>   And there my loved one comes,
> A southern paradise; none knows,
>   Except the talking parrot.
> Ah! talking parrot, though you know,
>   Do not reveal our secret!

He glories in his double life:

> I dwell apart in Potala;
>   A god on earth am I;
> But in the town the prince of rogues
>   And boisterous revelry.

But fear comes:

> Lo! the Serpent Gods and demons
>   Lurk behind me stern and mighty;
> Sweet the apple grows before me;
>   Fear leads nowhere; I must pluck it.

At that time a Mongol chief had a large military force in Tibet. Acting in collusion with the Manchu Emperor Kanghsi, he induced the young Dalai Lama to take the journey to Peking, assuring him that the Emperor had invited him to go there. Melodious Purity left Lhasa accordingly in the company of one of the chief's most trusted ministers, and died – being probably murdered – soon afterwards.[6]

When I discussed him with the late Dalai Lama, the latter said, "He did not observe even the rules of a fully ordained monk. He drank wine habitually. And he used to have his body in several places at the same time, e.g. in Lhasa, in Kongpo (a province seven days' journey east of Lhasa), and elsewhere. Even the place whence he retired to the Honourable Field (i.e. died) is uncertain; one tomb of his is in Alashar in Mongolia, while there is another in the Drepung monastery. Showing many bodies at the same time is disallowed in all the sects of our religion, because it causes confusion in the work."

"One of his bodies used to appear in the crowd in the Reception Hall of the Seventh Dalai Lama. One is said to appear also at my receptions, but I am unable to say whether this is true or not."

Whenever the Thirteenth Dalai Lama spoke to me, even on matters connected with the religion, he was eminently frank.

In spite of his disordered life, the Tibetan people display unflinching loyalty to Melodious Purity. They love his melodies, and will not hear a word against his purity. No; one of his bodies remained in spiritual meditation behind the closed doors of the great palace; while the other wandered forth into the highways and byways of Lhasa, to test the faith of his subjects. To outsiders he was a contradiction, but to the true believer he was one and the same Dalai Lama. The Tibetan faith, hitherto unquenchable, has withstood all attacks both from without and within.

During the seventeenth and eighteenth centuries Christian missionaries, mostly Jesuit and Capuchin, lived in Lhasa. The last were driven out in A.D. 1745.[7]

Of the remaining six Incarnations that preceded the late Dalai Lama, the Thirteenth, little need be said. The Seventh is regarded by Tibetans more highly than the others; he lived during the first half of the eighteenth century. The last four all died before coming of age, or soon afterwards. Each Tibetan Regent may have wished to keep the power in his own hands, and each Manchu Amban wished to avoid the advent of the god-king. For the Amban knows that if the Dalai Lama himself takes the secular power and learns how to use it, there will be far greater difficulty in controlling, or even influencing, him than a mere Regent, on account of the Dalai Lama's all-embracing authority over his own people.

A Regent is himself a tulku of the highest grade. The head of one of six leading monasteries at Lhasa, but not Drepung, Sera or Ganden, he is chosen for the post by the National Assembly. Such a one is just a high lama, surrounded by monks; he is quite ignorant of public affairs. He must recast his mental outlook, and gain his experience while he is carrying on his work in this new post, so utterly different from any work that he has done before. The Cabinet, three laymen and one monk, works directly under him for secular business; and the Ecclesiastical Council works under him for religious affairs. Some indeed of these high lamas regard the secular business as unclean, and refuse to accept the post of Regent. Others are delighted with their new power, and grow more and more ambitious in the exercise of it, as the years pass.

The last Dalai Lama came through the critical period of his minority, attaining manhood and gaining power over both Church and State. A Chinese officer of the period, more outspoken than his colleagues, remarked to a friend of mine that affairs had been managed very badly.

4 Discovering Him

When a Dalai Lama dies, or as the Tibetans say, "goes to the Honourable Field," by what means is his successor known? He does not succeed as a King succeeds, for a celibate monk can have no son. He is not chosen as a President or a Pope is chosen; it is not a matter for selection at all. No, it is a question of discovering where he is, for has he not promised to return to his helpless flock?

How then is he discovered? Well, it is believed that within a year or two after his passing, he enters some woman's womb, and in due course the baby boy is born. The popular belief in the West is that the successor is born on the day the Dalai Lama dies. But this is not so; in several cases the Dalai Lama was not reborn till eighteen months or more after death.

The Third Dalai Lama converted many Mongols to Buddhism. The year after he died, his successor was found in the infant son of a Mongol prince who had been one of the Lama's most powerful followers.

Since then many Tibetan saints have reincarnated in Mongol families, and vice versa. Thus are the two nations bound more closely together in the important matter of religion.

The discovery of the boy is difficult, for Tibet alone is twenty times the size of England. So religion is called in, to help the search.

Old Asia is the cradle of the world religions, and in this hermit kingdom in the heart of Asia there are many strange survivals of an age that has long passed elsewhere. You will find oracles, as of old in Greece. I sometimes found five or six in one large monastery alone. These oracles foretell public events, whether the crops will be good or bad, whether the year will be one of war or peace, and so on. They will also enlighten you on your private concerns, whether your wife will recover from her illness, and whether your next year's trading will be successful or the reverse. Among these oracles are two chief ones which helped in the finding of the last Dalai Lama; one at Nechung, four miles from Lhasa, and the other at the Samye monastery. Forty miles from Lhasa, Samye lies out on the sand dunes covering the northern bank of the Tsangpo, the great river of southern Tibet, the main source of the Brahmaputra in India. When I was there at the end of one September, I found the river three-quarters of a mile broad, and flowing in a swift current eleven thousand feet above the level of the sea.

A former Prime Minister of Tibet told me the story of the finding. Nechung gave out the names of the young boy's father and mother, and the whereabouts of their house. Samye made known that the mountain near the house was shaped like an elephant. That made a starting point for the council of monks who are responsible for discovering the right boy. Such a council includes the Panchen Lama, if he is of age, and includes also fifteen or twenty other leading lamas.

Tibetan Buddhism is a complicated religion. When the search for the Dalai Lama was about to begin, some authorities said he would be found in western Tibet, others in an eastern province, and others in Takpo, a province a few days' journey to the south-east of Lhasa. However, the State Oracle at Nechung came to the rescue. It pointed out that there are often three rebirths of a high lama, one of his body, one of his speech, and one of his mind. The first was the one required, and that was the one which must be found in the province of Takpo.

In this mystical land of Tibet there are several lakes that set out before one's eyes a vision of events to come. Tibetans, men and women, consult them a good deal. The most famous of them is one that lies to the south-east of Lhasa in that province of Takpo, where the late Dalai Lama was born. It is named "The Victorious Wheel of Religion," religion in Tibet being often likened to the turning of a wheel. A Tibetan friend, whom I met in China, had visited it, and described how the visions come:

"The water of the lake is blue. You watch it from the hillside. A wind arises, and turns the blue water into white. A hole then forms in this white water; the hole is blue-black. Clouds form above this hole, and below the clouds you see images showing future events."

Winds arise very suddenly on these lakes, and hot springs are numerous. My friend saw beneath the cloud some Chinese houses, and houses of the Calcutta type, before there was any idea that his government would send him via Calcutta to China.

High lamas are credited with the ability to keep their *la* – which for lack of a nearer term we may translate "soul" – outside their bodies. In such a case nobody can destroy the lama, unless he first catches and destroys the soul. A Dalai Lama's soul resides beneath the waters of this secluded lake, and so the Vice-regent of the Buddha should be particularly safe.

In these circumstances it was natural that this lake should help a great deal in finding the Dalai Lama. Armed with the pronouncements of the oracles, a high lama of the austere Gyü monastery in Lhasa, attended by several Geshes, was sent to look for a vision. But the whole lake was under snow; he saw nothing. However, the Wheel of Religion did not fail him. A wind arose – those tempestuous Tibetan winds are never far away – and dispersed the snow, leaving the ice clear before the lama, who was observing it from a neighbouring hill. Then he looked into it, as into a glass, and saw an image of the house and the land around it. He saw also a peach-tree in flower, several months out of the season for peach blossom. That night in a dream he saw a vision of the young Dalai Lama, then somewhat less than two years old, in a woman's arms. A few days later he came to the house seen in the lake and found the child in the arms of his mother, and the face of the boy was unmistakably that seen in the dream. The peach-tree in flower and a pail of milk, that remained full, however much milk was taken from it, were strong indications. All was as foretold by the oracles, the vision and the dream. The biography says that the lama told the parents "that they should take great care of the child, and keep him clean, and that a report would be sent to the golden ears of the Manchu Emperor; also telling them not to show him to any foreigners."

But all was not yet determined. The Dalai Lama is the Incarnation of Chenrezig who is the Buddha of Compassion. Now this particular manifestation of Chenrezig has four arms, and, sure enough, near the Dalai Lama's shoulder blades were two extra pieces of flesh indicating the other two arms of Chenrezig. Two other signs also he had, namely large ears, and an imprint like that of a conch shell on one of the palms of his hands.

Even these bodily marks did not finish the business. The young boy must also identify the property, especially the sacred possessions, of his predecessor, or rather of himself in his previous life. For instance, his hand-bell, his small drum, both of these being articles of worship kept continually on the small table in front of him. His rosary too, and the *dorje* shaped like a small dumbell, the emblem of power indestructible. And his drinking cup, one of his handkerchiefs, and other articles which he has used habitually. Two of these religious implements or other articles are placed side by side, one being that used by his predecessor, and the other an exact copy of it. Some Tibetans told me that all Incarnations undergo this test except only the Dalai Lama, but the Dalai Lama himself assured me that he also went through it. And this is confirmed by the fact that his successor, the Fourteenth, did so.

One may safely assume that the young Incarnation from Takpo found no great difficulty in the identification test. He had been indicated by the Nechung oracle; he was clearly and miraculously shown in the vision on the lake and in the dream. I was in fact assured that at a very early age he told his attendants that in his preceding life he gave the chief of the Litang district in eastern Tibet an image of Buddha. For fear of losing that precious image the chief had placed it in a golden urn and hidden it in a beam in his house. Let them send and see whether this was so. They did send; it was so.

This vision and remembrance of the past life is common to all

Incarnations, of whom there are several hundred in Tibet, being re-embodiments of saints, who, by the sanctity of past lives, have attained to this high position. When such a boy grows older, the vision becomes less clear; each worldly act lessens it just a little.

The discovery of the Dalai Lama's return was confirmed by the Nechung Oracle, and was reported to the Manchu Amban in Lhasa, who at first made difficulties about transmitting the information to Peking for the Emperor's confirmation, but was eventually persuaded to do so. There were no other possible candidates. The child was brought to Lhasa when two years old, and kept in a hermitage until confirmation was received that the Emperor accepted him as the Dalai Lama. This took about a year, and then he was formally enthroned. He was born in June, 1876, and enthroned in 1879. His successor, the Fourteenth, was enthroned soon after he was brought to Lhasa, Tibet having proclaimed her independence of China about thirty years earlier, so no confirmation was sought from China.

None of the troubles that gripped Melodious Purity entered into the young life of the Thirteenth Dalai Lama. His father and mother were separated from him soon after he was enthroned; and thereafter he could see them only from time to time. The faithful monk-servants of his previous life looked after him. Thenceforth neither his mother nor any other woman had the care of him; he was brought up entirely by men. The Master of the Bedchamber took his mother's place, fondling him in his arms and looking after him in every way. He also gave him his first education, and it was largely owing to him that the Dalai Lama later on became so learned. His mother died when he was about three years old.

The young boy's father and mother were ordinary peasants. None of his ancestors were of high birth; they had been peasants from generation to generation. When the Fourth was found to be the son of a Mongol prince. Mongolia was being steadily converted to Tibetan Buddhism; and no doubt when a young Mongol prince became the spiritual Head not only of Mongolia but also of Tibet, the conversion was quickened. But the "Great

Fifth" was the son of a peasant at Chunggye, two days' journey
south-east of Lhasa, and the later incarnations have almost always been taken from the families of the poor. A Dalai Lama's
family is ennobled and enriched. If therefore the boy is identified
in one already noble, the family is likely to become inconve-
niently powerful. Tibetans would not put the matter that way,
but it is a natural precaution.

What has been the daily life of the young boy's family before
he is discovered to be the Dalai Lama? His father, like all
farmers, rises before dawn and puts on his clothes. He does not
wash himself, for the climate is very cold, the wind is strong, and
the house is entirely unheated. He says a few prayers, such as he
may know. And now a drink of tea, taking some of his stock left
from overnight, a brew of tea made very thick and strong, and
into this he pours boiling water. A little after dawn he goes out
to his fields, or to the woods to collect fuel.

Let us assume that we are considering a day in summer.

About nine or ten o'clock the women of the household bring
breakfast out to the fields. If the field where the party are
working is near the house, and the workers in the field are but
few, the breakfast is brought ready cooked. But if a long distance
off, or the workers many, the women come to the field at about
seven in the morning and cook the food in a corner of it. For
breakfast they may have tea with barley meal or buckwheat
bread and some turnips or radishes. Maybe instead of these
vegetables they will have some cheese sprinkled on the bread.
The cheese has been kept in a closed jar for at least six of seven
months and perhaps even for two or three years. It has rotted
thoroughly and gives out a strong odour.

Breakfast lasts only twenty minutes to half an hour, after
which work is taken up again. The women stay in the field and
break the large clods with the backs of hoes, sow the seed, and
help in most of the other work except the ploughing.

At about two o'clock comes the heavy meal of the day. Meat
with turnips or radishes, or in some parts of Tibet, potatoes.
They may also have tea and beer, or distilled liquor, and the
whole meal will be somewhat longer than breakfast, lasting for

about three-quarters of an hour. Then work till dusk, the women again joining in, but of course leaving early to go and do the housework. For the farmer, whose name is perhaps Monday Long Life, would be justly angry should he find that the cows had not been milked or the fire had not been lit.

Supper around seven; gruel made from barley, bones well covered with meat, some dried leaves of turnips or radishes, tea, and possibly more beer. And those who have done the ploughing will get a little extra meat. The meal finished, Monday Long Life and his family remove all their clothes, wrap themselves up in blankets, and lie down to sleep on the hard, little Tibetan mattresses which are stuffed with barley straw.

Such till now is the boy's hard, simple life as he plays about the farm. But now that he has been discovered to be the Dalai Lama, he has suddenly become "The Great Owner," and the whole of Tibet belongs to him. His father becomes one of the great ones; everything is changed.

The ceremony of enthronement takes place in the Potala, the Palace of the Dalai Lamas. The Tibetan name for this enthronement is "The Prayer for the Power of the Golden Throne." It is in effect a petition to the Supreme Head to occupy again the throne which is his by right, and is the symbol of the power that he will exercise.

Sir Basil Gould, who was then the British Representative, witnessed the enthronement of the fourteenth Incarnation. Long before dawn, as is the Tibetan custom, the Ministers of State, many officials and monks attend, and there await the arrival of the returned Incarnation. He is brought in by leading lamas, lifted on to his large throne, and all do obeisance before him, prostrating themselves on the ground, while he, young though he is, gives each his blessing. The "All Covering Abbot," the head of those monks who are employed in the administration of the Tibetan Government, supports the tassel which the young Dalai Lama holds in his hand for blessing the people of lesser importance. The ritual is a long one, each person being blessed separately, and the Fourteenth was only a little over four and a half years old when he went through it. He was perfectly dignified. The ceremony is repeated for several days, in order that others also may be able to attend, and is in effect a proclamation to the people of Tibet that the young boy has been recognised as the returned Dalai Lama.

5 Training Him

The discovery of the Thirteenth Dalai Lama was a particularly clear one. Some of those before him were not above suspicion. In one case long ago the Oracle announced that the new Dalai Lama would be the son about to be born to a Mongol princess. The child indeed was born, but proved to be a girl. That was going too far, and afforded the Manchu Government an opportunity to intervene in the choice, and thereby increase their influence in Tibet. Accordingly the Manchu Emperor ordained that in future three or four boys should be chosen, and their names placed in the golden urn that he sent to Lhasa for the purpose. The Manchu Amban (High Commissioner) in Lhasa was to pick out one at random with a pair of chopsticks, and this name would indicate the new Dalai Lama. But in the case of the Thirteenth the Tibetan Government declined to use the urn. The divine indications being clear, they were convinced that he was the reincarnated Dalai Lama. He was given the name Ngawang Lobsang Tubten Gyatso.

This setting aside of the urn was one indication among others that showed the decline of Manchu and Chinese influence in Tibet. Since the early years of the eighteenth century the Manchu Emperors had from time to time succeeded in establishing a measure of power in Lhasa, for the Manchus believed in Buddhism far more than did the Chinese. But Tibet, large and mountainous, was difficult to hold against a freedom-loving people. Accordingly these efforts were not maintained for long; in general the Manchu authority was greatly limited, and often merely nominal, to be used by the Tibetans when convenient, and discarded when not.

As a young child the Dalai Lama was allowed to play only with his own brothers, of whom three were older than himself. No other children, and certainly no girls, were allowed to play with him. His personal attendants, who were adults, also amused him with toys and games. Locally made toys were of wood, such as horses and mules; the imported ones were toy trains and a great variety of mechanical devices. He went out for walks, accompanied by servants; and on the whole was treated more as a grown-up than as a child. He spent most of his time in the great Potala Palace, going to his country palace, the Jewel Park, only for a short time during the summer.

The personal attendants were the Master of the Bedchamber; the Chief Butler, who laid the food before the Dalai Lama, first tasting some himself; the Court Chaplain, who presented food offerings to the deities on the Dalai Lama's behalf; and the Master of the Kitchen. These were all monk-officials of fairly high positions. With them were associated the Chief Physician, and the "All Covering Abbot," so-called because he was the head of all the monk-officials. These attended to the boy's early education, and were responsible for his entire care and upbringing, and were held answerable for any harm that might befall him.

He began to learn reading and writing at a very early age, for the Tibetan biography tells us, "Reading and writing are the gates of all qualities." The biography also recognises that "Though he was Buddha, yet as he took human form, he must study as a human being. The scholar without learning and the sage without meditation will never do any beneficial work for a religious people."

Two learned professors were detailed to teach him; day and night he worked hard. He also used to meditate before an image of the Buddha of Wisdom, and make offerings to him. "He was still a small child when he retired for his first period of meditation. During these two months and twenty-five days nobody but his teacher was allowed to see him. After this period had passed, he mounted his throne and blessed, one by one, the monks and officials who came to visit him," so the biography tells us.

In addition to writing the language in its printed form, for the printed characters are the sacred ones, he learned also from the All Covering Abbot how to write in the running hand. From him, too, he learned arithmetic, and read with him the history of the Kings of Tibet and other books dealing with the general administration of the country. Besides these, he was trained as far as possible in government administration as well as in religion, as he was entitled to take over the temporal power when he came of age. Special tutors were responsible for this training, and as soon as he could read and write he was to some extent referred to in State affairs. However, the Dalai Lama himself informed me that when he took over the government he felt himself extremely ignorant, and spoke as though his administrative training in secular affairs had not carried him far.

From the beginning his education centred on religious studies, and before many years had passed his young mind wandered among the intricate mysteries of Tibetan Buddhism. He had to study the inner teachings in divers Tantricc works, as well as Buddha's Sutric open teachings. He was also said to have read through the *Kangyur,* the Buddhist Bible, in one hundred and eight volumes, as well as the Commentaries in two hundred and twenty-five volumes.

Eight Geshes used to debate theological subjects before him. When he was about thirteen years old he visited the three great monasteries near Lhasa in turn, and took part in debates there, in order to show that he was profiting by his instruction. During the remainder of his boyhood he frequently took part in these theological disputations, he on one side and a Geshe on the other. The technique of these debates is described later in the chapter called "The King's New Year." When thirteen years old, he also delivered a discourse on the previous lives of Buddha before a large assembly of monks. Certainly he obtained a profound knowledge of Tibetan Buddhism.

A large amount of time was spent in meditation. "The more he hears," says the biography, "the more he gains wisdom; and the more he gains wisdom, the more he comes to thinking and to meditation."

Towards the end of his life the Thirteenth Dalai Lama wrote his political testament. There are several books attributed to Dalai Lamas, but this is the only one of which it can be said with absolute certainty that a Dalai Lama wrote it.

In it he records thus concerning his boyhood:

"I was not identified in accordance with the previous custom of the golden urn. It was judged unnecessary, for from the prophecies and divinations it was clear that I was the true incarnation. And so I was enthroned. In accordance with the old custom a Regent was appointed for a time... ."

"I joined the monkhood. I became a novice. I read several books, for instance, *The Great Centre*, also numerous books on theological disputation, and the long succession of exoteric and esoteric discourses by the Lord Buddha with meanings as vast as the ocean. My instructors invested me with spiritual power. I worked every day as hard as I could, and thus attained to a moderate amount of knowledge and ability."

The Great Centre, alluded to above, is a book in five volumes on the metaphysical school of Buddhism in Tibet. During his childhood a Dalai Lama has to read a host of religious works.

It was a lonely boyhood with no real playmates. The village children play with no less mirth than children in Europe and America. But a limit must be placed on such things for the highest and holiest in the land. Deeply secluded was his life among the monks, study and study and study, mostly in the subtleties of this complicated religion. Of worldly matters he could know but little. Monks surrounded him, monks instructed him, and mundane affairs received but scanty attention. How could such a one administer the secular government of his country? Few previous Dalai Lamas had attempted to take over the secular side of the government, and none had administered it for very long.

The Tibetan biography makes known that when he was eighteen years old, he could no longer stand the slack discipline in the Church, and felt bound to tighten it up, for the lay population was becoming disgusted. So he summoned the heads of the largest monasteries, and his Chief Secretary made his warning known to them.

"Some rough men," he said, "committed to break the roots of perception, drink, smoke, and gamble. They roam about in various dresses, and they wander into the villages and oppress the poor villagers."

"If you, the chief officers of religion, do not punish them, good men will be discouraged. Putting the body under the head, you officers must be the silk-knot of religious rules. Do not mistake the choice that lies before you! In future, if you show slackness, your names will be destroyed."

We are told that after this injunction, "all gave up their evil doings and followed the right path."

As we have seen from the fate of the four previous Dalai Lamas, there were grave dangers in the boy's path, especially as the time drew near for him to take up the full power. His servants had always to guard against poison, though you will be told that "The Presence" need never die from poison, unless of course he wishes to depart owing to the wickedness of his people, or – as did the second in the line – wishes to cease from old age and to work again as a young monk.

The Presence must visit the holy lake, "The Heaven Lake of the Goddess," a hundred and fifty miles south-east of Lhasa, where he will see a vision showing the future events of his life and the manner of his passing away. That indeed is easy. But he must also visit Palden Lhamo, who is the goddess of the lake and the guardian of the Tibetan Government. Leaving his attendants outside, the lad penetrates alone into her chapel, which is furnished with stuffed carcases of wild animals and other fearsome objects, and speaks to her face to face. That requires skill as well as courage, for she is powerful and easily angered.

It may be interesting to note that many Tibetans held Queen Victoria to be one of the Incarnations of this goddess. They often used to tell me so while the Queen was still alive, and added that there was a prophecy that the British would not invade Tibet during her lifetime. The prophecy proved to be true, for it was not till three years after her death that British troops occupied Lhasa. A god or goddess may take several forms and have several emanations. Chenrezig the patron deity, has many emanations, of whom the Dalai Lama is the chief.

On his way from the lake back to Lhasa the young Dalai Lama is given a holy pill, "to renew his vitality and make his countenance shine." Of the four preceding Dalai Lamas, many Tibetans say that they died because they angered the goddess, being not sufficiently experienced to know how to speak to her. Others, outside the stronghold of the Tibetan faith, refer to the pill and speak of poison. The last Dalai Lama came through; he was older and of a fuller experience when he paid his visit. Besides he had a strong will and, as he used to tell me, was exceptionally fortunate in his servants. Reliable they were, always on the watch.

It may be that the lad inherited his strong will from his father. The latter was just a peasant, quite a poor man, but, as the custom is, was ennobled when his son became Dalai Lama. He then became "The Royal Father Duke," and received a large landed estate. Palhese met the duke in Lhasa, when the latter was somewhat over sixty years old, Palhese himself being a boy of thirteen. He describes him as a man of average height, without much learning, but bluff and honest and with a kindly mind. Holding the rank he did, he had, of course, a seat in the Tibetan Parliament, which was at that time under the domination of the huge Drepung monastery. Others hardly dared to express an opinion, but not so the peasant duke. Palhese told me feelingly how he insisted on justice for the Palha family, when a case against the latter was being decided.

Palhese's mother, in her kindness, had allowed Sarat Chandra Das, an Indian, to go in her train to Lhasa. At that time Indians, British, and natives of nearly all countries were barred from Tibet with the utmost rigour. He remained only a week or two in the Holy City, but the fact was discovered.

The Parliament were debating what punishment should be inflicted on the family. The heads of Drepung wanted to confiscate the entire Palha estates, granted from time to time during seven generations for good services rendered to the Tibetan people. None dared to speak against the views of the Drepung, till the ennobled farmer sitting on his little mattress on the ground – for it is the custom in this Parliament to sit when speaking – delivered his views as follows:

"You should not confiscate the entire estates. I noticed that when the property of a nobleman was confiscated some time ago, the Government received no benefit. Part was taken by a powerful monastery, the remainder by another noble family. If these estates are taken away, none of the large monasteries and none of the nobility should receive them. They can be taken by the Government itself; that is one way. Or they can be let out on lease to the Palha family (having been rent-free before), but none else should make request to hold them. This is what should be done, unless you judge it sufficient merely to impose a fine of one hundred *dotse*" (equalling £700).

These courageous remarks blocked Drepung. It did not venture to take the estates itself, or make them over – for a consideration – to others. The largest estate was indeed confiscated, but let out to the Palha family at a high rental. And this rent was paid to the Government.

The fact is that the large monasteries in Tibet – and there are many of them – are exceedingly powerful. Every layman of any position allies himself to one of these, giving valuable presents to it with the regularity of a subsidy, and receiving in return the strength of its support. The Palha house is in alliance with Sera, "The Wild Rose Fence," so-called because – as the books of the Tibetans tell us – when first built on small lines, it was surrounded by bushes of wild rose. Since then it has grown, and now, with Drepung, and Ganden ("The Joyous"), forms a trio known as "The Three Seats," the most potent monastic force in the Tibetan Government. But at that time, owing to the great power of Drepung, Sera was in temporary eclipse.

Part Three
Adversity

6   Dark Years

At eighteen the Dalai Lama comes of age and is entitled to succeed to the sovereignty of Tibet. This is not more than seventeen of our reckoning, for Tibetans count the year of birth and the current year. In fact, a child who might happen to be born on the last day of the year, would be two years old on the day after his birth. But the late Dalai Lama's succession to the sovereignty, as he himself told me, was delayed for two years, and the Tibetan biography confirms this. He was born in 1876, and succeeded to the temporal power in 1895. In this book the ages are given according to our European reckoning, except where it is stated that the reckoning is Tibetan.

There were serious obstacles in the young man's path. At this time the Regent of Tibet was a Tulku of high rank, the Abbot of the Tengyeling monastery in Lhasa. Tengyeling was among the seven monasteries, not large but very exclusive, one of whose heads – each being a Tulku – was usually chosen as Regent during the minority of a Dalai Lama. In consequence these seven monasteries hold an exalted position. Not even the Great Three, Drepung, Sera and Ganden, are endowed with that honour, though they are closely connected, for every Incarnation must receive his education at one or other of the three. This Regent employed as his Chief Minister his own brother, who made many enemies by his oppressive administration, even putting innocent persons to death, a double crime in Buddhist lands, where the taking of all life, guilty as well as innocent, is forbidden.

Now some time after the young Dalai Lama came of age it was

The Dalai Lama in Gnatong in 1912 on his way back to Tibet after his exile in India, top, and the Dalai Lama's State Palanquin, below.

noticed that he used to fall ill without apparent reason. Send for a doctor? No, in Tibet you should apply first to a lama or an oracle, who will see whether the victim is possessed by some evil force, and, if so, cast it out. In this case, the State Oracle of Nechung was apparently consulted. The Tibetan biography says, "The State Oracle, Nechung, was to the originals of all evil things like a finger-nail that was put on a louse." And then the discovery was made that a magical diagram in the form of a wheel had been written on a piece of paper and inserted into the soles of a pair of boots, a beautiful pair, which the Minister had presented to the young Dalai Lama. This diagram invoked the assistance of evil spirits to destroy the wearer of the boots. Associated with the Minister were his other brothers, one of whom was the abbot of a monastery. The conspirators were unmasked as the would-be murderers of the Vice-Regent of Buddha himself.

Great was the popular indignation. The Parliament wished to put to death these and other conspirators, among whom they included the Regent himself, believing that he had resorted to this plot to retain power. But the Dalai Lama from the first set his face against capital punishment, though it must be admitted that the penalties inflicted on the chief offenders were, according to Western ideas, perhaps worse than death. Sharpened bamboos were driven under the finger-nails, a punishment introduced into Tibet by the Manchus. Numerous floggings were inflicted with rods of willow on the bared back and buttocks, each of a hundred lashes or more. Terrible punishments these, but Tibetans do not feel as do the races of western Europe, and the Minister was receiving what he had often himself light-heartedly given. Jewel Long Life – for that was his misapplied name – managed to survive for a few years. The Regent, though apparently not subjected to the above tortures, passed more quickly to his end. The Dalai Lama, as he himself told me, believed the Regent to be in the plot. Various relatives were also punished; among others the wife of Jewel Long Life. She was a daughter of the noble family of Long Stone, thus named because their Lhasa house stands close to the famous stone pillar, on which, about twelve hundred years ago, was inscribed a treaty between China and Tibet – one of the earliest pieces of Tibetan writing that is known. But in spite of her high birth she was flogged and made to sit every day for a week in one of the main streets of Lhasa with her wrists manacled and a heavy board round her neck. She was afterwards sent into exile.

Then people remembered that former song of the women and the prophecy it conveyed. There are no newspapers in Tibet and people generally have to be extremely careful what they say. But men, and especially women, are encouraged to sing. So as they go about their work – whatever their work may be – carrying their loads along the streets, or stamping down the mud floors and the flat mud roofs, the women sing all the time. It may be just some ditty, but it may also be a prophetic verse. This is what the people remembered:

> As a mouth the pond is working,
> And the fish lie at the bottom;
> So this year the yellow gander
> May be driven to his ending.

The pond was the State Oracle at Nechung, the fish were the members of the Cabinet who moved the Oracle to the prophecy, and the yellow gander was the Regent, he being of the Yellow Hat sect. No more vague this than the old-time prophecies of Greece and other lands; and Tibet still lives in the days that we left behind several hundred years ago.

The holiest festival of the year in Lhasa is that of "The Great Prayer Festival," which takes place at the beginning of the Tibetan New Year in February, and lasts for about three weeks. When the women draw water at the wells, a goddess may appear as one of them, especially during this festival, and sing one of these verses. It is taken up by the others, and becomes one of the many that are sung up and down the holy city. The hidden meaning is weighed, and the prophecy discovered. So say the Tibetans, and we may infer that this is why women or men singing these verses are never stopped or punished. It is the work of a heavenly visitant. Sometimes the name of a powerful officer of state appears against a background of censure, and in all cases his identity is known. Should he come near to the voices, he and his escort will rein in their ponies, and find their way home by another street. Thus in this autocratic country do we hear the voice of public opinion; yet not so described, but as the inspiration of the goddess.

During the remainder of his life the head of the Long Stone family was barred from holding any government post, though, being one of the twenty leading families of central Tibet, he would ordinarily have held an important post as a matter of course. Some fifteen years later I used to meet him from time to time, and he always wore heavy spectacles. I was assured by other Tibetans that his eyesight was not really very bad, but it suited him to wear these in the hope of making others believe that he was physically unable to work for the government. I saw him last in 1934, when he was on the road to Lhasa, and only two stages away. He was then an old man.. I asked him whether he would now stay always in Lhasa.

"Yes," he replied, "it was the place of my birth, and I am now seventy-three years old. Every morning I shall go to the Temple. There I will meet the Lord, prostrating myself before the large image of the Lord Buddha, and receive the 'honourable cleansing water.' And every day I will go round the Inmost Circle (one of the three sacred roads of Lhasa) twenty-five times."

"And will you read the sacred books?"

"My eyesight is not good enough. I shall pray, just pray."

The legacy of bitterness left by this Tengyeling affair still survived more than forty years later. It broke out again at every opportunity. Whenever the Chinese troops fought with the Tibetans in Lhasa, the monks of this community, once so highly privileged, fought with the enemy against their own countrymen. And some of the lower monks started on its course a prophecy that this thirteenth Dalai Lama would be the last; another way of publishing that he was a sham incarnation. False prophecies, as Shatra, the Prime Minister, informed me, are occasionally manufactured to serve private ends.

In justice to the Tibetans, it must be mentioned that they do not visit the sins of the fathers upon the children. The Dalai Lama gave Long Stone's son a good post, and every prospect of advancement. And when I met him in 1934, he had been appointed as the head of an important mission to the Panchen Lama.

Thus the Dalai Lama came into the secular, as well as the religious kingdom, or, as the people call it, the twofold power. Here, too, as with the abandonment of the Chinese urn, mentioned in the preceding chapter, is seen the weakening of Chinese influence. Neither the Government of China nor their Amban in Lhasa want a Dalai Lama who exercises the secular power. The Thirteenth was the only one to retain the headship of both Church and State during the whole of his adult life, a period of nearly forty years.

Consider his upbringing. It had been entirely monkish, removed from worldly affairs. And now he was, if he wished, and he emphatically did wish, the head of everything; or, as the Tibetan couplet runs:

> The Lama of the Yellow Hats;
> The Ruler of the Black Heads.

The Yellow Hats, his own monks, he could control somehow or other, but what did he know about the laymen, the Black Heads? Small wonder that other Dalai Lamas had refused to exercise the temporal power for any length of time; the Fifth alone attempted it, and he had had to struggle in his early youth, and was probably better fitted than most to strike out a line for himself. They felt, too, those other Dalai Lamas, that their sanctity was tarnished by the dirt of worldly administration. And from the practical point of view they realised their lack of training, and recoiled from the almost insuperable difficulties of the secular government. Not so the last. His courage and energy were inexhaustible; he recoiled from nothing.

"I came into power," he said, "when I was twenty years old, but I did not know at all how to govern a country. For the first five or six years it was very difficult. I could see the administration was faulty in many ways, but I had no experience to guide me in making changes. However, within ten years I had in some degree improved the government."

As for the men of Lhasa, they tell of the skill, tinged with humour, by which he surmounted the obstacles that stood in his path. He was young and strong, and he worked continuously. In his political testament he points out to his subjects that the whole of Tibet, both deities and human beings, asked him to take up the power.

During February and March the largest religious festival of the year draws a great number of people, mostly monks, into Lhasa. It is called "The Great Prayer Festival," because prayer is then made to the next Buddha, whom Tibetans call "The King of Love," or Maitreya, to come quickly. It is believed that the reign of the present Founding Buddha Shakyamuni, has been fixed at five thousand years, and of that period fully half has passed already. As the moon waxes and wanes, so Shakyamuni Buddha's spiritual power declines during the second half of the period, and all things deteriorate. Cannot this period of decline be shortened? Yes, it may be shortened, if by holding continuous services and offering numberless prayers the next Buddha can be induced to come earlier, and start the world on the upward path again.

During the course of the Great Prayer Festival the maintenance of law and order in the city of Lhasa is removed from the hands of the mere laity, and entrusted to the monastic order. Two brawny monks of the Drepung monastery, each carrying an enormous staff of office, become the magistrates, and employ their own police. One can see what abuses may arise in an uprooting of that kind, and indeed they did arise. Confiscations of property were the order of the day, and the wealthier people of Lhasa were wont to fly from the capital, taking their valuables with them. For what says the Tibetan proverb?

> Every man thirsts for possessions;
> Every dog thirsts for blood.

The young Dalai Lama was not slow to recognise that this must be promptly checked. So he sent for the two monk magistrates, pointed out the sufferings of respectable members of the community, and asked them by what authority they did these things.

"By the authority of the Great Fifth Dalai Lama," came their reply.

"And who is the Great Fifth Dalai Lama?" queried the young pontiff. The burly monks were taken aback by the question. They hesitated awhile, but then realised that there could be no shuffling.

"Without doubt Your Holiness is he." The answer was subdued but clear, for none can question the Reincarnation, by which the Fifth and the Thirteenth and all the others are one and the same. Since that memorable interview the misuse of this priestly privilege was curtailed, and the good people of Lhasa were grateful to their youthful Head for his prompt reform. Here was a good thing for Tibet, a strong will working quickly in one whom they recognised as most mightily inspired from on high.

Nor did he leave the matter here. In future the monastery had to send up ten names, five from each of two out of the four colleges. From these he chose two, one from each college. In his choice the Dalai Lama was guided partly by their bodily physique, a good presence being necessary for this post; and partly by their ability to read letters quickly and in a loud voice, as they have to read proclamations, as well as to read out the prayers handed in by worshippers during the religious services at great festivals, when perhaps more than a thousand monks are present. The Dalai Lama also took into account their general administrative ability. But most of all he paid attention to their loyalty and trustworthiness.

All this time the Dalai Lama was fighting for Tibetan autonomy. During his early days, when the Manchu Amban at Lhasa thought he could over-ride the young Ruler, there was the case of Ramba, the nobleman. The latter was appointed by the Amban to be a member of the Tibetan Cabinet. Soon afterwards he received a call to present himself before the Dalai Lama, who said, "The Amban has appointed you as a member of the

Cabinet, but you are not one of my Cabinet." What was to be done now? It was impossible to disregard the word coming from the Ruler of the Black Heads. The Cabinet therefore did the best they could, reporting to the Amban that Ramba had died. The Amban knew very well that Ramba was alive and flourishing, but he took the easier course, reporting his death to the Emperor. Ramba's landed property is situated four or five days' journey from Lhasa; thither he went, and remained quietly and happily for a year. A little later the Precious Sovereign appointed a man of his own choice.

It was a common occurrence for the Amban to send false reports to the Emperor; so much so that at this time the Emperor became known to the people of Lhasa as "The Bag of Lies."

7   Diplomacy and War

The opening of the twentieth century was a time of trial and bitter experience for the young Ruler. During the preceding half-century Tibet had seen the British take possession of the Darjeeling and Kalimpong districts. Darjeeling was formerly a part of Sikkim, Kalimpong a part of Bhutan. There were reasons, of course, for these annexations, but not such as the Tibetan Government at that time would recognise. An Indian, Sarat Chandra Das, had made secret explorations of Tibet under the orders of the Government of India. These were detected by the Tibetans, and excited great alarm among them. People spoke of "The powerful elephants from the south." The Chinese, naturally anxious to prevent others from intruding on what they regarded as their own preserve, told the Tibetans that the British wished to abolish the religion to which they were so keenly devoted, and substitute Christianity in its place, and that no doubt the British had designs also on the Tibetan gold-mines. The Tibetan Government were keenly aroused.

But they were sadly ignorant of war and politics. A detachment of Tibetans occupied a mountain inside the Sikkim frontier, the lamas telling them that their magic would disarm any British troops sent against them. The Chinese did nothing to restrain them, for, though they claimed Tibet as their vassal, their suzerainty, if any, was purely nominal. After repeated remonstrances a miniature campaign followed, just enough to drive the Tibetan detachment back into Tibet. This display of force brought to India the Representative of the Manchu Government of China, and in due course Britain and China made a treaty, which recognised a British protectorate over Sikkim, and arranged for a trade mart a few miles inside the Tibetan frontier.

And now to establish that trade mart. "You cannot do it," replied the Tibetans; "we did not sign that treaty." In their hearts they were thinking, "You are an aggressive, disagreeable people; we will keep you out at all costs if we can."

It was therefore determined to establish direct communication with the Tibetans. Lord Curzon, then Viceroy of India, addressed a letter to the Dalai Lama. Six months later it was returned. "We cannot deal with it; we have no dealings with foreigners." Lord Curzon was not the sort of man to accept a rebuff of that kind. Accordingly, during 1901, the Government of India sent Kazi Ugyen to Lhasa with a letter from the Viceroy to the Dalai Lama. The Dalai Lama refused to receive the letter; it came back, unopened.

The Dalai Lama was now some twenty-six years old, having been in power for about seven years. In spite of his total lack of training in secular affairs, he had to some extent made good in matters of internal administration, for in that he was dealing with his own people, and their religious devotion carried him through. But in foreign politics he had to stand on his own feet. His ignorance led him astray; and the impetuosity and unyielding will, which were always strong ingredients in his character, pushed him still further on the road that led to disaster.

After refusing the Viceroy's letter, he cast his eyes towards Russia. That Power was indeed far away, but its vast domain overhanging all Asia from the north, the strength of its people, and its connection with Mongolia, combined to give it in Tibet a prestige higher than that of any country in the world.

In Siberia to the east of Lake Baikal lies an extensive country inhabited by a people called the Buriats, who are pure Mongols; but, for the last two centuries or so, they have been under Russian rule. One of these Buriats, a man named Dorjieff, was of wide learning and ability. He had studied hard in Drepung monastery, and won a high theological degree. Becoming subsequently a tutor for the Dalai Lama, he won the latter's confidence. When the Dalai Lama came of age, in addition to his theological duties, he appointed this tutor as "Work Washing Abbot," part of his duty being to sprinkle water, scented with saffron flowers, a little on the person of the Dalai Lama, but more on the walls of his room, on the altar, and on the books, as a symbol of cleansing. He was thus in a close relationship with the young god-king, now come into power.

Withal, Dorjieff was an ardent Russian. He appears to have told the Dalai Lama that, since their close contact with Mongolia, more and more Russians were adopting Buddhism in its Tibetan form, and even the Tsar himself was likely to embrace it. To have such a powerful Ruler united to him by the strong bond of a common religion, what more could the Dalai Lama desire? The professor of theology was clever and pushful, and the Dalai Lama was cut off from contact with the outside world.

Things were happening behind the barrier walls of the great palace, and Tibet's neighbours were becoming uneasy. The British Government believed that Russia was making a secret treaty to help China against those who were pressing her from different directions. Russia was to receive Tibet in return for her services. Nepal and other States on the northern frontier of India were alarmed at the news. Accordingly the Government of India despatched a political mission under Colonel Younghusband to put relations with Tibet on a satisfactory footing. The Tibetans then, as always, were opposed to the entry of foreigners; they refused altogether to deal with the mission, merely telling it to go back to India again.

Tibet was told that the British Government desired trade facilities in Tibet. Sikkim had recently become a British protectorate, but it was formerly under the Tibetan Government. The Maharaja of Sikkim and many of his subjects were Buddhists and regarded the Dalai Lama as the Head of the Faith. Accordingly the Dalai Lama wrote a letter to the Maharaja of Sikkim, himself a Tibetan. "Why do the British insist on establishing trade marts? Their goods are coming in from India right up to Lhasa. Whether they have marts or not, their things come in all the same. The British, under the guise of establishing communications, are merely seeking to over-reach us. They are well practiced in all these political wiles."

But to Britain the spectre of Russia stood behind. At length the mission became changed into a military expedition. The bravery of the Tibetans came as a surprise to many. But being armed mainly with antiquated muzzle-loaders, the fighting was one-sided; the British and Indian casualties being two hundred and two, and the Tibetan casualties not less than eight or ten times that number. From a reliable Tibetan source, it appears that the Dalai Lama prohibited his troops from fighting the British, but told them that they must check them. (The Tibetan way of doing things in the old days.) And, as I was told, "He wished to show that Tibet also has a little army of her own." Pathetic indeed was his ignorance as to how things were done outside his hermit land.

The chief difficulty experienced by the British-Indian forces lay in the transport of guns, ammunition and other supplies, as these had to be carried some four hundred miles through difficult mountainous country. The advance continuing, the four Ministers who constituted his Cabinet advised the Dalai Lama to come to terms with the British. But, far from agreeing with their recommendation, the Dalai Lama discussed them and interned them in the Jewel Park, his country estate outside Lhasa.

Eventually the British and Indian troops pushed their way to Lhasa; shortly before their arrival the Dalai Lama fled northwards to Mongolia. This was the first time that he had left his own country. He was now twenty-eight years old. He left his seal with a priest of especial learning and sanctity. Here at Lhasa, in September, 1904, with great patience and skill, but withal having his troops and guns behind him, Younghusband negotiated the treaty that laid the foundation of all our subsequent dealings with Tibet. Its main terms were that the Tibetan Government agree to recognise the British protectorate over Sikkim, to promote trade between India and three trade marts in Tibet, and to prevent other foreigners exercising influence in Tibet.[8]

The Chinese Government set up proclamations in Tibet deposing the Dalai Lama. These the Tibetans bespattered with manure, continuing to refer, as far as possible, all important matters to him for his orders.

China wished the Panchen Lama to become the Regent of Tibet during the Dalai Lama's absence. Lhasa maintains that no Panchen Lama has ever acted as Regent instead of a Dalai Lama. "Not even for a single hour," they say. In any case the Panchen Lama, who as I knew him at that time was a peaceful and spiritually-minded young man, though not devoid of worldly ambition, declined to take the post of Regent.

The Panchen Lama, whose residence is in the great monastery at Tashi Lhünpo, is the Incarnation of the Buddha of Boundless Light, the Dalai Lama that of the Buddha of Compassion. In one important respect Boundless Light is the higher, for he is the spiritual father of the Buddha of Compassion. Again, the Panchen Lama is the "Truth Body" (Chö ku) of a Buddha, while the Dalai Lama is the "Enjoyment Body" (Long ku) of a Buddha, which the sufferer can hold and so be drawn upwards!

However, the worldly rule over Tibet belongs to the Dalai Lama, and in this respect the Panchen Lama holds a subordinate position, as he controls only three or four districts out of the fifty or so into which Tibet is divided, and those he holds under the Dalai Lama. The town of Shigatse, only half a mile away from Tashi Lhünpo monastery, and after Lhasa the largest town in Tibet, together with the important district surrounding it, is kept under the direct control of the Dalai Lama's Government. It is not one of the districts under the Panchen Lama.

Besides, the line of the Dalai Lamas started before the line of the Panchen Lamas, and the Panchen Lama's monastery, Tashi Lhünpo, was built by the first of the Dalai Lamas. And this Thirteenth Dalai Lama, being the older of the two, was actually the spiritual guide of the Panchen Lama. The latter visited Lhasa in 1902, when the Dalai Lama administered to him the highest religious vows. And when the Dalai Lama returned from China to Lhasa in 1909, the Panchen Lama came to meet him on the way, ten days' journey north of Lhasa.

The Panchen Lama is identified in the same way as the Dalai Lama is identified; and the Thirteenth Dalai Lama, being the older, had the deciding voice in selecting the late Panchen Lama from among the possible choices. He told me that he chose the one who came, like himself, from the province of Takpo; their homes were not far apart.

Until the expedition of 1904 all foreign nations had carried on their diplomatic intercourse regarding Tibet with China alone. They had not consulted Tibet herself, and no diplomatic representative had entered, or could enter, Tibet, because the Tibetans would not allow them to do so. Now Tibet came to understand that China was not strong enough to protect her against powerful nations. More and more, therefore, she came to stand on her own feet, asserting that treaties giving rights in Tibet must be signed by her; and asserting that she was not and never had been under China.

8 The First Exile

What was happening to the Dalai Lama now on his flight to the north?

The first news that greeted the Younghusband expedition on their arrival at Lhasa was, "He has gone to Reting monastery, sixty miles to the north and across two high passes. He has handed over his seal to a Regent to carry on business." Nine days later, "The Dalai Lama has gone beyond Nagchuka to the north and is now eight days' journey distant, and therefore cannot be consulted." Four days later, "The Tibetan officials now say they do not know where the Dalai Lama is, but Dorjieff is with him."

It is a hard, bleak country through which His Holiness was travelling. In Lhasa he travelled often in the luxury of his golden sedan chair, carried by some six or eight carriers. But he was also fond of riding a pony or a mule, and discarded the chair when ceremonial did not require it. He continued the habit of riding even in his later years. At this time, being only twenty-eight years of age, he rode fast, until he had put a good distance between himself and the British troops.

In due course he reached the vast region known as the Northern Plains, where even the valleys are sixteen thousand feet above the level of the sea, and the fresh water of the lakes turns to salt, because they have no outlets into lower waters. Travelling on and on, he arrived in the country of the brigands, who rob all, high or low. But the Dalai Lama, the Head of the Faith, was a supreme exception. Far from robbing him, they brought him their offerings, and solicited his divine blessing and forgiveness, no doubt, for their misdemeanours. On and on he went with his large following, always with the thought in his mind that he was leaving the hated British behind, and approaching the territory of the Great White Tsar, who he hoped would help him against his enemies.

Eventually he crossed the border of Mongolia, inhabited by a race closely akin to the Tibetans, and covering an area more than one-third of the size of Europe. In November he arrived at the capital, Urga, fairly close to the Russian frontier in the north. Having seven hundred persons in his suite, his baggage was carried by a small army of camels. Over ten thousand citizens went several miles out of the town to meet him and prostrate themselves before him. Pilgrims flocked in from all parts of Mongolia, from Siberia, and from the steppes of Astrakhan, to do him homage. They left their homes and their other holy quests, for what place could be holier than this, where the Inmost One had come in his trouble. They brought him presents of food, ponies, cattle and money of all kinds, including lumps of silver, large and small. Few of them had ever before had the opportunity of seeing the Head of the Faith.

At Urga lived the Chief Lama of Mongolia. He ranked next after the Dalai and Panchen Lamas, and in Mongolia itself held a position in many respects analogous to that held by the Dalai Lama in Tibet. But he stood lower, for he did not occupy quite so high a spiritual eminence, nor wield so wide a secular power as did the Head of Tibet. Accordingly the Chief Lama of Mongolia suffered greatly both in revenue and reputation from the presence of the Supreme Head. Besides, the Mongol Holiness habitually drank wine, and drank heavily; he smoked, even in the presence of the Dalai Lama, and he had married a wife, three heavy sins for a monk, especially one of the reformed sect. Indeed, a Russian who knew him told me that he would frequently be drunk and incapable in public places. He would ask the Mongols, "How can you believe in a Divinity who is a drunkard?"

"You are not an inner man (i.e., not a Buddhist) and so do not understand," they would say. "He is not drunk, but acts like this to test our faith."

But the Dalai Lama did not accept this view, and relations between the two were sorely strained.

Messages received from Urga at this time show that throughout his stay in the Mongolian capital the Dalai Lama was carefully shepherded by the Russian Consul. During June, M. Pokotiloff, the new Russian Minister to China, reached Urga, and immediately after his arrival called upon the Dalai Lama, to whom he handed two packages of presents from the Tsar. Some leading Russians in St. Petersburg, who had the ear of the Emperor, attached great importance to these courtesies shown to the Dalai Lama, feeling that they would endear Russia to the entire Buddhist world. The correspondence of a leading English paper considered such an idea to be far fetched, but the Russians appraised the situation a good deal better than he did, for the Buddhists of Asia and Russia, and especially those of Central Asia, have an intense veneration for the Head of Tibetan Buddhism.

Indeed, the Russians gauged the Dalai Lama's position better than the British or Americans did. Their affinity to the Tibetans is much closer. They have annexed to their territory in Siberia several hundred thousand square miles of Mongol countries. They have inter-married freely with the Mongols, whose connection with the Tibetans is so intimate.

The chief medical officer with the Younghusband expedition to Lhasa was Lt.-Col. L.A. Waddell, who had written a thoughtful book on Tibetan Buddhism, and was one of the leading authorities on the Tibetan religion. At this time he wrote of "the hopeless character of the Dalai Lama," and "his ungovernable temper and incapacity for government," two estimates that proved to be singularly far from the truth.

About four years later the Dalai Lama was in Peking, and Dorjieff was there also. At that time the American Minister in Peking was W.W. Rockhill, a scholarly man, and one who had been interested in Tibet from the time of his college days. He spoke the Tibetan language and had travelled in eastern Tibet. In a letter to the President of the United States, Rockhill wrote that he had had a long conversation with Dorjieff. From this conversation Rockhill gathered "that the Dalai Lama cared very little, if at all, for anything which did not affect his personal privileges and prerogatives, that he separated entirely his cause from those of the people of Tibet, which he was willing to abandon entirely to the mercy of China. He did not care particularly concerning the contemplated administrative reforms, so long as he could feel assured that his personal honours and privileges were safe, and, if possible, slightly added to."

But here Rockhill erred seriously. As the years rolled on, few things were more clear to those of us who were closely connected with the Dalai Lama or with the affairs of Tibet than the Dalai Lama's strong wish to benefit Tibet. This was amply recognised by Tibetans themselves both before and after the Dalai Lama's death.

The Tsar, on the other hand, sent the following telegram to the Dalai Lama: "A large number of my subjects who profess the Buddhist faith had the happiness of being able to pay homage to their great High Lama during his visit to northern Mongolia, which borders on the Russian Empire. As I rejoice that my subjects have had the opportunity of deriving benefit from your salutary spiritual influence, I beg you to accept the expression of my sincere thanks and my regards."

The winter of Urga had proved severe for some of the Tibetans. The Dalai Lama used to tell me that he found the winter in Ta Kuren, as he called Urga, much colder than the winter in Lhasa. Though he had all the hardihood of the Tibetan peasant, he noticed cold a little more than the others did, because the home of his parents was in the comparatively warm province of Takpo, to the south-east of Lhasa. He spent the next winter also in Mongolia; but he quitted Urga, partly on account of the jealousy felt by the Grand Lama of Urga, and partly because when two personages of this high class live close together in Mongolia or Tibet, poor countries with scanty populations, the burden of maintaining them with presents of food and unpaid service entails great hardship on the farmers and shepherds in the neighbourhood. Law and custom prescribe that on such occasions food for the entire party – in the Dalai Lama's case several hundred persons – and for the transport animals with them, has to be provided without payment beyond a small gratuity. Service also – cooks, water-carriers, grooms, etc. – has to be rendered on similar terms.

Meanwhile the Dalai Lama despatched Dorjieff to St. Petersburg to see "the Great White Tsar," and to ask "for protection from the dangers which threaten my life, if I return to Lhasa, as is my intention and duty." He distrusted and feared the British invaders. To this message the Tsar returned a friendly answer, for the Buddhists who acknowledged the Dalai Lama as their spiritual Head were among the most loyal of the Tsar's non-Russian subjects.

In July, 1906, the Chinese Foreign Office told the British Legation in Peking half-contemptuously, "The Dalai Lama is wandering about. We hope eventually to find some temple where he can settle down." But Tibetans do not feel the need to "settle down," as the Chinese do, tied to their little patches of cultivation. Nomads as they are by instinct and inclination, the people of Tibet are accustomed to wander across mountains and valleys and plains for hundreds, even thousands, of miles. The nomadic spirit is still strong in them.

Three months later the Inmost One was at Kanchow in Kansu province; in December at Hsining, near the Tibetan border. "No, we have no intention," stated the Chinese Government, "of allowing him, as yet, to return to Tibet." At this time he visited also the "Monastery of a Hundred Thousand Images" (Künbum), the most famous monastery in north-eastern Tibet, for it is the birthplace of the founder of the reformed sect, and is therefore known to the Tibetans as the second birthplace of Buddha.

The fact was that His Holiness himself did not wish to return to Lhasa at present. He still had his eye on Russia. Meanwhile the Chinese authorities were careful to give him honourable treatment. When he arrived at Sianfu, all Chinese officials, including the Governor, went outside the city walls to receive him. He was accompanied by fifty Tibetan horsemen, some carrying flags and some carrying guns or rifles, with four hundred other followers, and five hundred camels.

But the hope of aid from Russia was dashed to the ground.

August, 1907, brought the Anglo-Russian Convention regarding Persia, Afghanistan and Tibet. In this Convention Russia agreed to leave Tibetan politics alone; Britain agreed to do so in most respects, but Russia recognised her "special interest in the maintenance of the *status quo* in the external relations of Tibet."

His efforts to obtain assistance from Russia having failed, the Dalai Lama turned towards Britain. Next January Sir John Jordan, the British Minister to China, received a complimentary letter from His Holiness. The envoy who conveyed this assured Sir John that "the Dalai Lama now desires friendly relations with India, and thoroughly understands the position of affairs; whereas in 1903 the circumstances which led to the rupture were concealed from him by his subordinates." At the same time the Lama wished to claim an independent position for Tibet. So his envoy visited the Russian Legation and those of other Powers. He would establish a link with other nations also. But could they help him? No; Tibet was too far away; they had no armies on her border, not even diplomats. China might help, if she wished, large, populous China, surging round her frontiers. And Britain, being established in India, might help. Could he rely on both, or either?

There was so much seriousness in his life, so little relaxation, that it is good to read in the Tibetan Government's biography that on one day, when approaching Wutaishan on pilgrimage, "he climbed up to the top of a high rock, and was in a care-free mood." The biography records plentifully his hardships and his struggles to improve the lives of his people, mainly on the spiritual side, but to some extent also on the secular. Only on this one occasion does it record that he himself was relaxed and care-free. We might have put it down to the fresh air and exercise. But the Tibetan biography will have none of this, saying, "He must have received some vision there."

Worldly politics weighed him down, but the holy religion could not be neglected. Everything depended on that, and it was for him to guide his people by showing them the two-fold Way, spiritual and material guidance. Thus it came that April, 1908, found the whole cavalcade worshipping at the shrines on the

Wutaishan mountain in the province of Shansi. This, the holiest place in all China to the Tibetan Buddhist, known to Tibetans as "Five-peaked Mountain," was even in those days only four or five days' journey from Peking. It is sacred to Manjushri, the Buddha of Wisdom, who ranks level with Chenrezig, the Buddha of Compassion. The Dalai Lama being an incarnation of Chenrezig, it was eminently suitable that he should show homage to Manjushri, whose incarnation is the Manchu Emperor. Compassion needs wisdom, and wisdom needs compassion; it is good for both.

Wutaishan has been sacred to Buddhism for more than fourteen hundred years; the Dalai Lama visited this site with all the fervour that Tibetans devote to objects of the highest sanctity. A holy being on pilgrimage. He lived in a monastery in great state and with a large retinue, for he was not only above all men, but above the lesser divinities also. Politics were of less account now; the atmosphere was religious, but there were occasional lapses. A German doctor visited His Holiness, and presented to him an illustrated book on the death-dealing weapons of German arsenals. He wished to show that another powerful nation would help him against the British foe. The Dalai Lama accepted the book, for to refuse a present would be a discourtesy. But he went no further in the matter. He felt that Germany was too far away to be able to help.

The Tibetan biography records that many a Chief in Mongolia sent to the Dalai Lama at this time to ask for the blessing of a son and heir; and it is claimed that the wish of each was granted.

He was to come to Peking for an audience with the Emperor, but religion comes first, and Peking in the height of the summer is unpleasantly hot for Tibetans. So September found the large gathering still at Wutaishan. The Chinese newspapers were displeased with them. According to the Peking correspondent of the London *Times*, "Chinese newspapers are waging a campaign against the Dalai Lama and his mission, and casting scorn upon his country. The provincial officials of Shansi, in which Wutaishan is situated, grumble loudly at the burden imposed on the provincial treasury by the entertainment of the Dalai Lama

and his following. The Tibetans complain quite as feelingly of
the treatment to which they are subjected by the Chinese authorities, and declare that of the sums alleged to be allotted by the
treasury only a small proportion reaches them."

Foreigners of several nationalities who visited Wutaishan during the stay of the Dalai Lama were impressed by the orderly
conduct of the Tibetans, and their friendly relations with the
people. The Tibetans, they said, had been made heartily welcome, and had brought much prosperity to the sacred spot,
which, on account of this visit by the Inmost One, had been
thronged by Mongols from all parts of Mongolia.

The Tibetans indeed were not much impressed by the Chinese
complaint. They remembered the acts of extortion practised by
the various Ambans during the last two hundred years, both
while travelling through Tibet and while stationed in Lhasa.
When a Chinese Envoy raised the complaint at a later date, the
Tibetan Prime Minister reminded him forcibly of the above
facts.

It must be admitted that everywhere the Dalai Lama treated
his Chinese escort with contempt. The Chinese did not help him
against the British. Why did they push in now between him and
his Tibetan followers, who were well able to guard him here? He
despised the Chinese soldiers. A high Chinese official was sent
to escort him to Peking. To him the Dalai Lama remarked, "The
Emperor of China has dismissed me." The official was greatly
ashamed and murmured that such a dismissal was impossible. At
an interview granted to the representative of an English newspaper he expressed friendly sentiments for Great Britain. Russia
was receding into the background.

He remained for five months at Wutaishan, communing with
the Lord of Wisdom, Manjushri.

9   Golden Peking

In September, 1908, the Dalai Lama arrives in Peking. His entry is made in state. The standard-bearers in the procession, the musicians, the yellow Chair of State, and especially the band of solemn monks clad from shoulder to foot in dark red robes, remind the European onlookers of a scene from the Middle Ages. The procession wends its way to the well-known Yellow Temple, one mile beyond the northern wall of the Tartar city, which is to the north of the Chinese city, these two together forming the whole city of Peking. In this Temple, built by a former Manchu Emperor for the Great Fifth, the Dalai Lama takes up his residence.

The reception is highly honourable to the Lama, but now comes the real struggle between him and the Government of China. There are two things to be fought for. He is to be received in audience by the Emperor on October 6th. The Government arrange that the Emperor will stand to receive him; the Dalai Lama will kotow, i.e., kneel and touch the ground with his forehead. Afterwards he will be given a seat on a low couch near the Throne. But His Holiness is not unmindful of the reception of the Fifth Dalai Lama, the only other Dalai Lama to meet the Emperor of China. The Thirteenth told me about this less than two years after his own sojourn in Peking. When the Fifth Dalai Lama entered, arrangements were made by which he could pass over the city walls instead of under them. For his people condemn the idea of anybody being over the head of Chenrezig's Incarnation. And at his audience with the Emperor the latter came down from his throne and advanced eighteen yards to meet him. The Fifth was greeted with all the ceremony that could have been accorded to any independent sovereign. At that period the temporal power of the Dalai Lama backed by the arms of a Mongol chieftain, and the devotion of all Mongolia, was not a thing for the Emperor of China to question. Notwithstanding the advice of his Chinese counsellors, who had intimated to him that he was the Lord Paramount, the Emperor fully realised that the Dalai Lama was the most powerful ally he could secure in establishing Manchu rule among the Mongols, and he treated him accordingly.

But Mongolia, as well as Tibet, is weaker now in material strength. Buddhism controls her conscience; military service has become sinful, for it involves the taking of human life, one of the worst possible sins for a Buddhist. Still, the Dalai Lama, the Vice-Regent of Buddha, objects to knocking his head on the ground. The audience has to be postponed, and when held a few days later, is made more acceptable. He is required ony to touch the ground with the right knee. The Empress Dowager and the Emperor receive him separately.

His second contest with his Chinese overlord is as to the future government of Tibet, and especially his own share in it. The Government of China would like to annex Tibet outright, carving it into provinces of China. Tibet, which up to the time of the Younghusband expedition in 1904 treated the Chinese suzerainty with half-veiled contempt, has been shaken by that expedition, and now lies at the mercy of China. Now, while he is helpless in China, is the time to put pressure on the Head of Tibet. But the Dalai Lama is wary, and is able to withstand any such extreme measure. However, his old title is modified to mark his new subordination. When he visited Peking as the Great Fifth, the Manchu Emperor of that period gave him a gold tablet inscribed with the title, "Most Excellent, Self-Existing Buddha, Universal Ruler of the Buddhist Faith, Holder of the Sceptre, Dalai Lama." The Government of China now describe his earlier title as merely "Most Excellent, Self-Existing Buddha of the West." They ignore those two inconvenient phrases, "Universal Ruler of the Buddhist Faith" and "Holder of the

Sceptre"; they smack too strongly of sovereignty. And the title is further changed to "The Sincerely Obedient, Reincarnation-helping, Most Excellent, Self-Existing Buddha of the West." A position of subordination must be marked out and proclaimed.

He tries to obtain the right to address the Manchu Emperor direct, that he may make known to the Throne his opinions on matters vital to his country. This right, refused in the past, is still refused. He is told that he must represent his case to the Manchu Amban in Lhasa; the latter will put the matter before the Government. The denial of this right had placed the Tibetan Government at the mercy of the Chinese officials in Tibet, until the young Dalai Lama had taken to ignoring the Amban and acting on his own initiative. But now, after the trouble with the British, he is powerless.

In his political testament – composed more than twenty years later – the Dalai Lama wrote, "The Sovereigns, mother and son (Dowager Empress and Emperor), treated me well beyond measure." He was courteous enough to write favourably of the Emperor in public, though he himself had on occasions received scant courtesy from the Government of China. But speaking to me in private, after the Chinese invasion of Tibet, he criticised the Emperor, doubting whether he was really, as supposed, an incarnation of Manjushri, the Buddha of Wisdom.

The Precious Sovereign – this is one of his Tibetan titles, but where is his sovereignty now? – during his wanderings outside his own country, has seen and heard a good deal about the Europeans who rule nations outside the limits of China. It seems that they are, after all, not so unreasonable or harmful. He cannot establish contact with all of them, but he will do so with the more powerful ones. Accordingly one of his emissaries calls on the British, American, French, German and Russian Legations. The American and French Ministers both call upon the Dalai Lama a day or two later, and are received in private audience. They stand outside, no doubt; but the Russian and British Ministers are more intimately concerned. They therefore hold counsel together, and decide that they will treat their respective interviews on similar lines.

Accordingly Sir John Jordan, the British Minister, accompanied by his full staff of twelve persons, visits the Lama at the Yellow Temple. After a considerable delay in the waiting-room, the party is summoned to the reception-hall in another courtyard of the building. At the entrance are two Tibetan soldiers armed with rifles. On entering the room they find the Dalai Lama seated cross-legged on yellow satin cushions, placed on an altar-like table about four feet high. It stands in a recess and is draped in yellow satin; yellow is the Dalai Lama's special colour for, while he is the Head of all Tibet, he belongs to the sect of the Yellow Hats. The Dalai Lama does not rise from his seat to receive the British Minister. For five of the Minister's staff, including the Minister himself, seats are arranged. When they enter, the Minister and each of the staff bow and present a Tibetan scarf of ceremony. The Dalai Lama turns the Minister's scarf over with his own hands, while an abbot, who stands at his right-hand side, performs this ceremony for him in the case of the staff. Now the five available seats are occupied, and the rest of the staff stand near the entrance.

The Dalai Lama speaks in Tibetan. This is interpreted into Chinese by an attendant monk, and into English by a secretary of the Legation who understands Chinese exceptionally well. The Minister's replies in English reach the Dalai Lama in Tibetan through the same circuitous channel. From the Dalai Lama's point of view, the object of the interview is, after referring to the fact that India and Tibet are neighbours, to send through the Minister a message to the British King-Emperor as follows: "Some time ago events occurred which were not of my creating; they belong to the past, and it is my sincere desire that peace and friendship should exist between the two neighbouring countries." The interpretation, however, of the Dalai Lama's message is at first bungled, and the Dalai Lama has to repeat it before it is made clear. The Minister says that he will certainly carry out the Lama's request.

A pause ensues. Has the Minister anything further that he wishes to discuss?

"No."

"Then I will bid the Minister farewell." And, when doing so, presents him with a pound or two of jujubes, certified to increase the length of his life. The reception lasts only for eight minutes.

The Dalai Lama's loose robes are maroon and yellow in colour, and his arms are bare nearly to the shoulder. His fingers work nervously the whole time, but the proceedings are carried out with perfect dignity.

In his letter to the President of the United States, Rockhill writes, "The special interest to me is in that I have probably been a witness to the overthrow of the temporal power of the Dalai Lama, which, curiously enough, I heard twenty years ago predicted in Tibet, where it was commonly said that the Thirteenth Dalai Lama would be the last, and my client *is* the Thirteenth." But this prophecy, as mentioned above,[9] was a sham one invented by some monks in the Tengyeling monastery. Indeed, the Fourteenth Dalai Lama was discovered a few years after the death of the Thirteenth and placed upon the throne. And the temporal power of the Thirteenth Dalai Lama and the Gelugpa or reformed sect, was not overthrown, but on the contrary, a few years after Rockhill's prediction, became stronger than it had been for many decades. It was indeed natural that in the circumstances of that period Rockhill should fail to recognise the strong will inside that small down-trodden figure, and the pertinacity of the Tibetan nation.

For a long time the Dowager Empress of China has deprived the young Emperor of his power, since he is inclined to the party of reform, a policy of which she disapproves. She is keeping him a close prisoner in the Summer Palace. Her death draws near, but the very day before she dies the Emperor himself opportunely dies, and she has the satisfaction of feeling that his policy of reform will fade away with him. Such evidence as is available of the happenings in the grim prison chamber within the high walls of the Forbidden City – at that time really forbidden – points strongly to the conclusion that she has caused him to be poisoned. The Dalai Lama conducts a religious service for their benefit in the Temple, much to the gratification of the Government of China. He receives the thanks of the Regent, together with presents both for himself and for all the monks who have taken part in the service.

The Lama on his side has several questions to discuss with the Chinese Government, but the death of the two Sovereigns, and the period of strict mourning that follows, renders all such discussion difficult. However, as he tells us in his political testament, "I represented fully the facts of the case" to the Emperor who succeeded.

On the 21st December he leaves Peking on his return to Tibet. He is escorted to the railway station by a number of Manchu and Mongolian princes and other nobles, all of whom march on foot. He enquires from the Regent whether he may leave some members of his suite to teach the Tibetan language to Chinese in Peking, and suggests that he should send from Lhasa some young Tibetans to study Chinese. The Regent welcomes both suggestions with alacrity; anything that will bring the two countries closer together is to the Chinese advantage.

The cost to the Manchu Government of the Dalai Lama's visit to Peking is between £30,000 and £40,000. A high cost, but it pays the Government, both on account of the Dalai Lama's power in Tibet and his compelling influence in Mongolia, two countries with scanty populations but a combined area equal to two-thirds of Europe. When the Dalai Lama used to tell me, "The Mongols have great faith in me," I noted that the Tibetan word for "faith" that he used on these occasions was not the word for secular trust, but that for spiritual faith (*te-pa*), the same word as a Tibetan would use for faith in Buddha. To have the Dalai Lama on their side helps the Manchu Government to control the Mongols as well as the Tibetans.

Why did China want the Dalai Lama at Peking? Mainly, no doubt: (1) To show him as a subordinate of the Dragon Throne. (2) To emphasise this by modifying his title through the addition of the words "The Sincerely Obedient," and marking it down in other respects. (3) To endeavour to force the Dalai Lama, while an exile in the Chinese capital, to agree to such changes in the Government of Tibet as would increase the influence of China in that country.

After the Dalai Lama's departure from China's capital, the correspondent of the London *Times* in Peking takes the opportunity of praising the good behaviour of the Tibetans during their stay. He writes, "During the stay of the Dalai Lama in Peking the demeanour of his followers has been excellent, and has given no ground for the outrageous stories of misconduct, nor any justification for such epithets as 'barbarian hordes,' applied to them by certain European newspapers. His visit has coincided with the end of his temporal power, but he has been treated with the dignity befitting his spiritual office."

In his political testament the Dalai Lama mentions his journey to "Golden Peking" and the hardship attendant thereon. "I went because the Great Fifth Dalai Lama and the Manchu Emperor had made an agreement to help each other in the way that a monk and a layperson help each other." There is no subordination in such a relationship; it is the duty of the layman (the Emperor) to help the monk (the Dalai Lama) in all worldly necessities. That was the line that the Dalai Lama and his Ministers always took when discussing with me the political relationship between China and Tibet.

10 Chinese Troops Invade Tibet

In 1904 the British Government had shown that it was both able and willing to send troops across the lofty Tibetan mountains and occupy the capital. True, after effecting their treaty, the British had retired. But the shock to China was severe; she feared that on some future occasion they might come again, and not go back the second time. She had not signed the treaty when Tibet did; and, later on, she consented to adhere to it only after several of its provisions had been whittled down. This new Convention between Britain and China was signed at Peking in April, 1906, and was followed by fresh Trade Regulations two years later. The joint effect of these was to establish Chinese power in Tibet more strongly than it had been before the British expedition went to Lhasa in 1904.

The Government of China now planned to conquer and control Tibet, in order to prevent the establishment of British influence. By degrees they pushed troops into the country. The Tibetans were weakened and disorganised by the previous British invasion; the Dalai Lama, the religious and secular leader, was far away.

In 1909 the Dalai Lama was returning to Lhasa from Peking and the religious side of his administration was taking up a good deal of his time. He found the discipline slack in the monastery of a Hundred Thousand Images (Künbum), near the large lake in north-eastern Tibet, known as Koko Nor. Accordingly he tightened the discipline in spite of opposition from the monastery itself. He visited other important monasteries that rank high in the history of Tibetan Buddhism. A good deal of time passed, but in any case the religion could not be neglected.

While the Inmost One was on his way to Lhasa in 1909, a new Chinese administrator, named Chao Erh-feng, was pushing his troops towards Lhasa.

The Tibetan biography says:

"Some of the infuential Chinese Ministers in whose hearts the devils dwelt, the Governor-General of Szechuan, and Chao Erh-feng, and the Amban in Tibet, all these having agreed upon an intrigue had played an evil trick like an underground thread. Attacks were launched in three different Tibetan provinces. They destroyed many monasteries. Sacred images were melted and made into bullets, and thousands of innocent monks were killed. The monastic properties were looted."

The Dalai Lama and his Ministers used also to tell me that the Chinese military officers had torn up the sacred books, the Tibetan Buddhist bible in one hundred and eight volumes, and used the parchment leaves for soling the boots of their men. This piece of sacrilege aroused the anger of the Tibetans even more than the killing of the monks.

On this return journey His Holiness heard of the new invasion. His Chinese hosts had given him no hint of it, although it was a breach of their peaceful arrangement with him in Peking.

Things look black for the Dalai Lama. How do the Chinese justify their invasion? This time they have imported into the Holy City a startling novelty – to wit, a newspaper published in Tibetan. In one of the issues the Tibetans read:

"Do not be afraid of Amban Chao and his soldiers. They are not intended to do harm to Tibetans, but to other people. If you consider, you will remember how you felt ashamed when the foreign soldiers arrived in Lhasa and oppressed you with much tyranny. We must all strengthen ourselves on this account, otherwise our religion will be destroyed."

Another paragraph tells them, "There are in Tibet some wicked, aggressive foreigners, with whom intercourse has to be maintained. For the purpose of doing various kinds of work, men who know English well are required to carry out the work."

China wished to unite Nepal, Sikkim and Bhutan against the British, "the wicked aggressive foreigners." She tells Tibet that they are "like men in one house." In a separate letter they are called "the molar teeth in a man's mouth." See them side by side, bestriding the high Himalaya between Tibet's frozen uplands on the north and India's burning plains down to the south. China wanted them as the southern barrier of Tibet; the British as the northern barrier of India.

At this time the Chinese were strongly pressing the Tibetan authorities to unite with Bhutan. Probably they had heard of the proposal of Claude White and myself for making a treaty between Great Britain and Bhutan. Some months previously I had visited Simla and secured the Government of India's acceptance of the terms that I thought best. These were to the effect that Bhutan placed its foreign relations under the control of the British Government, who on their side undertook to exercise no interference in the internal administration of Bhutan.

When at length the British Government in England gave their consent, I consulted with Kazi Ugyen, now the able Envoy of the Bhutanese Government, who lived at Kalimpong, thirty-five miles from Gangtok, my headquarters, across three low mountain ranges. I had met him during my pioneering expedition through Bhutan in 1904, and had gained his personal friendship during the intervening years. After securing his co-operation, I picked my track across the Bhutanese mountains, and gained the acceptance of the Bhutanese Government. This was composed of the Ruler, the subordinate Chiefs, and the High Lama. When the treaty was completed, the Ruler assured me in public that he and his Government were completely satisfied with its terms. From that day in February, 1910, to the present time Bhutan has turned a deaf ear to Chinese overtures. The treaty added to the British sphere of influence an area two and a half times the size of Wales, and filled a dangerous gap, two hundred and fifty miles long, in India's north-eastern frontier.

Why should Bhutan leave Tibet and China and join the British? Racially, they are the same as Tibet. True. Culturally, they go with Tibet. Yes, it is so. In religion – a still more important factor – they are the same as Tibet. Again, true. On the other hand, we may say that, economically, the draw towards India was becoming stronger. But the real deciding factors were two. Firstly, Britain's ability to protect them against aggression; China could not have done so. Secondly, Britain's promise that she would not interfere in their internal administration. This last condition I pressed strongly on the British Government; and it was this, coupled with British power, that won the day. Just as the Dalai Lama and nearly all Tibetans want home rule for Tibet – or, as they call it, "own rule" (*rang wang*) – so do the Bhutanese for Bhutan. The Chinese always attempted to introduce their own control – soldiers and magistrates – into the internal administration of countries related, however distantly, to China. In fact, China would not have left Bhutan's internal affairs alone, while we agreed to do so. In these circumstances Bhutan preferred to join Britain.

As he drew nearer to Lhasa the Dalai Lama found that the Government of China had broken their pledges to him not to interfere with his position in Tibet. They were actually attacking the heart of his country. What should he do in such a case? His knowledge of world affairs was almost non-existent. Pathetic were the cables which he forwarded to the British Agent at Gyangtse for despatch to "Great Britain and all the Ministers of Europe." "Large insects are eating small insects," which in Tibetan parlance means the oppression of the weak by the strong. To the Chinese Foreign Office in Peking he telegraphed his opinion of their representatives in Tibet, "We have acted frankly, and now they steal our heart."

At this time I had of necessity to be absent in Bhutan, having gone there to negotiate this treaty. The matter was urgent, because I could not but recognise the danger of China's pressure on this portion of the Indian frontier, a pressure that could show itself in various ways, which need not be detailed here. The treaty successfully accomplished, I was returning via India to Sikkim. But Bhutan being entirely innocent of post and telegraph offices, it was not until I was near the Indian frontier that I heard of the events that were happening in Tibet.

11   The Flight from Lhasa to India

In December, 1909, the Dalai Lama arrived in Lhasa, after five years' absence. Less than two months later the blow fell. Two thousand Chinese soldiers had arrived within striking distance of Lhasa, and soon afterwards an advance guard of Chinese mounted troops burst into the city, fired on the populace, and laid plans to seize the Dalai Lama and his Ministers. Had they succeeded, they would have put the latter to death, for a reward of one thousand rupees was offered for the head of each of them. The Dalai Lama himself, if captured, they would have held in close restraint, affixing his seal to their decrees and to the higher administrative acts of the new Chinese executive.

But the Ministers immediately joined their Chief in the Potala Palace, itself a strong building with massive walls lying up the face of a low hill. Here a hurried consultation was held with the result that they decided to attempt to reach India. Tibet is surrounded on all four sides by either Chinese or Indian territory. The former was obviously out of the question, and the latter is fortunately nearer, so it was to the land of their old enemy that they turned.

The same night they fled. Their way lay along the boulder-strewn track that leads from Lhasa to the Tsangpo, the great river of southern Tibet, forty miles to the south of the Holy City. It was February; the full blast of the Tibetan winter, twelve thousand feet above the level of the sea, was upon them, but their own lives as well as the future of Tibet were at stake. So they rode as they had never ridden before.

The following morning they reached and crossed the river.

Here the Dalai Lama's favourite young attendant, Chensa Nangkang, stayed behind with a handful of Tibetan levies, who, untrained and poorly armed as they were, yet contrived to hold back two hundred pursuing Chinese soldiers for a considerable time. Indeed in a letter to the Government of India the Dalai Lama asserted that in this guerrilla fighting seventy Chinese soldiers were killed. The villagers in that part of the country also managed, as the Dalai Lama afterwards informed me with boyish glee, to deceive the Chinese as to the route followed by the fugitives. The Tibetan levies dispersed into the recesses of the mountains, while Nangkang rode hard after his Chief. One who rides like this in the public service is entitled to borrow a pony from a village as he passes through, and change it from stage to stage, thus making greater speed and distance.

Gyan-tse, the third largest town in Tibet, lies between Lhasa and India, and at that time contained a garrison of Chinese soldiers. The fugitives therefore avoided it and took what may perhaps be termed a Tibetan by-pass, that is, a track running through the mountains between Lhasa and the Himalaya, some thirty miles east of Gyan-tse, and, incidentally, shorter than the main route. This enabled them to reach the Chatsa monastery on the lower slopes of the sacred mountain, Chomolhari. This last day when he crossed "The Plain of the Three Brothers," thirty miles long and fifteen thousand feet above the level of the sea, was the worst of the whole journey. The Tibetan biography laments that as they rode along, "snow fell heavily almost to the stirrups, and the wind pierced him continuously like thorns."

From Chatsa he went the few miles farther to Pari, for which visiting Europeans usually claim the distinction of being the dirtiest town in the world, as it is certainly one of the coldest. You do not step up into your house at Pari but down, for the houses there, built with sods of peat, are partly underground for the sake of warmth. July is the most summery month, but even in July you will sometimes ride or walk through falls of snow.

Pari had a small Chinese garrison but not large enough to arrest the fugitives, who were now escorted by a motley collection of Tibetan villagers, equipped with such antiquated weapons as they could lay their hands on. Here the party made their first contact with officials of the Government of India in the person of Mr. Rosemeyer, a quiet, efficient officer in charge of the telegraph lines in Tibet and Sikkim. Himself of mixed European and Asiatic parentage, he lived his lonely life in close contact with the Tibetans. On his own initiative he met the forlorn fugitives and took them to the governmental staging bungalow. Though no Indian soldiers were stationed in Pari, the Dalai Lama felt safer in this bungalow.

The party were now undecided whether to make for India or for the Himalayan State of Bhutan. The way to the former lay down the Chumbi Valley, and then a rough climb of five thousand feet to the Dzelep Pass, which forms the boundary between Tibet and Sikkim, the total distance from Pari to the Dzelep Pass being forty miles. The boundary of Bhutan lay only about two miles away over easy ground. The Bhutanese are of the same race as the Tibetans, follow the same religion, and venerate the Dalai Lama. The Ministers advocated coming to Bhutan. The Dalai Lama resorted to a very simple form of divination as to whether he should attempt the Chumbi Valley route. He shut his eyes, and put the tips of his two forefingers to meet across his forehead. The tips met; so he decided to face the forty miles instead of only two. When he came safely through, the Tibetans took it as another sign that he was a real incarnation of Chenrezig. In his own written account the Dalai Lama indicates that he wished to come to India, both because Buddhism having originated there, it is to Tibetans a holy land, and because he wished to use the mediation of the British Government for representing matters to China.

The next step was to Yatung, twenty-eight miles away, where there was a British Agent, Mr. Macdonald, with a tiny detachment of Indian soldiers. Sikkim, safe from the pursuing Chinese soldiery, lay only twelve miles beyond. The Tibetan Agent at Yatung, with the rank of colonel but a timid mind, went to meet the fugitive with such men as he could collect. The Tibetan retinue was now large enough to frighten off the local Chinese troops, who were of inferior quality.

Arrived in Yatung, the Dalai Lama stopped in the British Agency house there with Mr. Macdonald. The two slept in the same bedroom. But His Holiness did not feel safe, for the Chinese were hot on his trail, and so, after halting one day in Yatung, he rode on down the valley, then up and over the Dzelep La ("Lovely Level Pass") into Sikkim and safety. At this time of year the snow is very deep, and after crossing the pass they did not reach Gnatong, the first habitation, seven miles away, till five hours after nightfall. Gnatong, a cluster of rough-hewn log huts, lay snowbound in the hollow of the mountains. One of its chief features was the cemetery, where British soldiers lay buried. The other was the log hut which serves as a telegraph office linking Tibet and India. Most of these telegraph offices were manned by ex-soldiers; here there were two, Sergeants Luff and Humphreys.

It would be hard to imagine a duller life than that of the telegraphists at Gnatong, but it has occasional flashes of interest. One such came now, when the spiritual and temporal head of Tibet and his government came under the protection of two British ex-soldiers. Luff was in charge; he has told me what happened at Gnatong, which he describes with perfect truth as "one of the most bleak and lonely places of the British Empire, known for its most dangerous lightning, either raining or snowing, sometimes both." Detachments of British troops had been stationed there till 1895. Every such detachment had lost men who had strayed from the track in snow or mist, and had been unable to find it again. The snow remains at full depth for several months, and even in summer the mist does not clear for two or three weeks at a time.

"About the middle of February," says Luff, "we were getting persistent rumours in our small place that the Dalai Lama had fled from Lhasa and was on his way to India for refuge from the Chinese. I telephoned for information, but none came until some days later, when the Dalai Lama arrived at Pari safe, to the relief of us all. Later on, Mr. Macdonald telephoned to me to watch for his arrival at Gnatong, and give him what protection two military telegraphists could render.

"On the day he was to arrive we waited many anxious hours. It was very deep snow on the ground and still snowing. At half-past nine at night we thought he must have halted for the night on the road. It had been dark for over three hours, and you know how hard it is to find that narrow track in the deep snow even in the daytime. They could never come now, so we got ready for bed. Three-quarters of an hour afterwards we heard hammering on the office door.

"Who's there?' No reply.

"Again there was knocking, so we opened the office door, and found a gathering of Tibetans all in the most excited condition.

"I said, 'Who the hell are you?'

"They, 'The Dalai Lama.'

"I, 'Which of you blighters is the Dalai Lama?'

"They, 'He's coming.'

"I, 'Then who the hell told you to come here? Take yer Dalai Lama to the regular Dak Bungalow up there; it's much more comfortable than here.'

"But not a budge. They told us how they had held off their pursuers during the flight from Lhasa, and were rather too realistic swinging about their loaded revolvers, so we got them to put them away. Soon afterwards His Holiness turned up.

"One of the Tibs says, 'Here's the Dalai Lama.'

"I, 'Which blighter is the correct Dalai Lama? Yer all seem to think yer the Dalai Lama.'

"We again had it explained to him that this was only the telegraph office, and showed him where the dak bungalow was, but he asked to stay in our telegraph hut, so we let it go at that.

"We led him in, and gave them all hot cups of tea and such food as we had. There was no mistake he had been very scared, and showed signs of great relief on meeting us and getting under our roof. He sat down in front of the fire. Except one, whom His Holiness told to sit down, the other fellows all remained standing till dismissed; they wouldn't sit down in the presence of the Boss, even after their long day in the snow.

"After feeling better he looked round our office, finally settling in my bedroom, and after asking all about it and ourselves, asked if he might lie on my bed, a privilege I was only too pleased to grant. He saw I had a service rifle, and asked if we would give him protection if he was attacked during the night. We replied certainly, and Humphreys placed his rifle with mine. He was much relieved after this, and went to sleep. Two of his fellows slept in the bedroom in front of the fire, while both Humphreys and myself sat up to see nothing happened to him. Of course there were too many to stay in the office, so a number went out and slept in the veranda.

"Well, about those rifles. We had been given a transfer to Rungpo. You know Gnatong, sir, and how difficult it is get any transport even in summer, let alone in winter and snowing hard. So we had sent off our heavy boxes, and in them was our ammunition, and we had not a single round of ammunition for our rifles. However, His Holiness did not know, and slept soundly. He was absolutely worn out by fatigue and mental strain, which one could see was worrying him.

"Next morning he ate splendidly, and was very happy when we marched the first three miles with him, Humphreys in advance with his rifle at fixed bayonet at the slope, and myself behind likewise. Still minus ammunition. We wished him goodbye, and promised to keep the Chinese from following him. On leaving him there we both by strange coincidence remarked, 'Thank heaven we've got the Boss of Tibet off our bally hands safe and sound.' And we both heaved a sigh of relief, as the responsibility whatever one may say was risky and heavy."

Three miles beyond Gnatong the track descends abruptly into the heart of Sikkim, and Tibet seems far away.

Thus the chief spiritual overlord of central Asia made his first entry into the British Commonwealth, and spent his first night in the snowbound desolation of Gnatong, fortified by the protection and hospitality of two British sergeants. Neither they nor the Tibetans understood each other's language, but the British soldier is proverbially resourceful on such occasions. It was a strange setting.

A few days after leaving Gnatong the party rode into Kalimpong, the first considerable town on the Indian side. Among the many who went to see the lonely fugitives were their co-religionists from Bhutan and Sikkim, Nepalese, whose soldiers are known everywhere as Gurkhas, and traders from India. And among these were three little Scottish girls, daughters of Dr. Graham, the well-known missionary and founder of the Kalimpong Homes, that train European and Anglo-Indian children somewhat after the fashion of Barnardo's Homes in England, but with a splendid personality of its own.

Starting early, the girls rode three miles beyond the town, and were in time to see His Holiness and party arrive. He rode a fine mule sent by Raja Ugyen, the Agent of the Bhutanese Government. The animal was so covered with trappings that the Dalai Lama almost seemed to be seated Buddhawise on the top of it. They had come that day a short march of thirteen miles, making the usual early Tibetan start about sunrise, and arrived at Kalimpong while the sun was still low in the heavens. What a change from the snowbound wastes of Tibet! Here at 4,000 feet elevation, instead of 15,000, snow hardly ever falls, the mountainsides are green and brown, lit up here and there with the yellow splashes of the mustard crop, or the pink of the buckwheat.

It is not a slow, stately procession. The small, stocky ponies and mules do not move at a walk, nor even trot or gallop; but come at the amble or run, beloved of Tibetans, which takes them along at eight miles an hour. The three little girls slip in behind the great man himself, between him and his ministers, till the bazaar is reached three miles farther on.

Here the whole town turns out, Hindu, Christian and Moslem, lining the sides of the road, some bowing, some salaaming, while the numerous Buddhists among them throw their bodies on the ground, prostrating themselves in the thick dust of the roadway. All show respect, and many show reverence, to the forlorn Holiness coming on his second exile. The procession slows down; the little girls slip ahead to the staging bungalow a mile farther on, and wait by the house steps. Presently the greatest of all the Living Buddhas goes up, and, as he does so, passes his fingers through the golden hair of little Isa Graham, feeling it between finger and thumb, as one feels silken threads to test their quality and texture.

Now he goes in. No; he is out again, and comes down the steps to feel it once more, for till now he, "The Ruler of the Black Heads," as he is called by his subjects, has never seen hair of that colour. His attendants give that half-gasp, and put their tongues half-out of their mouths, the methods by which Tibetans show respectful astonishment.

The staging bungalow at Kalimpong was larger than most, and was comfortable. Here His Holiness halted two or three days, while the countryside flocked in to receive his blessing.

And then to Darjeeling, the summer capital of Bengal, perched along a ridge in the eastern Himalaya, seven thousand feet above the level of the sea. Any lower elevation would have been for them unhealthily hot, especially on their first arrival from the lofty altitudes of Tibet.

It was not long before the brave young favourite, who had kept back the Chinese troops, arrived at Pari, which was by then in Chinese occupation. A heavy price was on his head. The Chinese had placed men on watch at several of the bridges en route. The Dzongpöns of Pari sent some of their servants with him, and he managed to evade the watchers, and arrive in Yatung, twenty-eight miles away. Here he was put up in an outhouse belonging to one of Mr. Macdonald's servants. He carried two revolvers, and vowed that the Chinese should never take him alive; for if captured, they would certainly have executed him.

From Yatung he went with the postal runners, men who carry the letters and parcels between Pari and Sikkim. He did not wear the postal uniform or badge, but with his head no doubt bowed down a little under the load of mail, he was able to escape recognition, and to climb up through the snow to the pass, where he crossed the frontier into safety.

Thus the Dalai Lama arrived in Darjeeling, having ridden from Lhasa to Gnatong, a distance of two hundred and seventy miles, in nine days. Accustomed as he was to the dignified slowness of a Chair of State, this was for him a sterling achievement, more especially as the journey included four high passes and the chief river of southern Tibet. He had to ride over the icebound uplands in the depth of winter, the wind drove furiously in his face all the time, and culminated in that blizzard when crossing "The Plain of the Three Brothers." And with it all was the deep anxiety for his country.

Many British and other Europeans charged the Dalai Lama with cowardice, saying, "He should not have fled, but should have stood by his people in their time of trouble." But the Tibetans' view was completely different. They used to point out that, if the Dalai Lama had stayed, the Chinese, by imprisoning him, would have destroyed the independence of Tibet. As the Dalai Lama expressed it on another occasion, "It would have been like the rubbing out of a footprint." But by his hard ride to India he retained his own freedom, and was able to establish the freedom of his country, when the time was ripe.

We are now in February, 1910. When I was returning from Bhutan, a telegram arrived from the Indian Foreign Office summoning me to Calcutta. A brief stay there for consultation, and then to Darjeeling in time to meet the Dalai Lama.

12 The Second Exile

At first sight he did not look like a king. A squat figure, somewhat pockmarked, the features showed the plebeian origin of the farmer's son. But in Tibet things do not happen as elsewhere. Besides he was completely out of his setting. His kingdom gone, he was without the trappings of royalty. No palaces, no monkhood, not even the proper clothes; so sudden and rapid was his flight. Yet he was the spiritual and Secular leader-king of Tibet, the incarnation of Chenrezig himself.

It was my duty to look after this most unusual refugee; so I went to see him. The Darjeeling authorities, to whose district he had come, accommodated him in a hotel on a central and crowded site, overlooked by the road, which ran at the same level as its roof. His attendants had arranged a dais and a hurriedly contrived throne in one of the largest rooms. They seemed pathetically out of place in that European hotel with its European furniture and upholstery. But they were necessary. For in his own dominion and in the Buddhist lands that border on his own he remains exalted and aloof. When pilgrims pass near his palace, within half a mile or so, they prostrate themselves three times in the dust before it; and when he passes along, eyes are turned down towards the ground; they must not gaze upon divinity. Their only contact with him is when, humbly presenting their ceremonial scarves and other offerings to his attendants, the Presence touches their bowed heads with a tassel attached to a short rod.

However, in my case he made no use of throne or dais. To show honour to the British Representative he rose from his seat

103

and met me on the floor. Over my wrists he placed a gorgeous white silk scarf, and I one over his, the best I had been able to procure. For this is the recognised Tibetan form of greeting, and by placing the scarf, as he did, over my wrists, instead of round my neck, the Incarnation of Buddha disclaimed all superiority of rank. He then courteously showed his knowledge of European custom by proceeding to shake hands. He showed no sign of fatigue, but of course he would not have done so, however tired he might have been. That would not have been "The Way and the Custom," and even a Dalai Lama will seldom desert these.

The Dalai Lama was about five feet six inches in height, and therefore a little below the Tibetan average. His complexion was the darker hue of one of humble birth. The nose was slightly aquiline. The large well-set ears were a sign that he was an Incarnation of Chenrezig. Eyebrows curved high and a full moustache with the ends well waxed, accentuated the alertness of the administrator, rather than the monk meditating apart. His dark-brown eyes were large and very prominent. They lit up as he spoke or listened, and his whole countenance shone with a quiet eagerness. He had small, neat hands and the closely shaven head of the monk.

The Dalai Lama was thirty-four years old when I met him thus in Darjeeling, and already he moved with a pronounced stoop. For he had always to spend some nine hours daily seated cross-legged, of which four of five were devoted to religious study and meditation, in addition to the bestowal of blessings which, as the representative of Buddha, it was frequently his duty to give. His outer robe was of silk, yellow or red, and under it a thinner silk garment, white or yellow. Mongol boots, made of felt, reached to just below the knees.

I brought no interpreter into the room with me, and he seemed content that none should be present. The bowed figure looked up at me keenly, as if to say "What sort of a stranger is it with whom I have to deal from now onwards?" But before coming down to business, Tibetan custom prescribes that certain questions and answers, each to the other, must be gone through. One of these, when people go to call on each other, is, "Have you not had difficulty on the way?" From me to him seemingly ironical after his three hundred and sixty rough and dangerous miles; from him to me after a quarter-mile stroll along a trim Darjeeling road, absurd. But custom is inflexible.

There were several people present in the room when I entered, but as soon as the Dalai Lama began to tell me why he had to fly to India, all those present, including the Crown Prince of Sikkim, left the audience chamber, leaving me alone with His Holiness.

We spoke in the Tibetan of the Lhasa dialect, which is of all the most highly esteemed. He told me as follows:

"When the Bhutanese Agent presented the Viceroy's letter to me, I could not receive it since I had agreed with the Chinese to conduct Tibetan foreign affairs through Chinese intermediaries only. In like manner, when Colonel Younghusband wrote to me in the course of the Tibet expedition, the Chinese refused to allow me to send a reply. When in Peking, I received an assurance from the Emperor of China that I would retain my former power and position in Tibet, and that no harm would be done to the Tibetan people. This promise was broken after I came to Lhasa. The Chinese police already in Lhasa, and the forty Chinese mounted infantry who arrived there, fired upon inoffensive Tibetans in Lhasa, with the result that three of my people were killed and one high official was wounded.

"Then I fled. I feared that I would be made a prisoner in the Potala, and deprived of all temporal power. The Chinese sent four hundred soldiers by the direct route to Pari from Lhasa, and another party of three hundred along the road to Gyangtse, offering a reward to any one who captured me, and to any one who either captured or killed my Ministers. Some of the Chinese letters containing these offers fell into my hands.

"I have come to India to ask the help of the British Government against the Chinese. Unless they intervene, China will occupy Tibet and oppress it; she will destroy the Buddhist religion there and the Tibetan Government, and will govern the country through Chinese officials. Eventually her power will be extended into the States on the border between Tibet and India.

There are already two thousand Chinese troops in Lhasa and its neighbourhood; others are following, and so large a number of troops is not needed to garrison Tibet alone."

Thus he recounted the deceits and oppressions of the hated Chinese, but always in a low, quiet voice, varied at times with a cheerful laugh, as when he described how his people had turned the pursuing soldiers on to a wrong scent. Thus began a friendship between us that was to last until he died twenty-three years later.

Everything ahead seemed indefinite. The 'god-king' had come sailing out of the blue across the great mountain range into India. No such visitor had ever descended on India before. Meanwhile diplomatic usage rumbled along in its ordinary channels. The order came through from London that our attitude towards him was to be one of neutrality. Why certainly, for he was neither ally nor foe, though his flight was due to the Chinese invasion, which itself was due to the British invasion six years earlier. Our troops had withdrawn from Lhasa then, but the Chinese wished to gain control over Tibet, to make sure our people did not go back again.

Neutrality beyond a doubt, but meanwhile the fugitives had nowhere to go, and not much money. His hotel in the centre of the worldly round of Darjeeling was not only very expensive for his host, the Government of India, but also unsuitable for an Eastern deity and lama. Accordingly I obtained a house away in a wood for His Holiness, and one on the near edge of the town for the Ministers of State, now, alas! without a state to minister to.

They were invited to Calcutta. The Dalai Lama was to visit the Viceroy, Lord Minto; his entourage would see the wonders of a Westernised city. It was cold in Darjeeling to Britons who had come up from India; all were walking about in heavy overcoats. But to the Dalai Lama who had come across plains and passes more than twice the height of Darjeeling, the latter was thoroughly warm.

"Than this place, in Kalikata will the honourable heat be even hotter?" he asked.

"Than this, the honourable heat will be even much hotter," I reply.

And a little later came the enquiry:

"Does the great Viceroy of The White Expanse (India, where people wear white clothes) know how to speak Tibetan?"

It had to be admitted that even Viceroys are not omniscient. Although he had travelled in China and Mongolia, the Dalai Lama's horizon was still closely limited, but I was soon to learn that he was shrewd, and quick to enlarge his outlook.

We went down the little mountain railway. Many English people are as sick going down in this train as on a choppy channel-crossing. The "Protector of Great-Price" was fortunately immune, but a Minister of particularly high-born ancestry was ill and frightened by the swaying train, until his colleagues laughed him out of it.

On arrival in Calcutta vice-regal carriages drove us to Hastings House, the great Guest House where Indian princes paying official visits are entertained as guests of the Government. Just as the carriage conveying the Dalai Lama and myself was starting, with dignity but increasing speed, out of the railway station, some lesser servants of His Holiness rushed forward and attempted to climb up by the two Indian grooms standing on the back of it. They had never seen a carriage before, and did not approve of their Head being whisked away from them in the company of a foreigner. In their own Tibet they would at that moment have jumped on their shaggy ponies and ridden in front and behind in single file.

The fort fired a salute of seventeen guns in his honour.

"What is that firing?" said the Presence. I explained, and he expressed pleasure. At any rate, he, the harassed exile, was sure of a welcome and some recognition.

On the morning of the fourteenth of March His Holiness paid a formal call on the Viceroy, who returned the call at Hastings House the same morning. On the same afternoon the Dalai Lama returned to Government House for his business talk with the Viceroy. I interpreted at this, as indeed in all conversations with the Dalai Lama or his Ministers. He expressed his gratitude for the hospitality he had received and his reliance on the British

Government in his present difficulties, and continued somewhat as follows:

"Our former difficulties with Great Britain were due to China. Dorjieff, of whom the British Government are so suspicious, was a purely spiritual adviser. In this present case the Manchu Resident in Lhasa has disregarded the promises, made by the Emperor of China and the Dowager Empress, that my power would not be interfered with, and has shown clearly that he is going to take away all power from us Tibetans. Under the recent treaty the Tibetans have the right of dealing direct with the British, and I appeal to you to see that that right is not taken from us. I ask also that the Chinese influence may be withdrawn from Tibet, so that my position may be that of the Fifth Dalai Lama, who was an independent sovereign. The Chinese troops also should be withdrawn from Tibet. Those treaties of 1890 and 1906 were made by Great Britain with China; we Tibetans were not parties to them, and we cannot recognise them.[10]

"As for me now, the Chinese have cut me off from communication with the Regent whom I have left at Lhasa, although I and my Ministers are the Government of Tibet, and I have the seals of office with me. The Chinese are stopping all travellers between Lhasa and India and searching them. To get official letters through to my Ministers in Lhasa, I have to send them secretly; otherwise the Chinese confiscate them. And this although the Dowager Empress promised that there would be no interference with my jurisdiction. I will not return to Lhasa while matters are in this state. I wish to return to Darjeeling for the present; what my eventual destination will be I cannot say. As the Chinese have so completly violated the promises which the Dowager Empress gave to me, I will not trust again the written assurance of the Chinese Government.

"The Chinese Government and their Resident in Lhasa have adopted a hostile policy. You will find that they have designs on your border territory of Bhutan and Sikkim, and on Nepal as well. The Chinese have in Tibet now far more troops than they need for holding Tibet alone."

While I accompanied the Dalai Lama to the Viceroy and interpreted at the interview, Mr. Jelf, the under-secretary in the

Foreign Office, looked after the Ministers. He proposed a visit to the Calcutta Zoo.

"The suggestion is wonderful, but we cannot go to-day. It would be unfitting for us to see the elephants and tigers before His Holiness sees them."

So Jelf took them for a drive round Calcutta. Passing the Bengal Club, a palatial building, he indicated that he lived there. What the interpreter said I do not know, but an impression was gathered that the building was Jelf's private house, and he felt that his stock had risen greatly in consequence.

I was in an annex close to Hastings House, and a private telephone connected the two buildings. The Precious Protector liked talking on this. He enjoyed it so much that the conversation used to terminate in a gurgle of laughter from his end. Here I first learned the newly-coined Tibetan word for telephone. It was *kapar*, the "between-mouths."

Some time before the Dalai Lama's visit, a casket had been discovered, believed to contain three pieces of the bones of Buddha himself. These were found at the great chaitya or stupa of the Buddhist King Kanishka, near Peshawar, in north-western India. Kanishka was a Tartar of the Kushan tribe, and he ruled as King of Kabul, Kashmir, and north-western India in the second century A.D. The Dalai Lama with his Ministers and other members of his entourage visited the Indian Museum in Calcutta, where the casket was resting temporarily. Taking the casket in his hands, he blessed all the Buddhists present, including those of his own staff, the young princes of Sikkim and Derge, and my Buddhist associates, by touching them on the back of the head as they stood in a semi-circle in front of him, with heads deeply bowed.

It was a solemn ceremony, and all were both awed and pleased to have made so close a contact with the Founder of their religion through the medium of these precious relics.

Our visit soon ended, and we returned to Darjeeling. Poor Dalai Lama! First, a flight from the British expedition in 1904, resulting in five years' exile in Mongolia and China. And now a flight from the Chinese to the British, with apparently no hope of ever returning to his own country.

13 British Neutrality

After his flight the Chinese Government issued a proclamation deposing the Dalai Lama, just as it had done when His Holiness fled from the British. But the Tibetans paid no attention to this beyond bespattering it with mud. China also nominated the Panchen Lama again as the ruler of Tibet in the place of the Dalai Lama, but again the Panchen Lama refused to accept the appointment. His administration at the great monastery of Tashi Lhünpo, half a mile from Shigatse, is framed somewhat after the pattern of the Central Government, but on a reduced scale for it has charge of only three out of the numerous districts of Tibet. The spirit of the Tibetan constitution is against his acting as Regent, though it would be unsafe to assert that such an appointment could never be made. In any case a Regent has not the power of a Dalai Lama; he is largely under the control of the National Assembly in Lhasa. Thus were a Panchen Lama to act as Regent, there would almost certainly be friction between him and the Lhasan authorities, who would side with their National Assembly. The province in which Lhasa lies is known as "The Centre"; to the west is the province holding Tashi Lhünpo, and this province is known as "The Pure." The Centre and the Pure would be in opposition to each other, and great friction would result. The Panchen Lama was wise to refuse. I knew him, too, in the old days: though nourishing worldly ambition up to a point, his quiet, spiritual nature could not but shrink from a contest of that kind.

Meanwhile Tibet was deeply stirred in the subdued fashion that accords with the Tibetan nature. In Darjeeling, with its

Westernised ideas, meetings of protest were held by the Buddhists of Tibet and Darjeeling and the neighbouring Buddhist States. However, these did not have much effect on public opinion, for those assembled were neither numerous nor skilled in the organisation of protests. Besides, other people, knowing that China has been bullied by the European nations and by Japan, could not easily understand that she in her turn often inflicts extremely harsh treatment on her own outlying dependencies.

So much indeed has this proved to be the case that almost the whole of Mongolia has revolted against her methods of exploitation and fallen into the hands of Soviet Russia and Japan. This exploitation has taken two main forms. At frequent intervals Chinese soldiers used to drive the Mongol nomads from their grazing grounds, and make these lands over to Chinese farmers for cultivation In this way the Mongols have been despoiled of many thousands of square miles. Secondly, astute Chinese traders lured the simpler-minded Mongols heavily into debt, threatened the Chinese law, and so seized the Mongol's grazing grounds and cattle, and even bought their daughters as wives for themselves.[11]

Nobody in their senses would advocate that Britain should attempt to exercise over Tibet the close, though unacknowledged, control that the Soviet Union exercises over Outer Mongolia and Sinkiang. The conditions are entirely different. For the security of her northern frontier, India needs a Tibet that is as independent and strong as possible. Tibet's population is scanty; she is not herself strong enough to harm India, even if she wished to do so. As a matter of fact, for the last eight hundred years, since Buddhism, with its doctrine of peace, gained possession of her soul, she has never attacked any nation outside her borders. She herself wishes to be independent, and to live her own life. It was our duty to encourage and help her, as far as we could, without overtaxing our own national resources.[12]

However, the British Government of this period, 1910, among whom Lord Morley, the Secretary of State for India, was a leading member, appear to have viewed matters differently.

Briefly stated, the effect of their policy was to give China a practically complete control over Tibet, while insisting that we would not allow her to interfere in Nepal, Sikkim and Bhutan, those States in the Himalaya that lie along some seven hundred miles of the Indo-Tibetan frontier. That at first sight might to some appear a reasonable policy, but it contained two fundamental weaknesses. Firstly, these three States cover less than half of the Indo-Tibetan frontier. To the west of Nepal Tibet borders on Garhwal, the Simla Hill States and Kashmir; to the east of Bhutan it marches with Assam, the Assam frontier tribes and the region north of Burma. Secondly, China might be told that we would not tolerate interference in Nepal, Sikkim and Bhutan, but seeing us abandon Tibetan interests she was sure to interfere in those three States, whenever an opportunity presented itself, as indeed the Dalai Lama had always pointed out. "The Chinese way," he told me, "is to do something rather mild at first; then to wait a bit, and if it passes without objection, to say or do something stronger. But if we take objection to the first statement or action, they urge that it has been misinterpreted, and cease, for a time at any rate, from troubling us further. The British should keep China busy in Tibet, holding her back there. Otherwise, when the Chinese obtain a complete hold over Tibet they will molest Nepal and Bhutan also." I passed the Dalai Lama's views on to the Government of India as usual.

It was not long before his prediction was proved to be correct. As soon as they had consolidated their hold on Tibet, the Chinese Government claimed both Nepal and Bhutan as feudatory to China. The Ruler of Bhutan had permitted several adherents of the Dalai Lama to come to Bhutan. The Chinese Amban at Lhasa demanded an explanation from him. He also issued a proclamation that the Chinese coins which he was circulating in Tibet must be given free currency in Bhutan also. The Maharaja of Bhutan ignored both the demand and the proclamation, passing them on to us. We told the Amban that, as the external relations of Bhutan were controlled by the British

Government, we, and not Bhutan, would always answer such communications. The Maharaja relied loyally on our new treaty, and there the matter ended.

Well, here was the Dalai Lama in India. True, he was a fugitive from his own country and impoverished; but none the less he was the Dalai Lama. The British Government ordained that he should be treated in a strictly neutral fashion and receive no political favours. Still, as it seemed to me, we could not only afford him and his Ministers personal protection from Chinese assassins – a reward of one thousand rupees had been offered to anybody who would assassinate one of them – but we could also show him kindness and such hospitality as our limited funds allowed.

Kindness to a Dalai Lama is repaid a hundredfold throughout Tibet. Indeed, his influence extended not only over Tibet, but also over Mongolia, parts of China, the large tract east of Lake Baikal in Siberia, inhabited by the British Mongols, and even districts in European Russia, peopled by the Torgots and other Mongol tribes. As regards the Manchus, it was only the older ones who were Buddhists and looked with reverence on the Dalai Lama. The younger generation were greatly under Chinese and European influence and had consequently lost faith in him. Manchus seldom came to Lhasa. The Russian Consul General in India assured me that the Russian Government owed much to the Dalai Lama, for the latter's adherents were among the most law-abiding of the Tsar's subjects.

I rented a house for the Dalai Lama, our Government paying the rent. It was named "Hillside" and was in a wood away from the beaten tracks; neither Indians nor foreigners were sufficiently interested to seek him out. Within a fortnight of his arrival the excitement caused by such an unusual visitor had subsided, and the daily amusements of an Indian hill station, the tennis and the polo, the roller-skating and the dancing, went on as usual.

The Tibetan Ministers, having their house nearer to the town, were able to mingle with the life of the place, and more easily obtain their food and other supplies. I used to give to the Dalai

Lama and to them presents of food, e.g. mutton, rice, etc., every Monday, for in Tibet they used to give me presents of food, and in their impoverished condition such gifts were welcome.

The party were full of anxiety as to what the Chinese were doing in Lhasa. However, they had brought their seals of office with them, and hoped to establish a close relationship with Britain. They were well acquainted with the treaty that we had recently concluded with Bhutan, and wished to be put into the same position as that in which Bhutan now stood. They, too, desired that Tibet's foreign relations should be under the control of Britain, and their internal administration in their own hands.

But three months after their arrival in Darjeeling a heavy, and seemingly final, blow fell upon them. I was instructed to inform the Dalai Lama that our Government would not intervene between Tibet and China. When I delivered the message to him as we sat together in the quietude of his room, he was so surprised and distressed that for a minute or two he lost the power of speech. That deprecating look in his eyes became for an instant the look of a man who is being hunted to his doom. Quickly, however, he cast it off, and discussed the matter calmly and clearly.

At the conclusion of the interview I went downstairs and, as I always did, held a long conversation with the chief Ministers. When I informed them of the British Government's decision, they exclaimed, "Astounding! We do not know where to go, or where to remain; we cannot show our faces after this." For the whole day they would not even drink tea, a sure sign of utter dejection. Like other Tibetans of that class, they usually drank this national beverage thirty to forty times daily.

Tibetan tea, of which there are five different qualities, is grown in western China, and carried through Tibet on the backs of animals, yak, donkey, mule, pony, sheep, and by human beings also. What else can be done, when throughout this mountainous country, twenty times the size of England, there is no wheeled traffic? No railway, motor-car, carriage, not even a cart. The tea is usually pressed into the shape of bricks – but sometimes into the shape of cones – and may take three months to reach its destination.

It is not prepared for drinking by pouring boiling water on the tea leaves. The tea leaves are put into a cauldron with cold water and a little soda – found by the margins of lakes – is added to bring out the colour, and all are boiled together. It is then poured into a churn; butter and salt are added, and all is churned up. Tibetans consider European tea as indigestible.

Shortly afterwards the Dalai Lama appealed again to the British Government, but the appeal was rejected. Whenever our Government refused an important request, the Dalai Lama and his Ministers always wished to represent the matter again. They could not understand that such a refusal was definite and final, and they used to quote the Tibetan saying:

> Tibetan persistence
> Is the persistence of the simpleton.

Later on, as the Chinese gained more and more control in Tibet, there were some well-informed Tibetans who thought the Dalai Lama would find his way to the land of the Buriat Mongols in Siberia, east of Lake Baikal, and put himself under the protection of Russia. But his inborn persistence – certainly not that of a simpleton – put off the day, until, in August, 1911, relief arrived. And by personal solicitude and kindness we were able to ease the situation a little, though we had to be politically neutral.

This was the Dalai Lama's second exile, and much worse than the first in 1904, when he fled from the British expedition. The British army left Lhasa of their own accord, but the Chinese army stayed, took all government into their own hands, and oppressed the Tibetans. The British invasion was compared by Tibetans to a frog, symbolically regarded as a fierce animal by reason of its leaping and its peculiar aspect; but the Chinese invasion was figured as a scorpion, a creature far more virulent. Tibetans quoted the proverb, "When one has seen a scorpion, one looks on the frog as divine."[13]

Tibetans however are philosophers. They worry, but not overmuch. Their religion helps them, for it teaches the doctrine of *karma*, the law of cause and effect, that governs the lives of all Hindus and Buddhists, several hundred million people. Accordingly, they used to tell me that this oppression of Tibet by China would recoil on the latter; and all the more because Tibet is the "root" of China, and if the root is injured the whole tree suffers. Retribution, therefore, was certain sooner or later, and they hoped it might be sooner, as indeed it was.

14   Frequent Talks with the Dalai Lama

This close intercourse with the Dalai Lama was for me a unique experience. The mysterious divinity, the unknown Ruler of Tibet, had emerged from the seclusion of his mountain land. He had indeed been to China, but had not come into close touch there with Europeans and Americans. But during these two and a quarter years that he spent in India, I had some fifty intimate conversations with him. Each time that I came into the room, his welcoming smile softened the features that were somewhat hard in repose. Custom prescribes that he shall sit cross-legged as Buddha, on a lofty seat placed on a platform raised above the rest of the room. But it was not so now. Of his own accord he sat on a European chair. We were together at the same small table; everybody else, even the Court Physician, he sent out of the room.

Thus, the two of us alone together, he talked almost invariably with the utmost frankness, in spite of the refusals of our Government to give him the help for which he asked. Tibetan officials, especially those low down the scale, are afraid of saying what they really think, for fear of differing from those above them and being taken to task accordingly. But there was nobody above the Dalai Lama, and so he did not mind what he said. From time to time he gave me information – which I could never have obtained otherwise – as to what was happening throughout Tibet, far and near. We talked, too, on a wide range of subjects, and I only wish that I had kept more frequent and fuller notes of the conversations, but my work at the time was heavy, including not only Tibetan affairs, but also a close relationship with Bhutan, and the complete administration of little Sikkim. The Maharaja of Sikkim, for political reasons, had been deprived of his powers many years before I came. In due course the dear old man died, and I had the pleasure of installing his son with the full powers of government.

During the first three or four months I used to visit the Dalai Lama almost every week, sometimes more often. Should I come after a ten days' interval, he would remark with his deprecatory smile, "It is a long time since your last visit." Poor Dalai Lama! He was in great trouble, and the trouble was a little eased if the British Representative came often, and talked with him about this, that and the other. The Tibetan Government's biography alludes to my "many pleasant conversations with the Dalai Lama."

Diplomatically I could do very little for him, but he and his Ministers, among whom Shatra especially was a trained diplomatist, quickly realised the position of affairs. How often did I hear the expression, "The honourable responsibility is not yours." Some matters I was able to ease; and one way and another I gained their confidence. In due course I came to know him and the heads of his Government better than any Orientals of my acquaintance. If I could not go to Lhasa, one might almost say that Lhasa had come to me.

For coming as they did, fugitives and almost in despair, they opened their hearts freely and told me the inmost details of Tibetan politics – hitherto a subject closed to outsiders and so far as time allowed, about the mysteries of their complicated religion.

My calls were paid during the forenoon in accordance with Tibetan custom; it is at once more auspicious and more polite to go then while the sun is in the ascendant, rising in his strength. Upstairs I went, for the Dalai Lama of necessity lived on the upper floor; it would be considered impious for anybody to live over his head. Each visit was, of course, paid first to him; it lasted for an hour or nearly so. Most educated Tibetans in their conversation like to lapse into generalities and to employ proverbs and ancient sayings. I did not find this when talking to him. He came straight to the point and stayed there. When our talk was finished, I went downstairs for an equally long and absorbing talk with the Chief Ministers. The ordinary Ministers of State remained somewhat in the background.

During these conversations, and indeed when talking to any Tibetan above the lowest social classes, it was essential to use what they call "gentlemen's language." In this, as in so many other ways, I could not fail to recognise how great was my debt to Palhese. For he had from the first taught me the proper use of Tibetan honorific terms, a language which, as a member of the nobility, he had imbibed from his earliest years. Most of my British friends used to say that Tibetans did not mind if one failed to use the honorific language when addressing them, because they understood that it was not meant as an insult, but was the result of natural ignorance. Yes, they would certainly make allowances, but none the less every word that was spoken in that way would grate on the Tibetan lady or gentleman to whom it was addressed.

The Dalai Lama's chief butler holds high rank and has great influence. Soon after I entered the Dalai Lama's room he used to bring in tea, of course after the Tibetan pattern. He first poured some into the jade cup which he set before His Holiness, and then into the cup – of jade also, as far as I remember – set for me. Then he retired, leaving us two alone. We each drank a little of the tea, but not much; it was the conversation that I wanted, and the Dalai Lama showed clearly that he also wanted this. It was mainly no doubt political, China and Tibet, and then events inside Tibet, administrative difficulties and how he sought to overcome them. But it ranged further; events in Britain, Ireland, Germany, India and Japan, and the inner meanings of these events.

Five and a half years earlier the British had fought the Tibetans, invaded their country, occupied their capital, and driven the Dalai Lama into exile in China. Why then did he fly to India, a land controlled by his old enemies? The Russians had never shown him any hostility, and had in fact shown him honour in their letters. But the British were near and the Russians far away, and therefore the Dalai Lama and his Ministers had no option but to fly to India. A Tibetan proverb says, "Better an enemy in your own village than a distant friend." If you are in urgent need, the unfriendly neighbour may still help you, but whether he does or not, there is no time to go to the distant friend.

Faith is a precious possession. To the outside view it seemed that the Dalai Lama had been taken unawares, when he fled from the Chinese invasion of Lhasa. But the inner people, as Tibetans term Buddhists, knew better. They remembered an old prophecy, which Palhese had heard as a boy, twenty years earlier, "In the year of the Male Iron Dog there will be war with China." This prophecy was fulfilled in this year 1910, when the Chinese invaded Lhasa, and the Dalai Lama fled to India. Tibetans believed that the Dalai Lama knew this prophecy, and so took care to return to Lhasa before the Male Iron Dog year. He came to Lhasa accordingly in the year preceding it. For he had come to realise that British power was great, and that the Anglo-Russian agreement, concluded two and a half years earlier, prevented Russia from intervening in Tibet. For these reasons also he wished to improve relations with Britain.

While I was in Darjeeling with the Dalai Lama, a Russian professor came for an interview with His Holiness. I conducted him into the latter's presence and interpreted for him. The professor bowed to the Lama, and laid before him a white silk scarf such as is used in all Tibetan interviews and visits, and since he was presenting it to the Dalai Lama, one of the best quality available. He laid also before His Holiness the sum of twenty rupees. The Dalai Lama remained seated on his dais throughout the interview.

The professor was the President of a Committee that had built a Buddhist temple in St. Petersburg. He thanked the Dalai Lama for the presents that the latter had already given to it, said they hoped to build a Buddhist hostel and library, and asked for the assistance of His Holiness in procuring copies of old Sanskrit manuscripts from the important monastery named Reting, four days' journey north of Lhasa, and from another monastery near Lake Manasarowar in western Tibet.

At my next interview with the Dalai Lama, a few days later, he informed me that the Russian professor had brought also a letter from Dorjieff, written ten or eleven months earlier. The professor had conveyed it to the Dalai Lama through the Chief Secretary whom he met walking on the path above "Hillside." The letter asked His Holiness to permit the professor to come to Lhasa and to assist him in procuring copies of some of the sacred books. The Dalai Lama politely but firmly refused. Referring to the incident afterwards, he said to me, "It would have been difficult to grant that request, as the Chinese would not have liked a European to come to Lhasa, but as I have come to Darjeeling, the matter has been made easy for me."

I mention this incident as an example of the Dalai Lama's frankness. Dorjieff was then an object of great suspicion to the British authorities, and if the Dalai Lama himself had not mentioned this letter, I should never have been aware of it.

The more the foreigners have come into Tibet, the stronger has Chinese opposition grown, stronger even than that of the Tibetans themselves. The Chinese used to treat the Tibetans as a vastly inferior race. When the European came he treated Tibetans as friends, and showed them newer and gentler methods as contrasted with the oft-times harshness of the Chinese officials. Then the Chinese prestige fell; more especially as, from China's wars with Russia and Japan, Tibetans came to understand the weakness of their overlord. So China naturally wanted to keep foreigners out of Tibet.

It was here in the district of Darjeeling that the Dalai Lama and his Government first came into contact with the peasantry of India. He expressed admiration at their freedom and prosperity, compared with what he had seen in China. There, he told me, the Chinese have to supply wood and all sorts of things to their officials without any payment. He also expressed pleasure at the kindly way in which horses, cattle and other animals are treated in Darjeeling. I told him about the Society for the Prevention of Cruelty to Animals, and as the head of a religion which inculcates kindness to animals he was impressed. Tibet, no doubt, does not attain to S.P.C.A. standards as regards the comparatively few animals to which the S.P.C.A. pays attention; but the

Tibetan range is far wider, including almost all birds, beasts and fishes. Indeed the monks in many of the monasteries are kept indoors throughout the two months of the rainy season lest they tread on the numerous insects which then abound on the ground outside. Tibetans treat their animals far more kindly than do Chinese or Indians. The Hindus of India believe in the doctrine of rebirth, but Tibetans take this doctrine more seriously, feeling strongly that they themselves have been animals in some of their previous lives, and may be so again in some of the many lives that follow.

15 Life in Darjeeling

Tibetans are fond of exchanging presents with a friend, and are quite as pleased to give as to receive. The Dalai Lama and his Ministers and other Tibetans from time to time gave me presents. These I sent usually to the Government of India, but by an arrangement with the latter I was permitted to retain any that I wished, on condition, of course, that I gave in return presents of at least equal value. Various were the presents received when the party returned to Tibet, but here in Darjeeling, ousted from their own domain and cut off from their own property, they had not very much to give.

Among other presents that the Dalai Lama gave me were two iron ladles, one small and circular, the other larger and square, and each with a long handle. They have a symbolism of their own. When a man dies a sudden death, especially in a locality where he is not known, his consciousness may remain where he dies, unable to proceed to the next life and causing trouble to those in the neighbourhood. Then a lama, belonging to the mystic school, known as Tantric, will take oil or clarified butter in these ladles, and conduct his mystic service by which the name of the deceased becomes known and the consciousness is sent on its appointed way.

His Holiness gave me also a Tibetan grammar which, he told me, he himself had composed. I was surprised, though I did not say so. Somehow I did not visualise him as that kind of person. And his life appeared too full of incident to afford him time to sit down and write a grammar. But when I examined the book itself, I found that the Tenth Dalai Lama, who had died over

123

seventy years before, was recorded as being the author. This was a useful reminder that there have been not thirteen Dalai Lamas, but only one, in thirteen Incarnations. So though it was written by the Tenth, the Thirteenth Dalai Lama would naturally say he had written it.

Tibetan books have ornate titles. Here the title is, *The Amusement for the Bees with the Young Minds, being a Summary of the Thirty Five Ornaments of the Truth, from the Series of Books Known as the Recreation Lake of Sarasvati's Speech*. Sarasvati is the goddess of wisdom. We may hope that the students "with the young minds" found amusement in this solid book of two hundred and eighty-eight pages.

As the Tenth Dalai Lama died when about twenty years old, one cannot but feel that much of this book was written in his name by somebody else.

The present of a hundred Tibetan coins of a new issue seemed to indicate that the Tibetan Government was still carrying on a part of its work in spite of the Chinese seizure of Lhasa. The main Tibetan unit of coinage is the *trangka*, and it is curious how those of higher denomination often contain fractional parts of this *trangka*. For instance, these coins that I was given – about the size and weight of an English five-shilling piece – were worth six and two-thirds *trangkas*. At this time the *trangka* was worth one-third of a rupee, but, later on, it fell heavily. The Tibetan Government made too many copper coins. These were also forged in India, and smuggled by Indians over the Indo-Tibetan frontier.

Tibetans date their coins and general events from the year A.D. 1027. That was the year when astrology was introduced into Tibet. They divide the years into cycles of sixty. These coins having been made during the preceding year, on one side of each was inscribed "The forty-third year of the fifteenth cycle." Each cycle is composed of five elements, namely earth, iron, water, wood and fire, joined to twelve animals – dog, pig, mouse, ox, tiger, hare, dragon, serpent, horse, sheep, monkey and bird. Each element comes twice, first as male and then as female. Thus the elements end with the tenth year and the animals with the twelfth. Then the first element is joined to the eleventh and twelfth animals, the second to the thirteenth and fourteenth animals, and so on. This results in a cycle ending at the sixtieth year. It runs like this:

Fire Dragon
Fire Serpent
Earth Horse
Earth Sheep
Iron Monkey
And so on.

The Dalai Lama was born in the year of the Fire Mouse, i.e. 1876, and was therefore thirty-four years old when he arrived in Darjeeling.

Among the presents which the Dalai Lama gave me, I valued none so highly as two sculptured images of Buddha. Rarely, if ever, has any European received such an image of Buddha from the Dalai Lama himself.

He gave me the first one when the party had been only three or four months in Darjeeling, and when giving it, said, "I am having another and better image brought from Lhasa for you." A month or two later he gave me this second Buddha. Of each of these two the Dalai Lama said that it was brought from India to Tibet when Buddhism was being established in the latter country, that is to say, about twelve hundred years ago.

The first image is of bell metal, the second of copper-gilt. Of the second the Dalai Lama affirmed that it was of the same style and quality as the large Buddha in the Great Temple in Lhasa, the statue that was sent thirteen hundred years ago by the then Emperor of China as a part of the wedding dowry of his daughter given in marriage to King Straight Strong Deep.

"Mixed with the copper," said the Dalai Lama, "both in the statue of Buddha in the 'Head-Hand-Foot' (Tsuk La Kang, the Tibetan name for the great Temple in Lhasa) "and in this image which I am giving you, are gold, silver, turquoises, corals, etcetera, ground up together. This image has been kept in my private apartments in the Potala during my time and that of many preceding Dalai Lamas. There is no better image of Buddha in Tibet than this."

The statue in the Temple is believed to have been modelled from life. A remarkable fact about it is that it represents him as a boy of only eleven years old, twenty-four years before he attained to Buddhahood. He was then just Gautama, a lad of noble birth, destined apparently for the ordinary nobleman's life. It has a complacent, enigmatic smile. In Tibet no image of him as the Lord Buddha is so sacred as this one portraying him as a young boy.

When giving anything to the Dalai Lama or to the Panchen Lama, it should as far as possible be wrapped in yellow, for they regard yellow as sacred, and in Tibet generally the term yellow stands for the monastic order. If you give a book to either of them, it should be bound in yellow; if you give a photograph, it should be in a gilt frame. When giving my photograph to one of the Chief Ministers, he remarked that my eyes were sunk deep into my head, and added that this, according to the Kangyur, the Buddhist Bible, is a sign of longevity.

As presents to the two Lamas, as well as the Ministers and others, good English saddlery, field-glasses, telescopes and other modern marvels, were always welcome. By a layman nothing was so much appreciated as a rifle or revolver, but I did not often give these. Our Government felt that we had not yet established our friendship with the Tibetans on a sufficiently firm basis.

Although the affairs of State kept him busy, especially in Lhasa, the Dalai Lama was always devout in his religious observances. When travelling in India, the train would stop from time to time at large stations for meals, but if His Holiness was at the time engaged in his devotions, he would let the meal go. At Darjeeling, in the room below his, in that secluded wood, could be heard the low tones of the Lama invoking blessings on all living beings throughout the world, men, women, birds, beasts, fishes, or, as Tibetans term them, the "mind-possessors." Before the sun rose he might be heard and at intervals through the day.

It had always been the custom that when a Dalai Lama came out of his room any servants or officials who happened to be in the vicinity should run away and hide themselves. The Dalai Lama set this aside and told them simply to make way for him. He said that the former procedure gave unnecessary trouble to the servants and made him reluctant to appear, as he could not do so without causing so much inconvenience.

The Dalai Lama would frequently sit on a lower seat than a high Lama when learning religion from him, especially while the Dalai Lama was a very young man. Even at this time, when he was over thirty years of age, there were two learned Lamas whose seats were as high as his own. It should be explained that rank is indicated by the height of the seat above the ground.

Both the two Grand Lamas, the Dalai Lama and the Panchen Lama, are believed by the mass of the Tibetan people to be omniscient. When you read their titles, written on paper or carved on images, or marked out with large stones on the mountain-sides, you will often find "All-Knowing" among them. And yet it is quickly evident that this title cannot be sustained, and the Dalai Lama when speaking to me used always to point out any of his own mistakes or lack of knowledge. For instance, at one of our talks I had asked him where the Fifth Dalai Lama, when on his visit to China, had met the Manchu Emperor. He told me that the Emperor had not gone outside Peking to meet him. Later on he volunteered the information that he had since consulted some books and found that the Emperor had met him at a hunting seat one day's journey from Peking. Also when I asked him, "In which Dalai Lama's time did the first Panchen Lama live?" he replied that he did not know. But the most striking admission of ignorance came when he asked me, "Where is Bengal? We read this and other such names in our books, but we do not know where the countries are." He was actually in Bengal at the time, since Darjeeling is included in the province of Bengal. It is indeed not a part of the Bengali homeland, being inhabited mainly by Gurkhas, Tibetans, and other mountain races, but the district adjoining it on the south is altogether Bengali. The Court Physician was in the room when the Dalai Lama said this to me, and hastened to join in the admission of ignorance.

How then were these lapses to be explained? Talking once to Palhese about some unpopular measures of the Tibetan Government that fell heavily on the landed proprietors and the tenantry, he remarked:

"The Dalai Lama is not responsible; matters were misrepresented to him, and so he did not know how greatly the tenantry were suffering."

"But, Kushog (honorific title for one of his rank), is not the Dalai Lama All-Knowing?"

"Yes, he is All-Knowing, as being a Buddha, but by taking on the human form he limits this omniscience."

Here in exile the Dalai Lama's control over the administration of Tibet was immensely reduced, though his orders still carried great weight among his people there. They obeyed the Chinese as far as the Chinese soldiery compelled them, but no further. I asked him and his Ministers from time to time about his rule before this flight to India, and it was clear that, though still a fairly young man, he was obtaining a comprehensive control over Tibet. But he was at that time careful to consult public opinion.

The Tibetan Government employs three hundred and fifty officials on its regular staff, of whom half are ecclesiastical and half are secular. In the college where young officers destined to be secular officials were educated for a couple of years or so before being passed into the service of the Government, they were chiefly taught to write letters and other correspondence in the correct style; some arithmetic was also taught. The Dalai Lama raised the standards in all these respects, and insisted on proper examinations being held twice yearly, one in summer and one in winter. Of course, in a higly conservative country like Tibet there is an enormous power of passive resistance, but the young Dalai Lama did what he could, though it must be admitted that his title of "All-Powerful," like that of "All-Knowing," was subject to human limitations.

Tibetans did not always approve of British administrative methods. I remember talking to a Tibetan labourer in Darjeeling at this time. He was one of those who carry the chairs known as

"dandies," in which well-to-do Europeans and Indians are carried about the streets of Darjeeling. "I do not understand your
excise laws," he said to me. "I am told that the liquor shops all
pay revenue to the Government, and the more drink is consumed the more revenue they pay. The other day I was drinking
at one of these, and was sitting on the roadside singing; I was
drunk, of course. Well, singing is no crime; I don't sing any
worse than others. But one of your Gurkha policemen came up
and said, 'You are drunk.' Of course I was drunk, but there is no
crime in being drunk. 'You must come with me to the police
station; next Saturday you will be brought up before the honorary magistrate and fined five rupees. But if you give me one
rupee now I will let you go.' Why should I give him one rupee? I
was simply singing. And so the next Saturday I *was* taken up
before the honorary magistrate, and I *was* fined five rupees.
Now I cannot understand that; I was committing no crime, and
I was increasing your Government's revenue. And, besides, it
cost me two annas (twopence) to get drunk for that amount."

The Tibetan penal system is far harsher than that in India, and
Darjeeling district contained a great many Tibetans who had fled
from their country after committing serious crimes. Yet they did
not commit crimes in Darjeeling. "Why is that?" I said to one of
the Darjeeling Tibetans. "Well," he replied, "we often talk that
over, and think it must be owing to the good fortune of the
Great Queen (Queen Victoria)." In Tibet good fortune is regarded as a definite quality in a person, like brains or physical
strength. And so the good fortune of the Queen was able to
ensure this beneficent result in distant Darjeeling.

After the Dalai Lama had been about five months in Darjeeling I took a photograph of him, seated on a throne Buddhawise,
with crossed legs, and hands placed in the prescribed position; in
fact, as he would sit in his own palace at Lhasa for blessing
pilgrims and others. This was, I believe, the first photograph of
him seated in the Tibetan style. I gave him a large number of
copies, and these proved useful to him; he used to give them to
monasteries and to deserving people. These all used the photograph instead of an image, rendering to it the worship that they

gave to the images of Buddhas and deities. In subsequent years, when I travelled here and there in Tibet, I frequently saw my photograph of the Dalai Lama, but photographed down to a smaller size, standing among the images on the altar either in a private house or in a monastery, and revered along with them. In the private houses and shops of Darjeeling district and Sikkim one saw them everywhere; there must have been thousands of them receiving the adoration of the faithful.

A Tibetan painter in his retinue painted two or three of these photographs, and enclosed one of them in a frame made by a craftsman in the Dalai Lama's household from such materials as the exiles had with them. He painted them in the appropriate colours for his hat, his robes, his throne, the religious imple-ments, the richly brocaded canopy, known as "The curtain of heaven," and the silk pictures of Buddha which formed the suitable background of it all. At each of the four corners of the throne is a swastika, an emblem which has been used for many hundreds of years in Tibet. It is an auspicious symbol, a sign of good luck, derived from the Sanskrit words *su* (well) and *asti* (is). The sign is very ancient; it was known in India, China, Japan, Iran, Egypt, Greece, among the American Indians, and in other countries. It seems a great pity that this time-honoured symbol of well-being should, through the force of recent events, have acquired a sinister meaning among many nations of the world.

These coloured camera-portraits the Dalai Lama presented to me. He signed each of them in his clear handwriting. The signature runs, "In accordance with the Precepts of the Lord Buddha the Great Dalai Lama, Unchangeable, Holder of the Vajra, the Thirteenth in the line of Victory and Power." At the end of his signature he puts his square red seal with sides of about an inch and a half in length. This is known as the Inmost seal; it is the Dalai Lama's own, and stands apart from Chinese authority.

16   Political Struggles

Throughout 1910 and during the greater part of 1911 the troubles of the Dalai Lama and his Government increased rather than diminished. During the former year His Holiness appealed two or three times to Nepal for help. In 1856 Nepal had made a treaty with Tibet, by which she enjoys substantial privileges. Gurkhas in Tibet are entitled to be tried by their own, not Tibetan, magistrates. They are exempted from Tibetan taxation, and Nepal receives from the Tibetan Government a subsidy of ten thousand rupees a year. In return Nepal undertook to come to the assistance of Tibet whenever the latter was invaded. However, Nepal did not, at this or any other time, furnish any military assistance against China; the Dalai Lama, as Tibetans informed me, received only non-committal replies from the Government of that country. The Lama's appeal to the British King was similarly fruitless.

He appealed also to the Russian Tsar. The Tsar answered in a friendly vein, but his reply, which was non-committal, was communicated through the British Government, and it rested with me to pass it on to the Dalai Lama. So I visited him and communicated the message. He was struck with amazement that the Tsar should reply not direct but through the British. For a few moments he could say nothing. This was the only occasion on which I ever saw the Dalai Lama blush, but now he blushed deeply. He collected himself, however, within a few seconds, and replied that, though he had been compelled to write to Russia, because our Government had not given him the help for which he had pleaded, he had asked the Russian Government to work in conjunction with the British; and he had not told me of these letters because, firstly, it would have made the Russian Government suspicious that he might be acting on my advice, and secondly, it might have made the Government of India annoyed with me, thinking that I had advised him to address the Tsar! Certainly one could not term the representative of Buddha slow-minded.

It was indeed awkward for him that the Russian Government should inform us of his communication to them and send him no direct reply. The Anglo-Russian Convention of 1907, by which Russia recognised Great Britain's special interest in Tibet – although both agreed to abstain from interference in Tibet's internal affairs – had been concluded three years earlier, and by this action the Russian Government was loyally carrying out that agreement.

But on another occasion the Tsar did reply. The Russian Consul-General came to deliver the reply. He did not speak Tibetan, and I took it for granted that he would wish me to interpret for him. There was the Tsar's letter in Russian and a written translation of it in Tibetan, made by the Russian Government. Said the Dalai Lama to me, "Please ask the Russian representative to hold the Tsar's letter and translate it into English, sentence by sentence. Then will you, Great Minister, please translate each sentence into Tibetan. I will hold the Russian Government's translation into Tibetan in my hand, and compare it with what you say." We did so. All went smoothly until we reached the vital point as to whether the Tsar would help Tibet or not. The Consul-General's translation into English from the Russian was that he was precluded from doing so, and I translated accordingly into Tibetan. "Now it differs, it differs," said the Dalai Lama, who then read from the Tibetan written translation which held out some hope of assistance. I translated the Dalai Lama's remarks to the Consul-General, who merely said, "The writer of the translation has somewhat expanded the idea." I passed this on to the Lama, and there the matter dropped. Certainly Tibet's priestly Ruler knew how documents should be compared.

Nepal would not help Tibet in spite of the treaty of 1856; Russia, by the Anglo-Russian Convention, had in effect agreed to leave Tibet alone; and the British Government had tied itself by so many treaties that it was difficult for it to help Tibet, even had it wished to do so. The field was thus left open to the Chinese to do as they pleased. The line they took, as they always seem to take when dealing with their so-called dependencies, was to oust the Tibetans from their power and position in Tibet, and to endeavour to annex the country, to form it into regular provinces of China, and to govern it more and more through their own officials, as they gained sufficient power to do so.

Now Tibet down through the centuries has almost always governed herself, though the Chinese histories will not tell you this. In many respects Chinese historians deserve to rank high, but they are not at their best when they write about Tibet. They have always professed to regard the Tibetans as savages, though such few Europeans as are well acquainted with both usually say that educated Tibetans are often more civilised than educated Chinese.

As an example, the early Chinese history keeps telling us how Tibetans frequently made raids into China, but were almost in every case decisively defeated. This was untrue. Had it been the case, those invasions would not have continued with such increasing force, they would not have pushed in so far as they did, and they could hardly have succeeded in capturing the Chinese capital, from which the Chinese Emperor of the period escaped only in an eleventh-hour flight. In fact, we know from various sources that during this period the Tibetan armies overran a very large portion of China, as well as extensive territories in India and Burma. Those events occurred before Buddhism effected a hold on Tibet, forbidding the taking of life and preaching the gospel of peace. And - as has been shown in an earlier chapter – even while the late Dalai Lama was alive and governing Tibet, the Chinese representative in Lhasa sent to the Emperor in Peking such grossly untrue reports that the Manchu Emperor was known in Tibet as "The Bag of Lies." History based on reports of that kind cannot be true.

Such being the Chinese efforts to take the Tibetan Government from the Tibetans themselves, it was natural that the Dalai Lama should always be prone to criticise the Chinese character and their modes of action. The Chinese have usually endeavoured to exploit the Tibetans and the Mongols in so far as they have had the power. Tibet, with its high mountains and deep valleys, has not suffered to the extent that the rolling plains of Mongolia have suffered during the last fifty years. The Mongols of Inner Mongolia – that is to say, the strip of Mongolia that lies nearest to China – have been driven by Chinese soldiers from many thousand square miles of their territory, their tents burnt, their property plundered, and they themselves left to eke out their subsistence elsewhere.

These acts of violent exploitation are unknown to all but a few Europeans. Those who do know, Scandinavian missionaries and others, have been afraid to publish this knowledge – as some of them have told me – lest the Chinese take vengeance upon them. Some of the few others who know are perhaps opportunists, and prefer to align themselves on the winning side.

Soon after the Dalai Lama arrived in Darjeeling there came news of disturbances in China. His Holiness frequently spoke to me about these; one of my clerks, at his request, used to translate to him what the newspapers had to say about Sino-Tibetan affairs. It was clear that he hoped those internal uprisings would increase, and thereby weaken China's power in Tibet. He told me that he had stayed at Singan, the old capital of China in bygone centuries, in the palace of the Chinese Emperor, and found the buildings in decrepit repair. And as he passed through China he had been much struck with the great poverty of the Chinese farmers, but he noticed that some of the Chinese traders were very wealthy. He preferred the Manchus to the Chinese, for at that time many of the Manchus were still believed to be Buddhists, and therefore of the same religion as the Tibetans themselves. At the same time he candidly pointed out that the Chinese officials of the Young China party were more honest than their Manchu colleagues.

Meanwhile the Chinese were endeavouring to seize the power

throughout central Tibet. The Dalai Lama tried to block them as far as he could. While reviewing this period, the Tibetan biography says:

"The Dalai Lama sent to Tibet his attendant, 'Pure Moon, Subduer of Enemies' (the favourite, 'Clear Eye,' who received this new name after holding back the Chinese soldiers during the Dalai Lama's flight to India). He was to tell the Tibetans that they must oust the Chinese soldiers, and that all the Tibetan provinces must refuse to follow the evil China, and must keep the ten virtuous laws."

By his injunction, combining secular and religious authority, the Dalai Lama made matters somewhat more difficult for the Chinese invaders. I remember Pure Moon leaving on this mission, one that accorded well with his adventurous disposition.

The Lama was always wishful to learn about the military strength of other nations, especially that of his neighbour, Nepal. For Tibetans feared that the Gurkha rulers of that country, proud of their military strength, would seek some pretext to invade Tibet. In fact, relations between Tibet and Nepal were almost always strained while I was in Tibet. I did what little I could to improve them, for it is important that Britain and India should be friendly with them both.

Incidentally, I used to endeavour to point out to His Holiness and his Ministers the value of naval strength and the power that this gave to my own country, as compared with Russia and China. But how difficult it was to explain the value of naval strength to those who had never even been within sight of the sea, their own country being separated from it by five hundred miles of land and the highest mountains in the world.

From the above it wil be understood that the Dalai Lama was deeply interested in politics and the secular side of his work generally, and indeed this will become increasingly evident as the story proceeds. Brought up as a monk, it had been necessary for him, even when a young man in Tibet, to start learning about worldly affairs from the beginning. During the whole of his time in India he was increasing his knowledge of the West and enlarging his horizons.

The Dalai Lama and his Ministers used to tell me that they considered the Chinese an irreligious people, and therefore it would be difficult for Tibetans and Chinese to get on well together. To religion, not necessarily his own religion, a Tibetan attaches the utmost importance. When a mutual friend told me that the Dalai Lama regarded me as a religious man, I knew that this would bring us closer together. He wished all to be earnest in their own religions. Did not Khublai Khan, the great Mongol Emperor of China, think the same? And, in fact, it is the general attitude of the Tibetan mind.

It is necessary to write a great deal about politics in this life of the Dalai Lama, for he was developing into, and later on became, an absolute autocrat in both the religious and the secular administration of Tibet. He was genuinely fond of political affairs, and having taken up and retained the secular government, in addition to the spiritual government of Tibet, he had to take every opportunity of studying them.

He also thought, no doubt, that, when we were talking together, he should do what he could to increase his knowledge. Thus he used every effort to learn not only about China or Japan, but also about the chief European countries and America. I used to give him maps of the differrent continents in the world, with the places of chief importance written in Tibetan. When I showed him Sicily, he at once mentioned the earthquake that had shaken Messina. As to Germany and other leading nations in Europe, and America and Japan, he had gained a fair amount of knowledge about them all. He had not, during his youth, been taught the history or geography of other countries, but only of Tibet; but later in his life, after visiting China and India, he learned these subjects by personal observations, travels and enquiries. He was especially interested in the Great Powers, and learned all he could about the kings and different nations of the world. His officials in Lhasa and his agents in other parts of Tibet used to send him such news of India as they could gather from Tibetan merchants returning from that country, and of these there were many. Extracts from the English newspapers published in India, such as would be likely to interest him, were translated for his benefit.

The faithful Dorjieff sent him letters of information regarding events in Mongolia. When the Precious Protector was in that territory, in flight from the British expedition to Lhasa, he established a bank there; it was useful for keeping the numerous offerings that were made to him by devoted Mongol worshippers, and it was useful also in other ways. During the time in Darjeeling the agents of this bank still continued to send him gold and silver. These were often in the shape of a small horse-hoof, and were the proceeds of religious offerings made to him during that exile in Mongolia.

In India he did indeed observe British methods of administration and compare them with Chinese methods in both Tibet and China. The Chief Ministers were naturally interested in the revenues of Nepal, Sikkim, Kuch Behar and other States that they knew or had heard about. They were very emphatic that the Indian States, being made safe by the British power from external aggression, and granted freedom by the same power in their internal administration, were in an ideal position. They sighed and said, "That is how we should like Tibet to be."

As regards the question of independence for India, a Tibetan expressed to me the opinion generally held by the leading men in Tibet. He said:

"All nations should govern themselves, if possible. But in India, if the British left, the different religions and sub-races would strive for mastery. We Tibetans look on Indians as of one general race, but there are of course different sub-races, as in Tibet. In Tibet, however, we have but one religion, so we do not have this religious difficulty. And individuals would also strive for mastery; everybody would be as good as his neighbour; everybody would want to be a ruler. It would be as our proverb says:

When horses race, they start level.
When a tent is set up, the posts are of equal length.

Lawlessness would prevail; there would be great disorder. Everybody would want to be on top. The British Government is to India as the Dalai Lama is to Tibet. Nobody can be equal with either, and that keeps order in both countries.

"I suspect that the Gurkhas would come in, if the British left. They would turn matters of no meaning into matters of importance, and make them an excuse for war. They would, I think, annex Sikkim and the Darjeeling district, and gradually they would advance into Northern India, using one pretext or another for their advance.

"As regards the larger Powers, I think Russia might intervene, and invade India, because we Tibetans notice that Russia wants to obtain Tibet, and we being a country of but small population and resources, she must want us as a passage to India.

"When Gandhi was working his agitation and British goods were not being bought, we Tibetans thought that the Indians had got some other powerful nation behind them, supporting them. Later on, we realised that this was not so, and we thought the agitation doubtful strategy on India's part, for we knew that she could not stand alone.

"To me it seems that Indians see only the present; they do not see the future. It is as our saying runs:

If he drinks beer, his head aches;
If he does not drink, his heart aches.

"The Indians naturally want to rule their own country, but they will bring themselves into great trouble if they do so."

Thus and thus they noticed and remarked, but to the Tibetans India is primarily the home of their religion. In Tibetan plays we are often shown "The Indian King of Religion" and "The Chinese King of Astrology." The Dalai Lama's chief interest in the land of India lay in the holy places of Buddhism, and especially Bodh Gaya, where Gautama had attained to Buddhahood; and where he had wandered in his preaching, and finally had attained enlightenment."

And so in February, 1911, when the political situation, though still adverse, was less active, the party seized the opportunity of visiting Buddhist shrines in Nepal and India. It was noticeable that as the Dalai Lama travelled through the country not only Hindus, but Mahomedans also from time to time, solicited his blessing. Among others who did this was a

Mahomedan who had lived in England, studying and passing his examinations for the Bar, returning to India a fully-fledge barrister, a real Westerner so far as this is possible to Indians.

During 1911 preparations were in progress throughout India for the Durbar, held at Delhi in December, 1911, to commemorate the Coronation of King George V, at which Their Majesties themselves were present. Both the Dalai and Panchen Lamas wished to attend the Durbar, but it would have been wrong to invite them, for Tibet stood, and stands, outside the Indian Commonwealth. The Ruler of Bhutan came, now that we had made the treaty with his State.

17   The Tide Turns

During the first half of 1911 the Dalai Lama was still struggling against the seeming impossibility of escaping from Chinese domination. But during the last half of this year fate suddenly intervened in his favour. Revolution broke out in China. The Manchu Emperor of China was deposed and every vestige of Manchu rule was swept away. In several cities the Chinese massacred the Manchu garrisons.

In November most of the Chinese garrisons in Tibet mutinied. They killed a number of their officers and then moved about robbing the Tibetan population. The Tibetans rose against them, and fighting broke out between the Chinese troops and such few Tibetan soldiers as there were, aided by half-trained yokels from the countryside. A strong effort was made to expel the Chinese, for the Tibetan leaders were well aware of the Dalai Lama's views.

During these contests a characteristic Tibetan order was issued. A Chinese captain with two hundred soldiers had arrived at a Tibetan monastery where were quartered some Tibetan troops, whose officer telegraphed to the Ministers in Darjeeling asking for instructions whether to attack them or not. He received his reply:

"If they are stronger than you, send them on with soft words. If you are stronger than they are, cut them off by the root."

As this order had to go by the Indian telegraph line, needless to say it never went through.

During the campaign internal divisions and jealousies hampered the action of the Tibetan Government. The Panchen

Lama's subordinates were in secret relationship with the Chinese, as was the huge monastery of Drepung; while the monks of Tengyeling, in whose hearts burned the memory of the punishment inflicted on them, fought wholeheartedly for China. In this predicament the Inmost One exerted his spiritual power, reinforced by his own strength of character. His Ministers had frequently told me that the reason why the Chinese troops had found their recent invasion of Tibet so easy was that the Dalai Lama had sent instructions to the Tibetans forbidding them to fight. It is against the Buddhist religion to take life, except when the defence of that religion requires it, and then only as a last resort.

Now, however, there was a change. Not only had the Chinese invaded, but they had seriously threatened the holy religion. And the old Tibetan verse says:

> If there be an enemy to Buddha,
> His followers must put on armour.

Thus it was that the Dalai Lama authorised his Ministers to raise the country against the Chinese. Even then indeed he came in for much criticism from Tibetans, especially from those who, living outside Tibet, were free to criticise. Said the young Prince of Sikkim, "It is a sin for a Buddhist to take a share in destroying life, a great sin for a lama, and a terribly great sin for the highest of all the lamas." But the Dalai Lama had made up his mind and went ahead. His authority proved the strongest, and in due course the Tibetans obtained the upper hand. The Chinese soldiers were well armed, but in the revolution their discipline fell away, and the Tibetan yokels, though ill armed and untrained, were able to overpower them.

However, the Dalai Lama was not to have it all his own way. I was instructed by our Government to tell him to stop the fighting and save the lives of the Chinese. On the receipt of this message he was astounded and angry, because he felt that the British neutrality was applied when events were against him, but not when they were in his favour. If the Chinese could fight the Tibetans, in order to capture Tibet, why might not the Tibetans fight the Chinese in order to defend their country? His manner towards me was for a time constrained, but soon he became his old friendly self again. He recognised, as he always did, that my duty was simply to carry out orders, even though I thought that they went too far.

At length he said, "We must fight for the religion and our own freedom. The Chinese will be spared if they surrender their arms, but they cannot be allowed to retain them, since those whom we previously allowed to keep them used them to attack and plunder the country people."

I stressed the necessity of abstaining from putting to death any captured Chinese, as this would only antagonise the Chinese Government.

"That is undoubtedly the correct course. But I and my Ministers are firmly resolved to detain Len, the Chinese Amban (i.e., High Commission), in Lhasa, and Chung (the general in command of the Chinese troops there), because they are the origin of all the trouble."

I urged that they were only half responsible, since it was evident that the Chinese Government had itself determined to obtain a hold over Tibet, though no doubt Len had made matters much worse by his line of action.

It was necessary to persuade the Dalai Lama and the Tibetan Government to spare the lives of these two men, whatever their past history might have been, because if they put them to death they would thereby sow the seeds of great future trouble for themselves and for us. So I went so far as to say, "Even if a man oppressed me, plundered my goods, and killed my children, I should still try to keep calm and consider how it would be best to deal with the matter."

On this the Dalai Lama sat back in his chair, laughed consumedly, and said that he quite agreed. The Head Physician, who was in the room at the time, in his quiet voice and with head bent low before his master, interjected, "That is certainly true, but the Tibetan National Assembly are extremely angry, and do not reason matters out."

Eventually the Tibetan Government treated Len and Chung

and all the plundering troops with remarkable kindness. They deported them out of Tibet across the frontier into Sikkim, giving them plenty of food on their journey, and even providing riding ponies for those who were weak or ill. I arranged with the Sikkim authorities to send them across Sikkim into India, for if left near the Tibetan frontier they would have been a source of perpetual friction and danger. As a matter of fact, we heard afterwards that General Chung, when he reached China, was put to death by his own Government; why; it was difficult to understand. He had put up a very spirited defence when besieged in Lhasa. He could not achieve the impossible.

At this stage Tibetans were saying that the two most important benefits which the British had conferred on Tibet were:

(1) Retiring from Lhasa after the Younghusband expedition, and the general moderation in the terms then imposed on Tibet.
(2) Treating the Dalai Lama well in India in 1910-12, instead of regarding him as an enemy.

But in spite of this evidence of good will, the Dalai Lama felt that in present circumstances the British would not help him greatly in his fight for the freedom of Tibet. The deliverance of Tibet was due to the outbreak of the Chinese revolution and to nothing else.

However, His Holiness recognised that Tibet had none to depend upon except Britain. Accordingly he and his Ministers wanted to be under Britain on the same terms as Bhutan enjoyed in accordance with the treaty she had concluded with Britain two years earlier; that is, placing Tibet's foreign relations under the British Government, while the latter guaranteed that there would be no interference in Tibet's internal affairs. He had seen for himself that the oft-repeated Chinese allegation, to the effect that the British would destroy their religion and substitute Christianity for it, was untrue. For he had learnt about the conditions of British rule in India, and by travelling in that country had seen things for himself. But he found that we would not even begin to consider putting Tibet on the same footing as

Bhutan. This was a disappointment; yet it showed him and other Tibetans that Britain had enough territory of her own and did not covet theirs.

The Dalai Lama was pro-British and pro-Russian, but anti-Chinese; the Panchen Lama was pro-British but anti-Lhasa; the Dalai Lama's Ministers were simply pro-British; the All Covering Abbot was pro-British and pro-Russian. The two large monasteries, Sera and Ganden, were pro-British; the still larger monastery, Drepung, was mainly pro-Chinese, for most of the monks were Tibetans who lived near the frontier of China and feared Chinese power and influence. The bulk of the Tibetan peasantry had no political consciousness.

I endeavoured to persuade our Government to let the Tibetans import munitions from India. We wanted Tibet to be independent and strong, and how was this possible if she were not allowed to import munitions? Her industry being at such a primitive stage, she could not manufacture them efficiently herself, and she could not obtain them from elsewhere, as Tibet is completely surrounded by China and India. She had not only to defend her own frontiers, but also to maintain internal order throughout her mountainous regions. And it must be remembered that the monasteries are large and often turbulent. Other nations, or their subjects, sell arms to foreign nations. Tibet is friendly to us; why should we refuse to sell arms to her? But the British Government would not, at that time, accept my suggestion.

During these two years the Dalai Lama and his Government in exile had kept an eye on the Panchen Lama, whom the Chinese authorities were favouring in the hope of promoting discord between him and the Dalai Lama, so as to make it easier to maintain their own control over Tibet. The interests of these two high Incarnations were clashing in various ways, as they were almost bound to do. Tibet is still somewhat loosely knit together, though not so loosely as Mongolia, for the Dalai Lama's rule has had a unifying effect. But the tendency to split has never been entirely overcome, and this is especially true of Tashi Lhünpo.

My earliest personal experience of the upper strata of Tibetan politics had been a visit to His Holiness of Tashi Lhünpo. That was in 1906. Apart from formal interviews we had two conversations of three hours each in a pavilion on a sheet of water set well apart from other buildings. The conversations were, of course, in Tibetan; no interpreter was present, and he opened his mind to me. He wanted to be independent of Lhasa and to deal with the British Government as an independent State.

Such an action was likely to lead to friction with Lhasa unless the relationship between the two could be sympathetically controlled. To emphasise the importance of avoiding a rupture with the Panchen Lama in the interests of Tibet as a whole, I used to tell the Dalai Lama our proverb about the bundle of sticks, easily broken singly, but hardly breakable when united. Troublemakers, of course, there were, but the Dalai Lama I always found reasonable. To the Panchen Lama also, although he lived far away, I conveyed my suggestions from time to time, and he, too, was reasonable.

In fact, during all my time in Tibet he frequently sent his agents to me to ask my advice on many subjects, with complimentary remarks on my understanding of, and sympathy with, Tibetan affairs. Usually I was told, "The Panchen Lama says that six or seven words to you have more effect than a hundred to anybody else, as you deal with a matter from the depths, considering all the effects." Even when I returned for a two-year private visit to Asia, twelve years after my final retirement from Government service, he again sent his agents to me in Tibet and Kalimpong. While I was living quietly in England he had given out a prophecy that I would visit Gyangtse the following year. The prophecy turned out true, though at the time it was made, even I did not expect to go there. His officers were astonished.

When I went on from India to China and arrived in Shanghai, he heard of it, and telegraphed to his agent in Nanking to go and see me immediately. So also when I went on to Peking; in fact, all the time. "Advise me, advise me," was the purport of every such visit.

In June, 1912, the Precious Protector, with his Ministers, returned to Tibet. They had learnt well the bitter lessons of adversity, for, as the Tibetan proverb says: "Better than a hundred precepts is a single press on the nose."

A Tibetan mother who wishes to impress a warning on her child will often with her finger press the tip of the child's nose to make the warning more emphatic.

Two years earlier His Holiness had told me that the Chinese oppression of the Tibetans would recoil on themselves. An evil deed had been committed, and was bound to bring its own retribution sooner or later. *Karma*, irresistible *karma*, can never be over-ridden, and in this case the retribution came soon. A year and a half after the Chinese troops invaded holy Lhasa the revolution broke out in China, and the Emperor was deposed. And why? Because of his maltreatment of the Dalai Lama, his spiritual preceptor. What can a layman expect, if he treats his own root Lama in that way? Thus *karma* speaks! In his political testament the Dalai Lama puts this, the spiritual cause, prominently forward.

All was now full friendliness between ourselves and the Tibetans, high and low. The Tibetan Government wished to borrow some of our officials to help them in various branches of their administration: for instance, to establish telegraph lines in Tibet, postal services, and other administrative departments. To me the Dalai Lama said, "I will write to you from time to time after my return to Tibet, and I hope you will write to me. For now I know your mind."

The day of departure was drawing near; presents had to be given by both sides, especially by the departing guests. Among other things, His Holiness gave me the full dress of a monk of the reformed sect, complete in nine pieces. The Chief Physician, who himself held the rank of abbot, put each article on over his own clothes, while the Dalai Lama walked about the room, picking the things up to show them to me.

The abbot doctor was careful to tell me that the long skirt, dark maroon in colour, should always be put on over the head out of respect to Buddha. There were patches on it in imitation of the patched robe worn by Buddha himself, as he begged his food on earth. Hat and boots, everything was complete, including the small bottle for holy water encased in its covering of red cloth, with an iron spoon by which it was hung from the waistband, and the begging bowl of iron covered with red and yellow cloth. He gave me also a very fine suit of armour for a mounted soldier and his charger, made largely of iron and brown lacquered leather. It was three hundred years old, and people have lost the art of making it so well nowadays. I gave the armour to the South Kensington Museum, London, and the monks attire to the British Museum.

The Dalai Lama gave me also a very large gold medal, six and a quarter inches in circumference, weighing more than four ounces, and more than ninety per cent. pure gold, as a mark of intimate friendship. On the one side runs the inscription in Tibetan, "From the Dalai Lama who holds the Vajra, Lord of all the Buddhists on the earth. Given on the fourth day of the fifth month of the Water Rat year." On the other side is a partial translation in English, and the Wheel of Dharma in the centre.

Karma had checkmated the Manchu Emperor, and brought about his deposition. Was it not then *karma* that had turned the Dalai Lama out of Tibet these two times? No, because the fact that he was now able to return, and gained his power more than ever before, showed that his periods of exile were not fully ripening *karma*, but a lesser affliction known to the Tibetan monkhood as "Interruption," which could be, and was, removed by suitable religious exercises.

Part Four
The Two-Fold Power

18 The Dalai Lama Comes Back to Tibet

In June, 1912, the Dalai Lama of Tibet started from Kalimpong on his journey back to his own kingdom. I well remember that day, or to be more accurate, that night. For the astrologers of Tibet had fixed the auspicious hour of departure long before the earliest light of dawn. My wife and I set out for the Bhutan Residency, which the Agent for the Government of Bhutan, himself a devout Buddhist, had placed at the Dalai Lama's disposal during these few months' stay in Kalimpong. My wife was carried by four bearers in a dandy and I was mounted on an iron-grey Tibetan pony, this being one of the colours suitable for an official's pony. We left at half-past two in the morning, our sole illumination in the darkness being a little oil lantern of the type so well known to residents in India. The Kalimpong market-place was deserted, the open fronts of the shops all closed with the planks that are set up at nightfall. Not a soul was stirring, not even the pariah dogs. Only on the left the great snow mountains of the Himalaya flickered in the distance, as though externally on the watch.

We reached the Residency at three o'clock, a little before the time fixed for the departure of the returning sovereign. But now a characteristic hitch occurred. During their long visit His Holiness and his party had collected a great store of luggage. There were no trains in that part of the world, and practically speaking not even carriages or carts, or indeed any kind of wheeled conveyance. The main form of transport was by pack-mule, and the mules were still grazing on the hillsides and had not been caught. But none of the party worried at all about this; it was

Charles Bell, the Dalai Lama, Tibetan and other dignitaries at Hastings House, Calcutta, 1910.

nothing out of the ordinary. It was an hour or more later before His Holiness and his party left. But there had been no feeling of delay; rather, "Everything is ready; now let us go." Among Tibetans time moves freely; it is not harnessed to events.

The short figure, closely wrapped up, passed across the verandah in the dark. His shoulders were bowed from spending hours every day seated cross-legged, reading the sacred books of Buddhism. With him, among many others, went his Chief and lesser Ministers and other officials.

The Dalai Lama and I said our farewells to each other on the verandah, my wife standing at my side. She was careful not to speak to His Holiness, for that would have offended Tibetan custom. My wife never had an interview with him. In view of the gulf between him and the opposite sex, I did not think that would be right, a view which my wife shared.

Outside the verandah the golden Chair of State, brought down from Lhasa, was ready with eight bearers. Thus in the darkness of the night the Precious Sovereign was carried off to take up once again the rule of his wide domain. These departures before crack of dawn are quite the ordinary thing in Tibet, where as you lie in bed you hear the mules pass by your little bungalow, the bells round their necks tinkling as they go.

Soon after their departure daylight broke, and we could behold a gorgeous procession of men, joyful and determined, returning to govern their own land, very different from that forlorn arrival of tired men on tired ponies that was witnessed two years before.

In front are the personal servants with their flat, circular hats, completely covered with threads of bright red silk, astride their ordinary *ta* (ponies); behind these the minor officials, monk and lay, mounted on their honourable *chipa;* the *zhamo, chuba* and *lhamko* (hats, robes and boots) of the servants mingling with the more brilliant and richer hues displayed by the honourable *uzha, manza,* and *zhapcha* of the officials. The members of the Cabinet in their yellow brocades follow. And then the golden Chair of State, for the place of honour in a Tibetan procession is not at or near the head, but in the centre.

Behind the Chair ride the three Chief Ministers, each clad

from head to foot in a long cloak of bright crimson, muffled up round his face. These are rain-cloaks, for they are in a country with a rainfall more than ten times that of their own, and the valuable brocades worn underneath must be protected. Behind again are the lesser lights, tailing off into servants at the end.

The cavalcade is somewhat confined on the narrow, twisting mountain road, but it moves quickly, as if impatient to return to the homeland. Not only the *che* (tongues) of the servants, but the *ja* of the officers say little and speak low, for are they not in the presence of the Inmost One?

Some of the people living in Sikkim and Darjeeling, tracts of country which once were in Tibet but are now in the British sphere, said, "Yes, the Precious Sovereign is returning to rule his kingdom, but by living in all sorts of places and mixing with all sorts of people, including Europeans and others outside the Buddhist religion, his sanctity has been tarnished." Even these, however, spoke such words quietly, and did not publish them abroad, for, though the Dalai Lama's secular authority does not now extend over Sikkim and Darjeeling, his spiritual authority over them remains, and that, too, is a strong force.

"But that was unavoidable," said others. "Now the Inmost One returns to his inmost domain, and will resume his seclusion. And in the holy land of India, from which our Buddhism came, the Inmost One has been as constant in his religious observances as any Dalai Lama living in Lhasa."

Certainly His Holiness had been schooled in adversity, the first exile and now the second. But he had stood the test well. He had shown ability to endure hardship. And he had shown that cheerfulness in danger and difficulty which every Tibetan is expected to show. It was always with a gleeful laugh that he recounted the endeavours of the Chinese soldiers to capture him, and explained how he had outwitted them.

He had shown strength of will. The five years of exile, followed also immediately by a further period of two years, with his country snatched from him, apparently for ever, all these bowed him down but never disheartened him. Rather it stiffened his resolve to keep the Chinese power in check as far as he could.

Would the British help him? Certainly not with soldiers. If

they would not send soldiers, when the Chinese troops overran his country and drove him into exile, they would never send them. That was now clear. Even their so-called neutrality was not real neutrality, for they had not prevented the Chinese from invading Tibet, but seemed to wish to prevent him from driving them out again. Still, their officers in India had shown to him and his officers personal kindness, and afforded them personal protection. So he would see what he could do with the British.

When passing through the Chumbi Valley, the Dalai Lama told Mr. Macdonald that he would try to settle matters with the Chinese troops still left in Tibet, as requested by the Government of India; but that, failing such a settlement, he would ask the Government to depute me to assist him in that task.

The party did not go immediately to Lhasa, as General Chung and his troops had not yet been expelled from there. They awaited this event at the monastery called "Soaring Meditation," overlooking the turquoise-blue waters of the Lake of the Upper Pastures, some seventy miles on the Indian side of Lhasa. During my visits to the monastery later on I saw the room where he stayed. It used to be inhabited by the Abbess, who, strangely enough, is the head over this flourishing community of monks. Her title is Dorje Pamo, "The Vajra Sow." She is a very high Incarnation, and unquestionably the holiest woman throughout the length and breadth of Tibet. But since the Dalai Lama's occupation she has retired to a room below. It would be unseemly for her to occupy it ever again. And that indeed is the rule for all, monk or nun or layman, when once the Incarnation of Chenrezig has occupied a room.

Some months later he returned to Lhasa, and was welcomed with delight. Not only had he escaped the dangers from the Chinese invasion, but he had passed successfully through his thirty-seventh year. The thirty-seventh year (Tibetan reckoning) is always regarded as an especially critical year in a man's life. Every multiple of twelve with one year added is to some extent dangerous, i.e., the thirteenth year, the twenty-fifth the forty-ninth, and so on.

The Tibetan biography records, "Thus the great sun rose

again in the snowy land, and the light of happiness spread over the country." The Dalai Lama in his political testament, referring to this period of exile, attributes it to the wicked actions of the Chinese and his own religious action to combat them. "Religious services," he writes, "were held on behalf of the Faith and the secular side of state affairs. These insured the full ripening of the evil deeds of the Chinese, and in consequence internal commotion broke out in China, and the time was changed." He calls on the entire population of Tibet, both supreme beings and human beings, to witness these facts.

A few months after the Dalai Lama returned to Tibet, Yuan Shihkai, the President of the Chinese Republic, telegraphed to him, apologising for the excesses of the Chinese troops, and restoring the Dalai Lama to his former rank. The Dalai Lama replied that he was not asking the Chinese Government for any rank, as he intended to exercise both temporal and spiritual rule in Tibet. Thus the holy sovereign made clear his declaration of Tibetan independence.

As between Tibet and Great Britain there was now in our mutual relationship a complete change. In 1904 British troops had invaded Tibet and occupied Lhasa. Tibetans had naturally looked on this as an act of violence, the oppression of the weak by the strong, or, as their maxim runs:

Lion! Do not fight with dog!
Lion, though victor, is lion defeated.

Then the Dalai Lama and the skeleton of his Government had been driven by the Chinese into exile in India. We had afforded him and his Ministers protection from their Chinese assailants, and shown them hospitality and friendship.

This good treatment of the Dalai Lama and his Ministers had a better effect on our relations with Tibet than any other event. For all Tibet reveres the Dalai Lama, and everybody among them thought it very merciful of the British Government to have treated the Dalai Lama and his Ministers hospitably, and to have provided them with police guards after they had fought against us in Tibet during the Younghusband expedition six year earlier.

The total cost to our Government was not more than £5,000. China in similar circumstances would have spent a hundred times this sum.

All Tibet was pleased. Their Government would have liked their country to be turned into a British Protectorate on the lines of our recent treaty with Bhutan, but that – for us – would have been sheer lunacy, entailing the defence of a million square miles in High Asia. That we would not establish this Protectorate showed once again that we did not covet their domain.

The news of the good treatment given to His Holiness and his retinue penetrated quickly not only throughout Tibet, but through Mongolia, China, and Japan. When I visited distant Mongolia twenty-three years afterwards, I received a good welcome on account of my long connection with Tibet, and most of all by reason of my long friendship with the Dalai Lama.

Soon after his return to Tibet the Dalai Lama wrote to the Viceroy of India, and in the letter was pleased to say that I had "a vast knowledge of Tibetan affairs." He added, "In following out his duties to his own Government, he has been highly useful to me also, and has rendered me great assistance in the administration of Tibet."

Many were the invitations that I received from the Dalai Lama and his Ministers to visit Lhasa, and they wrote me numerous long letters about all their troubles. Large sheets of the Tibetan parchment paper, on which both the letters were written and the long reports that accompanied them, used to arrive every week or two. The reports were from their officials, high and low, detailing among other matters specific acts of aggression by the Chinese on their eastern frontier. Thus I learnt not only what was happening in Lhasa, but far afield in the distant areas of Tibet. From there the mounted couriers of the Government, having frequent changes of ponies, brought despatches to Lhasa with great rapidity.

The letters and reports were, of course, enclosed in a ceremonial scarf of thin white silk. And over all was the thick parchment cover, liberally sealed. Now and then, on the covers of letters from the Dalai Lama himself, there would be the order to the postal runners who carried them, "Do not stop even to take breath!" The Precious Sovereign did not lose time himself, and did not like others to do so.

It may be of interest to record the sort of phrases in which I began and ended letters to the Dalai Lama in accordance with Tibetan custom.

"To the golden throne of the excellent Dalai Lama, who is the protector and the unfailing refuge of all sentient beings, including the gods.

"Thanks very much for your health being good, like the King of the Mountains, by virtue of the accumulated merits of countless ages and your good deeds increasing like the stars in the sky. Here I am also in good health, and my affairs are going on as usual." (End of opening compliments. Now the business of the letter is written. The conclusion may be somewhat as follows.)

"This letter is composed and written by myself, and so do not be displeased if there are mistakes in it. Kindly take what is good, and abandon what is bad, for your health, and send letters to me, whenever necessary, like a divine river. Know. Know. Know. Know. Know.

"Sent with magnolia flowers by C. A. Bell, Administrator and Minister, on the eighth day of the ninth English month, a date of good omen."

My Tibetan work became twice as heavy as it had been before the visit of the Inmost One. But these letters, supplemented by visits from high Tibetan officials, afforded me a valuable insight into the highways and byways of Tibetan politics.

The Panchen Lama also used to press me to visit him again at Tashi Lhünpo. The Government of India did not permit me to accept any of these invitations, but I knew that if ever it changed its mind – as eight years later it did – a welcome in Lhasa and in any other part of Tibet was always awaiting me.

I could not but recall my first visit to the Tibetan frontier barely nine years before, when I was stopped peremptorily by sullen soldiers and angry monks. No change could have been more complete.

It was my time in Darjeeling with the Dalai Lama that opened to me all the forbidden places of Tibet. If my own Government had permitted, I could have gone anywhere and everywhere in that fascinating land. I obtained rather a good command over the spoken language, in addition to reading and writing it a little; and so when eventually I spent eleven months in Lhasa, the very centre of Tibetan life, I was able to talk, without an interpreter, on any subject to anybody, from the Dalai Lama downwards.

In February, 1913, eight months after his return to Tibet, the Dalai Lama seemed to be afraid that I was going to England for a period of leave. An extract from the letter that he wrote to me on this point reads as follows:

"Lately, when sending Lungshar of the fourth rank to deliver presents to the British Government, we were much inclined to request you to accompany him. He also made a request to the same effect. As however the affairs between the Chinese and Tibetans were still unsettled, we refrained from making this request, knowing that you are the only man who is so well acquainted with Tibetan affairs as to be able to help us in all matters of importance. We now hear that you are soon leaving for England, which, if true, will kill Tibet like a man who is strangled. We therefore request that, if it is not asking too much, you will defer your departure. We will continue sending you our representations, and request that you will continue helping us as usual.

"Sent with a robe of the gods[14] on the twenty-third day of the first month of the year of the Water Bull" (corresponding to February, 1913).

Many such letters I received, both from the Inmost One and from his Ministers. The close contact that was gained during their exile afforded a wonderful opportunity for helping towards the establishment of friendliness with the Government and the people of Tibet.

19 The Heads of the Tibetan Government

When he returned to Lhasa in 1912, the Dalai Lama had been absent from his capital, except for a few months in 1909-1910, for over eight years, having left it on his first flight to China when a young man less than thirty years old. He had then been in power for only a few years, having fought his way to a position in the secular government that had not been occupied for more than a month or two by any Dalai Lama, since the fifth in the order of succession had – through the support of a Mongol Chief – established the spiritual and worldly authority in himself. That was two hundred and fifty years earlier.

To understand the position of the Dalai Lama, or of anybody else in the Tibetan Government, one must realise that one of the root ideas on which Tibet is based is that it must not be too powerful in a worldly sense, nor exercise rule over foreign countries. The Tibetans believe that a powerful nation cannot be really religious. A Tibetan friend put it to me as follows:

"Rich and powerful countries can hardly avoid sinning. In their power they take possession of other countries by fighting and killing the inhabitants of those countries in battle. Thus, taking lives, they commit great sin. We always say that in a powerful country religion goes down. That was the reason why the sixth Dalai Lama – who, as you know, consorted with women – never had a son. If a son had been born to him, Tibet would have become powerful, and brought other nations under its rule."

His inflexible will enabled the Thirteenth Dalai Lama to go

even further than the Great Fifth. The latter had only held the power himself for a few years, and had then made it over to a Minister of singular capacity, who ruled in his name. But the Thirteenth consolidated his power so firmly that he did everything for himself, employing no substitute. He had indeed to be wary. Drepung monastery is not only large and powerful, but also wealthy; in fact, its landed estates are comparable in size with those of the Tibetan Government itself. And was always liable to disaffection. It was largely manned by monks from the eastern borders, close to populous provinces of China, with which it desired to keep on good terms as far as possible. Tashi Lhünpo, as always, was ready to use every means of increasing its own independence, and in fact during the Tibetan Government's contest with China had a secret relationship with the Chinese, and had to be compelled, almost by force, to take even a small share in the fight for Tibetan autonomy. As for the Tengyeling monastery, it had fought openly for the Chinese.

At this time Tibetans were saying that the Dalai Lama and Shatra were the two strong men in Tibet, the main supporters of the national party who were fighting for the independence of Tibet. Shatra was the first of the three Chief Ministers, and by dint of his authority among them may fairly be styled the Prime Minister of Tibet.

Another who exercised considerable power was Tsarong Shap-pe. The Shap-pes exercised less power than the Chief Ministers, being subordinate to the latter; and, acting together, may be termed the Tibetan Cabinet. Tsarong himself, however, was in a peculiar position. His father, as I understood, was a maker of arrows, i.e., about on a level with a carpenter. The young lad was the general body servant to the monk official who was in charge of the grounds at the Jewel Park, the Dalai Lama's favourite residence, one and a half miles outside Lhasa. After a time he obtained service under the Court Physician, and thus came to the notice of the Dalai Lama himself. When the Dalai Lama fled to Mongolia after the Younghusband expedition, the lad worked as one of the assistant valets to His Holiness. The latter adopted him as a favourite in his household, giving him the name of Clear Eye. It was usual for the Dalai Lama always to have one favourite, if not more; a boy or a young man whom he liked personally. Such were a recognised part of the household, and, if they remained in favour, gained afterwards considerable influence in the administration of the country.

Young Clear Eye had added to his good position with the Dalai Lama by his bravery and skill, when only twenty-two years old, in keeping back the Chinese troops who pursued his master during the flight to India. The Dalai Lama never forgot one who served him with faithfulness and courage. Two years later, when the Chinese and Tibetan troops in Lhasa were fighting for the mastery, Clear Eye was placed in command of the Tibetan troops. The head of the Tsarong family of that period was intriguing with the Chinese, and was put to death. Clear Eye married Tsarong's daughter and the widow of Tsarong's son, and so gained for himself the Tsarong name and estates. He appeared to be on excellent terms wtih both wives, and they seemed on excellent terms with each other.

Within a very few years the lad was a member of the Cabinet, thus gaining the rank of Shap-pe. He was also appointed Commander-in-Chief of the army and Master of the Mint. Thus, in spite of his low birth, the most severe of handicaps for a layman, he rose to one of the highest positions. The favourite of a king is a target for criticism, but this one made good, and something more.

The Tibetans have a saying, "Like the dog that ran round China." The meaning is that the dog just ran from one thing to another, looking here and sniffing there, but maintaining no continued purpose, and ending up with nothing important to show for its visit to such a wonderful country. As they say, "It went with a tail and came back with a tail." This saying is applied to a man who works aimlessly, accomplishing no definite purpose. Tsarong was the very opposite of such a man, none could have had a more definite purpose than he; none followed it more inflexibly.

From boyhood to age Tsarong was an unchanging friend of the British; to me he was always a firm friend. He was young and energetic; sometimes it seemed to me too hot-headed. Later on his impulsiveness got him into trouble, and he lost both his post in the Cabinet and his position as Commander-in-Chief. But even when his offices had fallen away Tsarong was one of the most influential men in Tibet. While rating very highly the physical ability of his people, he preferred British methods of administration. The Dalai Lama and those of his officials who had been to India approved of some of the British methods; those who had remained in their own country desired no change from Tibetan or Chinese ways.

On his return from India the Dalai Lama took a firmer control over Tibetan affairs. Meanwhile he had gained in knowledge and insight, and had become more wary through the bitter schooling of his double exile. He now knew not only what he could do with his own people, but also what he could not do with the nations across his mountain ranges.

The secular side of the Dalai Lama's task was not easy. The constitution of the Supreme Government consisted of himself at the top, then the Chief Ministers, of whom at this time there were three, but later on only one. Below these came the Cabinet and the Ecclesiastical Court, and below the Cabinet and this Court came the National Assembly or Parliament.

The Ecclesiastical Court deals with matters concerning the large body of monks, for, according to Tibetan ideas, it would never do to give the Cabinet full control over the monks, though even in the Cabinet one of the four is a monk. Still, having one ordained person among their members, the Cabinet can often settle a matter affecting religious interests.

The Cabinet is known to Tibetans as *Kashag,* and is composed of one monk and three laymen. Each Cabinet member is known as a Shap-pe, or more politely by two other Tibetan words which mean "Great Power of the Land." The Cabinet has a general controlling power over the internal administration of the country, whether in political, in revenue, or in judicial matters. It hears appeals from the decisions of the various judges and magistrates. But of course where a noble or high official is concerned in a serious case, those magistrates and judges have no jurisdiction. The matter is tried by the Cabinet itself; Tibet, being a feudal country, the nobility have large privileges. Both the Cabinet and the Ecclesiastical Court send their reports on serious matters to the Dalai Lama through the Chief Minister.

It is the rule in Tibet that all official bodies work as one. So is it with the *Kashag;* no orders are issued by them separately; if there are any differences, none are acknowledged. Their little square black seal is well known to all who have dealings with the Tibetan Government. To Tibetans it is known as "Officialdom, Yellow and Grey," expressed in Tibetan by four short syllables, for the Tibetan language is usually much more closely condensed than English is. Yellow denotes the clergy, as the reformed sect wear yellow hats; and grey stands for the laity, who are accustomed to wear grey clothes.

They are not allowed to use a red seal; that is reserved for the highest. The Dalai Lama and Panchen Lamas of course use red seals, and so does the Prime Minister. Orders go out through Tibet in the name of the Cabinet, and they write also to foreigners, who desire something from the Tibetan Government.

All reports on matters of importance go from or through them to the Prime Minister, who sends it on when necessary, as it usually is, to the Dalai Lama. The Cabinet, or the Prime Minister, often make alternative recommendations, and the Dalai Lama puts his little red mark against the advice which he accepts. It may be the appointment of some official. In this case the Cabinet must send up through the Prime Minister either two or three names to the Dalai Lama. The latter might accept none of them, and call for other names. He would always go on until he found before him the name that he wanted. A new Shap-pe, i.e., a colleague of their own, was appointed in the same way.

In the Cabinet Chamber was a shrine, in the centre of which stood an image of Tsongkapa, the fourteenth-century reformer of Tibetan Buddhism. To the left of this was the Dalai Lama's throne, a low one, on which he would sit if he came, at the Cabinet's request, to bless them and the officials working under them in Lhasa. Only the higher officials in Lhasa were allowed to come for this blessing, and none who worked outside the

Holy City. Actually the Dalai Lama visited the Cabinet Chamber only once, at any rate during the first fifty years of his life.

When I was in Darjeeling with the Dalai Lama, there were three Prime (or Chief) Ministers. By the time I went to Lhasa, eight years later, two of these had died, and one only, Shokang, was left. Thereafter one Prime Minister only was the rule.

20 The Parliament

One example of the semi-democratic influence in the Tibetan Government is provided by the National Assembly in Lhasa, which is the nearest approach to a Parliament that Tibet possesses. It is composed of all ecclesiastical and secular officials below the members of the Cabinet, or rather such of them as happen to be stationed in or near Lhasa. As already stated, the total number of officials in Tibet is three hundred and fifty, half of whom are lay and half ordained.

This Parliament was summoned by the Dalai Lama, who used to give the order through the Prime Minister. He would, as a rule, tell the latter to call it on the next day but one, but in matters of urgency on the very next day. The "arrow list" then went out, containing the names of those summoned to attend, and the date and hour of attendance.

The place of assembly is a large hall in the Temple near the office of the Cabinet. It was my good fortune to see this hall when in Lhasa in 1921. It was a large, bare room on an upper storey with plank flooring. Part of the room was on a higher level than the rest, two or three steps higher, this highest portion being the smaller. On this raised portion sit those who hold the title of *Kung*, *Dzasa*, or *Techi*, as well as the Grand Secretaries, the Financial Secretaries, and as many of the other fourth-rank officials as there is room for. High up on the walls are openings of wooden lattice work to let in light and air; but the proceedings cannot be heard outside, nor would anybody be allowed to go to the walls and listen.

The members sit on rugs on the floor, those of higher rank

being on mattresses raised, in the case of a *Kung*, some seven or eight inches, a *Dzasa* and a *Techi* being slightly lower and having mattresses of equal height with each other. These mattresses are bound with red woollen cloth and stuffed mostly with the hair of the musk deer, which is lighter than wool; though, of course, it is more expensive, and only the richer people, such as the landed proprietors and well-to-do merchants, can afford to buy them. *Kungs, Dzasas* and *Techis* have small tables in front of them, but those below them in rank do not enjoy this privilege. The other members, being of lower rank, that is to say, from the fourth rank downwards, sit on lower seats. The fourth rank have seats of coloured silk on the top, felt or white woollen cloth inside, and coloured cloth at the bottom. Then come those of the fifth and sixth rank, who work in Lhasa itself, such as police magistrates, subordinate judges, and so on. These sit on seats like those of the fourth-rank officials, except that on the silk tops of their seats squares of tiger-skin are inserted. Those of still lower rank always sit on long lengths of cotton cloth, with a thin strip of woollen cloth in the middle, and cotton cloth again below.

The abbots and treasurers of the three great monasteries, Drepung, Sera and Ganden, some twenty men in all, attend and exercise great influence, for they speak for twenty thousand monks, who are near at hand and may often be turbulent. Among those who do manual work for the Government, mostly carpenters and tailors, a few of their foremen receive the rank of civil official, and therefore are entitled to seats in the Parliament. They may also address it, though in practice they seldom do so, as they feel that there are so many people of much greater ability in it. However, if they speak wisely, this is recognised and members are not averse to agreeing with them.

The four heads of the Ecclesiastical Court, known as Grand Secretaries, take the lead among those members who are monks; three Financial Secretaries are the heads among the members who are laymen. The proceedings are opened by the senior Grand Secretary, i.e., the one who has been Grand Secretary longest, announcing the business which they have come to discuss. He ranks above the senior Financial Secretary because, other things being equal, a monk officer ranks higher than a secular officer. The Grand Secretaries and the Financial Secretaries do most of the talking, and the monks usually speak more than the laymen. The latter have given hostages to fortune, because they have families and hold large landed estates, and therefore cannot afford to offend the heads of the Government. The celibate monks have neither property nor family to consider; they say pretty well what they please.

There are no regular speeches, as we understand the word, but rather general conversation, each taking up the talk when another has finished. They remain seated while speaking. At the conclusion of his remarks the speaker may say, "Is that so?" or "Does that suit?" The lower officials are, as a rule, slow to assert their own views. But if another of the more important members disagrees with a former speaker, he may say, "It is not quite like that," and put his own point of view, and so on till all who wish to speak have stated their opinions.

The decision is not put to a vote of the members. From the way the discussion goes, it can be seen clearly in what way the opinions are at variance, and which is the opinion held by the majority, especially by the majority of the more important members. When its supporters speak, others say, "That is so," "That is true." In fact, the discussion continues until the minority, finding that the prevalent opinion is against them, forbear to press their views further. Then, when this prevailing opinion is put to the meeting, those in favour say, "It is so; it is indeed so," while those who are opposed hold their peace. Thus the decision has the appearance of being unanimous.

The proceedings usually last for two or three hours at a time. Tea is brought round, and members produce their own wooden bowls. The use of china cups is forbidden in all Government offices, even to members of the Cabinet. Later on, rice with minced meat may be brought round; it is taken in the same wooden bowl as was used for the tea. Later again, tea may be brought round once more, but that will be all. Tea, rice and meat are provided free of charge.

The reason given for this prohibition against china cups is that "Government servants are under the Government, and therefore they use the inferior wooden vessels for food and drink, instead of the superior vessels made of china." In their own homes many have cups of priceless china and jade.

After the Parliament at length came to a decision they reported it verbally to the Cabinet, who passed it on with their opinion to the Prime Minister, who in turn submitted it to the Dalai Lama. The Parliament kept no written record of their proceedings.

During the two and a half centuries which preceded the late Dalai Lama's coming of age, the Parliament exercised great power in Tibet. When a Regent is in power during the minority of a Dalai Lama, this Parliament is strong enough to hold the Regent in check, and sometimes even to depose him. Accordingly, during the first years of the Dalai Lama's rule, his instinct would hold him back from overruling it. In 1910 when His Holiness was still a young man, I asked him what happened when the Parliament and Cabinet disagreed. "In whose favour do you decide?" "It is good," he replied, "to make the larger number contented."

But later on he used rather to call together a committee of its leading members, and that with diminishing frequency. He did not often overrule their views, if he did summon them. When he wished action on any State matter under discussion to be delayed, or knew that they would give the decision that he desired, he might call them together. Those who disapproved of the decision and – being not under the close control of Lhasa – were bold enough to express an opinion, might perhaps then say to each other, though in the utmost secrecy, "The Precious Sovereign has wiped his dirty hand on the Parliament's sleeve." More often, however, a Minister would be blamed for having persuaded the Dalai Lama to take such action, by which the Precious Sovereign *seemed* to wipe his dirty hand on the Parliament's sleeve.

"The Parliament goes on talking, talking," the Dalai Lama would tell me, "and makes great delay in cutting the cord" (deciding). Especially was this so in disputes with other nations, though such disputes, if not settled quickly, caused much ill will on both sides.

Towards the end of his life, however, the Inmost One became increasingly autocratic, and would often disagree with the Parliament's recommendation.. He would himself then give another order, and the matter was finally decided in accordance with this order, none daring to object.

Thus the Dalai Lama, the Prime Minister, the Cabinet, and the National Assembly or Parliament, might be said to constitute the supreme Government of Tibet. The power of the Cabinet used to be great in matters of the internal administration, but in foreign policy they were controlled by the Parliament. And as the years went on the Dalai Lama took more and more of the power into his own hands, especially that relating to foreign affairs.

The Tibetan religion is wide in its spread. It includes not only human beings, but beasts, fishes, birds, insects, etc., in fact, all "living beings." A man in this life may have been an ant in the last; and if he does ill, he may be born a goose or a pig in the next. Your father or sister, who died some years ago, may now be a bird. It is believed that every year the birds hold their parliament at a large lake north of Lhasa, where justice is administered by their king, the cuckoo. The saying runs that law and justice will prevail among men and women for so long as there is law and justice among birds. Accordingly, the Dalai Lama's duties do not end with his human parliament, for he has come to earth to minister to all living beings. So he sends a yearly deputation to this parliament of birds. A lama addresses them on the importance of law and order, and at the same time gives them a present of food. As mentioned above, the human parliament is also fed at the Government expense when holding its debates.

Most Tibetans are fond of birds. Certainly the Dalai Lama was. Whenever I visited him, there was always a bird or two, not far away, perhaps a talking myna from India.

21   Difficulties in Government

Seals of state figure largely in the Tibetan administration. The
Dalai Lama explained to me the different purposes for which his
own were used. Beginning with the Fifth and ending with the
Eleventh, each Dalai Lama had received a separate seal from the
Emperor of China. Number Twelve, and my friend the Thirteenth, both represented that it was unnecessary for any fresh
seals to be given, an apparent indication that during those two
periods the Manchu power in Tibet was at a low ebb. Among
these seals the one most used was "The Golden Seal of Heaven
and Earth." This red, square seal bears on it the name of the
Manchu Emperor who ruled during the time of the Fifth Dalai
Lama. On any matter in which the Chinese are entitled to be
consulted, a Tibetan seal known as "The Inmost Seal," was
placed at the top and one of the seals from China at the bottom.

   It was not only from China that the Dalai Lama received seals.
"The Golden King," the seal which the Dalai Lama regarded as
the highest of all, was given by a Mongolian Prince to the Third
Dalai Lama, who lived during the sixteenth century, and converted Mongolia to Buddhism. That is why it was esteemed,
having been brought into use before the Chinese claimed Tibet
as a part of China. The Dalai Lama used to place it on the chief
acts of the internal administration, or in any important matter in
which the Tibetan Government did not consult the Chinese
authorities. For instance, the Golden King figured on the grant
by the Tibetan Government of a large estate, or the settlement of
a very serious land dispute. The seal, being of gold, was not itself
used, but a copy of it, made of iron.

When the Dalai Lama returned to Lhasa from China in 1909, at the end of his first exile, the Tibetans gave him a new seal, as from Tibet, not from China. For they looked on China as powerless to help them against a strong enemy, but able and willing to exploit them for its own purposes.

Seals of State and the other insignia of rule the Dalai Lama did indeed posses; but brought up as he had been entirely by monks, he found, especially during his years of early manhood, the administration of the secular Government to be no inconsiderable puzzle. He had almost no contact with the great mass of his subjects. He had studied books without number on theology, astrology, and the like, but these would not carry him far in the civil government. His very sanctity rendered him throughout his life somewhat inaccessible to his officials.

However, his early upbringing had taught him to be watchful. Though he was blessed with servants devoted to his person, he, too, from early youth had to be on his guard against poison or other devices which had brought to an early close the careers of his four immediate predecessors. He came soon to weigh the motives and characters of men.

Later on, he used his limited experience in trying to weigh up the political setting of other nations, and especially their strength and weakness. Mistakes there would be, but still he pushed on; his strength of will was great.

The difficulty in governing Tibet is partly due to the long distances that have to be traversed over high passes and across deep gorges. One must ride the little Tibetan pony, or walk. Thus it comes that it takes some three months' ordinary travelling to cross from one end of the country to the other. Many parts of Tibet are about two months' journey distant from Lhasa by ordinary communications; it may therefore be easily understood how difficult it was for the Dalai Lama or anybody to control these districts far away, and indeed difficult to know what was happening there.

Fortunately, however, the Tibetan Government have a system of mounted couriers, who can travel fifty to sixty miles a day across unbridged rivers and high mountain passes, and keep it up if necessary for twenty days or more, thus doing in one day what takes the ordinary traveller two or three. They receive a fresh pony at each stage of ten to fifteen miles, but themselves travel right through, so that there is no divided responsibility. Their posts are hereditary, and they are trained to the work and its attendant hardships from an early age. You can usually recognise one of them by the yellow bag on his back, in which he carries the letters. The ponies are supplied by the villages through which he passes, and they are bound to supply good ones. When I was in Lhasa, I was greatly impressed by the rapidity with which the Dalai Lama communicated his orders to the Chatreng monastery, two or three months' journey away, near the south-eastern border of Tibet, and obtained their submissive reply.

Away in the provinces the Dalai Lama found it extremely difficult to supervise the staff closely. The written proclamation, that the Tibetan Government have for many years past circulated to all *dzongpöns* (governors of districts), still held the field. This is known as the "Root Word" (*tsa-tsik*), and tells these district magistrates how they are to do their official work. All the people are categorically informed that "The real benefit of the world proceeds from religion alone, and religion depends entirely upon the lamas." Again, "If a *dzongpön* receives a complaint that the property of a traveller or pilgrim has been stolen, or that such person has been beaten or killed, or if an adult ill treat his old parents, an immediate report must be submitted to the Government. The owners of images of Buddhas, religious monuments, places where religious emblems or the golden scriptures are kept, must take great care of their property, and prevent other persons from injuring them. Money-lenders must not charge compound interest, nor take the landed property, the cattle, the ponies, or the donkeys of the debtor. It is forbidden to use false weights or measures. The *dzongpöns* must not impose heavy fines simply to benefit their own pockets. Nor must they demand things from their subjects in the way that a large insect devours a small one." And so on. Good, no doubt, but difficult to enforce.

Although supervision was difficult, the Dalai Lama met the difficulty in various ways. He installed his own squad of intelligence officers, so that interested parties could never be sure whether the Dalai Lama knew or not. As the years went on and his system became further improved, they found it safer to presume that he did. And litigants and other aggrieved persons, who felt that they suffered from injustice, could sometimes contrive to appeal to him direct.

Private interviews granted to privileged persons increased still further his sources of information from the outside. My friend Palhese had various interviews with the Dalai Lama. The last was less than a year before the latter died; at it they discussed sympathetically the hardships of the Panchen Lama and his party in the hot climate of China, and my forthcoming visit to Tibet. The Dalai Lama told the Cabinet nothing as to what transpired at this interview.

He allowed some, whom he trusted, to write to him direct, among these being his agent at Gyangtse, and Palhese. In the latter case it was partly to know what was passing in my mind.

Accordingly the district officials became more careful under the Dalai Lama's handling. And the raising of the literary standard helped to raise the level of their work.

One of the weaknesses of the Tibetan Government has always been their disinclination to keep their officers on their frontiers and in foreign lands informed of communications which passed between Tibet and other States. Their motive is to keep the power in their own hands, but the result is sometimes disastrous. For instance, Tibetan officers working on the Nepal-Tibet frontier were not supplied with the copies of treaties and other communications on which their actions should be based. They sometimes therefore violated treaty rights unconsciously, and brought the two nations within measurable distance of war.

The Dalai Lama made an advance here also. Nearly two years after his death, when I was in Peking, I used frequently to meet the three representatives of the Tibetan Government in China. Their verdict was as follows:

"The Dalai Lama used to keep us informed of all foreign events. If he sent a telegram to Chiang Kaishek or to Wang Chingwei or received a telegram from either of them, he sent a copy to us. The present Tibetan Government does not keep us so well informed. Sometimes, when communicating direct with the Chinese Government, they omit to forward us copies of such communications."

The rule used to be that public appointments could not be given to members of the Dalai Lama's family. That check, however, did not limit him fully, as they were allowed to hold private appointments that carried great influence. And later on, the Precious Sovereign went further. Little by little, as his power increased, he modified almost all rules that stood in his way. At an early stage he appointed one young nephew to a small position in the army. Towards the end of his life when he had long been an absolute autocrat, he set aside the rule still more markedly by giving another nephew the most responsible position of Prime Minister, in succession to Shokang, who held that post when I was in Lhasa. This nephew worked with, and was slightly subordinate to, Prime Minister Shokang for three years, and learned the work from him to some extent; but of course he had not the experience of one who had worked his way up from the bottom. He was only twenty-seven or twenty-eight years old when the Dalai Lama died, and so lacked general experience. Besides, the Dalai Lama really took all the responsibility, so that after his death the young Prime Minister was at a disadvantage, having to make the decisions himself.

The Dalai Lama must of necessity work through his officials. The lack of education in Tibet renders them ignorant. This ignorance, however, holds the people also, and in the case of the officials the Dalai Lama used to tell me that he had greatly raised the literary standard.

A more serious difficulty for His Holiness was the semi-indolent lives that the officials led on their large estates. The Tibetan nobleman or squire is a charming person to meet, courteous, hospitable and friendly; all the more so if one can converse with him in his own language. But, though keenly patriotic, few of them are inclined to work hard for the Government unless there is some pressing need. One who was appointed to the governorship of a distant district, feeling that

Lhasa was ever so much more pleasant as a place of residence, would often send a clerk or other servant of position to hold the governorship for him. So many of the Government posts in Tibet are really held, as it were, on contract. You pay what is necessary to the Cabinet, and you make what profit you can; both the payment – call it present or bribe, whichever you prefer – to the Cabinet, and the profit of the post being regulated according to certain rules that are well understood.

Tibet being still in the feudal stage, these landed proprietors, especially those with the largest estates, are tempted to lead easy, pleasant lives with hosts of servants. On the whole, they were unsatisfactory material for any Head of the Government to employ in his administrative work. The Dalai Lama used to degrade them frequently, and occasionally to dismiss one, but these were punishments that they did not mind very much, because their estates were seldom taken away from them. It was from their estates that they derived their incomes, their Government salary being trivial. Even a member of the Cabinet received as his salary a sum equal to only £250 a year. Besides, the number of available officials was limited, so that after a good lapse of time the degraded officer might expect restoration, and often indeed promotion, to some post or other. Twelve years after I left Lhasa I came to Tibet again on a private visit, some months after His Holiness had died. It had become then quite a joke for officials to ask each other how often they had been set down and raised again. One told me of an official who was twice degraded from his rank of colonel and twice reinstated, so that altogether he was appointed a colonel three times.

That half of the Government officials who were recruited from the monks worked much harder. They were, as a rule, self-made men, who had risen by their own exertions, and thought nothing of hard and continuous work. The monk official who, with a secular colleague, looked after my party during my year in Lhasa, had taken no holiday for twenty-five years. He had merely been absent for a day or two, now and then, when he was ill.

On account of the Dalai Lama's increasing supervision, those magistrates who took bribes and so gave what the Tibetans call "crooked justice," became afraid that their conduct would come to his ears. He did thus to some extent reduce bribery, by some Tibetans called "secret push," by others "the door of eating."

The huge size of many of the monasteries, and the turbulence of many of the monks inside them, was an abiding difficulty to the Dalai Lama during the whole of his life. The leading lamas have great influence by reason of their sanctity. Most of them, having worked their way up through all the stages of the monastic order, have shown themselves to be men of ability. And, as explained above, they are free to adopt a bolder course of action than even the nobles can do. The abbots in Drepung, Sera and Ganden, through their power in the Parliament, had a special influence of their own.

"The monks act straight off," said the Dalai Lama to me. "They do not consider the results of their actions."

"With the soldiers that you now have, and their improved equipment, you find it perhaps, Precious Protector, somewhat easier to control them?"

"Well, much more by choosing the right men to be abbots over them. I am careful in the choice of these."

When the Great Prayer Festival took place, and fifty thousand monks poured into the Holy City and remained there for two or three weeks, His Holiness kept the soldiers out of it, except on rare occasions, and thus avoided a clash between the old clergy and the rising power of the military.

When the young Dalai Lama decided to be not only the divinity of Tibet but also its autocrat in secular affairs, he headed into a great assortment of difficulties, and also burdened himself with a heavy load of work. But he had several advantages on his side. He was blessed with a hardy constitution, a love for work and authority, and a strong will. Besides, his very divinity, though it had prevented him from receiving the education that would fit him to be a king or minister, endowed him with unlimited authority, at least in theory. The Tibetans believe in the necessity of strong government at the top, though they manage to combine it with a good deal of local autonomy lower down. When I was in Lhasa, the Prime Minister used often to stress this point. Speaking of orders from the Dalai Lama, the Tibetan proverb says:

> If he tells you to strike a rock, strike!
> If he tells you to go to hell, go!

Pilgrimages to Lhasa increased the influence of His Holiness not only over Tibet, but over Mongolia and some of the tribes in China and Russia. Indeed his authority, when he learned how to exercise it, was supreme.

22   Judge and Historian

Although Tibet is a wild, desolate region, it is on the whole governed in an orderly manner. More so than the close-packed lands of China, ravaged as these have been by banditry and other disorders. Tibet is, as the Dalai Lama calls it, "the field of religion."

At the same time the Tibetan criminal code is drastic. In addition to fines and imprisonment, floggings are frequent, not only of people after they have been convicted of an offence, but also of accused persons, and indeed witnesses, during the course of the trial. For serious offences, use is made of the pillory as well as of the cangue, which latter is a heavy square wooden board round the neck. Iron fetters are fastened on the legs of murderers and inveterate burglars. For very serious or repeated offences, such as murder, violent robbery, repeated thefts, or serious forgery, the hand may be cut off at the wrist, the nose sliced off, or even the eyes gouged out, the last more likely for some heinous political crime. In former days those convicted of murder were put into a leather sack, which was sewn up and thrown into a river.

The ordinary magistrates in criminal cases are the heads of the districts, that is, the *dzongpöns;* and the landed magnates where their own tenants are solely concerned. Four other magistrates disposed of cases in the Holy City and immediate neighbourhood. One of these district magistrates may flog as much and as often as he likes, provided he does not kill the accused person. When property stolen has not been recovered, the accused is often flogged several times in the hope of inducing him to reveal where it is. There is no limit to the fine which the *dzongpön* may impose. He keeps the fines himself, except that once each year he has to remit a small portion of them to the Government. This portion is known as "The Tail of the Law"; it is a fixed sum, based not on the estimated receipts from fines, but on the total revenue payable to the Government for that district.

The magistrate may also sentence the prisoner to wear the cangue and iron fetters for three or four years; any longer sentence than this should be referred to the Cabinet. The cangue is taken off at night, except in very heinous crimes, when a somewhat lighter and smaller board is used during both day and night.

The Cabinet hear appeals from these magistrates, and themselves take cases which are beyond the jurisdiction of the latter. From the Cabinet an appeal lay to the Prime Minister, who had to report serious cases, including many cases of murder, to the Dalai Lama for decision.

When the Dalai Lama was a religious novice he used to try criminal cases. But when he became a fully ordained monk he himself tried them no longer, though he had to adjudicate on references from the Prime Minister. Though murder in Tibet is not uncommon, the Dalai Lama abolished capital punishment, except for an attempt to poison himself, or other very serious crime against the religion, such a crime occurring only once in every five or ten years. Until the time of his flight to India, while the ideals of youth were still strong within him, the Dalai Lama, as he himself informed me, allowed no capital punishment in any circumstances. Later on, however, as he became more and more immersed in the difficulties of administration, he found that capital punishment was occasionally unavoidable.

But considering all the murders in Tibet, this was very rare indeed. Not even Black Bönists were put to death. The Bön is the old animist religion of Tibet, existing before Buddhism was introduced. Tibetans divide it into White Bön and Black Bön. The White Bön have now become almost like the Buddhists, the differences between them not being reckoned as vital by the latter. "They are inner beings," said a Tibetan to me. "They have faith in Buddha, though they do indeed call him by a different name. There is no great harm in them.

"But the Black Bönists are non-Buddhist; they are heretics. They take life; they kill animals for sacrificial purposes; they work inner injury to human beings, so that they die, and in this way also they are guilty of killing. Many of the sorcerors and teachers of the Bönists were destroyed long ago, but some remained over, especially in the outlying parts. If anyone is found practising these Black Bön rituals by which people are killed, they are heavily punished. But the Dalai Lama does not allow even such a one to be thrown into the river.

His Holiness also discouraged severe punishments such as cutting off the wrists and putting out the eyes, in fact all forms of mutilation. Old Prime Minister Shokang, who from time to time passed orders of this kind, declared that when he passed the age of sixty and felt himself old, he disliked very strongly having to give such punishments. But custom, the overlord of the masses in Asia, was too strong for him.

Perhaps there is a riot, or other disturbance. The Ecclesiastical Court selects an ecclesiastical official, and the Cabinet selects one from the laity; these are to make an inquiry into the reason of the riot, and the punishment that should be inflicted. Their names are sent up to the Dalai Lama for his approval. In their findings they must agree; no divergence of opinion is permitted; the stronger will carries the day. Then they report through the Cabinet, who propose different alternative orders, sending their report to the Prime Minister. The Dalai Lama puts his red hand-mark opposite the order that he approves.

There is in Lhasa a tribe called Ragyapa, the lowest of the low. Convicts used to be put into their charge, as Lhasa is but scantily provided with prison accommodation. When, however, he was in India, the Dalai Lama saw how prisoners there were put to useful work in the prisons. Accordingly on his return to Tibet, he arranged that his subordinates should set many to work in the Government workshops instead of handing them over to the Ragyapa. His Holiness appreciated the fact that part of the expense of maintaining them was in this way recouped.

He also introduced a system of useful fines. One offender

might be sentenced to arrange for the repair of something like half a mile of the road between Lhasa city and his country house in the Jewel Park, costing the offender perhaps £40. Another was ordered to plant a thousand young willow seedlings in the Jewel Park.

Though he was opposed to cruel punishments, he was shrewd at maintaining order among the turbulent monks, who crowd in at the great religious festivals, and shrewd also at maintaining the morale of the rich laity, as happened during my stay in Lhasa, when things looked black and panic threatened.

In the civil, as well as in the criminal, law and the Dalai Lama found plenty of work. All civil disputes dealing with the title to, or possession of, land were referred to the Precious Sovereign for decision – even where small pieces of land were concerned – for land questions were always held to be of prime import-ance. The disputes were referred through the Prime Minister, and during my time in Lhasa the Dalai Lama was deciding, on an average, fifteen to twenty such cases every week. These were the cases in which there had been disagreement between the lower Courts. But even the numerous cases in which they had agreed were shown to the Dalai Lama for approval. Once a week all these cases were laid before him. Petitions of tenants for reduc-tion of rents went up to the Dalai Lama; the Prime Minister told me that even he had not the power to decide these.

If an applicant wrote the Dalai Lama's name on his petition in a lawsuit, it had to be laid before His Holiness. Not even the Cabinet or the Prime Minister himself could stop it. But if the petition was on a matter not considered worthy of the Dalai Lama's attention, the applicant was punished. The result was that not many petitioners abused this privilege.

As in the case of previous Dalai Lamas, the Inmost One had to supply materials for the history of his reign. It is a part of the business of Sovereigns to record important events at the time of their occurrence. The papers on which these diaries and notes are written are rolled up into bundles. Such is the theory, but it does not always work out in practice. The Tibetan biographer tells us what happened.

Some time after the Dalai Lama's death, when his mausoleum

was nearly completed, the Regent and his nephew the Prime Minister, as well as his other near relatives, asked the Incarnation Lama of Purchok – the Reincarnation of him who had helped the Dalai Lama during the latter's boyhood – to write the biography.

Purchok records, "I asked the inner attendants of the Dalai Lama to provide me with all the diaries and other notes that were useful for this work. But I found them only scattered pieces, and they were not arranged in order; and so I was greatly disappointed and confused." He feels, too, his own intellectual limitations.

But he remembers the old saying, "Though I have no teeth, I shall chew it with my gums."

He continues, "I copied most of his public work from his diaries. His private life I wrote from his private notes, without mixing them with my own ideas. I wrote such works as his meditations, preaching and reconstruction of old temples, in considerable detail, as I found these the chief parts of his work. But most of his commonplace work I wrote very briefly."

The Tibetan biography records only a few features in his secular work, and these briefly. It dismisses in two or three lines a treaty between Tibet and Britain, though the Dalai Lama himself regarded this treaty as important; and it gives barely one line to the Dalai Lama's establishment of a postal system in Tibet. It gives six times more space than both combined to a sermon that the Dalai Lama preached.

The biographer continues, "There was a break of one and a half years in my writing, as I had to go to the northern province to search for the new Dalai Lama. Thus, in about six years, little by little, I wrote this book, just as an ant-hill is put together, or a honeycomb."

This biography forms one of the Tibetan series known as *The Succession of Births*. Block prints were made, Tibetan printing being done, even nowadays, from engraved wooden blocks.

The older histories of the early kings are known as *The Succession of the Kings*. Such histories were compiled from a study of the earlier histories preceding them, and no doubt a large measure of reliance was placed on each *Succession of the Kings*. The stories and fables of olden days also found a place in the histories, but some at any rate of the historians were careful, and inserted only what they considered to be proved and true. Printed books in Tibet are held to be sacred, for it was in books that the Buddhist religion came to Tibet. Writers, therefore, hesitate to insert anything in a printed book unless they believe it to be true, for any mistake would be regarded by many as a slight on the Buddhist religion. Tibetans, however, have a love for miraculous events, and find no great difficulty in believing them. They have told me that they cannot understand why so many Christians should find a difficulty in believing the miracles recorded in our Christian Bible.

Since the time of the Fifth Dalai Lama all the important Government records, including the historical ones, as well as records of districts, revenues, etc., are kept mostly in the Finance Office at Lhasa. They are kept in large chests placed round the walls of the spacious room in which the Financial Secretaries and their clerks work.

Enough has been written to give some indication of the heaviness of the Dalai Lama's work on the secular side alone. He was able to get through it only because his industry was tireless and his will indomitable. He used to rise from his bed by six o'clock, but if the work was heavily in arrears, or a religious ceremony must needs be attended, or a journey be made, he might rise at three o'clock in the morning. Indeed, if the date was one of great sanctity in the Buddhist calendar, he might sit in meditation throughout the greater part of the night. In any case, during my time in Lhasa he never went to bed till after midnight. But he loved the work, especially until old age supervened, and he liked the power which the work gave him. At the same time he honestly felt that nobody but himself was equal to the headship, and believed that he alone could hold up Tibet among the powerful countries surrounding it. He used to tell me that his Ministers were constitutionally timid, and lacked driving power; they had no guts.

23   Finance

The coinage of Tibet is peculiar. The chief unit is the *trangka*, a silver coin with a large measure of alloy. It is divided into six lesser units, known as *ka*. Silversmiths used to cut round the centre and detach different portions, worth two *ka*, three *ka* or four *ka*. They kept the centre itself as payment for cutting the coin. In 1914 copper coins, worth one, two, three or four *ka*, were introduced, and then the cutting of the *trangka* became unnecessary. Lumps of silver, called "horse-shoes," and varying greatly in size, are used for the higher values; as well as treasury notes of five, ten, fifteen, twenty-five and fifty *trangkas* each, the issue of these notes being commenced also in 1914. Owing to over-coinage of copper coins, large quantities of which were counterfeited in India and smuggled across the frontier of Tibet, the *trangka* depreciated greatly, falling from sixpence in 1910 to twopence halfpenny in 1920, and even lower afterwards.

There was also a gold mint at Lhasa, whose machinery was worked by a water-wheel. It was in the charge of Tsarong Shap-pe, who reaped in it a part of his reward for saving the Dalai Lama during the flight from the Chinese in 1910. Tsarong was allowed to buy the gold at a fixed price and mint it at a value somewhat higher. It was no doubt a profitable post.

The public finance of the country over which the Dalai Lama rules has its peculiarities. Firstly, there is the Finance Office, controlled by three Financial Commissioners who, as already mentioned, unite with the heads of the Ecclesiastical Court in presiding over the Parliament. This Account Office does not receive the Government revenue. The officers in charge of districts and other collecting agencies pay, not to any central treasury, but to the different treasuries in Lhasa, or even direct to those to whom it is due. The Finance Office also has to manage the small and select Government college which trains young men for all branches of the Government service. When I visited this department in 1920 I found six young men studying under an elderly teacher in the same room as the three Financial Commissioners and four or five clerks were working.

There are four treasuries. The best known is the *Labrang*. It receives money from the tax-payers, but money is not the chief item, for the greater part of the revenue is paid in kind. Butter and tea from the landed estates, and gold from the mines in eastern and western Tibet swell its resources. Grain is also remitted in large quantities, and stored in Government granaries scattered all over the country. Its cold, dry climate helps Tibet in the storage of the butter, grain and other commodities. Grain keeps good for over a hundred years on earthen floors which have been merely rammed down by hand; on copper floors, with ventilators underneath, it keeps for many hundred years. There are several such places near the Lake of the Upper Pastures between Lhasa and Gyangtse. Were there a famine in Tibet, its inaccessibility and great empty spaces would prevent the import of grain in sufficient quantities; the granaries are the chief preventive against famine.

Another way in which this treasury earns revenue for the Government is by lending out money at the rate of fourteen per cent. yearly, more or less. This rate is somewhat low for Tibet, and the would-be borrowers must therefore produce two good sureties. Not only money is lent out, but grain also, adding still further to the revenue.

The treasury is managed by two monk officials and one secular, working as usual jointly. Their salary was equivalent to about £20 a year each, but worth much more in Tibet, where prices are very low. And their pay was of no importance, for their perquisites were greater than those enjoyed by other officials, as applicants for loans pay them to have these given at somewhat lower rates of interest, and applications from *dzong-pöns* for remission of revenue are also made through them. The greater part of Tibet is divided into districts, each one of which is in the charge of one *dzongpön,* or two acting jointly.

This treasury has twenty to thirty clerks, who put the things into it and take them out, and are known as "those who eat inside the treasury." They work under the three treasurers, who did not go often into the store-rooms, and so the clerks sometimes embezzled things, but later on the treasurers supervised them more carefully, no doubt under the Dalai Lama's watchful eyes. The practice always has been to lock up the treasury keys and the seal into a small box, the key of which is kept by one of the treasurers, while another treasurer seals the box with his private seals.

It may readily be imagined that the Dalai Lama's expenses are heavy. And indeed why not, for nominally the whole of Tibet belongs to him. He is the Dakpo Chenpo, the Great Owner. His household expenses are supplied from various departments of the Government in accordance with his requirements. He has full control in this as in other matters.

The second treasury is reserved for his own private use. It is known as the *Trede* and is in the Potala. The revenue schedules show what portions of the Government revenue are reserved for it. Money comes into it, and butter, oranges from Pari at the head of the Chumbi Valley, and lumps of gold from the mines in western Tibet, over a thousand miles away. Further, this treasury has its own landed estates, from which it receives the rent in money, grain, butter and other domestic commodities, the grain being stored on the estates themselves to be sold on behalf of the Dalai Lama as occasion may require.

Also, most of the gifts from the people to the Dalai Lama, an unending flow, are kept in this private treasury. Consequently he draws a great deal from it. The givers are not only Tibetans; a large amount also comes from devout Mongols who visit Tibet on pilgrimage, the holy shrines in Lhasa, Tashi Lhünpo and other places.

The third treasury is "The Treasury of the Sons of Heaven," and it, too, is in the Potala. It is a reserve treasury. Gold, corals, diamonds, etc., are stored in it, not to be used year by year, but to meet the exigencies of war or other calamities. This treasury also makes large loans, and its rate of interest as a rule is less, being about ten per cent., for the sums lent are large, and the security demanded is first class. The storage of goods in it or their removal is a transaction of public importance; the four members of the Cabinet must attend in a body on such an occasion. Very wealthy is this treasury; storing in it has proceeded steadily for over a hundred years.

In these treasuries there are separate rooms for storing silver, tea, butter, silk, gold, etc. The officers make good incomes, as *dzongpöns* petition them for an extension of time to pay arrears of revenue, and they are prepared to pay well for that.

The fourth treasury is for the army. Two of the treasuries are near the Temple; two are in the holy Potala. The religion overshadows everything.

As stated above, some of the revenue is not paid into any treasury or storehouse, but handed over direct to the person or institution to which it is due. For instance, the *dzongpöns* of Pari send to the Chief Oracle of Tibet, near Lhasa, a money value of £3 and some flags worth half that amount. They send a ton and a half of leaves, from which a dark red dye is made, to another place, where the Dalai Lama's clothes are dyed. To a temple near Paro in western Bhutan they send money, which is expended on butter to be burnt in the temple lamps. Bhutan, indeed, since the treaty of 1910, falls no longer within the rule or jurisdiction of Tibet. But what does worldly rule matter? The religion is the same.

The total revenue of the Lhasa Government in 1917 was approximately as follows:

In cash	£60,000
In grain, butter, tea, paper, yak dung, cloth, timber, meat, etc.	£300,000
Value of services rendered, i.e., carrying loads, lending ponies, mules, donkeys, and yaks, free of hire, and porters carrying free of cost for the Government	£200,000
Other miscellaneous revenue	£160,000
Total	£720,000

The compulsory lending of transport and porterage, all free of charge, is a heavy burden on the farmers and labourers throughout the land. It is much disliked, but the people are accustomed to it.

The monasteries hold vast estates free of rent, which, if levied, would aggregate about £800,000. In addition to the above, the different *dzongpöns* remit direct to monasteries butter, grain and tea in large quantities, and some cash, to help in the feeding and paying of the innumerable monks. These sums sent from the districts total up to about £70,000 every year. Then there are grants of grain, tea, butter, cash, etc., to the monasteries for holding special services, e.g. for preventing illness from falling on the Dalai Lama, for obtaining good crops throughout the country, for success in military campaigns, and so forth. During the first world war such services were frequently held on behalf of British arms, costing some £7,000, on account of the large number of monks and monasteries that joined for this purpose. The total yearly cost of all these special services might total up to £120,000 a year. Then we must not forget the gold and silver required for fashioning the vessels used in the temples, the images of Buddhas, deities and saints of past time, as well as the sacred pictures painted on parchment with their silk surrounds. Clothes also of various kinds, and silk for covering the seats in the Dalai Lama's palace, the Potala, and for his country house, the Jewel Park. These various items may amount to a cost of £70,000 a year. The Dalai Lama appropriated as a rule some £7,000 yearly for giving presents and the like; butter for burning in the sacred lamps in many monasteries and temples, and especially in the Potala and the Great Temple, absorbed about half this amount. Accordingly the monkhood of Tibet, apart from His Holiness, receive a good deal more than £1,000,000 yearly from this poor country, and prices being what they are, the grants made to them would be equal to about £6,000,000 in England. It will be understood that all my estimates of national revenue and expenditure are only approximate.

The secular officials, nobles, and others do not take so much from the State, but they take about £400,000 yearly, as many of their estates are not taxed at all. This is nominally in lieu of salaries, but actually has accrued through the giving of rent-free estates on a large scale in the past for exceptional services rendered. Besides, as each new Dalai Lama, or more correctly, as each new Incarnation of the one and only Dalai Lama succeeds, his father or brother receives a large estate, and this has happened several times.

However, each landed proprietor had to supply soldiers for the army in accordance with the amount and fertility of his land, and two complete outfits of clothing, boots, etc., for these soldiers every year. The Government paid salaries to the soldiers in grain and cash. Prior to my visit to Lhasa in 1920 the total expenditure on the army by the Tibetan Government was only £150,000 yearly, of which three-fourths was grain from the Government granaries, used for feeding the troops. After paying the monks and the soldiers, some £300,000 remained for all other governmental expenses.

The total expenditure was usually somewhat less than the total revenue, the balance being held in grain, which went to swell the storage in the Government granaries.

The enormous exemptions of revenue in favour of the monasteries and landed proprietors render the administration of public finance – if such it can be called – extremely difficult. When the difference in price levels is considered, the loss from the above exceptions would correspond to a loss in England of £8,000,000 or £9,000,000 every year.

Eastern Tibet, almost all of which has been recently seized by the Chinese, is the most populous and fertile part of the country, so that the Dalai Lama governs only between one and two million of his subjects on the secular side. His religious authority is, of course, far wider, but it brings him nothing except religious offerings, which cannot compete in value with the land revenue and other resources of a secular State.

There is no excise tax in Tibet, and no income tax, and hardly any customs revenue. The revenue from land, which in so many Oriental countries is the sheet-anchor of their finance, was, as we have seen, in large measure remitted, and brought in comparatively little.

In ordinary years this small budget was sufficient until the

Chinese seized eastern Tibet. The Dalai Lama had no wish to develop his country on Western lines; in fact, he had a horror of that. Still, he did wish to make certain changes which could not be done without extra revenue. Casting about for possible new sources, he leased out as far as possible all the Government lands that were lying untilled. A tax on wool, Tibet's largest product, added its quota; the newly established mint also brought in something. When Tibetans put on taxes they are fond of taking one item in every ten, and so they took one in ten out of the unending stream of bricks of tea that pour from western China into their country every year. In Tibet tea bricks are just as good as money for currency purposes. By these new taxes the Dalai Lama gained another small amount. Longingly he looked at those vast rent-free estates, but even he quailed at the idea of attacking such a citadel of privilege.

24   Full Control

Probably the most difficult of all the Dalai Lama's tasks in his home administration lay in restraining his own monks. They had been accustomed to exercise great power in the secular administration, but he was determined to restrain them from political activities, except within certain well recognised limits; for instance, in the Parliament. Indeed, this latter power he also held in check, because he seldom summoned the Parliament, when he was older and found his authority secure beyond all question. He would never admit the argument that religion and politics are inseparable. But religion was over all, Buddha was over all; and that was the rôle that he represented and filled. Himself a monk, he reduced the worldly power of the monks under him, and to that extent he increased the authority of lay officialdom.

The King of Bhutan, a neighbouring State, allows the Church no great influence in politics. This king and his people are of Tibetan stock, and follow devoutly the Tibetan religion.

In fact, the idea has long since passed into a Tibetan saying, "Religious affairs and secular affairs stand apart from each other." Ye cannot serve God and Mammon. The Dalai Lama undertook both, but he stood above the law; and even of him you would hear criticism on this account from those who were traditionally opposed to Lhasa, as in Tashi Lhünpo, and from those outside the range of his secular authority, as in Bhutan and Sikkim.

In the early years of his administration the Precious Sovereign no doubt stumbled and was brought down by the slings and arrows of foreign contacts. But educated in the way that he had been, and barred from the experience of outside nations by the great mountain ranges of Tibet, what could be expected? Gradually he acquired a due measure of experience, and with it businesslike habits; his instincts led him that way.

The Peak Secretary used to say, "We have no engagements at fixed hours in Tibet. We will send you word on each occasion, when we are ready to receive you. That is our custom."

But after he had seen what was done in India, the Dalai Lama introduced fixed office hours for the officials in Lhasa, a thing that had never been done before in Tibet. The hours indeed were not long, from nine to twelve, and then a lunch provided by the Government, but many stayed on till four or five o'clock.

Almost every Tibetan gentleman looks on Lhasa, with its social activities, as the Seventh Heaven, and the average country district as a depressing wilderness. It had long been the custom for officials appointed to distant and dull offices to send a relative, or even a servant, there to carry on the work for them and remit the profits to them. But the Dalai Lama stopped that. Henceforth the district officer had himself to go to his district and work there.

In his Political Testament the Dalai Lama writes, "This land of Tibet has become completely happy and prosperous; it is like a land made new." This was no idle boast; there was in it a large measure of truth.

The Precious Sovereign was impulsive and quick-tempered, but he did not readily nourish a grudge. What says the proverb?

> Although a lama may be quick-tempered,
> He does not retain his anger.

His disposition was by nature cheerful and kindly. A quick temper indeed does not necessarily injure a lama's reputation; Tibetan history records cases of lamas whose tempers were fiery, and places them among the highest of their time. Still, it does seem in the Dalai Lama's case that, combined with the extreme heaviness of his work, it did injure his health, contributing to a severe illness when I was in Lhasa, and eventually shortening his days.

It was partly due to his impulsiveness that the Dalai Lama used frequently to degrade his officials. But when he found that he had made a mistake, he would rectify it. For instance, he degraded the son of Shatra – who had held the office of Prime Minister during the last years of his life – from the post of Financial Commissioner to the mere headship of a district in the distant province of Po, a barbarous region which pays scant regard to the officers of the Tibetan Government. Later on, however, finding that Shatra, junior, was not to blame, he recalled him to Lhasa, announcing that he was to be appointed a member of the Cabinet, a post ranking higher than that from which he had been degraded.

The Dalai Lama did not work in the Government offices, but in his country palace. His chief secretary had great power, at times superseding the Prime Minister himself. Another valued officer was the chief librarian, who had not only to bring the books that His Holiness required, but also to explain the difficult passages in them; and therefore acquired, reasonably enough, a high reputation for book learning.

Matters that were quite trivial were often reserved by the Dalai Lama for his own decision. A young Tibetan was going to England for a further course of training in electrical engineering, and the Prime Minister asked me to request the Government of India to arrange for his journey.

"First or second class?" I enquired.

"Well, I cannot quite settle that point," said the Prime Minister, "but I will refer it to the Precious Protector."

Twice I suggested to the Dalai Lama that he should delegate a little of his power, to ease the intolerable burden that lay upon him. But until he was considerably older and almost worn out, he could not make up his mind to do so. Of government on Western lines he had only a hearsay experience, and slight at that. And he held but a poor opinion as to the competency of his own officials.

When the time has come for a young man to marry, his parents may perhaps consult the Dalai Lama, the Panchen Lama or other high lama, as to whether the girl proposed is suitable as his bride, and the revelation given out by one of these is shown to the parents of the bride to prove that everything is in order.

Every year before the crops round Lhasa, mostly barley, are reaped, specimens of the ears have to be shown three times to the Dalai Lama, and his permission obtained for the reaping. It was on September 12th, when in Lhasa, that I enquired about this. "Yes, they have been shown once already; the second time will be tomorrow or the next day; and the third or final time a day or two later. Then reaping operations will start in earnest."

Twice yearly the caravans come to Lhasa from far Mongolia, and from the province of Amdo in north-eastern Tibet, and even from Siberia, for the Buriats come too. The lands of robber tribes intervene, and the travellers therefore band together for mutual protection. Mongol monks naturally wish to come to the centre of their religion, and some will study for a course of years in the great Tibetan monasteries. Pilgrims come as well, and merchants with their camels and yaks and varied assortment of goods, including the famed ponies from Hsining in northwest-ern China, as these do well in Tibet, though the Mongol ponies do not. Having crossed the lofty northern plains, they halt at Nagchuka, until the Dalai Lama gives them permission to pro-ceed to the Holy City.

In one of those parties on their way down to Lhasa I saw a baby, less than two years old, strapped on a mule. He had come in this way for three or four months over the bleak wastes of northern Tibet, but his chubby cheeks and happy look showed that he was none the worse for the hardships and cold of the journey.

Enough has been said to show how varied was the work of the Dalai Lama in his internal administration, and how more and more – as the alert mind in that stumpy, bowed frame came to collate its experiences – he took care that the last word should be with him in every important matter; and sometimes even in petty details, if such were likely to serve as precedents for the future.

In 1912, when the Chinese invasion had been subdued and he returned to Lhasa, determined to extirpate Chinese domination from his country as far as possible, he took the control more and more into his own hands. "The Parliament talk and talk, but this matter cannot wait. I will not summon the full body; I will call together the small committee of it; they will be quicker and less obstructive."

As time went on, even the three great monasteris, Drepung, Sera and Ganden, though always to be reckoned with, did not carry the weight that they did before, because in the public estimation the Dalai Lama's word ranked immeasurably above that of all others. Further, by now the Tibetan Government had a larger body of troops, and these were better equipped and trained than before. They were therefore able to overawe any monastery that held up its head. As regards the ordinary laity, both the Dalai Lama and his Government paid less attention to what they thought.

Thus it came about that, as he grew older, the Precious Sovereign's power increased more and more. And the great mass of the people were well content to have it so. He was their Ruler in this life and in their lives to come. They had only one Authority to consider both now and in future lives; the problems of life were thereby greatly simplified.

The Dalai Lama did not disdain public opinion. On one occasion, at least, he sought it himself. When he returned to Tibet in 1912, he sent orders to each district in the two central provinces, those containing Lhasa and Shigatse, that each district should depute four representatives. These men were for the most part managers of landed estates, either Government estates or those of private persons. On arrival they were in effect asked by the Government representative who interviewed them, "Do you see any features of the internal administration that ought to be changed? And what do you consider is the best policy for Tibet to follow in foreign affairs?"

The reply came continually, "I am a man of no position. I do not understand these things."

"You must not say that; you must speak out your mind. Tell us your opinion.

With what Foreign Power or Powers should Tibet make friends?"

The usual replies to this question were either (*a*) "Make

friends with Great Britain; she is the nearest to Lhasa"; or (*b*) "Make friends with any one Power, and then stick to her. Do not change from one to another." (*c*) "Make friends with China; she has many people and is strong. Unless you can insure some other strong Power helping Tibet, China will take revenge on us later on."

Another question asked was, "Should the army be increased? If so, where can we obtain the revenue to pay for this?"

Some were in favour of increase. Hitherto soldiers had been paid by grants of land. "Stop that," said some; "pay them in cash, and give lands to their parents. Increase the amount lent to the traders from the Government treasuries and thus increase your revenue. You should lend from the Treasury of the Sons of Heaven as well as from the other treasuries."

A view occasionally put forward was, "The estates of the noble families and of some others are very large. Make them pay rent on those that they hold rent-free, and give salaries in money to those who serve the Government. Don't pay them, as at present, by rent-free grants of land."

Some indeed said, "Make the monastic estates pay rent, and give the monasteries subsidies in cash." But the great majority objected, "No; that would not do. The Three Seats are too powerful; they will not obey an order like that."

Since then the soldiers have been paid in cash; the Treasury of the Sons of Heaven has been included among the lending treasuries; and many rent-free estates of the nobility and gentry, but not those of the monasteries, have to pay rent. Had it not been for the fighting with the Chinese invaders in eastern Tibet, more action might have been taken on the opinions thus given by the representatives of the people. These stated their views more readily than one might have expected, for never before in the whole history of Tibet had people been summoned in that way to put forward their ideas on questions of government.

Formerly all titles in Tibet were granted by the Manchu Government in the name of the Emperor. From now onwards the Dalai Lama gave them himself. In doing so, he granted them for life only; no longer were they made hereditary, as they used to be.

To even a hermit His Holiness might grant a privilege. A hermit at Pede – a village well known to us who have travelled the road to Lhasa – served the Dalai Lama during the latter's stay in Mongolia and China. To him the Dalai Lama gave a high-sounding title, permission to use a square-shaped seal, as well as the privileges of decorating his horse and sitting on a threefold carpet with a pillow back.

The Dalai Lama's complete supremacy ensured order throughout Tibet. And it unified a large part of Tibet to an extent that it had seldom attained in earlier years.

The Dalai Lama was indeed an absolute dictator; more so as regards his own country than Herr Hitler and Signor Mussolini in theirs. To gain his position he could not make use of oratory, as they did; still less of the radio, even if arrangements for broadcasting had existed. But he had greater resources than either oratory or wireless. For he could reward or punish, both in this life and in future lives. "Does it not matter to you whether you are reborn as a human being or as a pig? The Dalai Lama can help to secure that you will be reborn as a human being in a high position, or, better still, as a monk or nun in a country where Buddhism flourishes."

Nothing is more important to a Tibetan than his birth in the next life, for indeed, if his life has been evil, and there is none to intervene on his behalf, he may even be condemned to hellish experiences for a thousand years or more. In these circumstances it will readily be understood that the Dalai Lama's power was almost irresistible. Yet even all this would not have given him that commanding position on the secular side, unless he had possessed a strong will, a good constitution, and a real love of politics and administration.

25   Gautama, the Buddha

The Dalai Lama was not only the autocrat of the State; he was the autocrat of the Church also. As already mentioned, he was regarded as a Deity, being an Incarnation of Chenrezig, the Buddha of Compassion. As Chenrezig is regarded as Tibet's patron deity, this gave the Dalai Lama an overpowering position in Tibet.

Since religion is to the ordinary Tibetan the most important object of life, let us consider what are the main features of Buddhism?

Gautama, the founder of Buddhism, was born a noble prince during the sixth century B.C. in Sakya, a small aristocratic republic, which lay in what is now Nepal. The kingdom of Nepal is inhabited by tribes, most of which are of Tibetan, not Indian, origin. In those days the population was probably still more strongly Tibetan, for the Tibetans were then a pushing nation and were descending down the Himalayan barrier into the plains of north-eastern India. Even at the present time the population of Nepal is more than eighty per cent. Mongoloid, and these speak dialects akin to Tibetan. So the historical Buddha may well have been Mongoloid (perhaps Tibetan) rather than Indian, by race.

Besides, as that outstanding authority, Sir Charles Eliot, pointed out, "The elementary simplicity of Buddhist principles – namely, that religion is open to all and identical with morality – made a clean sweep of Brahmanic theology and sacrifices, and put in its place something like Confucianism." Confucius lived shortly before Buddha.

Eliot continues, "But the innate Indian love for philosophising and ritual caused generation after generation to add more and more supplements to the Master's teaching, and it is only outside India that it has been preserved in any purity."[15]

Although Buddha Shakyamuni may well have been Mongoloid, rather than Indian, by race, his life work lay among Indians. His youth was spent on or near the border, and his later life in the interior of India. So his environment was mainly Indian.

Gautama's father was a leading man, perhaps the leading man, in the Sakyan republic. As a young man, Gautama came to learn of the sorrows of life, illness, old age and death. His feelings at this time he described, later on, to his disciples. He himself was rich and comfortable, but he reflected how people feel repulsion and disgust at the sight of old age, sickness and death. But was this right? "I also," he thought, "am subject to decay and am not free from the power of old age, sickness and death. Is it right that I should feel horror, repulsion and disgust when I see another in such plight? And when I reflected thus, my disciples, all the joy which there is in life died within me."

When twenty-nine years of age, he left his luxurious home and lived a life of stern asceticism, seeking always the riddle of existence. He continued this for six years, till he was at death's door. But the Truth lay not this way. He recalled then how in his earlier youth he had sat in the shade of a rose-apple tree, and entered into the stage of contemplation known as the first absorption. So he took food to recover his strength, and passed through successive stages of contemplation.

He obtained a vision in which he saw the whole universe as a system of cause and effect and rebirth. Finally he understood the truth of suffering and the cause of suffering, the cessation of suffering, and the path that leads to that cessation.

"In me thus set free the knowledge of freedom arose, and I knew 'Cyclic rebirth has been destroyed, the higher life has been gained, what had to be done has been done, I have no more to do with this ordinary world.' This third knowledge came to me in the last watch of the night: ignorance was destroyed, knowledge had arisen; darkness was destroyed, light had arisen, as I sat there earnest, strenuous, resolute." He was now thirty-five years old.

His enlightenment came at a place six miles from Gaya, the second largest city in the modern province of Bihar, in northern India. He was sitting under a large tree of the fig family, known to Indians as pipal. You will still find there a pipal tree, which claims to be a lineal descendent of the tree under which Gautama sat. It is known as the Bodhi tree, the Tree of Enlightenment, and near it is the Bodh Gaya Temple, where you may meet Buddhists from Tibet, Burma, Ceylon, Japan and other countries. It is strange that more tourists to India do not visit this place where Buddhism was born. A good road connected it with the railway at Gaya, when I used to visit the spot, and presumably does so still.

Gautama thus because Buddha Shakyamuni, the Enlightened One.

A few weeks later he preached his first sermon in the Deer Park at Benares. Five recluses, who had left him when he abandoned the ascetic life, listened to him. In this sermon he begins by saying that those who wish to follow religion must follow the Middle Way, avoiding self-indulgence on the one side and self-mortification on the other. The first is low, the second is crazy; neither of the two is the religious life.

"There is a Middle Way, O recluses," he says, "avoiding these two extremes." ... "And which is that Middle Way? Verily it is the Noble Eightfold Path. That is to say:

Right Views (free from superstition or delusion),
Right Aspirations (high and worthy of the intelligent,
    earnest person),
Right Speech (kindly, open, truthful),
Right Conduct (peaceful, honest, pure),
Right Livelihood (bringing hurt or danger to no
    living thing),
Right Effort (in self-training and in self-control),
Right Mindfulness (the active, watchful mind),
Right Concentration (in deep meditation on the truth
    of reality).

He then enunciated the four Noble Truths, which may be summarised as suffering, the cause of suffering, the cessation of suffering, and the method of effecting that cessation. The cause of suffering is Thirst, "the craving for the gratification of the passions, or the craving for the future life, or the craving for success in this present life." And the way that leads to the cessation of this suffering is the Noble Eightfold Path.

It will be noticed that this is a religion of conduct, not merely of belief; faith alone is not sufficient. By their fruits ye shall know them. And we have here a religion that is intellectual, rather than emotional. The cause of suffering is desire: this desire is due to ignorance. The thirst for the things of life causes rebirth after rebirth. The nature of this craving is explained in the chain of dependent relationship, of which we need only say that ignorance is the first cause, leading on through consciousness, contact, sensation, craving, and other links to birth and death. By ignorance appears to be meant ignorance of the true nature of reality and true interests of all beings. We were born into the world because of our ignorance in our last birth, and because of the desire for re-existence which was in us when we died.

Having followed the Perfect Path, the Buddhist can attain the status of an Arhat, and further, can attain final enlightenment. This was the aim of Buddha.

Wandering over a part of northern India – now comprised in Bihar and Uttar Pradesh – Buddha preached for some forty-five years, until his eightieth year. Moving from place to place, preaching to the people, but still more instructing his own disciples, building up and strengthening the religious communities, and deciding each difficulty as it arose, the days passed by. We seem to see a picture of one who was tolerant but authoritative, a born leader with a compelling personal charm of his own.

His teaching did not arouse violent opposition, though it differed so greatly from the varying Hindu doctrines of the time. He did not denounce the Brahmans as a class; indeed, he was singularly gentle and tolerant. When he converted a general, who had been a Jain, he permitted him to continue to give food to the Jain monks who came to him. He sat by the sacred fire of a Brahman and discoursed, but did not denounce the worship which the Brahman carried on.

Among laymen Buddha prescribed abstinence from the five sins of taking life, drinking intoxicants, lying, stealing and un-chastity. And they were to strive for pleasant speech, kindness, temperance, consideration for others, and love.

The aim was to be free from the round of worldly existences, to escape from the Wheel. Each must work out his or her own salvation; Buddha acknowledged no god-creator. The religious Order, or Sangha which Buddha founded, grew stronger and stronger, and became the dominant religion in India for several centuries. Later on, it became mixed with Hinduism and anim-ism, and was replaced by Hinduism, though the power of Buddhism lingered on in places till the twelfth century A.D.

26   What is Tibetan Buddhism?

Buddhism came strongly to Tibet in the eighth century A.D. It was then mixed with Hinduism, the worship of male and female deities, magical charms, and so on. At that time the Tibetan religion, called *Bön*, was based largely on worship of the forces of nature. But it was more than mere nature worship; it was strongly organised and resisted the newcomer for a long time. Buddhism succeeded only by compromising with *Bön*, adopting many of its ideas. Tibetan Buddhism is the result, and it has the strength belonging to all genuine expressions of the national character. The Tibetans found they could not do without somebody to worship. So they venerated Buddha and various deities, who, as the new teachers told them, were emanations of Buddha.

Monasteries and nunneries were formed; they grew and grew. This race of soldiers and raiders fought no longer in the material world. They became monks, and fought, instead, the evil forces around them.

There is much that is mechanical in Tibetan Buddhism. Prayers are written on strips of paper, and enclosed in little wheels that are turned by the hand; large cylinders are turned by the hand or even driven by water power, each containing many thousands of prayers and sacred writings. If you ask an intelligent monk what good there can be in machine-made prayer, he would answer:

"Turning a prayer wheel is in itself of no use, unless the person turning it concentrates his mind on good thoughts, thinking kindly of all beings and how he may help those who are in trouble. That is the rôle of the prayer wheel and its kindred; by no other means are the thoughts, especially of an uneducated person, so likely to be guided. It is the thoughts that are all-important."

The rosary is in general use throughout Tibet among men, women and children; monks and nuns and laity. Each rosary should have 108 beads, the Tibetan sacred number. The prayer wheel and the rosary, these the people carry everywhere; the former often in the right hand, the latter wound round the wrist of the left.

The old sects of the priesthood are allowed to marry and to drink wine, but many abstain from both marriage and liquor. Those ordained within the reformed sect, which was inaugurated five hundred years ago, neither drink wine nor consort with the opposite sex. None of the clergy are allowed to eat onions or garlic on the ground that they emit a bad smell from the mouth and make the air impure. A monk who takes garlic is not allowed even to put out a fire. The clergy are allowed to take fish, pork and eggs; but some abstain, as they believe that there is something holy underneath the skin of these. But the two things most strongly prohibited to the reformed sect, besides dealings with the opposite sex, are alcohol and tobacco; these are said to be the favourites of the devils.

Tobacco is looked on as far worse than alcohol. The Dalai Lama was strongly against it and forbade it, not only to all those ordained ones but to all the laity as well. The history of Bhutan, written long ago, attacks smoking violently. The Tibetan biography, too, is violent in its attack. It says, "There is no doubt that this plant is the cause of the destruction of India by the heathen."

Some Tibetans do indeed smoke, usually pipes with long stems and tiny bowls, but they smoke less than Indians do, and far less than the Nepalese. The Dalai Lama prohibited the sending of tobacco by post in Tibet, and the sale of it in Lhasa. He prohibited smoking privately as well as openly. Officers searched out all the tobacco, and mixing it with dirt to make it rot quickly, buried it in a pit in the sight of the public.

The people believe implicitly in the lamas, and call them in for spiritual help and for medical help too, for illnesses are as a rule ascribed to the action of evil spirits. It is the monks and nuns who go to the temple, rather than the laity, for they have three to five services daily in their monasteries, lasting four or five hours altogether. The sacred books are intoned, tea is brought round at intervals, and to the onlooker it all seems very mechanical. But one always has to remember that Tibetan minds differ greatly from ours, and they find in these services a deep unseen influence, which goes out and does good to all living beings, that is to say, human beings and all the animal world. The monks and nuns pray for all of these.

And what effect does their religion have on the Tibetans? Their whole-hearted belief in it may be seen in the fact that several thousands of them have lived for a long time in districts in India, where there are many Christian missionaries; Indians, Gurkhas and others are converted, but of Tibetans only an infinitestinal number.

Fear, no doubt, is an ingredient in a Tibetan's faith, but no more than it is with a believing Christian. They are more happy and care-free than the peoples of Europe or America. Their main characteristics have been described in some detail in the first chapter of this book.

Their religion puts a background of confidence into the Tibetan's life. They turn naturally to the lamas as their spiritual guides and helpers in times of joy, but especially in the times of trouble. No doubt the ordinary people hope to gain spiritual advantage from any good that they do, but so do those in all religions. The advantage for which the Tibetan hopes is a better rebirth in his next life; and, best of all, as a monk or nun in a Buddhist land, so that they may be able to follow the faith more devotedly.

The laity visit the temples and their own village chapels, especially on holy days, when they burn little lamps fed with butter, as offerings for the dead and for the living. They bow down before the images and throw white silk scarves over them, reciting prayers and passages from the sacred books as they do so. And most of all do they flock to the temples to witness the gorgeous ritual – with many resemblances to that of the Roman Catholic Church – and the ceremonies of this complicated religion. Here they receive interest and amusement, as well as religious instruction. They have no cinemas, and for theatres only occasional strolling players. The plays in the temples help to take the place of the theatres; all have a strong moral basis, with clowning and farce thrown in, for this laughter-loving race need their jokes when sitting through an eight-hour performance.

To the Christian, Love is the highest virtue; to the Buddhist, Wisdom. For, with the Buddha, they hold that ignorance is the root of all evil. This idea permeates all classes in Tibet. Even the beggar, soliciting alms, will not address you as "Kind Gentleman," but as "Learned Sir"! Love, however, ranks very high. There is no poorhouse or unemployment insurance, but no poor man, woman or child will starve; others will help as a matter of course.

The lamas, monks and nuns lead hard, austere lives. So much is this the case that few of the wealthier classes embrace the monastic life, except such as are recognised as Incarnations of those saints and others who have attained to Buddhahood in previous lives and therefore are on the earth only through their own unselfishness. Of these there are several hundred, and they live more softly than the ordinary monk, each taking the headship of the monastery ruled by the former Incarnation.

Almost all the people pray. Children of five years old often learn long prayers by heart. It must be admitted that they, and even many adults, are ignorant of the meaning of much that is in the prayers. For Tibetan education is primitive, but even these prayers turn their thoughts to higher things. Many laymen pray for more than an hour daily, part in the early morning, part in the evening; and some for three hours or more. The Prime Minister, in spite of his heavy work, prayed and read the sacred books for four hours daily.

They pray for all human beings, birds, beasts, fishes, the whole animate creation in all countries of the world; they pray that the crops may be good everywhere, that men may not fight and kill each other, but that peace may flourish throughout the world, and so on, and so on. They are told not to pray for themselves individually, since in praying for all they thereby pray for themselves; but undoubtedly many do pray specifically for themselves. They are told not to pray when the mind is angry.

> It is better to lie down with a mind at ease,
> Than to sit like Buddha and pray with an angry
> mind.

As for the Prime Minister, that experienced old administrator, his verdict was, "There are in Tibet a very large number of monasteries and nunneries, and innumerable monks and nuns; but the whole of their religion is summed up in this short verse that every Tibetan knows:

> Taking yourself as an example,
> Do good, not harm, to others;
> This, just this, is Buddha's teaching."

He added, "Our Buddhist religion is found in that saying, much more than in the temples or monasteries."

In fact, "As ye would that men should do to you, do ye also to them likewise."

No doubt it would be easy to criticize much in the lives of Tibetans, but they find it equally easy to criticize us.

After I had left Tibet, Palhese spent a year with me in England. When the year was ending I asked him to speak frankly on what he considered the defects among English people. Among other criticisms, he said:

"I read in the papers of cases in which husbands and wives kill each other. Such cases are practically unknown in Tibet. Children sometimes strike and even kill their parents. No Tibetan child would do that. Children should regard their father as they regard 'The Three Precious Ones' (Buddha, the Buddhist Scriptures, and the spiritual community).

"People are happier in Tibet than they seem to be in England. Everybody in my country can get work, and earn his little earning. Having done so, men and women sing and dance and play. For the people say:

> " 'Death comes later; to be happy for even one day is
> a profit taken.'

"So people work a bit, and play a bit, and practise religion, all three.

"Here in England," he continued, "people do not seem very happy. They are so often thinking how they can add to their money; so often they are full of anxiety. Amusements are set out everywhere, and the people go crowding to them, but they are mostly expensive. In Tibet we sing and dance, and it costs the party nothing except a few pence for beer. In England people must always be thinking of earning money to pay for their dwelling, their food and their amusement. In Tibet, out of happiness, many sing as they work; I do not find that here in England.

"Well, every country has its own customs. There is one thing in England, among many others, that all must admire, and that is the administration of justice, which is straightforward, and equal for those of high and those of low position."

In Tibet I used to be told, "Our Tibetan monks regard Europeans and Americans as having very little religion. They have often been informed that these frequently make war and kill many people, and taking life is one of the worst possible sins. Their churches are poorly attended; they worship but little. Instead of worshipping, they go off to their places of amusement."

Tibetans regard prayers, reading the sacred books, making certain religious offerings, going round a holy road in the neighbourhood, and such-like acts, as included in the most important part of religion. An example of such religious offerings is when beer or tea is offered to deities, beer for some, tea for others. Such offerings are made to accompany prayers on various subjects; e.g. before a man starts on a journey, or before a boy goes in for an examination. Holy roads are found in most places; maybe it is a path going round a monastery; the chief of them all is the one which goes round the holy city of Lhasa, four and a half miles in its circuit. But a merciful, good life is even more important than prayers or religious offerings. It is the state of the mind that matters; everything comes back to that.

One afternoon in Lhasa, Tsarong called on me. The conversation turned on the decreasing population of Tibet. "There is much empty land which ought to be cultivated," says he, "but on account of the enormous number of monks the people become less, and the land goes empty."

I replied, "That, Great Power of the Land, is a matter of religion on which I can make no comment."

With a wry smile he answered, "It is indeed a fundamental matter of religion on which I, too, can make no comment."

But in the side issues the laymen can step in. The young Tibetan colonel attached to my mission in Lhasa would not presume to sit down with us, when the Abbot of "The Tiger's Prophecy," a large monastery, called on me. But after a while he had no hesitation in telling the prelate to rise and take his leave; and the latter obeyed him.

At one of the monasteries which we visited, we were shown a tooth, some four inches long, and were told that it was a tooth of Buddha himself. The same young colonel doubted its genuineness, saying, "What must have been the size of the mouth that contained teeth like that?"

Yes, religion comes first in Tibet; it is at the centre of the ordinary Tibetan's life.

Here is the village, named Rock, in the valley of the Tsangpo, the great river of southern Tibet. Colonel Harnett and I stayed there in 1934. The landlords and the community have built a new chapel, and even poor people have contributed far more than they can afford according to Western standards. It is a solid chapel, complete with altar, and images of Buddhas and saints, sacred pictures, holy water, and the little lamps fed by butter. I can testify to these things for the villagers insisted on my lodging there, eating and sleeping, and drinking alcohol, if I wished. Harnett was free to do the same, though all these things were of course strictly forbidden to any Tibetan in this place of worship.

And why did they insist? Because it was the cleanest and most comfortable house in the village. Such is the tolerance of Tibetan Buddhism.

Tolerance allied to loving-kindness, and both based on Buddhist wisdom, that perhaps is the chief reason why the Middle Way of Gautama the Buddha has come down through two thousand, five hundred years.

27   A God on Earth

Such is the religious atmosphere in Tibet. Where does the Dalai Lama stand in it? Of others who have led saintly lives people will say that they are Incarnations of, or Emanations from, the celestial Bodhisattva, Chenrezig, the Buddha of Compassion. But the Dalai Lama is by far the highest of all these Incarnations, and Chenrezig is not only the patron deity of Tibet, he is the reputed founder of the Tibetan race.

When in the form of a monkey, Chenrezig met a she-devil. She importuned him thus, "By reason of my actions in my former life I have been born in a demon race, and being in the power of the god of lust, I love you greatly." He consorted with her, and they had six children. The Tibetan chronicle adds, "Those who took after their father were full of faith, diligence, love and piety, and were eloquent and meek; those who took after their mother were full of sin, contention and jealousy, and were greedy and mischievous. But all possessed strong bodies and courage."

This commencement of the Tibetan race is said to have occurred at Tsetang on the Tsangpo, the great river of southern Tibet, two days' journey south-east of Lhasa. In 1934 I visited Tsetang. The cave where the celestial father and the she-devil lived together is a vertical cleft in the almost precipitous side of the mountain, high above the plain below. When his descendents multiplied so greatly that feeding them was difficult, the Buddha of Compassion fed them on sacred grain, which, sown to-day, ripened tomorrow into barley. The first field to be sown is still pointed out by the inhabitants; it lies near the bank of the great

river. Through eating the barley, their tails gradually disappeared.

The Dalai Lama's religious position was supreme and unassail-
able. For, as already stated, he had power over others not only in
this, but also in future lives. The popular saying runs:

> The Ruler in this life;
> The Uplifter in the hereafter.

He is not only higher than all human beings; he is Master also
of the lesser deities. The State Oracle, four miles outside Lhasa,
is the master of all the lesser deities, and this Oracle is subordinate to the Dalai Lama. This is evident from the fact that when the
Dalai Lama preaches his annual sermon on the day of the full
moon in the first month of each year, the State Oracle comes and
makes his report to the Dalai Lama in the presence of a large
crowd of people. He tells the Dalai Lama, "Such and such an
occurrence happened, and I did so and so. Was my action
suitable?" He speaks in a very low voice; even the attendants
close by hear just a hum, but do not catch the words. The Dalai
Lama puts his hand to his ear, and bends a little forward, and
hears what the Oracle says, and gives replies, but nobody can
hear these; and later on the Inmost One does not tell anybody
what has been said on either side.

There is no doubt that Tibetans consider the Dalai Lama to be
omnipotent and omniscient, to possess all power and all knowledge. Up on the mountain-sides you will often see the inscription, marked in white stones, "Praise to the All-knowing Dalai
Lama!" Some of the better educated Tibetans, when pressed,
will say that his omniscience is limited by his sojourns on earth.
They are not prepared to admit that the Dalai Lama's power is
limited; if he did not adopt some remedy for a disaster, which by
ordinary human reason he ought to have adopted, they will
usually say that the wickedness of the world, or of a section of
his subjects – and his subjects are always ready to admit such
reasons – made him disinclined to exercise his power.

They believe that the Dalai Lama need not die until he wants
to. The four that preceded the Thirteenth all died young, a fact

which foreigners not unreasonably attribute to poison. But the Tibetans do not admit this point of view, for they will say that the poison would not have killed any of them, unless they had wished to pass on to the Honourable Field.

All recognise that he can multiply his body at will, for indeed every *tulku* has this power. But the late Dalai Lama, as already mentioned, condemned the use of this power, unless some real necessity existed, because it causes confusion in the religious work.

From time to time he was credited with the performance of certain miracles, including his footprint on a stone verandah in the Temple in Lhasa, and the imprint of his wooden staff on the sacred stone path around the Ganden Monastery, twenty-seven miles from Lhasa. But one hears very little about miracles performed either by him or anybody else. It is an accepted rule in Tibet that those who work miracles – and many are credited with the ability – should not work them, unless they fulfil some useful purpose. In any case, they should not talk about them, as that would be a sign of vanity, an evil thing. In fact, a miracleworker should not only not speak of his powers; he should not exhibit them in public, just to show what he can do. Any who do this are apt to bring on themselves an injury from a spirit, and shorten their lives. The Tibetan biography confirms the above views.

All Tibetans believe that the Dalai Lama has the power of foretelling events. These prophecies are not blazoned out to the multitude, but people talk about them among themselves, especially when the time of fulfilment draws near. In January, 1935, Palhese mentioned to me an application made by the Royal Geographical Society during 1933, for permission to make another attempt to climb Mount Everest. He remarked, "The Tibetan Government no doubt felt that the Dalai Lama would soon go to the Honourable Field, for the Dalai Lama himself had let this be known a year or two earlier. The Tibetan Government accordingly replied, requesting that the expedition should not be sent." And, incidentally, the Dalai Lama predicted that I would visit Lhasa some years before I went there, at a time when there seemed no chance of my going. He further foretold the work that I would do in Lhasa, and in this also his prediction was accurate.

A somewhat unusual example of the Dalai Lama's religious influence in Mongolia came to my notice soon after I went to Lhasa in 1920. During the course of a conversation about Mongolia, His Holiness said, "A Mongolian lama has collected a band of men with which he harasses caravans, and loots their arms and other property, so much so that Mongols are now hardly able to come to Lhasa by the overland route. This causes me loss, because the Mongols have great faith in me." The Dalai Lama's income from Mongolia was certainly large.

But although he blocked the road from Mongolia to Lhasa, and thereby involved the Head of the Faith in pecuniary loss, this lama robber talked of coming himself to Lhasa to visit the holy shrines, and prostrate himself before this same Head of the Faith. Incidentally, he wished to bring five hundred soldiers with him. He was told he might come, but must not bring more than twenty soldiers. There was no question of punishing the sinner for his wickedness, nor even of suggesting that such a large force of soldiers would be embarrassing in the capital. The number was limited to twenty, because "It would be difficult to feed them on the road." In those circumstances he did not come to Lhasa.

Far away in the north-east of Tibet the large Golok tribe, who trade peaceably for half of the year and rob caravans for the remainder, send religious offerings to the Dalai Lama in Lhasa once every four or five years. It was hardly possible for ordinary people to travel through this brigand area; but when the Dalai Lama crossed their territory in his flight from the Younghusband expedition, they flocked to him, imploring his blessing and pouring out their presents before him. The word *Golok* means "head turned round," i.e. "a religious people."

The seclusion behind which he was veiled, the mystery attaching to his person, and the miracles with which he was credited, increased his influence still further. Travelling to and fro from religious festivals in his sedan-chair, he was hidden from view. When presiding at the great religious festivals, he could sometimes be seen; as for instance, when he preached the aforesaid annual sermon in a crowded square near the Temple. But mostly he was in an upper chamber, unseen by the people.

This does not mean that he hardly ever saw anybody. His duties as the religious and secular head of Tibet necessitated his seeing many. But on such occasions his subjects usually saw him one by one, and their heads were reverently bowed. He was seldom seen in public; and seldom seen by foreigners, except by Mongols and a few Chinese. On the whole, he was secluded far more closely than the Pope.

It will be understood that his religious duties came forward not only during religious festivals and ceremonies; they claimed four or five hours out of every day, as we shall see when dealing with an ordinary day in his life.

He was exceptionally learned in the religion. One who is a *Geshe* has mastered the important branches – and they are many – of the holy books. Theology and the sacred literature are all within his sphere. Every year examinations are held for this prized position; these are attended by candidates who have been studying for fifteen or twenty years, sometimes even longer. Such as pass the examination are grouped in three classes. The Dalai Lama, when a young man, passed in the first class, and at the top of the first class. Many people will say, "Why, naturally; they would be bound to do that for the young vice-regent of Buddha." But this is not so at all. Some previous Dalai Lamas were placed only in the second class, and some even only in the third. The great reformer, Tsongkapa, the most important figure in the Tibetan religion during the last five hundred years, was in the third class.

The young Dalai Lama was keen. He thought that the standard for the first class, known as *Lharampa*, was not good enough, and raised it accordingly. Nor did he allow the *Geshes* to rest on their laurels. He would send for them from time to time and examine them, to see that they were not falling back. The better *Geshes*, if their characters were robust and trustworthy, he appointed as abbots of the different monasteries. This entailed much work on Tibet's spiritual ruler, but he found it well worthwhile.

He was not only the first *Lharampa* of his year; he was also highly skilled in both the metaphysical and the mystical schools. He improved the studies of the monks; he toned up the administration of "The Three Seats," Sera, Drepung and Ganden. Before his time their abbots were often ignorant and lazy, having obtained their positions through bribery. He put these through examinations, and dismissed those who failed. His own studies he kept up throughout his life; leisure was to him almost unknown.

The printing of books in Tibet is a laborious process, for each letter has to be carved on a wooden block. To set up the type may require four or five hundred thick wooden blocks with the words carved on both sides, a lengthy task. Great care is taken to make them accurate. When a volume is to be printed, the blocks are inked over, and the sheets of Tibetan paper laid on them; the sheets also are printed on both sides. Many books are written by hand; these usually are not so closely connected with the religion.

The Dalai Lama's libraries were in the charge of "The Servant of Philosophy," a successor of Dorjieff, who has held this post for several years. The Dalai Lama had several hundred books in his own libraries apart from the Buddhist Kangyur in one hundred and eight volumes, the Commentaries in two hundred and twenty-five, and other religious works. The Servant of Philosophy was reckoned the most learned of all in the whole field of literature.

What was the Dalai Lama's own attitude to his status in the Buddhist world? Did he himself believe that he was supreme among Buddhists, a god on earth? Among Tibetans and other Asiatics he claimed this supremacy in every word and deed. As for myself, it was undesirable and unnecessary for me to ask such a question. My chief duty was to promote friendship between Britain and Tibet, a duty doubly strong in these days when so many injure our fatherland by ignorant criticism of those whose forms of government or rules of conduct differ from our own.

Whenever the idea was in the background of our talks, he would look at me with a deprecating smile, as much as to say, "I know I cannot expect you to believe it." And he was always ready to admit a lack of knowledge or lack of power in the presence of a few daily associates, such as the Court Physician. But in public it was always asserted. On the medal that he gave me it is confidently claimed; in his Political Testament it is placed clearly on record.

The Dalai Lama was certainly interested in religions other than his own, though he probably did not know much about them, except Hinduism, and, in a lesser degree, that of the Mahomedans. What he chiefly wanted was that Hindus and Christians should follow their own religions devoutly, for he believed that each of these was near enough to Buddhism to be a good religion. Mahomedanism he distrusted, as do practically all Tibetan Buddhists, having heard of those Mahomedans known as Ghazis, who kill people belonging to a different religion just because they do belong to a different religion. Tibetans believe that the true spirit of religion cannot exist in anybody who is capable of taking life for such a reason. The Dalai Lama looked on the Chinese as lacking the religious spirit. But his most bitter condemnation was reserved for the Russian Bolshevists. He writes, "They have broken religion so that not even the name of it remains." Except for the hostile attitude of the Soviet towards religion, he, in common with most leading Tibetans, was fond of the Russian people.

Tibetans are keen observers of character, and he and all Tibetans noted closely which of the Europeans who came to Tibet held to their own religion in word and action. In Tibet, as in India, it is the ordinary Western layman, not the minister or clergyman, who is the real Christian missionary. For by their daily lives they show what religion really means to the race.

28   Controls the Religion

The administration of his Church, with its duties covering so much of the lives of his subjects, was a heavy task for the Inmost One. Supreme he might be, but he could manage the work only by long days full of hard toil.

He ordained monks, whether they were of the highest or the lowest birth. After he and the applicants had bowed before a figure of Buddha, the Dalai Lama catechized them as to whether they could perform such things as were necessary, and abstain from such things as were contrary to the ordained state. All replied to each question. At the end the Dalai Lama blessed each one separately, and dismissed him.

The Panchen Lama and other high lamas also ordained many

The blessings that His Holiness had to give involved no small manual labour. He did not bless crowds as the Pope does, but one by one. For instance, the Three Seats between them contain about twenty thousand monks. He did not bless these monastery by monastery, or even in smaller groups, but each monk separately. Any traveller starting on a long journey was entitled to his blessing. And when he himself travelled, the whole countryside flocked in. And they were blessed one by one.

On these occasions His Holiness sat cross-legged, Buddha-wise, on a throne placed on a dais. If the reception was public, the throne was higher; if private, it was lower. On occasions of urgency, however, he would stand outside on the ground, level with the suppliants who filed before him. At a public reception the suppliant removed his hat, went forward with lowered head, handed the scarf of white Chinese silk to the attendant, bowed his head right down to the ground at least three times, then took another step or two forward with the head still lowered, and received his blessing.

To bless those of the very highest ranks, somewhat less than two hundred in all, the Dalai Lama placed both hands on their heads. With one hand touching their heads he blessed all officials, priestly and secular, except the very highest, and every monk, even the youngest and lowest. As for laymen other than those mentioned above, he did not more than touch their heads with a tassel at the end of a short rod. All women received the tassel, excepting only the Incarnate Dorje Phagmo of Samding. Even the wives of the Prime Minister and the Cabinet Ministers received the tassel.

Let us now consider how Emanation Bodies are discovered, that is to say, those who are recognised as reincarnated lamas. In Tibetan they are called *tulku*. There are several hundred of these, and they form an extremely important element in the monastic world. Each rules his own monastery, which is often a large one.

Kusho Palhese had seen a good deal of this branch of ecclesiastical routine. He explained as follows:

"The monastery whose *tulku* is to be discovered, enquires of high lamas in whom they have faith, three to five years after the passing of the last *tulku*. These may indicate helpful details, such as the animal years in which one or both of the boy's parents were born, the direction, south, east, etc., towards which their house faces, the trees in their garden, the name of the district, and so on. For instance, one may say that the house of the boy's parents is in the province of Kongpo, that the door of the house faces to the east, and that the father was born in the Bird year. Sometimes, but more rarely, part of the names of the father and mother may be given; e.g. that the father's name is Dorje and the mother's Yangchen; and afterwards it turns out that the father's name is Dorje Tsering, and the mother's Yangchen Lhamo.

"If the answers differ one from another, the monastery follows the lama in whom they have most faith. If they cannot decide, they may represent the facts to the Dalai Lama, whose decision is final. In the case of all very high incarnate lamas the Dalai Lama decides. He might cast lots with dice, or tell by the beads on his rosary, or by having a vision.

"Strictly speaking, there are three reincarnations of every *tulku*, the body, the speech, and the mind. But it is the Body alone that is kept as the new *tulku.*

"When *tulkus* are being searched for, three or four boys are usually brought, in order to see which is the real body incarnation. Of two of the others, people will generally say that they are the speech and the mind. These two will often be identified as the reincarnations of other *tulkus*, and each installed at the head of his predecessor's monastery. Sometimes, however, they are not so identified, and then the parents may say that the boy must be the reincarnation of some *tulku*, and make a monk of him. This is when they are of low social position; when of the upper classes, they usually make a monk official of him.

"There was an instance of this in our family. My uncle, who was known to you as the Palha Kenchen and after you went to England was appointed as Lord Chamberlain, was one of those who as a young boy was among the three picked out as the *tulku* of the Iron Bridge Monastery. In accordance with the rule prescribed by the Chinese and followed by us Tibetans for a time, but now discarded, the three names were put into an urn, and his name did not come out. So he was kept at home and brought up as a layman till about eighteen years old, when he became a monk official. His head was then shaved, and he entered the monastic order. We of the Palha family and our servants knew that he had been picked out thus as a boy, but people generally did not remember it. The reason why lads like him do not enter a monastery in the ordinary way is that life there is so rough, and they would have to mix with boys of low family.

"Boys thus entering a monastery or the ranks of monk officials come in on the same level as others. They do not receive any preferential treatment as having been picked out when young.

"In some cases the boy is not put into a monastery or enrolled as an ecclesiastical official. It depends on his parents' wish. In this case the boy remains a layman when grown up. His family know that he was picked out, but others pay no attention to the matter.

"The Dalai Lama not only gave decisions as to which was the real *tulku,* he also gave indications towards their discovery. His indications were as a rule clearer than those of other high lamas; a good point this, because there is apt to be great vagueness in these indications.

"Let us suppose that a boy has been found. To his parents' house people come from the monastery, bringing religious articles and other things that the previous *tulku* has habitually used.

"A responsible representative from the monastery attends with a few monks at the house of the boy's parents. He is not necessarily the abbot, but is an oldish man of good knowledge and character, who understands how to conduct an enquiry. The boy's parents can attend, and members of the household. Along with these articles are set out others that do not belong, i.e. one false article with each true one. The boy, by way of identification, grasps his predecessor's things, i.e. his own in his previous incarnation."

I said, "Do a boy's parents ever coach him beforehand for this identification?"

Palhese replied, "Oh, no! They would never do a thing of that kind."

"One or two old servants, the teacher of the former lama, his assistant, etc., attend also; as these have known the old lama well. Sometimes the boy shows signs of recognising them."

The Tibetan biography mentions how, during 1915, the Dalai Lama gave indications for the discovery of the new Incarnation of the Abbot of the Reting Monastery, a very high incarnate lama. The monastery asked the Inmost One to guide them, and the latter's reply was as follows:

"About the Incarnation of him, you had better search in a country situated in the southern direction from Reting monastery, and in the exact southern direction from the Lhasa Temple, a prosperous country which has been blessed by many scholars and sages. There are three forests and a green meadow surrounded by a river which flows slowly. In the vicinity you may ask for a boy who was born in the year of Water Mouse (1912) to a father born in Hare year, and the boy may be a very wonderful one. If you examine carefuly according to this instruction, you will find the real lama, and he will do much beneficial work for Buddhism and for the people."

As a matter of fact, this young lama became the Regent of Tibet after the Dalai Lama's death.

Foreigners apply the term lama to all Tibetan monks but actually the title belongs only to *tulkus,* and to those – very few in number – who by outstanding knowledge or devoutness have gained the coveted distinction. These are known as "self-become" lamas. Adding even those who are accorded the title of lama out of courtesy by people living in their neighbourhood, the number of lamas is small in proportion to the total number of monks.

Occasionally a *tulku* falls from his high estate. There was one such, a member of the respected family of Taradoba. The Dalai Lama "made him follow the road of the grey men" (laymen). He took his *tulku* status from him, and turned him into a petty military officer.

Such are the main lines of the Dalai Lama's work in the administration of the Church. But of course there was much˙ other work to be done. When an important piece of furniture was to be chosen for a monastery, he would often be asked to decide on it. He kept a watch on many of the innumerable religious buildings in Tibet; it was not until his time that any of the old frescoes, beautiful but faded, were erased and repainted, and in the same exquisite colours. During the summer of my year in Lhasa the frescoes in the great Temple, describing events in the previous lives of Buddha, were being repainted. The Dalai Lama took great interest in this work; a hundred artists were employed under a chief teacher and seven assistant teachers; it took two seasons – each from April to October – to complete. During winter the work had to be suspended. I used to watch it being done; one of the Dalai Lama's secretaries, who came with me, explained that Chinese paints were used for the reds; Tibetan paints for the whites, yellows and blacks; and European and Tibetan paints were mixed for the blues and greens. European paints, he said, if used alone, do not last well. The Tibetan saying is that the blue and green paints should be prepared with the weakness of a sick man, but the white and yellow with the strength of a raging bull.

None but the oldest temples in Tibet have tiled roofs; the tiles were coloured blue, the art being learnt from Indians, who helped in building the earliest temples. The art of making these blue tiles had long been lost, but the Dalai Lama restored it.

His Holiness had also to decide disputes regarding property left by abbots and other high ecclesiastics. In fact, his duties in the religious sphere were varied and seemingly endless.

The Dalai Lama's task was not only heavy; it abounded also in difficulties. For, as already mentioned, the number of monks is immense; between a quarter and half a million out of the total population of Tibet, which may be estimated approximately at four millions. By their very numbers they are a force to be reckoned with; by their sanctity, especially of the higher lamas still more so. For monasteries and nunneries are as necessary as Buddha himself. Well known is the saying:

> Unless the Lama be to the fore,
> Buddha cannot work in the smallest degree.

Along with Buddha and the sacred books, the monasteries form the Buddhist Triad. Besides, the lack of worldly comforts adds to their influence with the mass of the people. For to Tibetans this form of self-sacrifice makes a strong appeal. These causes have brought it about that in no country in the world have the monasteries more influence than in Tibet, where they permeate every detail of the people's lives. Perhaps in no other country so much. Yet, as we have seen in an earlier chapter, the Dalai Lama succeeded in limiting severely the power of the monasteries in political affairs.

Although the Dalai Lama reduced the power of the monasteries, the monks still had greater power than the laypeople. In legal disputes between monks and laypeople, justice was apt to be strained in favour of the monk. Their vast rent-free estates and the additional subsidies from the Government gave the monasteries great resources, although these were heavily depleted by the huge number of poor monks, to whom they had to give the bare necessities of life.

The Precious Protector was determined to enforce a stricter standard among the members of this large and powerful body, but it was no easy task. Even after allowing for their three or four religious services each day, monks have more leisure than their lay brethren. More time, therefore – and more inclination – to get into mischief. Again, in the large monasteries, for instance, in Drepung, Sera, Ganden and Tashi Lhünpo, the discipline cannot be maintained so strictly as in the smaller ones. Some do not observe the monastic discipline properly, like "the sand mixed with the gold," as the people say. In the leading history of Bhutan – one of Tibet's daughter states in the Himalayan mountains – it is written that "after five hundred years of Buddha's influence has passed, the secular power will have to come and enforce religious discipline."

Especially during the great religious festivals, when Lhasa is packed with monks who have come from far and near, it is still more difficult to maintain discipline, religious or secular. A large number of the monks are bursting with superfluous energy, and spoiling for a fight. Foremost among these are the *dob dob*, the fighting monks. They keep their hair long and their skirts short, and paint their faces black.

A difficult task indeed for the Precious Sovereign! Later on, when we came to Lhasa, we saw how he dealt with the various disturbances that broke out during my time there. Putting the matter briefly, he chose as abbots men whom he could trust, he used his own great name, and in the last resort he had his little army.

Many years before, then His Holiness was only about twenty-four years old, the monks of the Lower Sera College, one of the three colleges in Sera monastery, went to realise some debts from peasants in the Chushü village, two days' journey from

Lhasa. As the peasants did not pay up promptly, the monks seized a lot of their goods and carried them off. The peasants petitioned the Cabinet, and the latter referred the case to the Dalai Lama for his decision. The Dalai Lama summoned the three Abbots – one for each college – and kept them standing for two days in his ante-room. He then fined the Abbot of Lower Sera heavily, and warned the three that if such a thing occurred again, they would all be dismissed from their posts. Of course, the news of this public disgrace travelled far and wide.

The Dalai Lama himself told me that the monks in monasteries were not allowed to cultivate land. At one time, as the Tibetan biography tells us, even Sera, Drepung and Ganden kept ponies, mules and cow-yaks, as well as dogs and cats, in their crowded monastic precincts. The monastic streets stank abominably. The Dalai Lama stopped these practices, restored comparative cleanliness and made each monastery once more a house of prayer and religious study. At the same time he ordered the cooks of the large monasteries to prepare the tea for the inmates very clean and hot, and sent officers frequently to examine it.

The monks were not permitted to stay out at night, but had to return to their own quarters every evening. However, they were given leave from time to time to go away to their homes, which might be some weeks' journey distant; at home they could help in the cultivation, and especially in the harvesting of crops. It often happens that in a monastery with a large number of names on its roll, only half or even less are ordinarily present.

If any monk of the reformed sect consorted with a woman, he was expelled from his monastery. Such a one was known as a "reversed monk." If the monastic authorities learned that any monk had been drunk, or otherwise transgressed the discipline, sure punishment fell upon him. In short, the Dalai Lama tightened things up.

If a monk committed a murder, the monastic authorities flogged him and turned him out of the monastery. He then became a layman, and was made over to the civil authority, who dealt with him as a layman. He was not favoured because he was a monk when he committed the crime.

The religion in Tibet is much more spiritual and powerful than among the Mongols in Manchuria or Inner Mongolia. Such is the verdict of Mongols themselves. The main reason for this appears to be that it has not been strongly exposed, as it has been exposed throughout Manchuria and Mongolia, to the adverse influence of Chinese and Europeans. But the Dalai Lama also played his part in holding up the religion. As says the Tibetan biography, he "restored Buddhism which is now always like a sick man."

Considering Tibet by itself, it is clear that the effect of the Dalai Lama's grip on Tibetan Buddhism was to infuse into it an increased spirituality. A strong Church needs a strong Head. In Tibet they have not always found such a Head, but in the Thirteenth Dalai Lama they did.

29   Boys, Baths and a Treaty

While he was in Darjeeling, I suggested to the Dalai Lama and to Shatra also, that they should send a few Tibetan boys to England for education, in order that on their return they might introduce such Western accomplishments as would be beneficial. Soon after his return to Lhasa in 1912 the Dalai Lama picked four boys, aged twelve to fifteen, to be sent. They all came from good families, though not the best, for he did not intend to embark on the adventure of sending the bluest blood, until he could see more clearly what this new experiment entailed. No applications were invited from parents; the boys had just to go, whether their parents liked it or not. A Tibetan official, named Lungshar, was in charge of them, and he took also his wife, who wanted to see England.

I was then at Gangtok, in Sikkim, and the Dalai Lama told Lungshar to bring the boys to me first, that I might give him any instructions that I thought advisable. My wife showed Mrs. Lungshar over the Residency. She examined it minutely and was delighted with it, exclaiming in conclusion to our orderly, who went round with them, that it was like a house of the gods. We took this at the time as a high compliment, but later on I was to learn that it was not altogether complimentary.

Some years later the Prime Minister of Tibet remarked to me, "We regard Europeans and Americans as of the gods' race." Palhese explained this to me as follows: "The Europeans and the Americans are very clean, and lovers of worldly pleasures. Their countries are rich, and they have long life and all the material things that one can need. But they have not much religion, so that in course of time, as with those in the world of the gods, their possessions and their bodies dry up, and they have to experience the fear of death and their subsequent rebirth in a less fortunate set by circumstances due to their lack of religion. Therefore Tibetans compare them to the gods."

Mr. (later Sir) Basil Gould, a young officer of the Political Department working in Tibet, took the party to England. As the boys knew nothing but Tibetan, they had to start learning English; but Tibetans are for the most part good linguists, and before very long it was found possible to send them to Rugby School. It was of course an experiment, more particularly as Tibetans could not understand what a long process Western education is; they thought that two or three years would suffice to turn boys – able only to read and write Tibetan, and with no further education of any kind whatever – into perfectly trained army officers, electrical engineers, telegraphy experts, or mining engineers.

They were delightful young fellows, very like British boys of the same age, and made friends everywhere in England. One of them was rather lazy; in his school report I read that he cared little for his books, but was well to the front when there was a town and gown row. On the whole, the move turned out a success, especially with the youngest, named Ringang, who has proved very useful to Tibet as an electrical engineer. Three of them are still alive, and they are usually in Lhasa, forming a little English-speaking island there, for even now hardly anybody in Lhasa can speak English, or indeed any language except Tibetan, Mongolian or Chinese.

After the return of the Dalai Lama's party to their own country, one might occasionally meet Tibetans with mules carrying a few zinc baths and buckets to Lhasa. As a result of the visit to India, many Tibetans of the wealthier classes were taking hot-water baths about once a week, and found their health improved by doing so. In fact, there was a rise in the standard of cleanliness among this section of the community.

The European almost invariably rails against Tibetans for washing so little. But it must be remembered that winds of almost hurricane force blow throughout the arctic winters of high Tibet. There were no fires in the houses and no glass in the windows. Instead of glass there was only cotton cloth or paper, white or off-white, tacked and gummed on, and sometimes oiled. Such were the windows in the houses of the wealthier class. These windows often ran down the whole length of a fairly large room, and the cotton or paper was apt to be torn and penetrated by the violence of the winds.

The poorer members of the population had small windows, with bars arranged vertically or in the form of a cross, over which some sort of cloth might be hung. All the above windows have wooden shutters, which are closed at night. In the poorest houses there were no windows at all, only the door and the smoke-vent in the ceiling.

Seeing that Tibet was becoming stronger under the Dalai Lama's rule, China despatched troops from the Szechuan province in western China to invade Tibet. They were at first repulsed, but afterwards succeeded in occupying two important districts in eastern Tibet. Consignments of rifles came from Russia, through Mongolia, to Lhasa, and the prestige of Russia grew at the expense of Great Britain, the Tibetans contrasting our inactivity with the Russian advance in Mongolia. A Tibetan prophecy, which I myself had heard many years before, "The British are the road-makers of Tibet," was recalled; it had always been interpreted to mean that the British would do pioneer work in opening up Tibet, but would lose their influence before very long.

The Dalai Lama sent me, with a letter, a private verbal message to the effect that he did not desire relations with Russia, provided that Britain could help them without Russian co-operation. They had written to Russia, because they thought that, under the Anglo-Russian Convention, Britain could not act without Russia. They had therefore written to Russia, urging her to co-operate with us. According to Tibetan custom, the most important messages are often sent verbally, as in the case of this one from the Dalai Lama. Sometimes the one who carries the message writes it in chalk dust on a small wooden slate, when it is dictated to him. If he encounters somebody inquisitive or undesirable, he can rub it out quickly. In times of stress a letter may be accompanied by a verbal message. The letter then is colourless; it is on the message that attention must be concentrated.

The Precious Sovereign also urged me not to accept promotion to any other post, but to stay on as the British Representative to Tibet for another ten years at least, but, if possible, longer.

In the autumn of 1913 a conference was held in India, at Simla, with plenipotentiaries from China, Tibet and Great Britain, to attempt to decide the political status of Tibet. The Prime Minister, Shatra, was chosen by the Dalai Lama to be the plenipotentiary for Tibet.

The terms which the Dalai Lama himself wanted were as follows:

1 Tibet to manage her own internal affairs.
2 To manage her own external affairs, consulting on important matters with the British.
3 To have no Chinese High Commissioner, no other Chinese officials, and no Chinese soldiers in Tibet.
4 Tibet to include all the country eastward as far as Tachienlu. All these districts are purely Tibetan, but some of them had been seized by China, and brought more or less under Chinese control during the last two hundred years.

The Dalai Lama had taken to consulting his Ministers only, not the Parliament. The latter was too slow in deciding the questions that came before it. Throughout his career the Dalai Lama recognised the need for promptitude in work, a characteristic for which his subjects have always been grateful, for the course of the Tibetan Government is usually very slow.

For six months the discussions continued, and in April, 1914, a Convention was agreed upon and initialled by all three plenipotentiaries. It was not found possible to turn the Chinese out of the large area of Tibetan eastern territory which they had occupied for two hundred years. For, scantily populated, Tibet cannot hope to stand up against the large armies of populous China in those parts of her territory that are near the Chinese border. Tibet's own army is insignificant. Accordingly, the Convention arranged that Tibet should be divided into Inner Tibet and Outer Tibet, the former being the part nearer to China. In Outer Tibet the Dalai Lama retained practically complete control. Inner Tibet was to a large extent opened to the Chinese, although the Dalai Lama retained full religious control, and the right of appointing the various local chiefs throughout the territory.

But now a hitch occurred. Two days after the Chinese, Tibetan and British Plenipotentiaries had initialled the Convention, the Chinese Government telegraphed repudiating it. Tibet and Britain, however, recognised it as binding on themselves. China, having repudiated the Convention, was of course entitled to none of the advantages, for instance, the opening to Chinese of Inner Tibet, which the Convention would have conferred upon her.

It was one of my duties to negotiate with the Tibetan Plenipotentiary the frontier to be established between Tibet and northeastern India, following for this purpose a line, eight hundred and fifty miles long, marked out on a map by the British Plenipotentiary, Sir Henry McMahon. I was able to gain Shatra's consent to the frontier desired by Sir Henry, which stands back everywhere about a hundred miles from the plains of India.

The Convention also abolished the existing Trade Regulations relating to Tibet. They had been made in 1893, and were followed by a fresh set in 1908. But both of these had been negotiated and signed between British and Chinese Plenipotentiaries, no Tibetan Plenipotentiary being admitted. Consequently the Tibetans, with their growing knowledge and growing power, had for several years refused to recognise them. It became then another of my duties to negotiate with the Tibetan Plenipotentiary a fresh Trade Treaty, to govern the commercial relations between India and Outer Tibet. In this, as far as I can remember, I was free to follow my own ideas.

In due course the British and Tibetan Plenipotentiaries signed the agreement in respect of the frontier, and that in respect of the trade regulations, thus making both a part of the Simla Convention.

When Shatra returned to Lhasa he found that the Dalai Lama was dissatisfied with his conduct of the negotiations. He was summoned to an interview at six o'clock in the morning, but His Holiness kept him waiting till five o'clock in the afternoon. Shatra and his friends kept the rebuke as secret as possible, but of course it came out.

Seven years later, when visiting the Dalai Lama in Lhasa, I made him understand the treaty better. He kept always a firm grip on the political issues that confronted Tibet, and, when he failed to understand, did not hesitate to ask. He was showing me his treasures in the Forbidden Enclosure of the Jewel Park. We were standing together in one of the conservatories, he and I alone, surrounded by rows of flower-pots, arranged primly line by line, and filled with pansies, marigolds, nasturtiums, and many other kinds of flowers.

Suddenly he turned to me and said, "Lönchen, why was Tibet divided into two, Inner Tibet and Outer Tibet, at the Simla Conference?"

"In my mind, Precious Protector, the matter stood thus. The Chinese wanted to give the parts of Tibet near China Chinese names, and treat them as provinces of China. We arranged for them to be called Inner Tibet, thus keeping Tibet's name on them. Later on, if your army grows strong enough to ensure that Tibet's rights are respected, you may regain the rightful possession of this part of your country. But not if the name be lost."

The Dalai Lama's face lit up as he said, "Yes, yes, I see; I had not got it in my mind just like that." Omniscience was always ready to admit to me a lack of knowledge. We resumed our walk among the flower-pots.

In due course he made it clear to his officials that this Simla Treaty was the one for Tibet to follow. He was not indeed fully satisfied with it, but he was pleased that he had made his own treaty, in peaceful conditions, direct with the British Government.

The Dalai Lama was not very sympathetic towards Shatra. Perhaps the latter's ability piqued him a little. Shatra on his side was thoroughly loyal to his master. During the Conference at Simla the Chinese Plenipotentiary argued that the Dalai Lama was the cause of the troubles that had fallen on Tibet. To this Shatra had replied, "It is false accusations like this that are in large measure responsible for the rupture between China and Tibet. It is solely through the gracious personality and the wonderful foresight of His Holiness the Dalai Lama that Tibet's faith has been kept intact, and the country has retained its individuality. So any attack upon His Holiness is something that splits our hearts."

Shatra had a large and generous mind, and his wife was a fine woman. His family was brought up well, as both Kennedy and I noticed. Kennedy, being a doctor, knew the women and children better than I did. I became well acquainted with two of his grown-up sons; they were splendid young fellows, keen, hard-working, with a strong sense of public duty, and plenty of common sense.

Towards the end of his life, Shatra was a lonely figure. He had climbed high, and as usually happens in eastern lands, many people wanted to pull him down. A few years later he died, mainly as a result of his service in the Himalaya, the mountain resorts of which, on the Indian side, are to Tibetans unhealthy. Shortly before his death he wrote me a letter, couched in terms of great affection. In the course of this letter he wrote:

"You are a dear and kind friend of mine and I have full confidence in you. I believe that this friendship is due to your prayers and mine in a former life."

Thus he showed clearly the Tibetan view as to the working of *karma* everywhere, the close connection of our earlier lives with our later lives, and of his life with mine. Tibetans believe that the friendship between two persons is often due to their prayers in their former lives. The same idea is found in Tibetan history and Tibetan poetry. The present life is just one fragment to be lived on the Wheel of Life. Each is based on the others; sowing and reaping always.

Shortly after the Conference ended, His Majesty the King awarded me a Companionship of the Order of St. Michael and St. George (C.M.G.). The Dalai Lama wrote me a characteristic letter which ran as follows:

"Letter from the Dalai Lama." (Various complimentary remarks follow here.) "And to the Tibetan Government, at the time of the Conference between China and Tibet and at other times, you have brought us the rain and the river, the help of a friend. Accordingly the great English Highest One, the Great King, has given you the title of C.M.G. By this occurrence there has come great joy to me; so, as a good omen, I send you a robe of the gods, to be a picture of prosperity and blessedness. I ask you in future also, as in the past, to devise means of bringing benefit to the territories both of Britain and Tibet.

"Sent with a robe of the gods (ceremonial scarf) on the ninth day of the twelfth month of the Wood Tiger year, an auspicious day."

"The rain and the river" are the two chief sources of prosperity for Tibet, a nation of farmers and shepherds, in a land where water is often difficult to obtain. For eight months there may be neither rain nor snow, and good rivers are then vital for irrigating the thirsty land. People say:

> In the sixth month full rain, full river;
> In the seventh the crops are risen.

The sixth month – Tibetan months begin and end with each new moon – falls during July-August.

A jovial Bhutanese – no lama he – wrote about the C.M.G. that, "The news gave me boundless joy, as the first call of the cuckoo gives to the maid."

30 Retirement After the First World War

Even while the negotiations at the Simla Conference were in progress, the Dalai Lama had to keep some ten thousand men under arms in eastern Tibet, to prevent the Chinese from invading his country. For although the Chinese Government had agreed to the Conference, and appointed their representative to it, so little idea of fairness had they, that they attacked a province in eastern Tibet while the Conference was in progress.

In those districts for some years the crops had been poor, and so it was difficult for the Tibetans to feed their soldiers. They had hardly any military budget at all, most of their resources being devoted to the upkeep of religious institutions. What little they had was mainly in kind; barley, tea, butter and dried yak dung. These resources were useful, but during a succession of lean years barley – which in Tibet takes the place of wheat – runs short; and in any case money is required for paying soldiers and for other purposes.

The Chinese general announced that he would carry his attack through to Lhasa, unless the Tibetans quitted the Conference to which his Government had agreed, and negotiated with him alone. "Otherwise," he said, "I will not leave even a dog or a chicken alive in the country." Certainly things were difficult for these untrained and ill-armed Tibetans.

Then, in 1914, the first World War broke out. In spite of his precarious position, the Dalai Lama immediately offered a thousand Tibetan soldiers to fight on the British side. Rather pathetically, when offering these men, he wrote that he could not send rifles with them. There were not many rifles in the whole of Tibet, and it would have been suicidal to let any of those rifles go. It was indeed not possible to accept this offer of soldiers, but many Tibetans joined the hospital and ambulance corps.

The Dalai Lama also ordained that certain special religious services should be held in the main monasteries throughout Tibet for the success of British arms. This may seem a trivial matter, but, as a matter of fact, the monasteries had to be paid for this service, and the expenditure on this by the Tibetan Government, hardly able to find money for its own needs, was considerable.

In one of the verbal messages that I received from His Holiness, while telling me about these religious services, he added, "We have transferred privately to the credit of the British Government a number of the services which have been held for the Tibetan Government. If we had held all of them for the British, our people would have thought that the British troops must be in desperate straits, and would have been greatly anxious as to the result of the war." It may seem strange to transfer religious benefits from one person or nation to another, as it were, by a stroke of the pen, but such a transaction is in accordance with the principles of Tibetan Buddhism. In Tibetan history you will frequently read of saints who offer to give up to others their own good *karma,* that is to say, all the spiritual merit that they have earned, their spiritual wealth, available for use not only in this life, but in future lives as well.

It was a wonderful change. Only ten years had passed since a British military expedition had invaded Tibet and occupied Lhasa, many Tibetans being killed in the fighting. Yet now Tibet offers troops which she can ill-afford to spare, to fight on the British side, and does what else she can to promote the success of the British arms. Seldom indeed can a change in the feeling of a nation have been so quick and so thorough.

Now that Britain was occupied in the world war, the Chinese were preparing to attack Tibet more vigorously. Accordingly, the little Tibetan arsenal in Lhasa had to strain every nerve to make as many cartridges as it could. It was in the charge of a capable monk, and though, of course, the cartridges were of mediocre quality, still they did the best they could.

Towards the end of 1917 the Chinese general in eastern Tibet broke the truce to which both sides had agreed in 1914. His attack was overwhelmingly defeated by the Tibetans, who drove him and his troops out of a large part of the Tibetan territory which they had hitherto occupied. The Prime Minister of the Gurkha nation, that race of warriors, was surprised at the Tibetan success, and regarded it as a fine military feat.

As the first World War went on, the Tibetans of Lhasa, and throughout the greater part of Tibet, began to think that the British were likely to lose. Chinese in various parts of the country, of whom some five hundred were in Lhasa, circulated reports that Germany was winning and that German troops were attacking Calcutta. The Tibetan Government accordingly took the most active among these Chinese and deported them across the frontier into Sikkim, and I saw to it that they were sent away from the neighbourhood of Tibet and moved through Sikkim into India, where, of course, I had no further control over their movements. The Dalai Lama, and with him some lamas of acknowledged authority, likened Germany to an elephant which it takes a long time to pull down, but is pulled down in the end, thus prophesying the ultimate victory of the Allies after great difficulties.

The Panchen Lama's Government, though unfriendly to-wards the Government at Lhasa, wished still to remain on terms of close friendship with the British. It is said that while these anti-British reports were circulated in Tibet, the Panchen Lama held religious services for killing the enemies of the British in the war. That is a dangerous thing for any lama to do, because it is believed that those who hold such services are themselves likely to die soon.

It was about this time that the Foreign Secretary summoned me to Delhi to discuss various political questions. He had a quick, clever brain, but had been brought up in the north-west frontier school, and was slow to believe that there was any need for a policy on the north-east frontier also. However, as Japan and Russia advanced in eastern Asia, the importance of India's north-eastern frontier was coming to be gradually recognised. But what a long time it took to persuade the authorities in India to recognise this!

When the first World War eventually came to an end, His Holiness telegraphed to His Majesty the King, congratulating him on the glorious result. During all the time the war was in progress, he had his own war against the Chinese troops encamped on his eastern territory, and not much in the way of arms or other equipment with which to oppose them. But the Tibetans held their ground, and more than twenty years later, when I came to Tibet on a private visit, were still holding on, keeping a force of Tibetan troops, sometimes larger, sometimes smaller, on the eastern border.

Each year I visited Tibet, and used to receive a letter of welcome from both the Dalai Lama and the Panchen Lama. They sent also invitations to visit them at Lhasa and Shigatse respectively; during one year alone the Dalai Lama sent me three such invitations. With these came presents, an ordinary sample of which would be three carcases of sheep, two leather bags of rice, three sacks of barley flour, five bags of mixed barley and peas, and six or seven dozen eggs. With them came a cloisonné bowl and several rolls of blankets; and, of course, the silk scarf of ceremony, which must always accompany a letter, a present, or an interview. The eggs were usually bad, at least four-fifths of them, for the Tibetan's taste in eggs differs widely from our own. The sheep had been killed nine months before, but the Tibetan climate being so cold and dry, were eatable. Tibetans kill their animals for food mainly in October, the meat freezes during the winter, and thus keeps within bounds for several years. Every bag and box or other object was sealed with the Dalai Lama's seal. The messenger who brought the things gave the list of them, also sealed with the seal of the Inmost One, to my clerk to read out, and showed him each package with the seal intact. The present from the Panchen Lama consisted of two boxes of sweetmeats and twenty sacks of peas, each sack weighing about fifty pounds. The peas were used for our ponies; that is the Tibetan custom. They thrive on this diet.

The Panchen Lama's messenger informed me that a new palace had been completed recently at Shigatse, which, excepting only Lhasa, is the largest town in Tibet, and lies half a mile from the Panchen Lama's monasatery of Tashi Lhünpo. He added that it would be placed at my disposal if I went there. I had, however, regretfully to decline all invitations, as the Government of India forbade me to accept any of them.

Certainly it was necessary to keep Tibet friendly, but I had to do the best I could without visiting either of the two leading personages in Tibet. It was a peculiar position. The British Government's representative had to maintain friendly relations with Tibet, but was at the same time forbidden to visit the Tibetan Government in their capital. It was as if an American representative in Australia was not allowed to go within five days' journey of Canberra.

Another work that the Panchen Lama was doing during the war was the erection of a huge statue to the Buddha of Love (Maitreya), Buddha Shakyamuni's successor. The Temple was four storeys high, and the statue rose through them all. As the Dalai Lama was his spiritual guide, and the two Grand Lamas were on fairly friendly terms in spite of the disagreements of their Governments, the Panchen Lama wrote to the Dalai Lama asking that he might come to Lhasa and receive the Dalai Lama's benediction there.

The Tibetan biography tells us that the Dalai Lama replied as follows:

"Near to the Panchen Lama, the All-Knowing One. This time I received your friendly letter, with a white scarf, and one *sang* (about one ounce) of gold. I was very glad and grateful to you. As I have already asked you to send me all the printed books of Tsongkapa and his two disciples, please send them if you have finished printing. I arrived here (in Lhasa) after visiting some monasteries. You, Panchen Lama, asked me to give you religious teaching and a benediction, informing me that you are receiving them only from your teacher, but being afraid of possible violation of religious vows, you did not intend to take any religious blessing from any other lama except myself. The best arrangement would be for you to come here secretly with a few attendants, in the coming autumn. I am classified in a very low degree regarding my education, on account of the worldly work which I have to do. But I bow to the feet of many great lamas in Upper and Lower Tibet with my head, and I have received from them many valuable religious instructions. I would like to give all of them to you, the great All-Knowing One. In any case I will serve you in any way that you wish, as I can never obtain any disciple greater and more suitable than you. So I am longing to see your golden face.

"But the difficulty is that I have to do many things during this coming autumn. I have not yet been able to bring to an end the war against the Chinese in eastern Tibet; and you also are working on the erection of the statue to Maitreya. Therefore I do not think you will be able to come during this autumn. If you can postpone your visit till next year, we can fix the proper time by correspondence.

"Regarding the matter of Engur monastery, I think the Noyön is guilty. But this is a trifling matter, and you must try to avoid making any harm to the owner or the lamas of that monastery.

"Please pay attention to the letters which I shall send you now and then.

"Offered with a white silk scarf on the 16th of the 7th month of the Wood Hare."

It will be noted that the Dalai Lama writes very humbly about his own education. This is in accordance with Tibetan etiquette when writing to a lama of equal spiritual merit.

The letter was despatched by the Dalai Lama in September, 1915. But during the following year he shut himself up in religious meditation for three years, and throughout this time he did not allow any officers to see him. Bundles of petitions he received daily, and he replied to them in writing with his own hand; he did not employ any officer or clerk to help him in the work. During these three years he had very little sleep. Except for this work, he spent the time in religious meditation. Accordingly it was December, 1919, before the Panchen Lama could come to Lhasa and receive the Dalai Lama's benediction.

It was about this time that Palhese was offered a Government post by the Dalai Lama. He, however, declined it, as the jealousy which is always so strong among Tibetan officials would have made him feel insecure. Palhese frequently told me, as did other Tibetans, that British officials work for the good of their country, while Tibetan officials work for their own good. Nevertheless, the Dalai Lama used to write direct to Palhese, and the latter would reply in like manner. This put him at the centre of things, establishing his status and influence with other Tibetans, and giving him access to true facts in public affairs.

Towards the end of the war the Dalai Lama asked me for a large number of copies, in a smaller size, of the photograph which I had taken of him in Darjeeling. He used to distribute copies to favoured disciples. I frequently found one of these little photographs on an altar in a chapel, being venerated in place of an image of His Holiness.

In April, 1918, I went on a year's leave, for I had been working year after year, and my health was thoroughly bad. During the following year, for various reasons, I retired from the service of the Government, who appointed Major W. L. Campbell to succeed me. He had officiated for me during the period of my leave. I remained in Darjeeling for a time, studying Tibetan literature and Tibetan Buddhism. Many were the letters that I received from the Dalai Lama, his Ministers, and other Tibetans, regretting my retirement. To Mr. Macdonald, my assistant, they wrote enquiring whether they would be permitted to ask the Government of India to induce me to continue my work, until the peace treaty between the Chinese and Tibetans should be settled once and for all.

Part Five
Storm and Calm in Lhasa

31 The Government Ask Me to Return

In January, 1920, shortly before I was leaving for England, the Government of India asked me to return to my work, although I had retired some eight or nine months earlier.

It seemed to me that perhaps now there might be a chance of being permitted to go to Lhasa, and do something there towards the improvement of the position between Tibet and India. Accordingly, I agreed to return to work for twelve months.

Rai Bahadur Achuk Tsering was still in the establishment. I had first chosen him for my service eighteen years before, when he was one of several clerks in a small countrified Government office. I had trained him as my confidential clerk, and later as personal assistant, for the diplomatic and administrative work in Tibet, Bhutan and Sikkim. Thin and smallish, quiet and shy, but shrewd always, he developed political insight that grew steadily year by year, and helped to train me in reply to the training that I gave him.

But Palhese had left, because he had always told me that he would leave when I did. To my request that he would come from Lhasa to my headquarters in Sikkim, I received this reply, "Though the Emperor of India may desire a good name, the Emperor of China cannot afford to bear a bad one."

"What on earth does he mean?" I asked a mutual friend.

"Ah, well; one of his tenants has brought a suit against him. He must stay in Lhasa till it is decided; otherwise he will lose both his case and his good name." Two months later he arrived.

Our friendly relationship with Tibet had weakened during

The Potala, the Dalai Lama's winter palace, taken from the Pargo Kaling, top, and the Potala from the north in the rainy season, below.

my absence. For when I returned to my post a year and three-quarters after leaving it, I found that the Tibetan Government had at length yielded to the pressure always being applied by the Chinese, and had allowed a Chinese diplomatic mission to proceed to Lhasa. This was an event that had never happened since the Chinese troops drove the Dalai Lama into exile in 1910, and it indicated a setback in the relations between Britain and Tibet.

The mission arrived in Lhasa from China shortly before I rejoined. Naturally it took every opportunity to lessen British influence and improve the Chinese position, by endeavouring to induce the Tibetan Government to negotiate with them alone and bar out the British. The Tibetan Government wrote to me asking for my opinion. Perhaps they were a little nervous as to what I would think of their action in admitting the Chinese mission. I advised them that they should tell the mission that they thanked them for their interest in the Yellow Hat religion; but that when negotiations were conducted at Simla in 1913-14, the Chinese broke them off without coming to an agreement; again during 1919, when the Chinese themselves re-opened negotiations, they themselves broke them off again; and therefore in these circumstances the Tibetan Government did not think any useful purpose would be served by sending delegates to China to negotiate an agreement. The Tibetan Government replied to the Chinese mission in accordance with my advice, and the mission left Lhasa shortly afterwards.

The Chinese Government then said that the mission was purely from the Government of Kansu; it was not accredited by the Supreme Government of China. That was the way that China used to proceed in such matters. If a mission failed, they said that it was merely some provincial move; if on the contrary it succeeded, they described it as a mission from the Supreme Government of China, and claimed the full result. In this way they reaped all possible advantage, and when they were unsuccessful, felt that they still "saved face." The Dalai Lama had explained this procedure of theirs to me several years earlier, and I found that it happened so every time.

That summer I paid my usual visit to Gyangtse. On my arrival, an official came to see me, and said, "Can you come to Lhasa now?"

"No; I have no instructions to do so." And none came while I was at Gyangtse; so I reprepared to return to Sikkim and England.

In September the Tibetan agent at Gyangtse came riding urgently with his escort to my quarters in the staging bungalow, and delivered to me another letter from the Dalai Lama to the following effect: "I hear from my agent in Gyangtse that you are returning to England. There is no other Sahib that understands every issue of Tibetan politics as you do. It will be a matter of the deepest grief to me if you leave before the issues between China and Tibet are settled. Please consider the matter. This letter is despatched with a white silk scarf on a date of good omen."

To Palhese also the Dalai Lama wrote. An unusual procedure, especially when a request was likely to be unsuccessful. But even in this custom-ridden country, "The Way and the Custom" were pushed aside by a will that recognised no obstacle. This letter was on the same lines as that to me, concluding with an order to Palhese to press me with all his strength to remain. Poor Palhese! What could he do? He was known in Tibet as "two-headed," because he had to serve two masters, two countries. It was possible for him only because I found that on most of the main issues the interests of the two countries lay very close together.

Discussions between the Government of India and myself were, of course, always in progress, and therefore on my return from Gyangtse I waited in the Chumbi Valley, just inside the Tibetan frontier, expectantly. There, before long, orders came from London instructing me to accept the repeated invitations of the Dalai Lama, and take a diplomatic mission to Lhasa. Briefly stated, my instructions were to convey to His Holiness the Dalai Lama friendly greetings from the British Government, and to explain the international state of affairs then prevailing.

So on the first day of November, the day after my fiftieth

birthday, I left the Chumbi Valley for the Holy City. It would be cold going over the passes and the high plains at that late season. I asked my clerks and servants whether they regretted the move. "Not at all," was the reply; "our good fortune is great that we can visit 'The Place of the Gods'[16] and meet the Lord in his Temple."[17]

32   We Go to Lhasa

We went to Lhasa by the ordinary route, namely, Pari, Gyang-tse, the Lake of the Upland Pastures, and Chaksam. Our party included Dr. Dyer, the Government doctor in Sikkim. It included also Rai Bahadur Achuk Tsering, now promoted to the post of Personal Assistant. Palhese, the invaluable, came also.

I had arranged with the Government of India that my old friend, Lieutenant-Colonel R.S. Kennedy, D.S.O., M.C., of the Indian Medical Service, should be the doctor of the party. He had been stationed for two or three years in Gyangtse, and had accompanied me on my mission to Bhutan some ten years earlier. But he had to come from a station far away on the plains of India, and therefore did not reach Lhasa till a few days after us. Dr. Dyer then returned to Sikkim.

How lucky I was to have Colonel Kennedy as my sole European companion! His warm-hearted Irish nature fell naturally into sympathy with the Tibetan people, while his knowledge of the Tibetan language and customs enabled him to use that sympathy to the best advantage.

An exceptionally virulent type of influenza was raging at Pari, and though we did not halt there – the usual halting-place – for the night, but only for half an hour or so, changing our transport, yet three out of my party of thirty died later on, as a result of coming through this zone of infection. Even in ordinary circumstances, breathing is difficult at fourteen thousand feet above the sea level; and when influenza takes hold of anybody, it often turns to pneumonia, and at such a high altitude breathing becomes almost impossible.

However though the season for the storms of winter had arrived, we have exceptionally favourable weather. On the "Plain of the Three Brothers" a blizzard had raged until the day before we arrived there.

Two weeks later we crossed the last pass, the Kampa La, over 15,000 feet high, in glorious sunshine and no snow on the ground. That night a blizzard arose, and the pass was submerged in deep snow.

I remarked how fortunate we were. "No; it is because you, the leader of the party, have a good mind."

"How do you make that out?"

"Why, this is a verse that every educated Tibetan knows:

Deeds white and black, for minds are clean and foul.
Is the mind clean? Then earth and sky are clean.
Is the mind foul? Then earth and sky are foul.
For'tis upon the mind that all depends.

This was far more pleasant to hear than the common Western saying, "You have the Devil's own luck."

Insistence on the power of the mind runs deep in Tibetan thought. They believe that it greatly influences external events. A man who is out of the common may be expected to influence things round him; for good, if he is good; for bad, if he is bad. A good man of this kind, making a visit to a foreign country, will probably have good weather on his journey, will keep good health, and the crops of the country that he visits will be improved. And the good weather was taken also as a favourable omen for the success of my mission.

After leaving Gyangtse there are no Indian staging bungalows, because Gyangtse is the furthest Indian trade mart in this part of Tibet. We were coming to Lhasa at the invitation of the Dalai Lama and the Tibetan Government. Accordingly, from here onwards we were completely looked after by the Tibetan authorities. They had deputed a cheerful but somewhat wayward official, named Netö, one of the two magistrates at Gyangtse, to accompany our party to Lhasa, and see that we had transport and food and lodging accommodation on the way.

Forty miles from Lhasa, after we had settled into our staging bungalow, a secretary of the Dalai Lama himself was ushered into the room. With courteous bows he explained that His Holiness wished to provide for me either lunch or dinner, whichever I might prefer, on the day of my arrival in Lhasa. His Holiness would not be present at the meal, but wished to save us trouble. He wished to give me either Chinese or English food, according to my choice; and if the latter, would I be good enough to send my own cook to prepare it? A most natural request, for what should a Tibetan cook know of European dishes. Enough that he should be acquainted with Tibetan, Chinese and Mongolian food. My health being, as usual, unreliable, I chose English food on that occasion, and sent my cook ahead before arriving in Lhasa. I had other servants who could cook well enough meanwhile; most hillmen can cook a little. This secretary's name was "Wisdom"; he was one of the ten secretaries employed by His Holiness. All are monks and known as "Secretary at the Peak," i.e. at the Potala. My "Wisdom" was exceptionally alert and intelligent. He was also of an unflagging industry; during more than twenty years' service he had taken no holiday, and had been absent only a day or two when incapacitated by illness. He and Netö, the officer who conducted us from Gyangtse, were attached to my mission when I arrived in Lhasa. A monk and a layman; they often work in pairs.

Tibetans never speak of the Potala simply as the Potala, but always refer to it as Peak Potala, because it is built into a small hill, about four hundred feet high. Similarly, the word "Peak" is inserted before the designation of all those who are in personal attendance on the Dalai Lama, because he is identified with the Potala, and so they, too, are identified with it. Indeed, the whole body of ecclesiastical officials – who constitute one-half of Tibetan officialdom – are known collectively as the "Peak Officials."

After crossing the river, the main river of southern Tibet, the Brahmaputra of India, we halt for the night at Chushur. We halt the next day also at the Dalai Lama's request, in order that we may arrive at Lhasa on the 17th November, which happens to be an auspicious day. That is absolutely necessary according to Tibetan ideas, and all the more because the Dalai Lama and Tibetan Government wish to discuss with me political questions which, for them at any rate, are of vital importance, namely, the independence of their country in the face of the Chinese invasion and attempts to take their freedom from them. But in all things, small as well as great, Tibetans consult omens, good and bad, as did the Greeks of old. We are to call on the Dalai Lama in Lhasa on November 19th, which is the eighth day of the tenth Tibetan month, a day of very good omen in the Tibetan calendar. So these essential preliminaries are happily arranged.

A few miles before reaching Lhasa the valley bends at a ridge coming down from the right. Here is an enormous cairn of stones, to which devout worshippers are continually adding fresh ones, for here one catches the first glimpse of the Potala, the Dalai Lama's great palace at Lhasa. All Buddhists in our party throw themselves on the ground; the place is known as "The Ridge of Reverential Prostration." A long name in English, but in Tibetan only three short syllables, Chaktsegang, the Tibetan language being so closely condensed.

Our entry into the Holy City resembles a triumphal procession. All and sundry come several miles outside to meet us. Representatives from Nepal, Bhutan and far Kashmir – the last indeed ride forty-two miles outside Lhasa to greet us. Representatives of the powerful nobility, especially the Houses of Palha and of Long Stone.

Our party grows larger and larger. There is a kindly sun, but a frost-biting wind of almost gale force. The endless, unresting dust of Tibet rises thicker and thicker, and goes scurrying down the track. Two miles outside the city we are welcomed by the delegates of the Dalai Lama, of the Prime Minister, and of the Cabinet, the last being represented by my young friend Shatra, the late Prime Minister's son. Conducted to a large tent, we are regaled with tea, biscuits and rice, all after the Tibetan style. Rice is a luxury in Lhasa, as it has to be brought from Bhutan or Nepal, fifteen to twenty-five days' journey over high passes, being carried by pony, mule and donkey, by yak and bullock, as well as by man. But an occasion such as the present one demands it. We stop ten minutes and pass on, the delegates joining in the cavalcade.

By the reception tent a Gurkha Guard of Honour, few in number for there are not many Gurkhas in Lhasa, lines the roadway. Further on a hundred Tibetan infantry are drawn up under their officers. And now a fresh party of Ladakhis stand to greet us; their ancestral homes are three months' journey distant across the wind-swept, icy plains and passes of western Tibet.

The crowd grows more and more; indeed, the greater part of Lhasa seems to have turned out to see these strange Europeans, who are coming to live for a time in the Tibetan capital without any of their soldiers to protect them. "That," they say, "is a new thing; they are coming like brothers."

Lhasa at last! The Dalai Lama and Tibetan Government had wished it, and I had wished it, and at length our mutual wish was fulfilled. It was an especial pleasure to think that I was the first European who had ever visited Lhasa at the invitation of the people themselves, in fact, after repeated invitations from the Dalai Lama and his Government. As matters turned out, I was destined to stay there longer than any other Westerner had stayed for a hundred and seventy-five years.

Before reaching the Potala we turn to the right and are conducted to a little house belonging to a former Regent of Tibet, the Abbot of the monastery of Kündeling, who had died the preceding year. It lies by the river in its own extensive grounds, known as Happiness Park. The owner, though a hardy Tibetan, used it during the summer only, regarding it as too cold for residence during the winter. It is one of the type known as a "pleasure house," a small house set in the grounds of the main residence, a house in which the owners will stay for a few days off and on during the summer, enjoying the outside air, and maybe entertaining their friends at archery parties. Though here by the side of the river it was exceptionally cold, I could not have been provided with more comfortable quarters than were afforded by this country villa. To it was attached, more than in most cases, a large park, in which were other houses which my assistants and clerks occupied.

Throughout our year there the climate was wonderfully regular. The last frost of winter came during the first week of June, the first frost of the next winter during the last week of September; so that there was frost, with occasional intermissions, for eight and a half months. During seven months frost was continuous, not missing a single night. There were never more than forty-two Fahrenheit degrees of frost; the chief thing that made it cold were the violent winds, which blew at their strongest during winter, coupled with the lack of heating in the house, the plentiful windows, and the absence of glass in them.

A tiny garden adjoined the house, and was surrounded by a very high wall, which turned it into a sun trap, so that hollyhocks, twelve feet high, and other flowers bloomed luxuriantly in the summer. Roses did not do well; most of the buds rotted and withered before coming into full flower. The Tibetans do not prune them, nor manure them; those in our garden here were planted also in beds too small and stony and under the eaves of the house; and of course were never weeded. But the large white peonies were a delight to the eye.

Hollyhocks, marigolds and asters are all popular in Tibet, having been grown there from time immemorial. The single marigold is known as "The Saffron-coloured," the double marigold as "The Great Gold," the aster as "The Flower of the Pure Age." An apple tree also grew in our miniature garden; its fruit, too, was miniature, hardly bigger than a walnut.

Charming was the water garden with its various channels winding through belts of slim willow-trees. Here a pair of moorhens and a pair of solitary snipe made their nests and reared their families during the spring of 1921.

On the branch of the river which flowed close by our house were flocks of bar-headed geese, gadwall, mallard, and the yellow-bodied Brahmany ducks (ruddy sheldrake), all tame and friendly, for the Tibetans never kill them. The last-named, a high Tibetan lama of the Red Hat sect told me, "were formerly white, but by teaching religion to the birds, their bodies turned to yellow." Yellow is, of course, the Buddhist colour.

The large number of willows and poplars that grew in the ample grounds outside the high walls kept out of our house the insanitary dust of the city.

The house had a large room, thirty feet by twenty, on the ground floor, which we used for our numerous receptions and for our own meals. In my study upstairs the owner used to work, eat and sleep. Tibetans often use just one room; during the latter part of his life the Dalai Lama did the same. I used an inner room upstairs for washing; during December and January its temperature remained always below freezing point, even during the middle of the day. But washing was a thing we did not overdo.

I had brought a few cylindrical oil-drums, which we fitted up as rough stoves, burning in them yak dung, reinforced by some small pieces of wood. Tin piping led out of these and through the thin cloth that covered the window space. Thus we in the main house, and my clerks in their houses outside, were able to warm up a bit. I was usually able to prevent the thermometer in my study from falling much below fifty degrees Fahrenheit, for several hours of writing in a lower temperature is uncomfortable for anybody like myself, whose blood circulation has always been bad.

The staircase between the two floors was a ladder, after the usual Tibetan style, very steep. Every Tibetan comes down these ladders with his or her back to the ladder. I once saw an Englishman in a monastery come down facing the ladder; he excited surprise and mirth among the monks who stood there watching him. The rungs of the ladder in our house were rounded and slippery from the countless feet that had trod them, and you came on two or three that turned round and round in their sockets. The house was fairly new, but the ladder was not.

When a governmental mission from any country visits Lhasa, the Tibetan Government, always hospitably inclined, treats it as guests, supplying a house or houses for its accommodation, and giving a large measure of the daily food required by the members of the mission, as well as fodder for their ponies and other animals. They wished to do the same for us during the whole of our stay. I pressed them to allow us to meet our own expenses, but they insisted on supplying a portion during the first one and a half months, and then only with considerable difficulty were persuaded to allow us to pay for everything.

In accordance with long-established custom, the Tibetan Government gave to the Chinese mission, that was in Lhasa from December, 1919, to April, 1920, a large part of their supplies during the whole of their stay, and also during the long journey inside Tibet to Lhasa, and back again to the Chinese frontier.

On the whole our food, though naturally monotonous, was sufficient, but there were a few difficulties. During the warmer months our bread arrived mouldy, for it was a month on the road; but we ate the bits between the mouldy places, and so did not lose it all. Kennedy was of opinion that, having come over an altitude of 16,800 feet, the harmful germs had been destroyed. For a month it was all mould and quite impossible; at that time our cook made us chupattis – a kind of griddlecake – after the Indian style, but sparingly, as our supply of flour was but small.

There was also a difficulty about green vegetable. During December the cabbages that we had buried became absolutely uneatable. From then onwards we had no green vegetables until the following April, when Kennedy discovered on the Lhasa plain a weed which he had eaten at Gyangtse. The Tibetans do not care whether they have green vegetables or not, but we could not go as far as that. There was no fruit to be had except occasionally, dried apricots.

The water of Lhasa is notorious throughout Tibet; it upsets even Tibetans who come from other districts. Fortunately I discovered this shortly before I arrived, and found out also that the Dalai Lama's water supply was much the best. "The Lhasa water is like a heavy weight," said Palhese's uncle, fifty-five years of age. It causes toothache and pain in the temples among those unaccustomed to it, though it does not bring on bowel complaints. I am accustomed to it, as I lived in Lhasa when I was a boy, and therefore it does not harm me much. But if I go away for a long time, I feel it for a month or two after my return."

Accordingly, we obtained our water from the Dalai Lama's

water supply, for he readily gave his consent to this. It became the duty of one of my orderlies, a simple-minded but thoroughly trustworthy Lepcha, to take the mule-driver and his mules every day to it, as often as necessary. It would not have done to send the mule-driver unattended; he would have filled up his wooden buckets from the nearest roadside puddle. Jungly, so-called from his simple-mindedness, was a real treasure. He would not willingly join us even in the most gorgeous religious ceremonies or in the most entrancing holiday festivities in case anything went wrong with the purity of our water supply. He absolutely refused to leave his job.

While he was still young, his father and mother had died, so that he had never learnt to care much for religious observances. Indeed, two of Jungly's sons had died only a few years before we came to Lhasa. His friends ascribed these calamities to the fact that he had never learnt from his parents the names of the gods and demons who dwelt in their family. He had therefore been unable to worship the one, or propitiate the other. People in such cases often suffer three or four calamities before they discover the family gods and demons. The Lepchas, though nominally Buddhists, still cling to the roots of the old *Bön*.

33   A Cordial Welcome

Here in the Holy City the Dalai Lama lived his life mainly in the seclusion of sanctity. I used to see pilgrims who were passing along the track near our house in Kündeling, turn and face left towards the Dalai Lama's Jewel Park Palace that stood half a mile away. Then they prostrated themselves at full length, and laid their foreheads in the dust of the road that led to it. Three times would they do this before they moved with deliberate steps on their way to the Great Temple and other goals of pilgrimage.

With one hand the pilgrim tells the one hundred and eight beads of his rosary; with the other he turns the prayer wheel with its hundreds of prayers and sacred sentences packed tightly inside the little cylinder. And as we pass by we hear the favourite prayer, *Om mani peme hum* (Om! The Jewel in the Lotus Hum) endlessly repeated. According to the popular Tibetan belief, *Om* is a word that cleanses; as it denotes the summing up of all the Divine Powers. Tibetans have written volumes to explain the meaning of this mystic sentence.

The Dalai Lama's State journeys were made in his yellow sedan chair screened by curtains. Only six or seven persons are allowed to use sedan chairs in Tibet, and of these only two, the Dalai and Panchen Lamas are allowed to use the Buddhist yellow.

Kennedy and I were now to see the Dalai Lama behind the veil in the Holy City.

The date of my first call on him had already been fixed, a day of especially good omen, but the hour had still to be settled.

Shortly before reaching Lhasa, Palhese had pressed me to let him know what hour would suit me best. I had suggested 10 a.m., if it suited the Dalai Lama, because, as already mentioned, calls should be made before midday, after which the sun begins to decline and grow weaker, and the omen is not so good. On the day after my arrival the Dalai Lama's Chief Secretary called on me and said that His Holiness suggested 10 a.m. as the hour of my call on him, but that any other time that suited me would suit him. It is in accordance with custom that suggestions or instructions of this kind should come from the Dalai Lama, and should meet with acceptance; and this is how the matter was arranged to suit my convenience.

Indeed, apart from cases of national emergency, the Dalai Lama would never make a request that might be refused or modified. Steps were always taken first by subordinates to make sure that the request was acceptable.

On the following day, therefore more than eight years since we had last seen each other, the Peak Secretary conducted me to my first interview with the temporal and spiritual leader of Tibet in his own capital. What a contrast was this, after that approach through a non-Tibetan population, and the sad reception in the European hotel in Darjeeling! The Peak Secretary, wearing his robes of State, and accompanied by his own servants, came with me and my own small retinue. This included Achuk Tsering, Palhese, and a few orderlies and grooms, all of us mounted on our small, sturdy Tibetan ponies. I always rode a pony a little larger than the ordinary, and of iron-grey colour, for this and a yellow-brown shade, with a black line down the centre of its back, are deemed good colours for a secular official, as is white for a lama. These rules are by no means always followed, but the observance of the best usage is advantageous in a country where etiquette is so closely watched.

Our destination was not the Potala Palace, but the more comfortable and secluded country palace, the Jewel Park, Norbu Lingka, one and a half miles out of Lhasa, and not far from our house. Former Dalai Lamas lived in the Potala. But my friend, even before coming to Darjeeling, ten years earlier, used to live in the Potala during the winter months only, and in the Jewel Park during summer. During the four weeks of the Great Prayer festival he had to stay in the Temple. That being in the heart of Lhasa, he was unable to obtain privacy or to take exercise, for the streets are crowded. In this land of strongly-rooted custom the partial abandonment of the holy Potala Palace was a bold step to take. But after his return from Darjeeling to Lhasa, he lessened his residence there still further.

"I find no privacy while living in the Potala," he would tell me, "and no exercise except by walking on the roof. There are many steps to climb, as it is built into the hill. I do not like so many steps, and they merely take one down into the streets below. Besides, it is near Lhasa, which is full of that kind of dust that is dirty and smelly and causes sickness. Illness came often to me there."

It was not the Dalai Lama's habit to over-state a case, nor did he do so in this instance. There are ten or twelve religious festivals every year at Lhasa. In the larger ones the city popula-tion of some fifteen to twenty thousand may be swollen to five times that number, and so remain for two or three weeks. Let it be remembered that there are no sanitary arrangements of any kind. In the houses a hole in the floor; outside, just dark corners by the streets, and the surrounding fields. And the raging winds of Tibet carry the plentiful dust of this dry climate and the germs with it.

As we passed down the new well-made road, crowds of Tibetans lined the sides, to catch a glimpse of the strange foreigner. At the entrance to the Park a military guard in work-manlike khaki uniforms stood at attention as we passed in.

I was received in the Dalai Lama's private apartment. He and I sat alone together, and I was told that being received thus at my first interview was an especial honour, due to the Dalai Lama having known me so well in Darjeeling; and intended also to show the friendship subsisting between Britain and Tibet. The room, of course, was cold, as are the rooms in Tibetan houses, for we were there in winter at an elevation of twelve thousand feet above the level of the sea, without a fire or other kind of heating. But the Dalai Lama's room had one supreme luxury; there was glass in the windows, so the arctic Tibetan winds could not force an entrance.

He had not aged much since I first knew him in Darjeeling, except that his eyes had become watery, a condition which his subjects regard as a sign of Buddhahood. He was now forty-four years old. It is after fifty that most Tibetans begin to age rapidly, and by sixty they are in old age. Perhaps living always at an elevation of the higher mountains in the Alps, and even higher, is a strain on heart and lungs to which nature cannot accustom them. You may be told that the man or woman who is perfectly virtuous will live to be a hundred and eight years old, the sacred number in Tibet. But this is merely a pious joke.

My reception was delightful, that of one old friend welcoming another. He was not seated on his throne in accordance with a Dalai Lama's custom. As I entered the room, he came forward to meet me. I gave him my scarf of ceremony. He took it over his wrists as it is taken by one equal from another, and gave me his scarf over my wrists. Then he grasped both my hands in his own, and held them for a time, smiling happily at me. "What a pity you could not come in the summer, when the flowers are out! Now there are no flowers, and the trees are nearly all bare."

He was dressed simply; a robe of red silk with a yellow silk jacket underneath, and high boots of which the prevailing colour was white. The room in which he received me was large, with one or two European tables, and a few chairs to fit them. But a large altar with its images of the different Buddhas and saints faced me as I sat – always in the same chair and exactly the same place – about three feet from the Dalai Lama at a small round European table. Round the walls hung sacred pictures, painted on parchment with silk surrounds, resembling Japanese kake-monos up to a point, but with greater exuberance of detail. And some other, but not all, the appurtenances of a Tibetan chapel.

My servants brought in my few presents and laid them before him. When meeting Tibetans you must give presents freely, and when meeting those of exalted position you must indeed be lavish. But I had come here at short notice on instructions cabled from London, and I had started on my journey from the Chumbi Valley, far from the resources of civilization. So I followed the procedure proper in such a contingency, and handed to the Dalai a list showing the presents that I was now giving to him, and those that I would give afterwards. Then I handed him a letter from the Viceroy, standing up to give it, and His Holiness stood up to receive it.

He spoke of the residence he had selected for my party and myself. "The Cabinet suggested that you and your staff should be accommodated in the large mansion of Lhalu, where Colonel Younghusband and his staff were acommodated during the war in the Wood Dragon year (1904). But I wish you to be near me, so that you can visit me easily. Besides, a residence in or near the town of Lhasa you would find smelly and dusty, whereas in the park, in which your house lies, you will be troubled by neither smell nor dust, and will be assured of complete privacy. During my stay in Darjeeling I came fully to understand that the British like their houses to be very clean. It was feared that it might be too cold, but I chose it because it is near me and is clean."

After thanking him, I tell him that when I come for my next interview I will deliver the official message from the Government of India (contained in a letter separate from the Viceroy's letter). I have purposely avoided bringing it with me at this interview, because at the first of a series of interviews you should not discuss political matters at all; it is just a visit of ceremony.

Before leaving, I say, "At later visits, bit by bit, I will tell you, Protector of Great Price, what is in my mind regarding the best policy to follow so as to benefit both Tibet and India, but these ideas will be purely my own, and not in any way those of my Government. After returning from Lhasa to Sikkim, I expect to retire very soon, if not immediately, from the service of the Government. Accordingly, my one idea in coming to Lhasa – apart from the pleasure of meeting you again and my Tibetan friends – is to do what I can for the mutual benefit of India and Tibet."

Several times throughout our talk the Dalai Lama said how

glad he was that I had come to Lhasa at last. His whole attitude was one of great relief, and of pleasure at a hope at last fulfilled. When I left, he shook hands in our Western style.

In a letter from Rai Bahadur Norbhu Dhondup, O.B.E., that experienced officer who served in our Political Agency for thirty years, he writes that, in the case of my successors the Dalai Lama sat above them on a raised dais. Norbhu adds that he, or Kushog Ringang, interpreted for my successors. Excellent interpreters they must have been, but it is still better to have none at all.

What a contrast between the Chinese mission to Lhasa of 1919-20, and mine seven months later! During the four and a half months of their stay they had only two interviews with the Dalai Lama. And each member was unceremoniously searched, to make sure that he was not secreting arms on his person. They were kept waiting at the Jewel Park Palace for two hours, while this search was made, and were then conducted into the Precious Sovereign's presence, and conversed through an interpreter.

Soon after I arrived, the Chief Attendant would bring in Tibetan tea for us both. At calls and receptions with Tibetans ordinarily the servant stands behind and refills your cup whenever you drink. But the Dalai Lama wanted us to be alone, and not to waste time. So the Chief Attendant always left after he had filled our cups. I would take two sips, to satisfy the Tibetan standard of politeness, and then neither of us would drink any more; we were both absorbed entirely in our discussions. Thus we were left completely alone together. There was no third-party risk.

Our subsequent conversations ranged over many lands and subjects, even more than in Darjeeling, for by now I knew much more about Tibet, and was in Lhasa, the heart of it all. We usually talked for about an hour.

When I came out of the door there would be nobody within twenty yards of it. And then at the further end of the long verandah was always the group, seated and chatting together. As I walked down the verandah they would rise and give me a friendly smile, as though to say, "Here is one who talks direct to our Dalai Lama, just the two together."

34   The Dalai Lama's Private Life

After leaving the Dalai Lama I called on my old friend the Prime Minister, who worked in another house in the grounds of the Jewel Park. From him also I received an extremely cordial welcome.

I enquired whether the Tibetan Government would have any objection to my wife joining me in Lhasa. So I said in the Tibetan style:

"If the little lady wife comes, would that be suitable?"

So far and no farther, custom prescribes that I should use honorific language regarding my wife. He, of necessity, replies with the full honorific.

"If the honourable divine wife comes, that will be what is good, good" (repeated thus in Tibetan), he replied. "She would promote great friendliness by exchanging visits with the wives of the nobles and other officials."

However, before the weather was warm enough, events had rendered Lhasa dangerous for us Europeans as will appear later. It was unsafe for her to come.

During our conversation the Prime Minister gave me a piece of thoroughly sound advice.

"Lönchen," he said, "I advise you to conduct all your business direct with His Holiness the Dalai Lama; not with the Cabinet, and not even with me. Otherwise all sorts of people will come to know secrets which should be kept from them, and harm will result."

This was the course that I followed. My successors conducted their business with the Cabinet. Such would have to be referred to the Prime Minister, who would pass it on to the Dalai Lama. I was fortunate in being able to deal direct with the Ruler of Tibet, owing to Providence having thrown us together in Darjeeling, and established close friendship between us. Working in this way, secrets were better kept, matters were dealt with promptly, and often settled finally; for the Dalai Lama was an unquestioned autocrat, and one that knew his own mind.

By his choice of the Jewel Park and the manner in which he laid out the grounds, the Dalai Lama showed his desire for privacy and rural surroundings. He did not care for the endless salutations, though dutifully submitting to them. People were still telling the story of the old farmer. The Dalai Lama was riding towards the Sera monastery, and met the farmer, who was the worse for drink, at a bridge. Being hustled by some of the retinue and not recognising the Sovereign of Tibet, the farmer burst out angrily, "You are not the only official in Tibet. I have met many, but none who treated me as badly as this. You might be the Dalai Lama himself, if swagger could make you so." His Holiness thoroughly enjoyed the joke, and told his people to let the man go without injury.

The grounds of the Jewel Park were almost square, each side being about half a mile in length. They had been planted somewhat thickly with trees, mainly willows, but poplars also, including the attractive white poplar. The surrounding wall combined with the trees to keep the house and grounds free from the polluted dust that the strong winds blow down the streets of Lhasa.

But though desiring privacy, the Dalai Lama liked to see things going on. During my year in Lhasa he had a house built in English style on the outskirts of the grounds, and kept very clean, as were all his houses and rooms. It was known as "Clear Eye Palace." He used to do a good deal of his work in this house; but being near the boundary, it had a clear view. So he would stop work occasionally and take a telescope or field-glasses – from among the many presents that people were constantly giving him – the better to watch the traffic pass down the road and the daily round in the fields outside.

Inside the Jewel Park is a second square enclosure, surrounded by loftier walls, twelve feet high, and some two hundred yards long on each side. It is forbidden ground to everybody, except for one or two intimate attendants. Nobody, not even members of the Cabinet, or the Prime Minister himself, is allowed to enter. My second visit to the Dalai Lama was on the morning of November 30th, and I received his permission to go over this forbidden enclosure the same afternoon. When I came near to it, and was visiting one of the members of the Cabinet in the outer grounds, a messenger came to tell me that His Holiness wished himself to show me round. Meanwhile the Peak Secretary and Achuk Tsering and I waited in the enclosure reserved for the higher monk officials – servants are not allowed to enter the Jewel Park – till His Holiness was ready. We were accompanied here by two of his "room stoppers," tall, strongly-built monks who guard doorways.

The Dalai Lama met me at the entrance to his conservatory. In and just outside the conservatory there were many flowers in bloom, including pansies, petunias, asters, geraniums, marigolds, nasturtiums ("the rope flower"), chrysanthemums, phlox, stocks and a few roses. It was a fine show of colour for the last day of November, but the high walls concentrated on the plants the strength of the sun, which in Lhasa is powerful, being only thirty degrees north of the equator. A number of his flowers, however, were poor, probably from being grown from his own seed. So I procured fresh seed for him from Calcutta, twenty-five varieties, and the same from England, and they turned out well. He was especially fond of sweet peas, hydrangeas, hollyhocks, marigolds, zinnias, petunias, chrysanthemums, pansies and stocks. He loved the scent of the stocks. Most Tibetans are fond of flowers; with the Dalai Lama this characteristic was strongly marked.

A large part of the scanty leisure of the Precious Sovereign is spent in his gardens; and as he sows and plants with his own hands, the gardeners are stirred to greater efforts. But they are ignorant, and consequently I advise him that two lads should be sent to the Residency grounds in Gangtok to be trained by my head gardener there. Later on, he agrees to this, and asks that the lads may join my party when I leave. This is done.

There are walnut, apple and other fruit trees, besides willows. Under the trees, which are planted thickly, a few animals are tied up. I notice two barking deer and a musk deer; also a male burrhel, one of the smaller variety of wild sheep with spreading horns. One cage holds a leopard, another a Bengal tiger with a magnificent coat, due to the cold of the Tibetan winter.

In a corner of the garden are half a dozen big brown monkeys from the province of Kongpo, seven days' journey east of Lhasa; these are fierce. Also a couple from India; these are milder. In one cage are three porcupines; in another the large Tibetan snowcock with some Chinese pheasants. All the animals and birds, whether in cages or not, are well cared for.

Large Tibetan dogs – used for herding yaks and for guarding houses and tents – with their long black hair, and collars of thick hanging wool, dyed a dull red, and chained up here and there. Incessantly they tug at their chains, as they try to spring on you, and bark with the deep, low note which Tibetans tell you should be like the sound of a well-made copper gong.

The Dalai Lama is fond of this breed. To be able to give such a dog to him people will pay a great sum of money, the earnings of several months. One of these dogs in the enclosure is a particularly fine specimen; it comes, as the Dalai informs me, from his own district, Takpo. He is proud of that dog, but indeed he is fond of all animals, especially of birds. We walk by the Bengal tiger's cage; it is a large cage, but how flimsy the bars look! Hardly sufficient to confine the king of the jungle.

He likes very large or very small dogs; their novelty and strange ways amuse him. Had he been a Westerner, people would have said "He has a way with animals," but Tibetans, of course, put it higher than that. In their estimation his spiritual influence moves the animal world; for animals also are sentient beings, and are, or should be, on the Path to Buddhahood.

A large artificial lake spreads an atmosphere of peace over the whole. A hundred geese of the bar-headed variety, and different kinds of ducks, float lazily upon it. Built up in the lake on strong stone platforms are a small temple to the nagas, and a pavilion. The Dalai Lama conducts me over each of these. The pavilion consists of an outside verandah-like room with an inner room beyond. In both of these rooms are magnificent specimens of porcelain, jade and cloisonné, and pictures on silk, mostly given to him by the Manchu Emperor or the Manchu Government. In the verandah is a rug laid over a small Tibetan mattress. Beside this is one of the low Tibetan tables, with a jade teacup standing on it, used by His Holiness for drinking the numerous cups of tea that Tibetans drink every day. High up on a stand at his back is a porcelain figure of the mythological lion of Tibet, with his foot on a ball. On his left side a delicately-traced cabinet of lacquer, and at the foot of this, a large vase of Chinese porcelain.

Beyond this again three stone steps lead up to the inner room.

"I often spend the day in this verandah," he tells me; "I go into that inner room only for small receptions. Here I am away by myself, and can work in peace."

He does his religious work, both devotional and administrative, and he does it all conscientiously and efficiently. He has had all the training necessary for it, but it is clear that his interest centres largely on secular affairs.

He loves beautiful surroundings; he loves privacy – to see a good deal, but not to be stared at himself; he loves the open air; and he loves his work.

The interest of this visit is increased by the knowledge that I am the first European to enter the forbidden sanctuary. But subsequent visits during the brief Tibetan spring and summer – sometimes by the permission, and sometimes at the request, of the Dalai Lama – enable me to note how the flowers of England and other temperate lands can flourish twelve thousand feet above the sea. Not that they are called English flowers. All of these, except a few kinds, among which are hollyhocks, marigolds, and asters, long established in Tibet, are known as "Indian flowers," because their seeds are brought up from Calcutta.

Occasionally I am told by Tibetans, "The climate of Lhasa is warmer than it used to be."

"Why is that?"

"Because so many Indian flowers and plants have been brought here."

On May 18th very few of the flowers are out. But at a subsequent visit on July 30th they are in full bloom. There is a fine array of pansies. These are known as "The Threefold Protectors." The light blue represents the Buddha of Compassion (Chenrezig), the purple is the Buddha of Power holding a vajra (Chana Dorje), and the yellow is the Buddha of Wisdom (Jampeyang). These are the three deities whose earthly representatives are the Dalai Lama, the Panchen Lama and the Emperor of China. In Tibet all comes back to religion sooner or later, and sooner rather than later.

In front of the Palace of the Nagas a monk is making a sacrificial offering of barley meal, and is reciting prayers, all for the benefit of the trees and the flowers, for these are under the jurisdiction of the Nagas. In another small building in this Inner Garden a monk sits quitely and happily by himself, working at silk embroidery in many different colours, for the benefit of his monastery.

Our first month in Lhasa was largely occupied in receiving and paying visits, and exchanging lunches, teas and evening dinners with old friends and new. Thus we increased our acquaintance with Tibetans of various kinds. We met some Mongols also, and Gurkhas and Bhutanese, as well as Mahomedans, these last from the Indian State, Kashmir.

At the end of each lunch with a Tibetan I say, "Now we petition for leave to go," the regular Tibetan phrase for goodbye. Then Palhese, in accordance with invariable Tibetan custom, gives our host's servants a present amounting to a few rupees, but in Tibetan copper coins which, being depreciated in value, fill his hand and seem a large amount. This is always done in the presence of our host, who stands and looks on unconcernedly.

We also visited many monasteries, small and large, one of them being the largest monastery in the world. We visited various temples, the Dalai Lama's great Potala Palace, and other places of absorbing interest in this hidden and unique capital in the heart of Asia. The great Temple, named "Crown Hand Foot," and the Potala, I visited several times.

Apart from these more formal visits, we had time also for quiet rides and walks, observing the country and people, and talking with all and sundry. By reason of my friendship with the Dalai Lama and many others, all were willing to converse. The Tibetan is fond of talking, when he knows you or hears well of you, and so I learned the views of Lhasa and Tashi Lhünpo, of monks and laymen, of civil and military, of official, merchant and peasant. Speaking Tibetan is often hampered by the differences of dialect in this mountain land, where railways and motor-cars are not, no carriage nor cart, nor wheeled conveyance of any kind whatever, so that communication between one part and another is slow indeed. As the proverb has it:

> Every district its own dialect;
> Every monk his own sect.

However, I had always spoken the dialect of Lhasa, which is regarded as the most correct form of Tibetan speech. Almost all people, with even the smallest education, can understand it sufficiently, at any rate when you meet them in Lhasa or the neighbouring districts. All wish to understand it; you are not in the swim unless you do.

One afternoon, strolling along the river bank, I met nobody until I suddenly came on the Dalai Lama, walking also and accompanied by only one attendant, who walked a few paces behind him. His Holiness was attired in very simple robes, and carried an English umbrella, though there was no possiblility of rain. He gave me a welcoming smile, but I took care not to interrupt him; he needs greatly his times of leisure, for his work is almost overpowering. When I returned home, I told my servants:

"I have been walking by the river. I met the Protector of Great Price, and nobody else did I see the whole time."

"Word was sent round that His Holiness would walk there

this afternoon, so of course everybody was careful to keep away."

How quietly, but efficiently, orders are conveyed among his subjects! But when religious festivals require him to reside within the town of Lhasa – as happens during the Great Prayer Festival, which takes place in February and March – he can have no privacy outside his residence.

On my way back I pass a dozen Mongolian camels, which have been presented to the Dalai Lama by one of his Mongolian disciples. Their double humps are well covered, as are the whole of their bodies, with winter's thick growth of hair. During the day they graze along the dry bed of the river; at night they are kept within the ample grounds of the Jewel Park. Among them is the camel which the Dalai Lama rode in 1909 on his way back to Lhasa from the north. It is named "The Spirit of Abundance."

Numerous are the animals which are thus given to His Holiness. When too many, the excess is handed over to this nobleman or that. They usually do not want them, but have to provide a home for them with as good a grace as possible. Later on, when visiting the mansion of one of the leading nobles, I stroll over to the "pleasure house," a cottage in the park. There is a box in the verandah, and in the box a pair of guinea pigs.

"Where did these come from?"

With a wry but good-humoured smile comes the reply, "They belong to the Inmost One. He does not want them, and has told us to look after them."

The bystanders laugh heartily.

35   Recall from Lhasa Postponed

Four hundred ponies and mules belonging to the Dalai Lama found stabling in the Jewel Park; some fifty-five more in the village at the foot of the Potala. Among them were some magnificent mules from north China. One of these he had given to me several years previously, a black mule, with white round the fetlocks, and 14.2 hands in height. Mules, at any rate in India, have a reputation for being vicious, but I have never had anything to do with a more gentle and tractable animal than this riding mule. My wife usually rode it. Riding up the steep mountain tracks of Sikkim, the only possible pace was a walk, and its walk was faster than that of almost any pony. A few years later when it died, the Dalai Lama sent me another, equally handsome and well-mannered.

He himself, especially during his latter years, was fond of one of the smaller breeds, that which comes from the province of Kongpo, a week's journey to the east of Lhasa. A great many Tibetans like this small Kongpo variety of mule, because they are very clever on the rough Tibetan tracks, and really more manageable there than an animal which is over fourteen hands high. When riding, the Dalai Lama went usually at a slow amble. This amble, slow or fast, is a kind of run, and is the pace preferred by all Tibetans. A Tibetan never trots; he thinks it a most ridiculous pace; men, women and children find it difficult to avoid laughing when they see Europeans proceeding in this manner. And in fact they are wise not to trot, for their animals are mostly under thirteen hands, and trotting is therefore slow and uncomfortable. The Mongol, whom he resembles in so many respects, is fond of galloping, but not so the Tibetan; nor does he usually go at a walking pace, except in difficult country. Ambling, as he does, he travels at the rate of about six miles an hour, and neither he nor the pony tires. Twenty to twenty-five miles a day is a normal march, for the accompanying transport moves more slowly. But the Dalai Lama was not in the habit of travelling so far in a day's journey.

We ride sometimes round the marsh on the plain on which Lhasa lies. It is about ten miles round and goes close up to the Potala. A large amount of marsh grass is cut from it, and is reserved for the ponies and mules in the Dalai Lama's stables. It looks unappetising, and I am told that it does not agree with the animals at first, but when they become accustomed to it, they thrive on it, as it has strength-giving qualities.

In earlier chapters I have given examples showing how the honorific branch of the language is used. This honorific language is carried very far. Though we must call the gentleman's horse *chipa*, we do not have to go so far as to give the honorific word for the horse's tongue; but in the case of the Dalai Lama or the Panchen Lama we must indeed refer to the honourable horse's honourable tongue (*ja*). As a matter of fact, to the Dalai Lama and the Panchen Lama are accorded other honorific terms that are not extended to anybody else.

A few days after my first call on the Dalai Lama I paid my official visit. At this I explained the instructions I had received from the Government of India. These were to give His Holiness friendly greetings from the British Government, and to explain the present political position, which was far from good. I do not wish to burden this book to an unnecessary extent with the complications of Tibetan politics; any who wish to understand this subject will find it referred to fully in my *Tibet Past and Present*.[18] Suffice it is to say here that the British Government and the Government of India had often protested their friendship for Tibet and their desire to help her against Chinese domination. It seemed to me that they were not doing enough. So much so, that some time after I had retired from Government service, the Dalai Lama had admitted – as already related – a

Chinese mission to Lhasa, and was considering the possibility of obtaining Japanese rifles, machine-guns, etc., as the British Government refused to allow munitions to go to Tibet through India. This would have meant in the long run not only control by China or Japan of Tibet herself, but also their strong influence over the States and tribes that constitute the bulwark of India's mountain frontier in the north-east, north, and part of the north-west; that is to say, a distance of two thousand miles from the tribes north of Assam to far Ladakh in the State of Kashmir.

When the governmental instructions had been suitably conveyed, we discussed various matters, among others the question of an expedition to climb Mount Everest.

Three or four months before I came to Lhasa, the Royal Geographical Society and the Alpine Club had asked our Government to use their best offices to obtain from the Tibetan Government permission for this. Everest being the highest mountain in the world, the wish was a natural one. The mountain lies partly in Tibet and partly in Nepal. Nepal, though our ally, had refused permission. Tibet was not our ally; indeed a few years before, out troops had invaded her territory and occupied her Holy City. These two countries, Tibet and Nepal, equally fear the exploration of the Europeans, lest it lead ultimately to the curtailment, or even the loss, of their independence.

When the Government of India asked me for my opinion on this subject, I felt sure that, if I wrote to the Tibetan Government about it, they would grant the permission to climb the mountain, for I cannot remember the Dalai Lama ever refusing me anything that I asked him. But even if permission were granted, there could be no doubt that the scheme would give cause to a deep-rooted suspicion in the Tibetan mind. One cannot explain things fully in letters; the Tibetans would not understand the plea of geographical or scientific knowledge, and would unfailingly suspect that something sinister lay behind this new proposal.

Now Mount Everest is not sacred to the extent that many

mountains in Tibet are sacred, such as Kailas in western Tibet, or Tsari, near the Tibet-Bhutan frontier. But a mountain with permanent snow on it has always an added sanctity, because the permanent snow is looked on as something old, and age is always respected in Tibet. Besides, every place in Tibet, from north to south and from east to west, has its own spirit of the district. An expedition of foreigners, who did not believe in Tibetan spirits and stood outside the Buddhist brotherhood, would of necessity disturb the spirits of the place. I therefore recommended that the Tibetan Government should not be asked for permission. The Government of India and the Home Government agreed with my views.

But when I was coming to Lhasa, the Government of India re-opened the matter, leaving it to my discretion whether I would ask for permission or not. I felt that now I could explain to the Dalai Lama the ins and outs of the question. Conversation removes many misunderstandings. I explained to him that the ascent was expected to have scientific results which would benefit humanity, and that a good many people in Britain wanted Britons to be the first to climb the highest mountain in the world. I knew, I said, that Tibetans might well be suspicious about expeditions of this kind, as they would not understand the scientific reasons which prompted it, but, as far as I could see, no harm to Tibet was likely to result from it, and His Holiness knew me well enough to realise that I would not say this unless I really meant it, and that during my long service on this frontier I had always worked, as far as I could, for the welfare of Tibet.

I showed His Holiness Mount Everest on the map, and left the map with him. Subsequently Achuk Tsering discussed the map in detail with the Dalai Lama's Chief Secretary.

At a subsequent interview, seven days later, the Dalai Lama received me in his conservatory in the Inner Enclosure at the Jewel Park. But meanwhile a hitch had arisen. When I had been only three weeks in Lhasa the Government of India ordered me to come away again.

Now that I had come to their capital, the Tibetans were hoping that we would give them some substantial help against

Chinese aggression on Tibet. They admitted no Chinese sovereignty or overlordship of any kind. "China," they said, "can show no treaty or other document proving that Tibet is under China." The Dalai Lama and his Government expected that when I was here in their capital, the political relations between Tibet and Britain would be examined thoroughly. Such examination was bound to take a long time, as the British Government and the Government of India were busy with many problems.

Accordingly, the prospect of my departure had thoroughly alarmed the Tibetan Government. At this interview the Dalai Lama pressed me to stay on in Lhasa. The old Prime Minister came hurrying round to my house. He said he was astounded, and unable to believe the news. "Everybody will say that you are annoyed with us," he said, "or that the British Government has fallen out with the Tibetan Government. I was ill, but your coming here has made my illness much better. We are old friends. While you were away in Sikkim, I used often to look at your photograph, the one that you gave me, praying that you would come to Lhasa. You know the Dalai Lama gave out a prophecy that you would come to Lhasa, and settle out Tibetan difficulties. So when I heard that you were coming I believed that the prophecy was coming true. If you go now," he concluded, "you, my old friend, will be rubbing my face in the dust."

The day following the Prime Minister's call the four members of the Cabinet called, and pressed me to stay on. Shortly afterwards the chief representatives of the Parliament, the monks as well as the laymen, called and urged me very strongly to remain in Lhasa. The Prime Minister and the Cabinet also urged that the Dalai Lama, they themselves, and the Parliament must all consult as regards the reply to be given to the Viceroy's letter, and in that case I should not leave till this reply could be handed to me. Indeed they thought it essential that I should remain for several months longer, until their problems had been eased.

The All Covering Abbot said to a mutual friend, "We will first beg Lönchen Bell with folded hands to stay. If he does not agree to stay, we will throw our arms round his neck to keep him. If he still insists on going, we will hold on to him with our teeth, so that he will have to knock our teeth down our throats before he will be able to get away."

The Government of India ultimately agreed to my remaining in Lhasa until the following April. This postponement put the Tibetan Government at ease. As for myself, I felt at ease also, because I knew that long before April our Minister in Peking would become aware of what I was doing in Lhasa and would approve. I felt also that the Home Government would have time to understand and sympathise with my ideas. And that was just what did happen. In fact, by April everybody seemed to want me to stay on; so much so, that when spring and summer had passed, I had in the end to press for permission to leave. My work was then done, and it was time that the Tibetan Government had the field to themselves again.

Two days after my previous interview with His Holiness I called again. He expressed his unbounded pleasure that I was staying on in Lhasa.

At this interview the Dalai Lama of his own accord brought up the question of the expedition to Mount Everest through Tibetan territory, and told me that he gave his consent. When saying so, he handed me a small, unsigned strip of Tibetan paper containing the following words, "To the west of the Five Treasuries of Great Snow Mount (Kangchen Dzönga) in the jurisdiction of White Glass Fort (Shekar Dzong) near Inner Rocky Valley (Dza Rong Buk) monastery is the district called 'The Southern Country, where Birds are Kept' (Lho Chamalung)." This strip of paper was apparently a note made by one of his staff, giving the name of the district in which the mountain was situated, and other details. To His Holiness and staff, as to other Tibetans, the British name "Everest" was unknown.

A conversation some months later with that alert and widely-read man, the Peak Secretary, happened to turn on the mountain and the country surrounding it. He told me that the Tibetan name for the mountain was Kang Chamalung, adding that Chamalung is short for Cha Dzima Lungpa. (It is the usual practice in Tibetan to shorten names in this way.) Kang means "Snow Mountain"; Cha means "Bird"; Dzima means "taken care of"; Lungpa means "Country." Thus the name at length means "The Snow Mountain in the Country where Birds are taken care of." Or "The Snow Mountain of the Bird Sanctuary." The word Chamalung is sometimes used by itself as the name for the mountain. The Peak Secretary told me that an old and well-known book, the *Mani Kabum,* records that in the times of the kings of Tibet, during the seventh and eighth centuries of the Christian era, a large number of birds were fed in this district at the expense of the king. The people will sometimes tell you that in the good old days – yes, in Tibet, as elsewhere, we hear of those good old days – the people were so prosperous that none would accept alms, and charity was mainly devoted to the feeding of birds.

Shortly afterwards I received from the Tibetan Government a passport in official form, which granted permission for the climbing of Mount Everest. This was a marked instance of the friendliness of the Tibetan Government towards the enemy of sixteen years earlier, for it was a great change from their former policy of discouraging all explorations. Tibet, the old enemy, granted what Nepal, the unswerving ally, would not grant.

During the last three weeks or so the Parliament have been debating on the reply that they will give to the letter from the Viceroy of India to the Dalai Lama; both the Dalai Lama and they will send replies; such is the Tibetan custom. The Dalai Lama sends "Wisdom," the Peak Secretary, and Palhese to me to ask my opinion as to how these communications shall be delivered to me, for in the Tibetan mind etiquette is of the first importance. His Holiness suggests that they shall follow the same procedure as they used to do when delivering communications to the Chinese High Commissioner in Lhasa, a suggestion to which I readily agree. He considers that this procedure is suitable, and that it will act as a restraint on Chinese aggression, for it will certainly come to the ears of the Chinese Government. And, later on, the signs prove him to be right.

Two days afterwards the Dalai Lama's reply is brought by one of the Grand Secretaries, a hard-featured man and capable, accompanied by the Dalai Lama's Chief Secretary. As soon as they leave, a deputation from the Parliament brings the latter's reply. This deputation is composed of three Grand Secretaries who are monks, two Financial Secretaries who are laymen, as well as an Abbot each from Drepung and Sera monasteries. From Ganden, the other member of the "Three Seats," comes a lesser representative, for Ganden is more than an ordinary day's march distant.

The representative of Nepal in Lhasa is uneasy at my coming to Lhasa. "Why is the British agent here?" he wants to know. The Prime Minister says that the officer in charge of the Nepalese escort calls on him and remarks, "I suppose Lönchen Bell is discussing matters of importance with you?" The Premier gives a non-committal reply. Some months later Kennedy lunches with the Premier and in accordance with Tibetan custom remains for several hours discussing various topics. Before he leaves, his host says, "Many people will pester me with questions as to what we have talked about today. I shall tell them that we have talked about two matters, namely, the wonderful improvement in Lönchen Bell's health since he came to Lhasa, and your prescriptions for my own health." The Prime Minister enjoyed a joke.

36 Increase the Army?

Soon after I reached Lhasa I decided to give to the Great Temple, as one of the presents from the Government of India, a butter lamp, such as Tibetans place on the altars of their temples and chapels. The wick of this floats in butter, and burns until the butter is consumed. I decided to give one made of gold.

The Dalai Lama heard of my intention and arranged for one of his best goldsmiths, of whom a large number were always in his employ, to make it for me. I was accordingly able to give a larger and better one, for the money I had set aside for it all went into the material; and I had nothing to pay for the manufacture. Its weight was that of fifty-six and three-quarter rupees (twenty-three ounces), and this fact was duly recorded on the lamp. Whenever I visited the Temple – sometimes on the spur of the moment when I happened to come near it – the lamp was always burning in the Holy of Holies on the altar in front of the image of Buddha, brought by the Chinese princess more than a thousand years ago, the most sacred image in Tibet.

During one of my visits to the Temple in Lhasa, among other sights, I saw in a central courtyard eleven sheep. Kind people had bought them from those about to kill them, and offered them to the great image of Buddha in the Temple. They were then sent to the Jewel Park and the Dalai Lama made them over to attendants, who saw that they were treated well and allowed to live out their full lives. Another custom is to take the animal, usually a sheep, round the Park Circle. It is then kept in comfort for the remainder of its life.

During December Achuk Tsering died suddenly from a heart

attack, brought on by influenza contracted in the deadly epidemic which we encountered at Pari, on our way up to Lhasa. This was a very great loss to me, at the outset of my work, and a sad blow to all of us to lose so good a friend. Being a follower of the Tibetan Buddhist religion, his brother clerks and others who were of the same religion, made a petition to the Dalai Lama to help him in obtaining a good rebirth, and the Dalai Lama gave a favourable reply.

It was about this time that Mr. David Macdonald paid a short visit to Lhasa. Often and often he had begged me to let him join me in Lhasa, if ever I went there; and now that I had come he renewed his entreaties. He had helped the Dalai Lama greatly on the latter's flight to India, and there was consequently friendship between them. His father Scottish, his mother of a race akin to the Tibetans, and himself endowed with a patient and kindly temperament, he never failed to get on well with Tibetans. He found our house much colder than his quarters in the fort at Gyangtse, and his servant, a hardy Tibetan, said that he would die if he stopped another night in it, and wanted to lodge in another house further from the river. However, both stayed on without ill effects.

In spite of the cold, life had its compensations, small as well as large. We heard of some bacon stored in the Supply and Transport Department of the military authorities at Gyangtse. It had been condemned as unfit for human consumption, but we found it excellent. Having been condemned, it was being sold at one-third of the authorised price.

Lhasa is not a purely Tibetan city. Here are Mongols from the borders of Siberia and from Siberia itself, Chinese from many provinces of China, men from Nepal and Kashmir, men from Chinese Turkistan, as well as Tibetans from outlying parts of Tibet, that one hardly ever sees in Sikkim or Darjeeling.

Riding round the marsh on the Lhasa plain, a ten-mile circuit, we saw a number of lammergeier under the high hills. Golden eagles abounded, also ravens and magpies and flocks of sparrows. In this land of live and let live the golden eagle sometimes came quite near. I remember one on the way to Lhasa that took up a position nearby, interested in my lunch. But with only a few sandwiches and a slab of chocolate, I left nothing for the poor bird.

During my many talks with the Dalai Lama we discussed everything that seemed to us likely to affect Tibet. One of his main preoccupations was how to protect his country from Chinese invasion and Chinese domination. He had suffered from both in the past, and was determined to prevent them in future, so far as lay in his power.

When I came to Lhasa there were about six thousand soldiers in the so-called regular army, scattered throughout Tibet. These men were indeed hardy, accustomed to travel, and to live for many days on a small bag of barley, carried on their backs. But they had received no military training worth the name. Their rifles and ammunition were poor, having been mostly manufactured in primitive workshops a few miles outside Lhasa, where an Indian was in charge. They had received a consignment of fairly modern British rifles a few years before, but these had been badly kept. They had no artillery. And of course it must always be borne in mind that Buddhism, with its prohibition against taking life, makes the work of a soldier difficult.

Shortly before I came to Lhasa, Tsarong Shap-pe had proposed an increase in the army, but his proposals had not been acted on. Having risen from a family of low social position, he was regarded with jealousy by the nobility and gentry. As Commander-in-Chief, his forceful personality roused the hostility of the powerful monasteries, for they suspected, naturally enough, that the army would in time lessen their own power.

I was not aware of Tsarong's proposals, but during one of my early conversations with the Dalai Lama, in which he is discussing the danger of Chinese invasion, I point out that six thousand men, untrained and ill-equipped, have very little chance of protecting his country from a Chinese attack. I make it clear that my ideas are simply my own, and not in any respect the instructions of my Government. It seems to me that he should increase the army gradually to about fifteen thousand men, which indeed is itself a small number, but Tibet, with its straitened finances, cannot at present afford more. We may expect that difficulties of terrain in such a mountainous land will help a great deal. The army would be one purely for self-defence, against China as far as may be, and also against Nepal.

The Dalai Lama puts before the Parliament the suggestion I had made, not the full Parliament, but the committee of higher members, that is to say those who may be expected to have some knowledge of foreign affairs. They are to discuss my suggestion and report their opinion to him through the Cabinet and the Prime Minister.

Meanwhile I come soon to understand the opinion of the people regarding my remarks. Tsarong, the head of the army, and his subordinates, are pleased, as is natural. But what is surprising is that the Gurkha representative, the unfriendly neighbour to the south, holds the view that the Tibetan Government should aim at increasing their army to thirty thousand men; and that they should send officers to India for training, as if British, Indian or Gurkha officers are sent to Tibet to train them, China may object.

But the general reaction of the people is one of strong opposition, especially among the monasteries. One of the leaders in the opposition is a monk from Sera Monastery, named Chamön, whom fortunately I met two years earlier when he was with the Dalai Lama in Darjeeling. "This proposal to increase the Tibetan army," he tells me, "is strongly disliked by the monks, who feel that it is against the Buddhist religion." I put the point of view that unless the increase is made, an outside nation, e.g. China, may invade the country and injure the religion, as she did before, when the Chinese High Commissioner in Lhasa tried to reduce the number of monks and turn them into soldiers. He urges that Britain should protect Tibet, because she is "an intermediary and witness" (*parpang*) in the treaties between China and Tibet. He thinks that to this end Britain should be prepared to send soldiers, in any case to protect Lhasa. He adds that if the Chinese attack Tibet, every monk and layman will fight to the last. It is useless to remind him that during their recent occupation twenty Chinese soldiers, armed with modern weapons, kept at bay the six thousand monks in his monastery.

Many Tibetans know that Tibet is useful as a barrier to India.

They claim that the Tibetan Government will keep Russians, Chinese, etc., out of their country, if they are assured of protection. Therefore they consider that they have a claim to British protection. Some simply say, "What is the good of making friends with the British if we have got to raise an army and fight the Chinese?" Such are the views that govern the minds of the monks, and, through them, of the uneducated laymen. Chamön, who carries great influence in his own monastery, has told his colleagues, "It is of no use increasing the army in Tibet, for it is written in 'the books' that Tibet will be conquered by foreigners from time to time, but they will not stay long." As recent proofs of this he mentions the British, who went away again after the Younghusband expedition, and the Chinese troops who were driven out of Tibet in 1912.

Asking Ngarpö Shap-pe what would be his reply to such an argument, he says, "No doubt there is an appointed time for everything. The years of a man's life may be fixed at sixty. But if he does not take medicine when ill, he will die before the appointed time."

Among the mass of the people strong rumours abound to the effect that Lhasa and the neighbouring districts are going to be combed to raise the new soldiers; and that the estates of the landed proprietors, and even those of the monasteries, will be taxed to help in providing the cost. Mr. Macdonald is leaving Lhasa at this time, and will have an interview with His Holiness before he leaves. Through him I send word to the Dalai Lama that if he decides to adopt this, my opinion about increasing the army, he should arrange to increase it gradually, say five hundred to one thousand men each year; and that the soldiers should be recruited from outlying districts rather than from the vicinity of Lhasa, because Lhasa is always a centre of excitement; that I doubt the desirabilty of taxing the lands of the landed proprietors, unless lightly, at this stage, and that I think it is altogether undesirable to tax the monastic lands. I ask Mr. Macdonald to remind His Holiness once again that my opinions are purely my own, and do not emanate from the British Government. The Dalai Lama returns word to me through Mr.

Macdonald that he agrees with all my suggestions. He says also that he wishes to see me in three or four days' time, after he has received the report from the Cabinet, in order that he may ascertain my views upon the report.

On the 25th January, 1921, I make this visit to the Dalai Lama. He tells me that the Parliament have completed their debate on the raising of soldiers. It appears that they propose that five or six hundred shall be recruited yearly until eleven thousand more are raised, bringing the total to seventeen thousand altogether; and that the monastic estates, and the estates of the nobility, shall be taxed to provide for the pay of the soldiers. These proposals of the Parliament cause alarm among the people, who fear that not only will taxes be increased, but that monks will be recruited as soldiers, and the religion thus dishonoured.

I repeat to the Dalai Lama the suggestions that I asked Mr. Macdonald to convey to him a few days ago. I suggest that the people should be definitely assured that the monks will not be recruited as soldiers.

The Dalai Lama says that he agrees with me, and in due course will let me know his decision on the whole case. "I shall think it over quietly," he says; "it is necessary to put through this scheme in a gentle manner."

The scheme is finally adopted by the Dalai Lama. Five hundred to a thousand men are to be recruited yearly. No monks will be permitted to join as soldiers.

It had seemed advisable to record the above discussions in some detail, for on the increase and improvement of her army depends Tibet's only hope of maintaining her independence against Chinese aggression.

The payment and equipment of this little army is for various reasons a matter of difficulty. One reason is that the British Government has constantly prohibited Tibet from importing munitions from India. At this time also an Arms Convention is in force, which still further prevents such importation. Accordingly the Tibetan Government, thus denied and denied, has in despair arranged to import Japanese rifles and machine-guns from distant Mongolia. Eventually I am able to persuade the British Government to allow a moderate import from India. Otherwise Tibet will be at the mercy of China, and must turn from Britain to Japan, for Britain, while professing friendship, seems almost always to refuse assistance.

Another difficulty, which lies with Tibet herself, is the obtaining of efficient officers for her army. The nobility and gentry in this country do indeed often fail to make efficient civil officers, but it is still more difficult to make good military officers out of them. The nobility look on military service as a degradation.

There are many signs of this feeling; here is just one. A lad of sixteen years old, was one of two Tibetan officers who were appointed by the Tibetan Government some time ago to train with fifty Tibetan soldiers, under the British military officer at Gyangtse. This lad belongs to the old noble family of Long Stone; his father and mother have left their beloved Lhasa for the first time for over twenty years, and come to one of their country seats, three miles out of Gyangtse, in order to be near their son. My wife and I were in Gyangtse at that time.

The parents tell me how cast-down they are by their son being made a military officer. They call on me and tell me of their woes. "For untold generations we of the house of Long Stone have always been officials in the civil service; it is a blow to us that our son, our only son, has been made a military officer." I point out how throughout Europe and other lands the military profession ranks second to none in honour, how healthy the outdoor life of an army officer is, and how Tibet, being on the whole a peaceful country, the casualties from warfare are but few; and I ask his mother not to be anxious. "But I am very anxious," she replies. And when I leave the room presently to arrange my camera for taking a colour plate of our guests, both Long Stone and his wife beseech my wife to urge me to write to the Dalai Lama that their son may be transferred to civil employ. This feeling of degradation is very strong.

However, the Dalai Lama was always quick to grasp the essential needs of his country. Accordingly he determined to put the plan through, in spite of the strong opposition it entailed and the other difficulties that lay in the way. Thanks to his strong will, the plan proved one of the chief methods – perhaps the chief method – by which he was able to preserve the independence of his country.

37　Casting Out the Evil of the Old Year

Meanwhile the Dalai Lama was busy with many other matters, especially as the festival of the Great Prayer was approaching. He would sometimes find a slight recreation in watching me skate on a backwater of the "Middle River" (Kyi Chu), using a telescope for the purpose. As my skates had lain by and not been sharpened for over twenty years, my skating on the rough Tibetan ice, scarred with dust, and sometimes in ridges and hollows from the force of the wind, may well have caused him some amusement.

The Great Prayer Festival is the largest and most important of the many religious festivals that take place in Lhasa throughout the year. The Precious Sovereign must now leave his comfortable home in the Jewel Park, and live for a time in the historic Potala. The entry is made in state. The bodyguard and the Lhasa troops line the foot of the Potala hill, all in serviceable khaki serge and equally serviceable fur hats to keep out the February gales. A small contingent of Gurkha troops is drawn up in honour of the Dalai Lama. The caretakers of the houses of the nobility are grouped at the foot of the hill, clad in their long, red cloaks. A little further away stand the ladies from the leading families of Lhasa, in their gorgeous silk robes of different colours, aprons with many-coloured stripes, and head-dresses sewn with corals, turquoises and seed pearls. They wear top-boots of various hues. Countless ornaments, too, including square charm boxes of gold or silver, whose contents are guaranteed to ward off illness and accident.

Parties of townsmen and villagers occupy the lower slopes of the hill and the mile-long route between this and the Jewel Park. Monks from the Muru and Shide monasteries hold up the sacred "Banners of Victory" on iron rods ten feet high. All is now in readiness for the solemn event.

But just before the procession appears, a caravan of little Tibetan donkeys, carrying their wares to Lhasa, plods patiently along the road. Nobody resents their appearance at this supreme moment, or seems to think that they may interfere with the cavalcade that is to follow. One is reminded of the appearance of the solitary Indian sweeper who appeared at the great Delhi Durbar in 1911 to sweep the royal track, dressed in his every-day clothes and holding his every-day broom, when all were in uniform or their finest attire, prepared for the arrival of the King-Emperor and his Consort.

Waiting on a convenient ridge overhanging the road, we see smoke rising from the stone-built incense-burners by the road-side. That means that the Dalai Lama is starting. Servants of officers, clad in their best robes and wearing the handsome "Mongolian hat," shaped somewhat like a tam o' shanter with red silk threads radiating over it, come clattering down the road. Then parties of minor officials in gorgeous costumes of all colours, which glisten under the clear Tibetan sky. And at last a slow, dignified, procession half a mile long, and in the middle of it the sedan-chair of the sacred yellow colour, in which the Inmost One is carried. The spectators bow their heads and turn their eyes towards the ground. Even in the crowd he is secluded.

In front of him ride the four Members of the Cabinet. The Lord Chamberlain and the Dalai Lama's own nephew, a lad of eighteen, are in attendance on the Chair of State, and two soldiers with drawn swords are immediately in front. And so the solitary figure in the Chair passes slowly by, looking out wistfully on the ceremony for which he has but little liking, though patience and training, combined with all-powerful custom, enable him to go through with it.

Immediately behind the Chair, which is borne by sixteen carriers, rides the bowed and dignified Prime Minister. Most of the ecclesiastical officers ride in front of the Chair; most of the lay officers behind it. All have special uniforms for the occasion, made up of costly silks from China, and all harmonise, except perhaps the yellow coats and breeches of the high military officers, which seem to strike a jarring note. But there is no doubt as to the workmanlike appearance of the rank and file of the troops. The sacred yellow umbrella over the Chair is turned round and round the whole time, and close to it is the Peacock Umbrella, presented to the present Dalai Lama by the former Manchu Emperor.

The procession passes to the left of the *chöten* that forms the ordinary entrance to Lhasa, and round the northern face of the Potala. Here the crowds are larger and all sections of the people are represented, monks, nuns and beggars, peasants and tanned shepherds in their homely sheepskins, country dancers, strolling players, and all the rest.

As far as I know – with the possible exception of Manning, over a hundred years ago – we are the first Britons to see either the Sacred Dagger of the Sera monastery, which we saw this morning, or the State Entry this afternoon. The latter was certainly a brilliant and typical Tibetan ceremony.

One noticeable reform which the Dalai Lama made on the religious side of his work was the restoration of old theological ceremonies that had been curtailed or slurred over during the preceding two hundred years. His secretary used to point out these bits, as I witnessed one festival after another in Lhasa. The Dalai Lama believed in pageantry; it was good for the religion, for the country, for himself. Kennedy told him that it appealed very much to us British. At this he showed pleasure, as he always seemed to do, when he discovered resemblances between the British and his own race.

Two days after he comes to Lhasa from the Jewel Park, His Holiness presides over the great monastic dance at the Potala, held to cast out the evil of the old year, so that the new year may start fresh and clean. It is known in Tibetan as "the sacrificial offering of the twenty-ninth," represented in Tibetan by two short syllables, *Gutor.* Being the twenty-ninth day of the twelfth month, it is the second last day of the old year.

We of the mission attend it, and are accommodated in a room with a balcony, overlooking the great courtyard in which the dance takes place. Opposite us is the high building, with the Dalai Lama on the top floor, screened by a yellow curtain and grille. On the floor immediately below him are the Cabinet Ministers, and to the right of them, with a separate room and balcony, is seated the Prime Minister.

In our European and American theatres the wealthier class are on the floor near the spectacle; the poorest high up in the gallery with a far inferior view. Here the Dalai Lama is at the top, farther from the spectacle than the gallery in the highest theatre. But none may sit or stand over the head of the Precious Sovereign, and those next in rank to him must be on the next floor below.

Before the dance commences, scenes are enacted by the old-time soldiers of Tibet, the braves of King Gesar's time, with their chain armour and flint-lock guns. This is in the period before Buddhism came to Tibet. Drawn up in two lines, one is represented as engaging the other in mortal combat, exchanging the taunts and replies that are found in the Gesar Saga as well as in the Iliad of Homer.

Then follows the "Spear Play" (*Dungtse*) of the same warriors. Fresh combats take place. And so we are shown the first period of Tibetan history, the time of fighting Gesar, the time of the Warrior Kings, these latter being known as "The Three Religious Kings, Men of Power."

Round the actors in these two scenes are drawn up, in a circle round the courtyard, others dressed as soldiers of the same period. The soldiers' parts, both actors and chorus, are taken by laymen of Lhasa and the neighbourhood, for it would not be fitting for monks to take such parts. These laymen are known as "little soldiers." Each is rewarded at the end of this part of the performance with a measure of barley-flour, which they receive for the most part in little skin bags. An official distributes this in a corner of the courtyard.

The scene now changes. From the lowest floor of the high building in which the Dalai Lama and his Ministers are seated there issue seven figures. In the centre is one of gigantic size with still more gigantic mask over his head. This is the Mongolian, Jinda Hashang, and with stately steps and slow he moves towards the steps leading down to the courtyard. His large body denotes his strength, his large head old age and prosperity. One on each side of him, are his two small children, beyond each of them an Indian Brahman, and at each extreme end a skeleton representing the guardians of the places where dead bodies are cut up and given to the dogs and vultures.

The Mongolian father is the emblem of strength, so often associated with Mongols, and he is also an example of charity, for the word Jinda denotes a layman who supports the monks and nuns with his alms. Before he descends the steps he scatters a handful of barley flour and the sacred *tsampaka* flowers as an oblation to the gods. All descend together into the courtyard and make their obeisance to the Dalai Lama, and perform a solemn dance. Thus it is shown that, after the time of the fighting kings, Mongolians and Indian priests entered the land, the next main period of Tibetan history. The actors in this and subseqent acts are monks, as befits the religious scenes enacted. They are members of the "All-conquering College," which is housed in the Potala, and supplies the monks in the private service of the Dalai Lama.

It is a pity that Europeans and Americans almost invariably describe this and other monastic dances as "Devil Dances," and so mislead their readers. Out of the numerous dancers that take part in this ceremony not one represents a devil.

Now begins the main portion of the dance, the object of which is to cast out the evil of the old year, while it also symbolises the growth of Buddhism in Tibet.

First a stag and a buffalo descend and dance, then two goddesses. Later on, four grim skeletons, scattering flour over each other, cause merriment in the audience, seated round the outer fringe of the courtyard. These are guardians of the cemeteries, if the term cemetery can be applied to the grounds, where corpses are given to the birds and beasts. The guardians represent Brahmans from India; their duty is to prepare the ground, and to drive out the evil and mischievous spirits, that the dance may go forward without interruption or mishap. As they dance, and the wind becomes stronger, the robes of these and subsequent dancers from time to time become disarranged, but monks in attendance step forward and put these right, and then the play proceeds. The skeletons dance round a picture which has been placed on the ground, representing the Evil of the Community.

After this follow various solemn dances with comic interludes. In one of the latter an old Mongolian is seen lying on a carpet. The street urchins come to steal his fruit. But though old, is he not a Mongolian, and therefore so strong that he can slay a horse or a bull without a weapon in his hand? His name is The Long-Lived Protector. And he belabours the urchins with his stick, so that they flee precipitately, though ever returning to the place when his back is turned.

At length the Black Hat dancers appear. The "Master of the Dance" is in the centre, and all take their steps from him. He, the Chief Magician, is endowed with the power to call up spirits and to command them. He summons the Spirit of *Karma,* and quickens the spirit's action. The Evil of the Community is already there on the ground, awaiting judgment.

Soon afterwards the "Protectors of Religion" enter, including a second gigantic figure, representing Damchen Chögyal, the guardian of Tsongkapa. They have come to help the Chief Magician to bring the Evil One to justice. They frame the charges against him, recounting how he misleads all sentient beings (i.e. animals as well as human beings and gods who are still on the Wheel of Transmigration) and hinders them from obtaining deliverance.

The wind blows high as the dance proceeds, and this is a good omen, for it shows that the powers of evil, angry at their impending destruction, are stirring up all the trouble that they can before they go. We are frozen by the wind, and scarred by the dust; but the omen is good, and so what matter?

At last the executioner, with the head of a stag, descends into the arena. In spite of his heavy, cumbrous clothes and his stag's mask, he dances with quick and tireless steps. Hither and thither he darts to make sure that the demons of evil have all been collected on the picture in the middle. From time to time he settles on the picture, swinging his body rapidly from side to side. He is a manifestation of the Lord of Death.

For the part of Jinda Hashang the biggest monk is taken, and for Damchen Chögyal the next biggest. For the part of the executioner a young monk, aged about seventeen, is chosen, one of superabundant energy.

The powers of evil now collected are represented by a figure on a square of paper, and are thrown into a large cauldron of boiling oil, which has been strongly heated on one side of the courtyard with piles of flaming brushwood, collected for the purpose. The Chief Magician takes also a human skull filled with spirit, and throws the liquor into the oil. The flames rise thirty feet into the air; the crowd clap their hands. This in Tibet does not signify applause, but is done to help in driving out a devil.

The evil is now finally cast out. The Dalai Lama explains later that when the flames and smoke shoot up in one mass, as they did this year, it is a good omen. There will be no war or other great calamity. Sometimes the flames shoot out sideways and injure a number of people; that portends a disaster.

During the ceremony, which lasted from eleven to four, the Dalai Lama sent us cups of tea three times. When we left, we sent him a ceremonial scarf by the Peak Secretary. A most interesting spectacle, the finest monastic dance that I had seen so far during my eighteen years in Tibet and its borderland.

Thus the Tibetan monks cast out the evil of the old year. And one remembers how men and women seek the midnight service on the last day of the old year in Christian churches that they may repent of the sins committed during the old year, and start fresh in the new.

But the play has also its esoteric aspect, and we should understand something of this too, for it goes to the root of the matter, and the secluded figure seated up there in the topmost storey, understands it all. It shows how Hinduism in India paved the way for Buddhism, how the latter triumphed over the old *Bön* beliefs in Tibet, and how it developed from a system of rational ethics into a mystical, soul-satisfying religion of a kind that meets the need of the Tibetan people. It shows also how the Tantric mystic is endowed with the power of accelerating the action of the Forces of *Karma*, by means of which he can utilise even the very passions to help him on his upward progress, and how he may himself be of benefit to sentient beings by assisting them to gain salvation.

Various other meanings have been read into this religious drama, but the above is one that has gained a wide acceptance.

38   The Potala

There is not space in this volume to describe the religious ceremonies or the different buildings and other sights of Lhasa, nor would it be pertinent to do so, except in so far as they concern the Thirteenth Dalai Lama or his Incarnations in his previous lives.

But something must be said about his palace on the top and along the sides of the Potala hill, for it is beyond question one of the most impressive buildings in the world. It rises abruptly from the plain as these little hills so often do in Tibet. Here there are two hills side by side, the Potala Peak which is now covered by the great palace, and the Iron Hill on which the Temple of Medicine stands. Between them is a large *chöten* through which passes the western entrance to the Holy City.

During the seventh century A.D. the first of the great warrior kings of Tibet, named "Straight Strong Deep" (Song Tsen Gampo), made use of Potala Peak, then known as "Red Hill," to build a *dzong* or fort-residence, surrounded by a wall. On the Iron Hill he erected quarters for his queens and the other ladies connected with his court. "After his death," says a Tibetan chronicle,[19] "many people came from China to worship at the tomb, and the troops of China arrived in Tibet, and destroyed these buildings."

It was the Regent of the Fifth Dalai Lama who re-erected the Potala, but on a scale larger than that of King Straight Strong Deep. That was during the seventeenth century. This energetic and capable man, himself a lama named "The Ocean of Buddhahood," was the real ruler for many years during the time of the

Fifth Dalai Lama, who conducted the secular administration for a few years only. Tibetans say the Potala was originally modelled on Shigatse Dzong, then, as now, reckoned the finest of all the *dzongs* that form the headquarters of districts. Shigatse Dzong was also the residence of the king whom the Fifth Dalai Lama superseded. But the Potala soon quitted this model, for it was governed by the shape of its own hill. While it was still being built, the Fifth Dalai Lama died. The Regent concealed his death for nine years, for stones had to be carried and other heavy work to be done, all without payment. The faithful would do this for their Divinity, but for nobody else. Thus the Regent was able to complete the Potala, making use of his master's name. It was over forty years in building.

The unorthodox sixth Dalai Lama, bringing his artistic sense into play, enlarged and enriched it.

Since that time small additions have been made, for after a victorious war it is customary to add to the Potala. For instance, a dispute arose between Nyarong and Derge, two States in eastern Tibet. Nyarong invaded Derge, but Lhasa came to the assistance of the latter, subdued Nyarong, and brought it under Lhasan administration. A building was then added to the Potala. This was in the Tibetan year of the Water Hog, in our style 1863.

The accumulated result is not a mixed jumble of buildings but a magnificent creation in stone. Nine hundred feet in length, it covers the top and much of the sides of the Red Hill. It rises far higher than the dome of St. Paul's Cathedral in London, or the Capitol in Washington; and like some other buildings in Tibet and Bhutan, seems to have grown out of the hill itself, so natural and artistic is its setting.

Every September the huge southern wall, massive and sloping inwards as it rises, receives a fresh coat of whitewash. The central topmost portion is coloured a dark crimson, a sign of added sanctity, for here are the chapels. Here, too, a yak-hair curtain, known as "The Curtain of Heaven," adds to the sense of religious seclusion. Above this central crimson is a margin of maroon, bordered above and below by a narrow strip of white.

This is the universal sign of a religious building in Tibet. Every monastery has it, and every chapel, large or small; just a mass of small branches and twigs very closely packed, pointing their ends at you, and covered with the dye from a shrub that grows plentifully in Sikkim and Bhutan. Near the middle of this maroon margin, making an admirable colour contrast, are four large monograms of embossed gold – two and two with a space between them; and to the right and left a line of smaller ones. Still further above, on the summit, are sheets of gold roofing, covering the pagodas that are set here and there on the flat roof of the huge edifice. Below, in summer, is a sea of green and gold, grass and ripening crops, dark-green poplars and light-green willows. And above the whole the wonderful deep blue of the Tibetan sky. What a magnificent harmony is here!

The Potala dominates Lhasa, and by its bulk and beauty dominates the broad valley for miles around. And on each side are those mountain peaks and ranges, with their clear-cut edges, rising another six thousand feet into the rarefied air.

The Potala is always beautiful; morning, midday or evening, in summer or in winter. During the rainy season in July and August, when the purple light of afternoon fondles its glittering pagoda roofs, the grandeur of the scene leaves one almost breathless. This Potala in the heart of high Asia is not of a kind to be judged by the standards of Europe or America, both so far away and unknown. Indeed, it is not possible to describe it adequately; the architecture has its own baffling magic.

The palace was named Potala after a hill on the southermost tip of India, a hill sacred to the cult of the Buddha of compassion, known in Sanskrit as Avalokiteshvara, and to the Tibetans as Chenrezig, whose chief earthly Incarnation is the Dalai Lama. As already mentioned, Tibetans do not call it Potala, but "Peak Potala" (Tse Potala), or simply "The Peak."

The interior is dirty. That is due in large measure to the countless feet that have trodden its floors, impregnating them with dirt from the city; and due also to the droppings of rancid butter all these years from the sacred lamps on the numerous altars. The dirt and the odours furnish some of the reasons why the late Dalai Lama disliked living in it.

But the interior is undoubtedly of great interest. The chapels and other rooms are innumerable. Three officials have charge of the buildings in the Temple in Lhasa, and three have charge of the chapels in the Potala. But whereas two out of the three in the Temple are secular, the three in the Potala are all monks. In both buildings these officials go round at least every evening, as a precaution against fire and theft, and to see that nothing is amiss.

Among the rooms is one representing the living apartment of the Warrior King, Straight Strong Deep, who built the first Potala. Another is the one which was occupied by the Fifth Dalai Lama. Another contains numerous images most of which came from India many centuries ago. There is also the large hall where, in 1904, Younghusband made his historic treaty with Tibet.

Two of the four treasuries are in the Potala, the *Trede* Treasury, and "The Treasury of the Sons of Heaven." The wealth in them, gold, silver and precious stones, is immense. They have been described in an earlier chapter.

In the Potala is housed the Dalai Lama's personal monastery, known as "The College of Victorious Heaven." It contains one hundred and seventy-five monks, who lead a life less hard than the monks in other monasteries. To it, therefore, flock those sons of the nobility or upper social classes, who become monks, but after a luxurious childhood are unwilling to face the hardships of ordinary monastic life.

The most spectacular section of the interior is along its western side. Here are placed the mausolea of the Dalai Lamas, from the Fifth onwards, except the Sixth, as he did not die in Lhasa. The First is entombed at the great Tashi Lhünpo monastery, which he built and inspired.

The mausolea are shaped somewhat like *chötens*, masonry structures more or less of a conical shape, containing relics of saints, images or other dedicated objects. That of the Fifth is about sixty feet high. All are covered thickly with gold, the framework of many being said to be of solid silver. In them are set corals, turquoises, sapphires, diamonds and other precious stones. On each side of a tomb are placed large and beautiful porcelain vases and cloisonné jars, magnificent specimens of their kind. In another chapel is kept the actual boot of the Fifth Dalai Lama, encased in a thick gold covering.

The mausoleum of the Great Fifth in the Potala was the finest of them all. Every day of the year from sunrise to noon a religious service is held before it by the lama in charge. After midday, it is closed to all.

The Eighth Dalai Lama died about 1804, the year of the Wood Mouse. At the foot of his tomb, among the porcelain and cloisonné pieces, is one of enamel, worked on metal with representations of English people in the dress of between one and two hundred years ago, and with English houses and scenery. It has a Chinese mark on the bottom, and is evidently a specimen of the work done for the East India Company. Some years before the passing of the Eighth Dalai Lama, Warren Hastings, that famous, far-seeing Governor-General in India, had twice established a connection with the Panchen Lama by sending British envoys to his Court at Tashi Lhünpo; Bogle in 1774, and Turner in 1783. It may well have been through this connection that this curious piece found its way into the Potala.

At the foot of the tomb of the next Dalai Lama we see a very common little looking-glass among the priceless old cloisonné and enamel. The Peak Secretary tells me that it is prized as a thing of beauty, and has been kept there for many years past. In their own arts and crafts, Tibetans are endowed with a keen artistic sense but when appraising the products of Europe their tastes wander sometimes along curious lines.

It was cold during those winter visits. The large bowls of holy water on the steps of the tombs were frozen from top to bottom at midday.

Each Dalai Lama accumulates during his lifetime a large part of the gold, silver, precious stones and other wealth required for his own tomb. The Fifth, who lived to a good old age and held high prestige, accumulated much. During my time in Lhasa the Thirteenth was collecting his own store. He, too, had the advantages of a fair span of life and high prestige; and by holding the secular power throughout, he had no doubt an added advantage. I was often told by Tibetan friends that his growing store would provide the largest tomb of all.

Thus the Potala houses its own monastery, its chapels and sacred images, and the tombs of its Dalai Lamas. It is the official residence of each Dalai Lama. But in spite of this – or because of it – he who rebuilt it during the seventeenth century built it again on the lines of a fort, as his predecessor had done a thousand years earlier. In certain connections it is still known as "The Fort." A horse race, held on the plain to the north, is known as "The Gallop behind the Fort"; and the beautiful chapel in the small sheet of water below its towering northern face is "The House of the Nagas behind the Fort." Many of the monastic buildings in Tibet might almost be forts; some are still surrounded by their defence walls with turrets and loopholes. Tibet was of old a land of fighters and raiders; however hard it may try, it cannot change easily into a land of unbroken peace. Tradition is too strong. It has attacked no nation beyond its frontiers for a thousand years, but internally there is occasional unrest.

In Lhasa, the people will tell you, "Hail is not allowed to fall on the Potala, the Jewel Park or the Great Temple." There is in Tibet a class of sorcerors known as Ngagpas. These are credited with various powers, and one of them is that of preventing hailstorms from coming to places under their protection. A Ngagpa is armed with a horn, which has been taken from a bull, or a bull-yak, red in colour, which has killed another bull in a fight. This he fills with the seed of the white mustard, and blows incantations into it. The mustard seed thus acquires great power, so much so that the horn has various figures on it, to enable it to cope with the power inside. Among these are figures of scorpions, which are believed to turn the mustard seed into vajras when thrown against the hail.

There are two Ngagpas in Lhasa, who have to prevent hail from falling on those three holy places. But when I was in Lhasa hail fell on all three. As a punishment, the Dalai Lama made them plant a number of willow trees, a sensible penalty in a land where the trees are insufficient. He was all for useful punishments.

An admirable foil to the great palace is provided by the village that lies humbly at its base on ground that is almost flat. This is

Shö, a word which means "Below." The magistrates of this village exercise jurisdiction for some twenty-six miles up the valley, and nineteen down it.

In Shö there is a prison. When I entered it I found some of those prisoners that were confined for lighter offences, wandering about. But when they saw me, they went and sat down by the stocks, to be ready for the warder, who soon arrived and fastened them in.

A murderer was confined in a room, dark and airless. He had been there for three years and would remain till he died coming out only for calls of nature. At a small upper opening of this room, on the flat roof, his groans could be heard. To a Tibetan friend I put the question:

"Does not punishment of this severity kill a man soon?"

"Yes, it often does."

"Does it not, anyhow, make him mad?"

"Mad? No, why should it do that?"

Tibetans are not driven to madness by treatment of this kind; they have nerves of iron.

Capital punishment has long been rare in Tibet. The late Dalai Lama tightened up the prohibition against it. As far as possible, none should destroy the precious gift of a human life, the best opportunity for working towards Buddhahood, however far away from him his Buddhahood may be. Except in very rare instances, such as a deep crime against the religion, to take life is a terrible sin. But shortening life by severe treatment is not regarded as destroying life. At any rate it gives more time for repentance.

In this little village at the base of the Potala was born the late Grand Lama of Mongolia. The identification proceeds on the same lines as those of the Dalai Lama, and other Panchen Lama tulkus. He died several years ago, but the Russians have prevented any successor from being chosen. They fear, no doubt, that he would prove an obstacle to their authority in Outer Mongolia. His predecessor was the son of a servant, a water-carrier, in the Palha household in Lhasa.

39　The King's New Year

Having cast out the evil of the old year, the Iron Monkey, the Tibetans now enter the year of the Iron Bird. The Dalai Lama is kept very busy as usual. On the first day of the year, the 8th of February, a time of great cold and wind and dust-storms, the Ecclesiastical New Year is ushered in, for the monks and nuns must come first. The Prime Minister, the Members of the Cabinet, and the leading lamas make their obeisance to the Dalai Lama in the Potala. This ceremony appears to be mainly on the lines of that which we witnessed next day, but in briefer form. I met a number of abbots and others returning to Drepung after the ceremony. Among them was a boy, thirteen or fourteen years old, with a pink and white complexion, as fair as any English boy. He was an incarnation born in the Lhoka province, south of the Tsangpo and south-east of Lhasa.

On the second day of the New Year takes place what is known as "The King's New Year," being the day for the lay officials. It was instituted by the Dalai Lama in his fifth Incarnation, and pictures events of the time of the Religious Kings and others, especially during the reign of King Straight Strong Deep.

Long before dawn those entitled to attend set out to climb the ascent to the Potala, where, in the main audience hall, the Reception is held. It is a large square hall, supported by massive, painted pillars. Sacred pictures hang on the pillars and walls, showing but faintly in the dim light. The Dalai Lama's throne is about six feet high, and is set against a high screen standing several feet in advance of the centre of the northern wall. Over the throne is an inscription in large gilt Chinese letters with a

Tibetan translation below it, the meaning of which is "The Excellent One, who Draws Up, is Merciful, and sheds his Light in all Directions." It was presented to the Fifth Dalai Lama by the Manchu Emperor.

Kennedy and I, with Palhese, and young Norbhu, who had taken the place of Achuk Tsering, and our servants, attended the Reception. The Peak Secretary and Netö accompanied us, and took us to our Tibetan seats, which are somewhat like sections of hard mattresses covered in red cloth. These were at the top of the row running down the room to the left of the Dalai Lama's throne.

Kennedy and I wore uniform, and my staff were in their finest attire, for this annual Reception by the Dalai Lama stands out above all other receptions; and it is believed that something of the kind was held even in the days of the Religious Kings, more than a thousand years ago. We were, I think, the first Europeans to witness this unique ceremony.

Next on our left was seated the Nepalese agent with his staff, and behind us were the Envoys from Ladakh, in Kashmir, whose mission to Lhasa takes place alternately every two and every three years. These also had their staff.

To the right of the Dalai Lama a small throne, raised between two and three feet above the ground, was for the Prime Minister.

After some time a narrow strip of cloth is laid from the entrance of the hall to the Dalai Lama's throne. Accompanied by the Prime Minister and Cabinet Members, and to the sound of musical instruments, the Dalai Lama enters, supported on one side by the Lord Chamberlain and on the other by an official clad in gorgeous robes with a succession of large turquoises reaching from his left ear to the shoulder, and on the centre of his chest a capacious round box set with large turquoises. Round his neck a chain of corals and a second chain of amber, corals, etc., reaching down to his middle, the lower stones being of enormous size.

As the Dalai Lama enters, all rise and remain standing until he is seated. Then the Prime Minister comes forward and makes his threefold obeisance with clasped hands, head touching the floor three times. He makes an offering to the Dalai Lama of an image of the Buddha of Long Life, a religious book, and a *chöten*, representing respectively the Body, Speech and Mind of Buddha. He then receives the Dalai Lama's blessing.

The Prime Minister and the Members of the Cabinet are dressed in Mongolian clothes in recognition of the fact that the Mongolian Chieftain, Gushri Khan, gave the Fifth Dalai Lama the overlordship of Tibet.

After the Prime Minister's obeisance we have a religious service, held by the monks of the "All Conquering College," the Dalai Lama's private monastery. In this service they pray for long life for the Dalai Lama and prosperity for Tibet. There are eight parts, one part for each of the "Eight Auspicious Emblems," the Precious Umbrella, the Golden Fish, etc; and when its appropriate service is in progress, that emblem is held up. The eight who hold up the emblems are dressed in gorgeous robes of the same kind as those of him who helped to conduct the Dalai Lama to his throne. Two others stand as sentinels at the foot of the Dalai Lama throne, and another serves His Holiness with tea. In addition to the eleven there is a leader, making twelve in all. They are known as "The World's Most Beautiful Ornaments," and represent the high nobility of Tibet in the time of the King of Rimpung, who was ousted by the King of Tsang, who in turn was ousted by Gushri Khan in favour of the Fifth Dalai Lama. His Holiness therefore introduced these costumes into this ceremony.

Now the Dalai Lama sends his Chief Secretary to ask me whether I am in good health. I stand up to reply, *"La Chung"* ("Yes, thank you"), the stereotyped reply on this occasion. A similar enquiry is then made to the Nepalese Agent, who rises smartly to make his reply. Some days before the ceremony I was asked whether I would have any objection to making that reply and standing up to make it.

The service over, the Cabinet Members make their prostration before the Dalai Lama and receive his blessing. Other officials follow, and their servants. Then I go up, present a ceremonial scarf of the first quality to the Lord Chamberlain, who stands by the throne, and bows; then I present a scarf of the second quality (there are eight qualities of ceremonial scarf) to the Prime Minister, and return to my seat. When I present my *kata* to the Lord Chamberlain, the Dalai Lama shows his two hands to me, palms outwards, a very high honour, which he has never accorded even to the Prime Minister. Kennedy follows me, then the others. After us, the Nepalese Agent, then the Amban of Ili, and then the Envoys from Ladakh. Thus Tibetans come up first; foreigners afterwards.

Now appear thirteen young boys, who perform a dance, each with an axe in his hand. They are said to represent the sons and daughters of gods who appeared to King Straight Strong Deep. These lads are recruited, whether they or their parents wish it or not. From time to time likely boys are taken from the streets of Lhasa, and the Dalai Lama picks out some of them. Some fathers, however, manage to get their children off by saying that they are making monks of them, as it would not be right to forbid a spiritual career. For the actual dancing only twenty are required, but a larger number is maintained, to take the places of those who are ill, and to work as messengers.

The stage is next taken by eight "Protectors of Religion," who execute a dance with slow, measured steps. After them four men give a sword dance. Each has two swords, which he twirls simultaneously with skilful turns of the wrist. These men are said to represent deities of the fierce kind, who appeared to the early kings; but possibly they depict the warfare of the old fighting days, prior to the advent of Buddhism into Tibet.

After this a large number of low square tables are brought in and placed in the centre of the room. On them are laid fruits, cakes, sweet-meats and dried carcases of sheep, and the head of a bull. These articles of food have all been blessed by the Dalai Lama, and are meant for the sweepers, grooms, sedan-chair carriers, and other servants of His Holiness, that these poor folk also, though not admitted to the ceremony, may share in the general rejoicing and in the general blessing. The doors are thrown open, and in they rush. With them also crowd in a number of outsiders, eager also to gain some of the food, not because they are poor – most of them are not – but because the food has been blessed by the Dalai Lama. These thrusters are belaboured by the doorkeepers, stalwart men, from six feet to six feet six inches in height, who lay on with thick sticks, one stick breaking in the process. The intruders, however, seem to care but little for this, provided they can gain the blessing that comes with the food. It reminds one of Jacob, wrestling with the angel, and, though hurt, refusing to let go until he received a blessing.

In the intervals between the various ceremonies the stage is often taken by two Geshes, who conduct a theological debate. One is from Sera Monastery, the other from Drepung. The discussion goes on vehemently, especially on the part of the Sera Geshe, a thin, sharp-featured man. He is at present asking questions of the other one, who is seated. As he puts each question, he slaps his right hand on his left, stamps his right foot on the ground, and then slides his right hand away from his left, close to the head of his opponent; then waits for his answer. He then walks away a few feet, and with a fresh question returns as before to the charge. This procedure is in order to drive the points home. The Dalai Lama smiles from time to time at the points made. The Drepung Geshe is somewhat taller and more broadly built, and carries a calm, confident expression on his well-filled face. In the end he seems to have much the best of the argument. We frequently hear him say, with a smile and in a loud voice, "*Ona Tsa*," which means "That settles you; you can't answer that."

Afterwards a Member of the Cabinet, when asked what the debates were about, replies, "I did not understand a word of them, nor did anybody else, except the Dalai Lama and the disputants themselves." I am told later by the Lord Chamberlain that the Dalai Lama awarded to the Drepung Geshe the first place among all the Lharampa. There are four grades of Geshe Degrees, the Lharampa being the first grade. Our Drepung disputant is thus assured of a high career. The Dalai Lama will probably give him an exalted post in the Gyü Monastery from which he may rise in due course to be "The Enthroned of

Ganden" (The Ganden Tripa). Both he and the disputant from Sera are Mongols, being chosen for this high occasion, in preference to all the Tibetan Geshes. Mongol monks usually study hard when they come to Lhasa. They have come a long way and wish to make the most of their time. And they do not have to think about friends and relations, but can devote themselves entirely to religion.

All the officials, except the Prime Minister, are in the white caps which the lay officials wear at all important ceremonies. These white caps were introduced by King Straight Strong Deep and represent the turbans worn by Indians. The Cabinet Members wear them today, but today only.

The ceremonies ended, the Lord Chamerlain and the Dalai Lama's nephew holding each one hand of His Holiness, the procession files out of the room. On his way out the Dalai Lama stops the procession, while he turns round to give me a friendly smile. Further down the hall he repeats this action. This is considered an unprecedented honour; he has never done it to anybody before. Several Tibetans come and speak to me about it.

Such a gesture on the Dalai Lama's part may seem a small matter, but it was, in fact, a help to me in my mission. I had aroused hostility among a number of the influential monks by recommending the Dalai Lama to increase his army; but I was able to turn much of this hostility aside by learning Tibetan customs and observing them carefully; and here was the Dalai Lama's public recognition of my doing so. The recognition by the mass of the people would naturally take longer.

We then go to the roof of a house in Potala Shö, and witness three dwellers in the province of Tsang, one after the other, slide down ropes attached from one of the houses in the Potala to the obelisk on the ground inside the Potala precincts, a distance of perhaps 250 feet and a descent of 100 feet. Each first offers a prayer in a loud voice, and scatters an offering of barley flour as he stands on the flat roof of the house from which he commences his descent. Then, strapped to the rope by a leathern thong, he descends. The first two come down easily, but the third turns upside down after one-fourth of the descent and hangs with his head down for a long time before he can put himself right side up again, when he comes down easily enough. The Dalai Lama told Kennedy later that this contretemps caused him great uneasiness; he felt himself partly responsible if the man should fall and be killed. Besides, it would be a bad omen for the year just beginning.

This ceremony refers to the defeat of the King of the Tsang province – which lies west of the Lhasa province – by Gushri Khan, who gave the sovereignty of Tibet to the Fifth Dalai Lama. It is intended to prevent the Tsang province gaining power again, for descending without ascending is an inauspicious omen for Tsang. However, to prevent bad fortune falling on Tibet as a whole from this inauspicious performance, one of them ascends the rope again a short way.

In former times the rope used to go from the top of the Potala down to the village below its foot, a much longer distance than that in this year of the Iron Bird. But the stomach of one of those coming down was ripped open; his intestines came out and he died. After that, the present shorter rope was used.

Kennedy and I were the only Europeans who have seen this time-honoured but dangerous feat. For, later on, the Dalai Lama abolished it, and substituted another in which a man first stands on a tiny platform on the top of a pole fifty feet high; and then, tying a bobbin-shaped piece of wood to his stomach, fits this over a short iron rod attached to the top of the pole, and with arms and legs outstretched spins round and round. He repeats this performance several times.

And then through a dense crowd, and in a tempestuous dust-storm, we rode home. Soon after my arrival, a letter came from the Dalai Lama thanking me for observing Tibetan custom during my attendance at this ceremonial of the New Year. Also another letter saying that he was giving Palhese a lease of the Serchok estate for a further period of three years, perhaps as a reward for having taught me the Tibetan language and customs so well. With these letters came sweetmeats, blessed by the Dalai Lama. I distributed them to the clerks and servants, who received them with great eagerness.

I heard later all Tibetans were pleased with the British Representative for observing the Tibetan customs when attending this reception, e.g. standing up when the Dalai Lama arrived and left, standing up when His Holiness sent his Chief Secretary to enquire after my health, and bowing to the Dalai Lama when giving him the ceremonial scarf in the same way as one bows to the Viceroy of India. "The Nepalese representative," the Tibetans say, "used to only half rise from his seat, when the Dalai Lama sent to enquire about his health, and this was taken as a public insult to the Dalai Lama. But this year, as you stood up, he stood up and salaamed, and we think he will have to do this in future years also."

40 People Urged to Kill Us

The "Great Prayer Festival" (*Mönlam Chenmo*) lasts for about three weeks after the commencement of the New Year, and is followed by sports and games. The prayer is for the good of all beings, human beings and the whole animal kingdom, throughout the world. Especially it is for the good of the Dalai Lama and Panchen Lama, the Tibetan Government and the people of Tibet. Their belief is that the Buddhism of Shakyamuni Buddha has passed its peak, and is gradually declining. But the Great Prayer Festival will shorten this period of decline, and prevent the latter end of it, when human beings would otherwise live to be only ten years old. For it will hasten the coming of the new Buddha, Maitreya, who will establish his kingdom on an ascending scale. The decline of Buddha Shakyamuni's kingdom will be a thing of the past.

But though the object of the Great Prayer Festival is blessing and happiness, and though the monks should be the main supporters of this good object, many of them are apt to make a contrary course. Most of them indeed are devoted to their religion. The higher Geshes have a wider knowledge of Buddhist theology in all its ramifications than the most learned divines in Japan, as is testified by Kawaguchi, the studious Japanese priest who spent three years in Tibet, and was generally hostile to Tibetan Buddhism. Many, too, of the simple ones, recruited from the Tibetan peasantry, are spiritually minded, though their features may not show this.

But a large number of the monks, who lack either the brains or the will to study, are professional fighters. They keep the hair on their heads long, and their skirts short, and paint their faces black. People hire them for purposes of attack or defence; in fact, lamas travelling in places infested with robbers may take some of them as bodyguards. These *dob dob,* as they are called, are especially liable to break into fighting during the crowded festivals.

For the last month or two there has been great friction between the monasteries and the soldiery in Lhasa. All are afraid of a clash between the two, and many are hiding away their property in the villages round Lhasa. It is rumoured also that the British Government is sending troops to the Holy City to aid the Tibetan soldiers there against the monks. Feelings are acutely inflamed; the atmosphere, in fact, is electric. The great monasteries are on the point of breaking out into rebellion.

Many of the monks are asking who it is that has brought the British to Lhasa. Placards are put up secretly one night at various places in Lhasa, telling the people to kill Kennedy and myself. One of these is affixed to Turquoise Roof Bridge, across which all persons entering or leaving Lhasa from the north, south or west habitually pass. The placards are all pulled down before we see them, and the Tibetan Government assures me that what they contained was a complaint against a lama in the Dalai Lama's private monastery in the Potala. I thank them for this assurance, but, later on, it becomes evident from people in Lhasa itself – where some of the placards were put up – that they were directed against us. The Nepalese tell us the same, with undisguised satisfaction. And by degrees reports come in from places on the Indo-Tibetan frontier saying that we have been assassinated. The Superintendent of Indian Post Offices, with headquarters in Darjeeling, hears that the whole mission has been massacred, and telegraphs to the Indian telegraph office at Gyangtse to ask whether this is true.

And, unfortunately, a bad omen has occurred. When coming to Lhasa for the Prayer Festival, the two monk magistrates bring banners of the chief Oracles with them. This year the banner of one Oracle broke on the journey in. That happened once many years ago; and on that occasion the monks broke loose and attacked the Nepalese traders in Lhasa and looted their shops. For this reason the people more than ever are fearing an outbreak during this Prayer Festival. Some fifty thousand monks will be collected in Lhasa then; they will heavily outnumber the lay population.

Palhese, by his upbringing in the inner circle and mingling plenteously with the different outer circles, is an adept at sensing the feeling of the people. He urges me not to grant any private interviews without consulting him first. Such indeed has been my usual practice since we came to Lhasa, but he wishes to make sure that it is followed regularly.

The Dalai Lama is nervous. The friction between the monks and the soldiers is in the forefront of his mind, and there are other danger spots. I suggest to him that now that he has six thousand soldiers, it must be easier than before to keep the large monasteries in order.

"But still more," he replies, "by my choosing carefully their heads and the heads of the colleges into which they are divided, choosing men that I can depend upon. The mass of the monks do not consider their actions; they act without thinking (*lit.*, "act straight on"). I am always afraid that they will cause bloodshed at the great festivals in Lhasa.

"There was the Nepalese affair many years ago when I was young. The last few years have passed without disturbance. But when thousands are collected, it is difficult to say afterwards who has started a fight. I am thinking of employing soldiers this time to keep the peace.

"There is a Chinese trader in Lhasa, called Shalo, who is failing to pay his debts. Some of his creditors may quarrel with him during the Prayer Festival and cause a disturbance. Accordingly I am not allowing creditors to realise their debts in full, as there is not enough to go round. He owes many people money; to myself also a little, between two and three hundred *dotse* (£1,200 to £1,800). I think we should all lower our rate of interest, so that it will be the same for all. It is of no use killing the cow that gives the milk, as our saying goes. The meat won't last long. It is better to continue taking the milk."

The Dalai Lama knows well how easily, at this time of excitement, a disturbance might grow into a serious outbreak ending in many deaths. He therefore sends an order to the two magistrates of Lhasa, enquiring, "Why are people hiding away their valuables? A Sahib (myself) has come to Lhasa with the object of making a treaty. The British are not going to make war on Tibet. If any other nation is going to make war on Tibet, let me know which nation is going to do so. Or if there is going to be civil war in Tibet itself, I require to be told who is going to make such war. But if there is not going to be fighting, why are people hiding their property without cause? Every householder must sign a written statement for my perusal, stating whether he has sent away his property or not."

On this everybody has signed to the effect that he has not removed his property, whether he has done so or not. For each one fears that, if he says that he has sent away his property, he will be compelled to show where he has hidden it, and will in any case be punished. It is believed that the Dalai Lama's order will ease the situation in some degree. People will be more careful about spreading rumours.

The festival of the Great Prayer has now arrived; fifty to sixty thousand monks, many in a savage mood, are gathered together in the streets of Lhasa. Parties of them parade the streets, shouting "Come out and fight. We are not afraid to give our lives." The peace-loving laity respond by barricading their houses.

Women of the labouring class have started singing a new verse in the streets of Lhasa, a verse which refers to the heated feeling between the monks and the soldiers. It runs as follows:

> I bought in the Lhasa market
> An old pair of Chinese boots;
> The right foot danced well,
> But the left raised a cloud of dust.

Though an outbreak threatens, all the observances of the Prayer Festival continue as usual. To have abandoned any would, to Tibetans, be unthinkable. The Dalai Lama attends all, or nearly all, the religious ceremonies, but when doing so is seldom visible to his people. He may be on the top of a high building. Or, as happens twice, when the ceremony takes place at the entrance to the Temple, he views it from the screened balcony of an adjoining house.

However, on one exceptional date, the fifteenth day of the first Tibetan month, the Dalai Lama comes out into the public view during the early morning, and again after nightfall. Tibet keeps the lunar calendar, and the fifteenth of each month is the day of the full moon. So on this, the holiest day in the chief religious festival of the year, the Precious Sovereign preaches his yearly sermon to the people. First, he visits the chapel of the goddess Palden Lhamo, the special guardian of the Tibetan Government; that duty he performs at five o'clock on this icy morning of February 22nd. The temperature is nearly down to zero on the Fahrenheit scale, and a light wind is blowing.

An hour or so later, when sunrise is approaching, he crosses the short distance to the large square near the Temple and mounts a throne five feet high on a platform, itself four feet above the ground. On the platform, seated in reverential attitudes, are the Prime Minister, Members of the Cabinet, those holding the high title of *Kung, Techi* or *Dzasa,* the higher Incarnate Lamas, and the Abbots of Drepung, Sera and Ganden. That reverend, dignified figure, the Enthroned of Ganden, is also there. He is the head of all those who are not yet recognised tulkus, and by reason of his great learning and piety is more highly revered than nearly all those who are. In the square and vicinity are seated some five thousand monks of the Three Seats.

This service is called "The Spoken Religion." The Dalai Lama reads from a book with yellow pages and black print. He reads the commands of Buddha, e.g. that monks should dwell in solitary places, not seeking human society, shows, or other human pleasures, that they should not drink wine, nor consort with women, that they should pray frequently, both aloud in the religious services and privately in their hearts. That all people, monks, nuns and lay, should do good to others, not harm. He reads the story of how Buddha in a former existence cut off a piece of his leg to feed a starving tiger. After reading, the Dalai

Lama preaches to the people, explaining the meaning of what he has read, for the book is in archaic language, hard to understand.

Letters are passed up to his Chief Secretary from persons who have given donations to monasteries, asking for the Dalai Lama's blessing and protection. He reads out two or three of these. During the service trumpets are blown from time to time by representatives of the soldiery of the Tibetan kings who lived a thousand to twelve hundred years ago, and conquered large portions of China, India and Turkistan, before Buddhism became a power in Tibet. It is interesting to note how often these representatives of the ancient soldiery of pre-Buddhist Tibet take part in the religious ceremonies of the present.

Some women also, attendants of Palden Lhamo, take part in the service; they are chosen from different places in Tibet and are known as "The Clean Ornaments."

At half-past eight the service ends and the Dalai Lama leaves on the arm of the Lord Chamberlain on one side and his nephew the Yabshi Kung on the other. The assembled monks give a loud cry, which is interpreted as expressing their applause and their pleasure at meeting the Head of the Religion. During the service, however, they were not particularly attentive; the temptation to turn their heads and gaze on the foreigners, seated just behind them, was too strong.

In an interview with the Dalai Lama shortly afterwards, he asks me whether preaching in "the English religion" is at all like his preaching, and confirms what I have written above about his explaining the hard meanings in the book. I tell him that in our Church also we have reading of Scripture and preaching.

It is cold sitting out of doors at six or seven on a February morning with the thermometer registering twenty-five degrees of frost. But this does not trouble the Tibetans, who hold that in the early morning the mind is fresh, whereas during the warmth of the day it becomes clouded. Besides, sunrise is an auspicious time; things going upwards are of good omen, and particularly is this so of the mighty sun beginning its ascent.

41 The Butter Festival

There are three Sacred Ways in Lhasa. First, the Inside Circle which goes round inside the Great Temple. Second, the Intermediate Circle, which encloses the Temple. Third, the Park Circle, which surrounds the city and the Potala, and is between four and five miles in length. Normally it would have been called the Outside Circle as opposed to the Inside Circle; but the word "outside" (*chi*) has a sinister meaning, for an outside man means one who stands outside the pale of Buddhism, in fact, "a foreign devil."

In order to prevent accidents, people are generally prohibited from riding on the crowded Intermediate Circle during the Prayer Festival, though exceptions are made in the case of the higher Government officials who habitually ride to their offices in Lhasa.

In the evening following the Dalai Lama's sermon, the holy night of the full moon, this road is the scene, of a typical and splendid display. We must see this rare sight; the opportunity is not to be missed, and the Dalai Lama will be there.

Tsarong Shap-pe has invited us and our clerks; we go to his house at six in the evening, to see the offerings arranged round the Intermediate Circle. We are shown to an upper room, twenty-five feet above the ground, where Tsarong's younger wife joins us, as well as Ringang.

Opposite us are the offerings of two Members of the Cabinet, Künsangtse and Tsarong himself. Each of these offerings – as indeed are all the offerings – is in the form of a triangular wooden frame, forty to sixty feet high, with a sharp apex.

Leather is stretched over this, and on it are figures, pictures, etc., fashioned in butter, painted in various colours, and many of them covered with gold leaf. On each side is an ascending dragon, and in the middle a circular flower or wheel, usually red. Below this wheel are groups of figures, often representing long life after the Chinese pattern; e.g. "The Long-Lived Man," "The Six Long-Lived Ones," and so on. The whole is tastefully and elaborately designed, the figures are carefully moulded – all made of butter.

At the base of the triangle in a little throne of his own is the figure of a man, usually Jinda Hashang. On each side of him may be arranged Indian gods or goddesses, perhaps a dozen altogether. The absence of Tibetan deities among these figures is noticeable, though occasionally a Tibetan Oracle will be found. On the top of all stands a red umbrella, made of frilled silk. Of these huge offerings there are eighty or ninety altogether.

This is the famous Butter Festival of Lhasa. To the Tibetans themselves it is known as "The Offerings of the Fifteenth," this being the fifteenth day of the first Tibetan month, which in this year falls on February 22nd.

At a quarter to seven the lights in our room – a large silver chandelier and a paraffin lamp – are extinguished, for the Dalai Lama is coming soon, and it is forbidden to be seen looking on him, especially from above. Servants of the Cabinet Members come along the street, then soldiers, lay officials, ecclesiastical officials, and the Cabinet Members themselves. And now the Dalai Lama in a "dandy," a kind of open chair borne by three or four porters, and used by ladies and old men in Darjeeling and its neighbourhood. Formerly he used to go on foot, a strip of white cloth being laid for him to walk on, all the way round the Intermediate Circle. Since his return from Darjeeling and Kalimpong in 1912 he goes round in a dandy.

Many large Chinese lanterns, gaily decorated, are carried in the procession. Künsangtse has darted ahead and stands by his offering, which is just opposite our window. The Dalai Lama inspects it with the help of a lantern, which is hardly necessary, for the full moon, the torches and the numerous butter-lamps, arranged along the street, give sufficient light. The Minister makes three obeisances and offers a scarf. The Precious Protector gives him the double-handed blessing, to which, as a Cabinet Member, he is entitled, and the ceremonial white scarf is put round his neck. This done, His Holiness passes on, examining briefly the best offerings.

More soldiers follow, all in double file, with buglers trained after the British model. There are twelve hundred soldiers altogether in Lhasa and the Jewel Park, and nearly all of them are in the procession.

Now come a number of monks, about four hundred altogether. They are mostly from the three *lings*, Kündeling (where we live), Tsomoling and Tsechokling. *Ling* in Tibetan means a place apart and independent. Applied to a monastery, it means one that may be small, but is independent of other monasteries; an unusual condition in Tibet, where most monasteries are branches from a parent stem. These three *lings*, all in or near Lhasa, are especially favoured; they are three out of the five monasteries from which is usually chosen the Regent of Tibet during the minority of a Dalai Lama.

Townspeople and countrymen follow, many singing and carrying torches. If these go out, they can easily be relighted from one of the numerous butter-lamps. There is an air of merriment abroad; it is an occasion for general rejoicing. There is plenty of singing, but very little drunkenness.

Tsarong now arrives in a highly excited condition. While walking by the Dalai Lama's side with the other Ministers he felt safe. But being so strongly hated by the monks, he felt afraid to return to his house with only one or two servants, after he had left the Dalai Lama. He feared lest a monk in one of the dark little rooms should assassinate him from behind, either by throwing a heavy stone on his head or in some other way. There are several fanatical monks who would like to kill Tsarong, even though they knew they themselves would be caught and executed. A layman would fear, in addition to his own death, the confiscation of his property and the ruin of his family, but monks of the reformed sect have neither family nor property.

We naturally wish to see this uncommon spectacle; we could not see the details well from our window. And we judge it not unwise to do so, as we have seen the sights on previous days, and if we do not see those this night, our absence will be noticed. Any show of nervousness will lessen my influence with the Tibetans, who have no respect for timid people.

Tsarong is greatly upset and full of fear on our account also. He carries a loaded revolver, which he presses Kennedy to take, but the latter declines. He sends a dozen soldiers with us. The Peak Secretary now arrives and is also nervous for our safety, thinking it very risky for us to go round. So he takes half a dozen stalwart monks armed with thick poles. Our clerks, too, are excited and nervous as they follow behind us. Unknown to me, they carry loaded revolvers.

We then go out and go round the Intermediate Circle, round the outside of the Temple buildings. The crowds stand at the side as we pass, singing often in their light spirits, lost in merriment and wonder. In some of the offerings the figures on the plaforms are made to move by strings pulled from behind and below. A stag and a garuda bird nod their heads at each other. In another, an ecclesiastical official and a lay official nod at each other; then a fluffy Oracle rushes out and belabours them both; anon, an Indian Brahman comes out and does the same, and the scene ends with a procession of monks in single file winding through a pillared hall. This – the offering of the most learned and ascetic monastery in Lhasa, where the monks are allowed only one meal a day – is the finest offering of all, with the possible exception of that put up by the Government treasury. The countrymen stare agape at this marvellous performance; some of them, especially the boys, look on it as a miracle. The sophisticated town lads laugh, but enjoy it just the same. The very name of such a performance, however, gives it away, for it is known as "The Secret String."

After completing the round we dine with Tsarong, Ringang making a fourth. From time to time during dinner we hear the shouts and songs of the revellers in the streets. We leave at a quarter to ten; the people are still numerous and happy, but we see no signs of rowdiness. Tsarong sends a file of twelve soldiers with us. They have to return to the Jewel Park, and our residence, Happiness Park, is on their way. The revels last till dawn. As the night wears on, drunkenness increases, and there are occasional street fights.

The offerings are taken down at four o'clock in the morning, before the sun can melt the frozen butter. The butter is thrown away, for having been painted, it is unfit for further use. The wood and leather are kept for next year. The expense of the whole festival totals up to about four thousands pounds, and the show is a short-lived one, though a fine spectacle while it lasts. Some of the donors of offerings find the expense a heavy burden, for the standard of living in Tibet is far lower than in plutocratic Europe and America. But they must of necessity spend in accordance with their social position; and where the religion is concerned there can be no turning aside.

Later on, the Dalai Lama told me that – apparently on Tsarong's suggestion – he ordered that soldiers as well as a guard of monks should go round with us, though he himself considered that a guard of monks was sufficient. The latter, he said, was necessary, as monks are headstrong, and one never knows what may happen with numbers of them at night. Indeed, with the narrow streets and the unlighted houses, a fatal blōw or a shot would be easy.

As for the various State ceremonials, none are omitted or modified, however threatening may be the atmosphere of unrest and rebellion. For each ceremonial is an indispensable part of the all-embracing religion.

We went everywhere in Lhasa, and without guards. A few days later to the Temple, to see and hear the theological disputations by learned Geshes. How the audience jeer when one is unable to reply! The learned ones come from the Three Seats. Two abbots preside; when a Geshe from Drepung is answering the questions, the judges are abbots from Sera and Ganden; and on similar lines for other answers. These judges classify both questioners and answerers, and submit their recommendations to the Dalai Lama. Those who do well may hope for a vacant abbotship at one of the Three Seats; or – an even higher honour – at Upper Gyü or Lower Gyü, the two branches of the tantric monasteries, in which they can rise eventually to the exalted position of "The Enthroned of Ganden." Those who do well receive also rewards of money and clothing from the Inmost One, who, however, as he himself told me, takes into anxious thought many other qualities besides learning, before appointing to the position of a leading abbot, with all the influence that such a position brings. And this the abbots know well.

Men and women throng the galleries above to watch these disputations; they are from the country. They of course do not understand the discussion, but besides being a novelty for them, it is considered a work of spiritual merit to attend them. Here are farmers from eastern Tibet whose homes are two months' journey distant, herdsmen from the far north, and brigands from the Golok country in the far north-east. For these men of Golok, who rob travellers and even caravans passing through their own country, come also to Lhasa and other parts of Tibet as peaceful or semi-peaceful traders, and are tolerated as such. They want to see all that is to be seen. And among the spectators are several Mongols, who have come three or four months' journey from their own land. Of the inhabitants of Lhasa hardly any attend; they have seen these disputations so often before.

Five days later the Dalai Lama presides at the festival known as Torgya, when sacrificial offerings composed of grain, butter, etc., are made in order to subdue evil spirits and avert evil from the Tibetan Government. It is perhaps hardly necessary to note that sacrificial offerings in Tibet do not include the sacrifice of animals; such a sacrifice, far from being a religious act, would be regarded as one of the greatest of sins. We, as usual, are invited to the ceremony, and are accommodated in an upper room overlooking the square outside the Temple. The Dalai Lama is seated in a balcony directly above us, screened by a curtain of yak hair. Our room forms a part of the Temple buildings, the main entrance to the Temple being directly below us, only a few feet away.

Some hours later, when the proceedings are ended, His Holiness leaves. The monks, free now that he is no longer there, surge forward into the Temple square, and stare at the two foreigners seated in the room above. And then we also go. A way is immediately cleared for us through the dense masses of monks and laymen.

Three days afterwards, on March 4th, follows the direct invitation to the New Buddha, Maitreya, to come soon. A procession takes place a little before sunrise, as an invitation to him to come quickly, and to appear, as the sun is about to appear, in his might.

The next event is a pony race, which follows an hour later at half-past six o'clock. We accept the invitation to this, and ride out from Happiness Park. The thermometer registers eighteen degrees of frost on the Fahrenheit scale and a north-easterly wind is blowing. This, say the Tibetans, is good; everybody will be fresh in mind and body.

The chief peculiarity of the race is that the ponies run without riders. They start from near the Drepung monastery, race along the road to Lhasa, through the city, and on to one of the parks at "Dust Heap Ridge," a distance of between five and six miles in all. Occasionally they stop, or try to turn up a side street, but the grooms ride behind each pony or set of ponies from the same stable, to urge them on, and to make sure that they do not go astray.

Entries are compulsory. Those who hold official rank in Lhasa, from the Ministers downwards, have each to enter a prescribed number of ponies, in accordance with their rank. The Government itself enters a large number. Occasionally some of the Government men drive a competitor's pony off the course. But this is done quietly, so that their offence does not come to the Dalai Lama's ears. Tsarong is the winner in this race.

Some of the ponies slip away before the starting gun is fired. For this the owners are not only disqualified, but fined in addition.

We are accommodated in an upper room of a house in Lhasa, not far from His Holiness and on the same level; not at the finishing point, but more than a mile away from it. A Government delegate of good rank goes there, and hands out for each pony a small piece of wood, bearing a number that shows the order in which the pony finished. A groom or other servant carries this in his upraised hand back to the square in Lhasa, where we view the race.

A foot race over the same course follows. The first competitor to pass the Dalai Lama's seat amuses the crowd by the delight that he shows. He bows three times, and then, with a caper of delight, runs on at a good steady pace. The later arrivals run stolidly by, without bowing to the Precious Sovereign. Belated ponies in the first race continue to arrive among the competitors in the foot race; the people drive them on, aided by the police with their long willow rods. A little dog, running up the street with the solemn air of a competitor, provokes a roar of laughter, as does a woman who, when crossing the street, falls down with her baby on her back, and is unable to recover herself without assistance. It is a merry crowd, easily moved to laughter.

There follows a competition in lifting a heavy stone; only one man succeeds in this. The proceedings end with wrestling competitions.

The Dalai Lama remains for all these events, for they have a spiritual significance. The racing denotes speed; the weight-lifting and wrestling denote strength. All, therefore, are good omens accompanying the invitation to the next Buddha to come quickly and come in power.

The Great Prayer Festival is now finished. As they quit the Holy City and wend their way to their homes far and near, people repeat the refrain:

> Lhasa's Great Prayer Festival now is ended;
> And the Buddha of Love invited.

42   Rebellion is Threatened

A few days before the invitation to the Buddha that is to come, and for two days afterwards, ceremonies and sports, mostly on horseback, are held on the plain north of Lhasa, but the Dalai Lama does not attend these; on the third day, March 7th, to his great pleasure, he returns to the Jewel Park. The return is made in state, and he asks me to have some photographs taken of this ceremony. I tell my little orderly, Rabden, to do his best, but the early morning light is too weak to produce good results. It takes place at seven o'clock in the morning, less than an hour after sunrise.

The procession back to the Jewel Park is similar to the one out to the Potala about a month ago. This time we see it from close quarters. It is noticeable that the Dalai Lama cannot be seen inside his sedan-chair.

The New Year ceremonies are now over. His Holiness tells Kennedy that they are of ancient origin, and wants to know whether we have any like them in Britain. Kennedy is able to point out some resemblances.

Though he has returned to his favourite home, ceaseless work and worry await him there. The political situation is deeply disturbed. During some of the Parliamentary debates, which were directed towards the disbandment of an extra levy raised by the military authorities, the Financial Commissioners, who are responsible for summoning the members to the meetings, purposely refrained from summoning any military members. Some of the latter tried to get into the meeting, and made a scene with one of the Commissioners who reasoned with them the feelings between the monks and the military party have become more bitter, and people are fearing an outbreak by the monks against the army officers, and especially against Tsarong. The officer in charge of the Dalai Lama's bodyguard has served out a hundred rounds of ammunition to each soldier in it. The populace of Lhasa is greatly excited on this account.

The Dalai Lama instructs the Prime Minister to enquire into the situation. The latter tries to settle it in accordance with the feelings of his kindly old heart. But the Precious Sovereign evidently thinks the matter so grave as to demand more drastic treatment. He puts on his Chief Secretary to make an investigation independently of all the ministers. Now he has received the Chief Secretary's report and come to a decision, but this is kept rigorously secret till it is made known at a Presence Tea.

The Presence Tea is a gathering held each afternoon at the Jewel Park, and lasting for about half an hour. All ecclesiastical officials in Lhasa from the Grand Secretaries downwards must attend it. The Dalai Lama himself seldom does so; his Peak Secretaries and room-stoppers take charge of the gathering. Tea is drunk, for the giving of tea is an auspicious omen; just as in a household the servants should be entertained periodically by their master, to increase the happiness and prosperity of the household. But no talking is permitted, except in low tones. It is in effect a kind of roll-call, to ensure that the monk officials at Lhasa shall not go away on pleasure or business of their own. If an official is absent from it one day, nothing is said; if two days consecutively, his absence is remarked; if three days consecutively, he is reprimanded.

On March 26th the Presence Tea is evidently of unusual importance, for the Cabinet Ministers have been ordered to attend it. What is the reason? It soon becomes known. The Chief Secretary reads out the Dalai Lama's orders. One of the Cabinet Ministers, Künsangtse, is dismissed. He has been found guilty of being at the bottom of the trouble, and of hiding his own property. He is also convicted of pushing the interests of his relatives at the Government's expense. These are the reasons given out for the present. Two other Members of the Cabinet are fined. Three colonels are dismissed for taking part in the quarrel with the Financial Commissioners. Two junior military officers, one of them being the Dalai Lama's own nephew, are fined for lesser offences. One of the Financial Commissioners is fined heavily for his share in the quarrel with the military officers. Some others on both sides are punished in lesser degree.

Künsangtse has to take off his minister's uniform, hat, robe and boots immediately. One of his colleagues, Trimön, manages to procure for him the dress of a lesser member of the nobility to go home in. Künsangtse had apparently no inkling of what was in store for him. On the way to the Jewel Park he passed Kennedy and waved his hand cheerfully to him.

The Chief Secretary, on the Dalai Lama's behalf, has also warned the monk magistrates to keep the monks under strict control during the Tsonchö. This is the second religious festival of the year, and is to take place shortly. He has impressed on them the injury that would result to the monasteries if fighting broke out, and left them under no doubt that the Dalai Lama would punish them severely.

The whole of Lhasa is talking over the matter. There has not been such heavy official punishment for nearly twenty years. By many of those who are sufficiently educated to take an interest in politics, Trimön and Künsangtse are looked on as the ablest of the Ministers. And a few who wish to criticise the Dalai Lama but dare not do so directly, talk discreetly about the intelligence of the fallen Minister.

A month later I hear on first-class authority that Künsangtse was really dismissed by the Dalai Lama on account of treasonable dealings with China. A lama of a monastery forty miles outside Lhasa left it some time ago, giving out that he was going to Mongolia. He did not go there; he went to Peking, where the Chinese Government paid him a salary, and made a lot of him in other ways. He was a great friend of Künsangtse, and has been in accordance with him lately on the subject of establishing Chinese influence in Tibet. The two misdeeds – promoting an outbreak in Lhasa, and treasonable dealings with China – are closely connected, for a rebellion in Lhasa would give the

Chinese a pretext for sending troops into Tibet, saying that they must restore order. And this although the Tibetan Government on the whole governs Tibet in a much more orderly manner than the Chinese Government governs China.

This otherwise painful affair has one humorous aspect which causes much quiet merriment among many of the people. The Dalai Lama has ordered that all secreted valuables are to be left where they are. They may not be brought back except after petition addressed to the Government, in which it must be explained "Why, without reason, they hid their goods," and the name of the receiver as well as of the petitioner who has hidden the goods, must be stated. It is expected that on such petition being made; both will be fined; but when anybody is caught bringing back their goods without Government authority the punishment will be very severe.

On receiving the report from his Chief Secretary, the Dalai Lama – in accordance with his usual procedure – first gave a verbal judgment, imposing the punishment and giving reasons for his decisions. The Chief Secretary reported this to the Ecclesiastical Court, which, after the Lord Chamberlain, is the highest authority among the monk-officials, and is composed of the four Grand Secretaries. These, acting in unison, formulated the judgment in writing, and submitted it to the Dalai Lama, who placed his red hand-mark on it.

"The Precious Protector's power is very great nowadays," says Palhese, pleased and somewhat surprised that the Dalai Lama should be able to go as far as he does.

The women, too, take up the matter, and the effect lasts a long time. Four months afterwards I am riding with Palhese along the broad road from the Jewel Park to the Potala. It is crowded with monk officials and their servants returning from the daily Presence Tea, and with labourers returning from their day's work. A party of a dozen women labourers are singing as they come, the words of their refrain being as follows:

> Though he from Heaven's centre be cast down,
> Grieve not, ye turquoise bees!

They sing loudly, so that all the road, high and low, can hear.

It is indeed a heavy fall from Heaven's Centre, the Tibetan Cabinet, and the ladies of the household might well be grieved. Everybody of course knows to what this verse refers, but nobody restrains the women from their lusty singing. It would be against custom to do so. Sometimes even the name of the dismissed official is sung:

> Künsangtse, Great Power of the Land,
>   Pressed his power too far;
> So now he has laid aside the Minister's coronet,
>   And wears the hat of the people.

This is sung by men and women, especially those of the labouring classes. Künsangtse seldom leaves his house; he is so ashamed.

During this upheaval occurs the anniversary of the death of the Ninth Dalai Lama. It is observed as usual. In the evening the sacred butter-lamps are lighted in the Potala and the Great Temple, and musical instruments of various kinds are sounded.

There may be unrest and disorder in the city; and even rebellion may threaten. But the spirits must not be neglected. None knows this better than the Peak Secretary. He has lately been consulting his Birth Spirit. The Spirit to be approached depends on the quarter of Lhasa in which the family house is situated; the Peak Secretary's house is in the southern quarter.

"What did you consult him about?"

"I thanked him for his protection last year, and asked what fate is in store for me this year. The Spirit replied that I shall have sickness this year, but he will help me. When anything bad is going to happen, we thus get warning of it and can hold religious services to ward it off. Birth Spirits should be consulted, as a rule, once a year."

The feeling against me seems to be gradually cooling down. The Dalai Lama honours me, and I am gaining the goodwill of the people by studying and observing Tibetan customs, as well as Tibetan etiquette, which to them is so important. Since approaching within one hundred miles of Lhasa, I have not allowed any members of my staff to shoot or fish. For several years I have myself abstained from shooting or fishing in Tibet. Nor have I smoked in or near monasteries. Of course, in my own Lhasa home, the Park of Happiness, I smoke as I please.. Besides all this I have been able to show the Tibetan leaders that I want to help their country in every way I can. And the increase of the army is being put through, as the Dalai Lama promised me, "in a gentle manner."

43 The Temple

The Great Temple is the holiest spot in Lhasa, the holiest in Tibet. I used to visit it from time to time at various hours of the day. The three last visits were on the full moon of my last three months in Lhasa, the first being during the forenoon, the second in the evening, and the last during the afternoon, when I dropped in for a short visit on my way back from my Sunday ride. The day of the full moon being the most sacred day in the month, the Temple was consequently crowded then, especially in the evening.

It would take too much space to explain this holy place in detail; a brief description must suffice. The Temple is a large collection of buildings. The entrance is architecturally unimposing, but in harmony with the secluded sanctuaries within. There are large courtyards and innumerable chapels, each with its own special image or images. The "Inmost Circle" runs round inside the Temple, and there are various Government offices included in the outside portions, so closely linked together are the religion and the secular administration.

The Temple was build by King Straight Strong Deep. Where Lhasa now stands was then a lake or marsh, which had to be filled up before the building could be begun. This was done partly by bringing earth on the backs of goats, which abound in Tibet. So the King named the spot Rasa, "The Place of Goats." Later on the name was changed to Lhasa, "The Place of the Gods." Thus it is recorded in the *Clear Mirror of the Line of Kings*, a Tibetan history of which the Dalai Lama gave me a careful copy on first-class Tibetan paper, so that the Tibetan characters stand out sharp and distinct.

The site of the Temple is thus the real Lhasa; the buildings round it, which grew into a town, are mere appendages.

The holiest chapel in the Temple is the one in which is kept the image of Buddha, known as *Cho*, "The Lord," which was brought from China to Tibet by Straight Strong Deep's bride, the Chinese princess. In its head-dress are several very large turquoises; the general effect is one of turquoises and gold.

At each visit to the *Cho*, Palhese offers for us the white silk scarves of ceremony or worship, and puts his head to the feet of the image while he prays silently. He takes holy water from the copper vessel held by a monk, and drinks a little. The rest of the party rub it over their eyes, and put some on the backs of their heads. I put mine on my head.

Behind the *Cho* sits another image of Buddha, facing the *Cho's* back. The tradition is that it is the image which used to hold the place of honour in this chapel, but when the *Cho* was brought, it spoke and asked to be put behind. Some of the images in Tibetan temples are termed Speaking Images; these are said to have spoken from time to time, usually at very long intervals.

Among many interesting and beautiful objects in the Temple are a large number of frescoes depicting the earlier lives of Shakyamuni Buddha. These, being nearly three hundred years old, are being erased and repainted under the Dalai Lama's orders by about one hundred artists, guided by one chief teacher and six or seven assistant teachers. The painters do not commence painting until one of the teachers has sketched in the outline. Tibetan paints are mainly used; the result is beautiful. One can find no difference between the old and the new, except in clearness; and even in that respect the difference is not great, for I have seen frescoes still clear in this dry, cold air, though painted twelve hundred years ago, and never repainted.

Another work of the highest importance and entailing a long period of toil was commenced by the Dalai Lama during 1920. The Kangyur, the Tibetan 'Bible', the holiest book in Tibet, consists of a hundred and eight bulky volumes. The Tibetan system of wooden blocks with the letters incised on them, a block to each page, has been described. There were only two sets of blocks throughout Tibet for printing this sacred work. One was at Nartang, near Tashi Lhünpo; the other in the State of Derge in eastern Tibet. Copies of the Kangyur are constantly being printed; the Nartang blocks, nearly two hundred years old, had therefore become blurred. The Derge blocks are printed on metal, and consequently clearer; but it is difficult to obtain copies of them in central Tibet.

The Tibetan biography says, "The existence of the Kangyur should be considered as equal to the very presence of Buddha himself in the Snowy Land" (Tibet). Accordingly the Dalai Lama determined to make fresh wooden blocks for the entire Kangyur. The immensity of the task may well be imagined. Making a very rough estimate, the number of blocks may be put at more than thirty thousand, and the number of letters at more than forty million, each letter to be carved with clearness and accuracy.

Some lamas and laymen gave large sums for the work, and a great deal was collected in smaller subscriptions, rich and poor contributing according to their means for a project of such all-embracing importance. We learn from the biography that "The Dalai Lama spent the entire amount on the work. Thus the gravy vanished into the meat."

A room in a monastery or in a private house that keeps the Kangyur needs to be large. But to store all the solid blocks, from which the pages are printed, requires a far larger amount of space. So the Dalai Lama built a house in front of the Potala. "It had a verandah, and was three storeys high. It contained many rooms, and among them dwelling-rooms for the guards. Also there was a room and a kitchen for himself." In the centre was a statue of the Coming Buddha, the Buddha of Love. Walls were decorated with frescoes on sacred subjects. The Inmost One named the house "The Island, the Storehouse of all the benefits and happiness of the Snowy Land."

The work took seven years to complete. Now for the first time Lhasa, Tibet's Holy City, has its own materials for printing Tibet's holiest book.

During my last visit to the Dalai Lama I have been discussing with him a highly important Tibetan treaty, in respect of one of its leading provisions. He says that he will call for the original treaty from the offices of the Cabinet. He will give the Cabinet such and such a reason (not the real reason, which might stimulate undesirable curiosity) for wishing to see it.

When he has done so, the Dalai Lama tells me that he does not think the provision in question does the harm that was feared; but he intends to send the original treaty for me to read.

A few days later his Chief Secretary not only brings me the original treaty, but, in accordance with the Dalai Lama's orders, proposes to leave it with me for a few days, while I have it copied. He brings also the original of a second treaty supplementary to the first, and proposes to leave that also with me. The second treaty is unknown; and is therefore not included in Aitchisons's Treaties, that series of solid volumes in which are collected the treaties and other engagements relating to India and neighbouring countries, the official record of the Government of India.

I ask the Chief Secretary not to leave the treaties with me, but to keep them in his own custody, and I will send my two Tibetan clerks to copy them. The Dalai Lama's trustfulness certainly goes far. It may be doubted whether any nation has ever proposed to leave the originals of two highly important treaties in the hands of a foreign representative.

As a rule the higher the rank of the man I talk to and the more often I converse with him, the more frank he is. The Dalai Lama has always been frank, for there is none who can rebuke him or punish him for what he has said. And the Prime Minister and some others have become almost as frank.

It is about this time that the second great festival of the year takes place. It lasts for ten days, and is known as "The Offerings of the Assembly." Each day a fresh religious ceremonial is displayed. The festival was instituted by the Prime Minister of the Fifth Dalai Lama after the latter's death, and in honour of his master.

Some three weeks after this festival ends, the Dalai Lama gives refreshments consisting of tea, cake and sweetmeats to all officers from the Prime Minister downwards, who have ridden with him from the Jewel Park to Lhasa and back again. The entertainment lasts for about three hours, being either in the forenoons or afternoons; this year in the afternoon. It takes place on three successive days, and each officer must attend on at least two out of the three days. Tea is passed round three times; any one who does not come in time for the second cup cannot enter; he must go away again. The Dalai Lama himself does not attend.

Two days after this festival is finished, I happen to visit the Temple with the Peak Secretary and Palhese. There is a slight imprint of a foot on the paved verandah of the large Temple courtyard. People say that the Precious Protector was sitting there during the last Great Prayer Festival while a service was in progress in the courtyard. Being of the opinion that the service was not being properly conducted, he rose from his seat, stamping his foot impulsively. Thus the footprint is said to have been made.

The place is marked off with a small wooden railing, to prevent people treading on it. It is not the subject of much talk; in fact, I did not hear of it until now when I happen to walk by the spot a month after the miracle was performed. Footprints and impressions of wooden staves on the stones and rocks have always been favourites among the minor miracles of Tibetan Buddhism.

Quick-witted himself, the Dalai Lama does not bear patiently with the dullards or the lazy ones. Some of the impetuous temperament of his youth still remains, though he is now forty-four years old. But he has learnt much, and the rashness of youth has grown less. That rashness was largely due to the close seclusion of the early days, for it delayed his gaining a knowledge of the outside world, and especially of those nations that dwelt far beyond his borders with their – to him – strange ideas.

44 The Dalai Lama's Favourite in Danger

The Dalai Lama's household is fully staffed. The chief members of it are the All Covering Abbot, to whom reference has already been made; and the Chief Secretary, who, like nearly all the Dalai Lama's chief assistants, is a lama. He ranks somewhat lower than the All Covering Abbot, but exercises by far the greater influence, as he is the intermediary between the Dalai Lama and those desiring audience with His Holiness. Each petitioner states his request to the Chief Secretary, who goes into the presence of the Dalai Lama and lays the request before him. In due course he brings back to the applicant the order which the Dalai Lama has passed. Very few persons are allowed to make their requests direct to His Holiness. Before the appointment of a Prime Minister, several years ago, the members of the Cabinet used to come in all together, and the four Grand Secretaries did likewise. But since then this privilege of the Cabinet and the Grand Secretaries has been cancelled; nowadays they consult with the Prime Minister, who alone is admitted for submitting such reports to His Holiness.

However, Tibetan obstinacy is proverbial. Now and again, when a case has been decided unjustly by a magistrate or delayed for a long time by the Cabinet, a petitioner will submit his personal appeal to the Dalai Lama. He may come forward when the Inmost One is on the road, or he may creep into the Jewel Park, and jump up and down outside the window of the Dalai Lama's room. In either case he is seized, roughly handled, and put in prison for breaking the law; but he has a good chance of a favourable decision afterwards.

The Chief Secretary has ten secretaries under him; these, too, are all monk officials. When the Dalai Lama grants an interview, the Chief Secretary pours into his cup the tea which is an inseparable part of all ceremonies and interviews. Before offering the tea he must first taste it himself. He naturally makes a large amount of money from the applicants whose requests he conveys to the Dalai Lama. I have never heard him make anything approaching a joke, and he never gives secrets away. This thin, sharp-featured man with hawk-like eyes has many enemies.

Other influential members of the household are the Master of the Bedchamber, the Chief Attendant, the Court Chaplain and the Master of the Kitchen. The Master of the Bedchamber is responsible for the clothes of His Holiness, and has charge of much besides. He has two valets under him. The Chief Attendant is responsible for the food arrangements; he has six assistants. The Court Chaplain hands to the Dalai Lama the religious implements required for worship, e.g. the bell and the vajra (dorje), this latter being a small piece of metal shaped like a dumb-bell and emblematic of durability. And many other implements there are. The Court Chaplain's assistants are monks picked from the one hundred and seventy-five inmates of the Dalai Lama's private monastery in the Potala. These serve in relays of twelve at a time.

The monks in Tibet being innumerable, large numbers are always available for any form of service or ceremony. At a religious service in the Prayer Festival in Lhasa I have seen as many as twelve thousand monks in attendance. They filled the courtyards of the Temple and the buildings round these courtyards, four thousand here, two thousand there, and so on. In Tibet the monks, not the laity, form the congregations. A few of the laity wander in and out to see how the service is going on, but take no part in it.

But the monks must attend strictly to the service. One of them laughs quietly; a monk policeman immediately hits him from above on his shoulder, with a heavy pole, hard enough to cause a serious fracture. But Tibetans are constitutionally tough, and wear a lot of thick, loose clothing, especially in winter. And seeing where the blow would fall, the offender rapidly threw his thick monk's shawl over the place.

The Dalai Lama's chief cook has about seven assistants; there are eight servants in charge of his water supply, four "room-stoppers," i.e. orderlies, who, besides guarding doors, ride in front of the Dalai Lama's sedan-chair when he goes out, carrying whips with which they can, if necessary, clear the way. The bearers who carry the sedan-chair are under two chiefs; when His Holiness rides his pony or mule, an officer carries the sacred umbrella of yellow silk in front of him. His Holiness has also two superintendents of the stables, and the superintendent of the dancers who dance and play music at important festivals. This last is a layman, as are the superintendents of the stables and those in charge of the sedan-chair. The others are monk officials.

When the faithful Master of the Bedchamber died, the Dalai Lama fell into deep sorrow, and, knowing how vital this post was, put his own younger brother into it.

During my year in Lhasa the Precious Sovereign's chief favourite is Tsarong. So firmly does the Dalai Lama support him that for part of the time Tsarong's power outweighs that of the Prime Minister. His manner is somewhat ponderous as compared with the quiet and dignified courtesy of the blue-blooded Tibetan nobles. If his wife is present, she teases him gently, or otherwise restrains him. But he brings a vigour to the lay nobility, which is lacking in many of them. When the Chief of the Po country, semi-independent and semi-barbarous, wanted a wife from the nobility of Lhasa, it was Tsarong's younger sister who was sent to him. None of the best families were willing to send a bride to Po, which was not only lawless, but a long distance from Lhasa. The rulers of Sikkim indeed are able to obtain wives from the best families – the wife of the present Maharaja of Sikkim comes from one of the highest families of all – but Sikkim, though distant, is quiet and law abiding.

Tsarong and I have many talks together. He believes fervently in the superiority of his own people. He considers that Tibetan soldiers are hardier than British soldiers or the soldiers of other countries, as all they need is a little barley flour and they will go all day on that. "They are better at digging," he says, "and the Tibetan workmen are best of all at making things by hand, better than British, Chinese, or the people of any other nation." I express pleasure at the supereminence of the Tibetans.

One informal call on Tsarong found him dressed in an old English lounge coat of poor material, trousers of blue embroidered Chinese silk, and a pair of cheap, white canvas shoes. What a change from his beautiful Tibetan costume! He is greatly interested in Gandhi's movement in India, and especially in the supernatural powers with which Gandhi is credited.

The line he has taken as the head of the army had brought him into strong opposition with the powerful monasteries, who persistently demand that he resign either the post of Commander in Chief or the membership of the Cabinet. The windows of his house in Lhasa are broken by monks during the festival which takes place at the beginning of April. And later on, his wife's jewellery is stolen to the extent of over two thousand pounds. This theft, however, is believed to have been committed during his absence by some of his soldiers in collusion with one or two of his servants. The soldiers are on the whole good fighters, but their discipline is lax, their pay is small, and many of them are recruited from the lowest classes.

Tsarong is so unpopular now, and his life so often threatened, that he has applied for permission to resign his three posts under the Government, i.e. those of Cabinet Member, Commander in Chief, and Master of the Mint. When his resignation is not accepted he repeats his request. Again, for the third time he asks for leave to give up all his governmental posts. His application runs on the following lines: "I am a man of the common people; I am not a member of the aristocracy. I am a man without learning. Thus I am unable to render good service. I therefore beg to be relieved of my three posts. If not of all three, then of two. If not even of two, then at any rate of one."

He has submitted this application direct to the Dalai Lama, who has referred it to the Cabinet for their opinion to be rendered to him through the Prime Minister. But even on the third attempt, the resignation is refused.

The labouring classes do not spare him either, as they sing on the road. They want to know why the colonels and other army officers were punished so heavily, while he was not touched. The decision was the Dalai Lama's, but he, of course, is above criticism. "The King can do no wrong" is the law in Western lands. How much more in this Oriental theocratic State must Chenrezig's Ruling Incarnation be held free of all blame! The Ministers no doubt have given wrong advice; it is they who are to blame. So the verse can be heard:

> Our Ministers in consultation,
> What have they in their minds?
> We thought they should cut out the root,
> But they only peeled the branches.

45   A Day, an Illness and an Angry Monastery

We have seen the work that the Dalai Lama has to do; it will be of interest to consider how the time of an ordinary day in the Jewel Park Palace is apportioned.

Rising from his bed before six o'clock, and often between four and five, he drinks two or three cups of tea. What Tibetan could do without that tea? Then his religious devotions begin. He reads out of the sacred books, invoking the Buddhas of past ages, for Tibetans look on Shakyamuni, the historical Buddha, as being only one from a long line of a thousand Buddhas. He is the fourth, and nine hundred and ninety-six are still to come. A long period, but the Buddhists of Tibet, like the Hindus of India, are apt to deal in vast aeons of time. The Dalai Lama calls down blessings on the whole world, human beings, birds, beasts, fishes and all. On an ordinary day these devotions will last for about two hours. He always has his rosary in his hands or round the left wrist when engaged in his religious devotions or receiving visits.

Then into the grounds to get a little fresh air, maybe playing with his dogs. Breakfast follows, perhaps rice with melted butter poured over it, curds, vegetables and possibly meat. Now he takes his ease for a short time, and then gives orders on his private and semi-private concerns. A new piece of furniture is wanted in the Jewel Park Palace; a religious emblem in the Potala is not quite correct, and must be altered. And other things of the same kind.

Next he may deal with ordinary Government business. His

Ministers send in their reports; he peruses them and makes his decisions quickly. While all this official work is going on, and indeed throughout the day, letters come from all parts of Tibet, written by the relatives of those who have recently died. These letters make offerings to His Holiness and entreat him to exert his influence for the soul of the deceased, so that the latter may obtain a good rebirth, and especially may not be consigned to one of the hellish realms, of which there are cold as well as hot ones. His Holiness then stops whatever work he is engaged on, whether this be Government business or even the religious services of the morning or the midday. After he has performed what is necessary, a statement to that effect is recorded on the letter, his seal is affixed, and the letter is returned to him who has brought it. Such letters are constantly coming in, and take up a considerable portion of each day.

It may well be imagined that these presents on behalf of the dead are often of great value. One such offering is of the kind known as "the present for frying," the meaning of which is that as barley is improved by frying, so the deceased by the Dalai Lama's power will be purified and rendered fit for further good work, and thus saved from going to hell.

About midday the Dalai Lama sometimes holds a religious service with a number of monks who sit in a row below his throne. These read prayers aloud, His Holiness replying at intervals with "Let it be obtained," "Let it be performed," or other suitable and satisfying response. Many of his religious devotions, therefore, cannot be described as "prayers," for he is the one who grants. But speaking of himself, he often says that he prays for this or that.

Round about one o'clock he has his lunch, and he likes to have it in Clear Eye Palace, where he does so much of his work. Lunch may consist of the pastry puffs known as *momo*. His *momo* contain vegetables, cheese, raisins, and possibly meat, all mixed together. Barley bread is also taken, and fruit, for of fruit he is especially fond. And with it all the inevitable tea, of which he takes about forty cups, of ordinary teacup size, each day. This is a moderate amount for a Tibetan; for many drink sixty or seventy cups daily.

After lunch he sometimes draws or paints for a short time, or amuses himself with some of the boy monks. Then he continues working till about four o'clock. The tedium of the daily task is occasionally relieved by watching the traffic go along the road or through the fields, and for this he finds his field-glasses and telescopes useful. For the Dalai Lama is intensely human. He knows he must observe the restrictions that fence off his divinity, but he feels deeply the isolation to which it condemns him. At about four o'clock he returns to the Jewel Park. Afterwards he takes a walk in the countryside round, or maybe works in his garden, or strolls among his animals, sees how the tiger is getting on, and admires his fierce, black watchdogs.

At about five o'clock he dines. A typical dinner would be macaroni soup, bread and fried vegetables. Also cakes, as he has become very fond of European bread and confectionery.

It will be understood that the above hours vary greatly, for Tibetans never allow themselves to be tied to the clock. When I was invited to festivals and ceremonials, I used to ask at what time I should come. The Peak Secretary would say that he would come to conduct me when they were ready. At last he said to me, "We Tibetans have no fixed times. When the Dalai Lama has finished the preceding ceremony, he will take up this one; it may be nine o'clock, or ten, or eleven."

After dinner, chats with members of his household staff give the Dalai Lama a pleasant interlude. Some of the dogs or other household pets, but especially the dogs, are brought in, and a little time passes in this way. Then private prayer, meditation, and the reading of holy books till about eight o'clock. Thus more than four hours are spent daily in religious devotions.

Work follows and continues till midnight, or a little later. During this night work he is alone, and so can take up the heavy and complicated work on which he needs to think deeply and undisturbed. For his work he has three rooms one for dealing with religious matters, one for the secular work, and the third for his own private business. In whichever he is working at this time, two favourite attendants sit outside the door, but neither they nor others may enter, unless the Precious Sovereign rings his bell. Quiet reigns throughout his country palace till he opens his door again. During his evening meditation and the heavy work that he does afterwards in these peaceful hours of the night, not even applications for succouring the souls of those who have lately died are allowed to be brought to him.

This daily programme is not a matter of cast-iron routine; there are variations. He sometimes rises as early as three a.m. This happens when (*a*) he is starting on a journey; (*b*) has a ceremony to attend; (*c*) has arrears of work to get through. On days of importance in the calendar of Tibetan Buddhism he will sit in meditation throughout most of the night.

The All Covering Abbot tells me that some days the Dalai Lama spends a lot of time in reading. He himself always has to be prepared for the Lama's calls, and so he seldom gets more than four hours' sleep. Throughout the winter at Lhasa the Dalai Lama prayed regularly for my health. So did the Prime Minister. During the whole of my thirty years' service under the Government of India the weakness of my health was notorious. But during my year in Lhasa I kept well.

It is a strenuous life for the Inmost One, with but little relaxation. Some of his officers, especially the monk officials, work from year to year without taking any interval of leave, but it may be doubted whether any work under such a strain as their Head, for he carries in addition the burden of high responsibility. Courageous, strong-willed, impulsive and humorous, he often smiles in conversation and laughs too, but a serious purpose is always close underneath.

The Dalai Lama does not take part generally in social life. He enters monasteries, temples, and other sacred buildings; but he hardly ever visits private houses. Personally I knew only one instance of such a visit; that was when he visited the house of a wealthy resident in the village of Cheman in the Chumbi Valley, on his return from his exile in India. There he held a short service for the benefit of the household, and received in return an offering of three thousand rupees (two hundred pounds). At this time he was short of funds from having been shut out of Tibet, and this may have been the reason for his visit.

However, he grants interviews to many people, not only on

matters of Church or State, but also regarding the family and domestic affairs of the caller. Not more than fifteen or twenty minutes are allowed for such an interview. He is able to understand a layman's point of view, and will generally take the lead in the conversation. He may give advice to the man before him how to educate his children and manage his estate. Of others who come from afar he makes enquiries as to how their country is faring, and how they themselves are faring.

He takes an intelligent interest in their families and all other matters. To the fathers he may say, "You must send your children to school, and educate them." To the old people, "Devote yourselves to pious acts, and be charitable." He may ask the merchants, "How is trade going on? Pray that trade may prosper." If the man to whom he talks seems stupid or slow, the Dalai Lama does not become angry, but carries on the conversation gently and with patience.

Day by day and night by night his heavy work goes on, and his energetic nature brings its own worries with it. It is therefore not surprising that during this first week in April he falls ill, so that I have been unable to present to him the letter from the retiring Viceroy, Lord Chelmsford, bidding him good-bye. His own doctors are treating him – he never calls in Colonel Kennedy – and therefore it is not possible to say definitely what his illness is. Even the Prime Minister does not know. The All Covering Abbot informs me that it began when he was occupied with the threatened outburst between the monks and the soldiers, and was due to the strain thrown on him by this. High fever set in, accompanied by a slight cough, and his legs became painful.

This morning, April 12th, his Chief Secretary calls on me and says that the Precious Protector is worse after going to Lhasa to attend the recent ceremonies there; and especially after having to bless individually two thousand of the monks of the Ganden Monastery. He had to do this on the ninth; the following day the monks were due to return to Ganden. Could he but bless, as the Pope blesses, a whole crowd together, the physical exertion would not amount to much; but blessing a large number of

people, whether monks or laymen, one by one, is a great
exertion for a sick man, as the right hand and arm must be held
out the whole time. I ask the Chief Secretary, and similarly have
sent word to the All Covering Abbot, to ask His Holiness to rest
from all work as far as possible until he is well again. This on
Kennedy's advice. The Chief Secretary thanks me and says that
he himself wanted to advise the Dalai Lama strongly to this
effect, but has not dared to do so.

On the following day I hear he is at present taking Kennedy's
advice; he is due to attend a religious service in the Potala to-day,
but has decided to give this up. However, he is so set on doing
his work thoroughly that he does not follow the advice for more
than a day or two. A few days later he goes to the Potala and
works there, and becomes still worse. The All Covering Abbot
does not know what to do, so, bowing his head to the ground as
usual, he addresses the Dalai Lama as follows:

"Precious Protector, please instruct me what you intend to
do. I asked you not to go to the Potala to conduct the ceremony,
but you went there. I keep asking you to rest, but you continue
working. Do you intend to change your body (that is to say,
give up this present life) or to remain with us?"

The Dalai Lama laughs and replies, "Harm there is none; give
me your medicine." The Precious Sovereign becomes more
careful now; in fact, he is too ill to work, whether he wishes to
do so or not. For two days, his doctor tells me, he was danger-
ously ill. As far as possible his illness is kept secret, for if it
became known there might be grave uneasiness throughout
Tibet.

This severe illness causes us all great anxiety, for everything
depends on the Dalai Lama. If he dies at this time when the
monks and the soldiers are ready to fly at each other's throats, a
serious outburst may result, weakening Tibet so much that the
Chinese troops could invade her again, and destroy her autonomy before her little army is established. Such outbursts have
occurred in Lhasa at intervals, though usually at long intervals.
Fortunately, the constitution which he has inherited as a peasant
of this mountain race, combined with his persistent courage and

the will to live, enables him to recover after three weeks of illness.

It was just seven years ago, when we were at the Conference in Simla between Tibet, China and Great Britain, that the representative there of Drepung monastery told Achuk Tsering that the monastery was not far off from rebelling against the Tibetan Government, for they felt the latter had punished the whole monastery for the fault of a few. Achuk thought that, unless the Tibetan Government treated both more leniently, Drepung and Tashi Lhünpo might combine against the Tibetan Government and bring about civil war in Tibet.

This threatened revolt of Drepung seems close at hand now. Some time ago the Dalai Lama banished two of the treasurers of the Loseling College, which is much the largest of the four colleges in the monastery, for it contains five thousand monks, as many as the other three colleges put together. They have been sent to Lhoka province, on the further side of the Tsangpo (Brahmaputra river), south of Lhasa. They were efficient in their work as treasurers, but they intrigued with the Chinese at the time when the Tibetans fought and drove out the Chinese during 1911 and 1912. The monks of this college are composed largely of eastern Tibetans near the borders of China, and some of them would be likely to combine with China against Tibet. He is therefore replacing eastern Tibetans by those from other parts in the head posts of this college. But the whole monastery supports Loseling.

Now the women are heard singing:

> The two jewels of the house
> Have been sent on the track to the south;
> The Drepung nunnery
> Now wears her rosary as a head-dress.

The name of nunnery, thus applied in an opprobrious sense to this great monastery, was first given to it during the British military expedition of 1904. When supplies of food for the British and Indian troops were demanded from them, the populace of Lhasa thought that they were easily frightened and yielded too readily, comparing them with Drepung, who are held to have been less timid towards the troops opposed to them. The Tibetans also say that Colonel Younghusband gave Drepung a letter, promising that the British would help them afterwards if they were in need. Thus this monastery, the largest in Tibet, came to be stigmatised as a nunnery.

And the stigma goes yet further. The reference to a head-dress shows that Drepung has even dropped into the laity and become a housewife who has taken Britain, a foreigner, to be her husband. Head-dresses are not worn by nuns. The rosary, mentioned in the song of the women, refers to the fact that the Dalai Lama has recently given a rosary to each monk in Drepung, Sera and Ganden.

This song shows the extent to which the freedom of the women's singing is carried. Who else in Tibet, from the Prime Minister downwards, would venture to criticise publicly the largest home of religion in the country?

A few weeks after the Dalai Lama has recovered from his illness, while I am riding with my groom and one attendant, I meet two thousand of these monks from Loseling on their way from Drepung to the Jewel Park. They intend to demand an interview with the Dalai Lama himself about these happenings. To me they show no hostility; it is not the rising army that they are concerned about, but their own personal politics, and the troubles that result therefrom. Whenever I am at all crowded by their large numbers, they go down the raised road to the fields below.

Having reached the Jewel Park, they demand to see their Head, but this is not allowed. The Ministers arrive hurriedly from their office in the Jewel Park, and such troops as there are in Lhasa march in.

"Shoot," say the monks, "we are not afraid to die." Thus would they die for the Faith, and obtain good rebirths in their next lives. At length they are persuaded to leave.

The Dalai Lama is firm in the attitude that he has taken up. No doubt he knows his own people.

46   Bringing the Rain

It is morning in the middle of May; the strong sun is drying up the light frost of the night. The cuckoo has been heard for the first time during the last two or three weeks, and many remember the verse of "Melodious Purity," the Sixth Dalai Lama, which begins:

> Now the cuckoo from the lowlands
> Comes, and comes the yearly moisture.

But this time the yearly moisture has not come. The land is parched, for throughout the last eight months we have had no rain; only two insignificant snowfalls, and they were long ago. The young crops of barley, peas and mustard – and in the lower lands, wheat – are in great need of rain.

Their morning services ended, the monks of Sera, sitting in the sunshine, discuss the long drought. One of the leaders bursts out, "What can you expect with these miscellaneous kinds of people in Lhasa?" He adds indeed that he was in Simla for the Tibet-China-Britain Conference, and that there I worked harder in the interests of Tibet than most of the Tibetan officials themselves, and he does not think that I would willingly harm Tibet. However, in his opinion the rain deities are angry because I have come. The feeling against me was passing, had almost passed away, but now it is coming forward again, especially among the monks.

The Tibetans have their own system of irrigation, but irrigation alone does not secure the crops; the rain also is necessary. Talking to me, Netö, our secular guide, says, "It is vital to get

349

some rain in the fourth Tibetan month (that is between the middle of May and middle of June, and this year commencing on May 10th). Rain during the fifth and sixth months will not compensate for absence of rain in the fourth. Unless, therefore, a fair quantity of rain falls early in the fourth month, the Dalai Lama will order high lamas to hold the 'Rain-Bringing' services. They will go to various places, including the sacred springs round Lhasa, those where the *nagas* dwell. These are serpent spirits who live underground, and have charge of water, trees, crops and flowers. At these springs, often situated near willow trees, the lamas will hold religious services on the appointed day from morning till evening, read the sacred books, and feed the fishes in the adjacent pools with barley meal, milk, butter and fruits. Indeed, almost anything may be offered except meat."

When the services have started, I ask cheery, light-hearted Netö whether he is praying for rain. His little yellow hat, like an undersized tam o'shanter without a tassel, bobs up and down on his head, and with a half-humorous sigh he replies, "I do not see much use in prayers for rain when the sky is clear. I hold with the view of Uncle Tömpa."

"Uncle Tömpa? Who was he?"

"He was a clever man who lived in the Pempo country, one full day's journey north of Lhasa, a long time ago. He was not much good in ordinary prophecies, but he had studied the rain question and understood it. He refused to pray for rain, when there appeared to be no chance of it, but used to say that the proper time to hold these services was when the clouds were going from the south to the north. That is the time when the rain is most likely to fall. So even in the present day people repeat the saying:

> When the southern clouds go northwards,
> Uncle Tömpa prays for rain."

But the Dalai Lama has no sympathy with such spiritual laziness. When the rain does not fall, he sends a message to the Cabinet to enquire whether the services are being properly carried out. The Cabinet sends men to enquire in the different places, for the prayers are going up not only from the monasteries in and near Lhasa, but far and near throughout the countryside, and especially from Drepung, Sera and Ganden. Any monastery found to be lazy in conducting the services is fined forthwith.

During the first week in June the long desired rain falls, and continues on and off for several months, with the result that the crops are well above the average. I point out to a Tibetan friend that I was blamed for the fact that the rain did not come in May. But the crops have ended up very well; so shall I receive credit for this happy result? "Oh, no," he replies. "Had they been bad, everybody would have said, 'The sahibs have come to Tibet, and so the crops have failed.' The crops being good, many pay no attention to the matter, while those who do pay attention say, 'The sahibs came to Tibet, but no harm has resulted.' This is how our people speak."

During July the river at Lhasa rises so high that a little more will flood the Jewel Park. Accordingly the Dalai Lama sends instructions to the Enthroned of Ganden, who conducts a service for preventing this danger. The water goes down.

The problem of the army has now become easier for the Dalai Lama, and, incidentally, for myself. There is in Lhasa a community of Mahomedans from Ladakh in far Kashmir, numbering several hundreds. An army sent from Kashmir attacked western Tibet in 1841; these Mahomedans are descendants of prisoners captured by the Tibetans in that campaign. Khan Sahib Faizulla, the head of this community, comes to tea with me in the middle of June. He says that the people are pleased with me now. When the question of increasing the army was agitating their minds, the feelings of many were hostile; but now the people are easier in their minds about this.

Parkang, the deputy of the monk in the Cabinet, comes to lunch. This monk is Commander in Chief of the Tibetan troops facing the Chinese in eastern Tibet, and a highly efficient general he proves to be. For when the Chinese general, without any warning, broke the truce that was being observed by both sides, this Tibetan monk repulsed the Chinese everywhere. Then he took the initiative and gradually drove the Chinese out of the territory which they had previously occupied, and recaptured the greater part of eastern Tibet. Parkang, as his deputy, ranks as equal with the members of the Cabinet.

He says that the idea of the Cabinet is to increase the army by five hundred men every year. I suggest it will be better not to bring the fresh troops under training to Lhasa. He agrees and says they would be an extra burden on the people of Lhasa in various ways. Besides, the troops are not yet properly disciplined and are apt to rob the people. He would like them to be trained in an outlying district, and brought to Lhasa later on for a short time for fuller instruction.

One soon learns that it is necessary for the ordinary administrator to treat Lhasa tenderly, because it is so much the heart of Tibet that it can react powerfully against inconsiderate treatment. Meanwhile the Cabinet is discussing ways and means of meeting the expenditure, a difficult feat in Tibet, where so much of the national revenue has been alienated.

Another of the members of the Cabinet comes to lunch with me about this time. This is Ngarpö, who has lately been appointed to his high post, middle-aged, steady, and sensible. He is over an hour late for lunch, but that is unavoidable, for today the Cabinet have been discussing the opinions of the Parliament on different matters connected with the raising of the new army. They are going through lists of revenue in order to ascertain how they can find money to pay the new army and provide equipment for them. They agree that the increase of the army should be gradual, for they reckon that with the British rifles in their possession five hundred Tibetan soldiers can keep out a thousand Chinese soldiers.

He adds, "We have increased our revenue of late. Among other increases, due to Shatra, the late Prime Minister, a man of great wisdom, we now let out on loan the grain in our Government granaries. The farmers are thus benefited as well as the State, which gains the interest on these loans; the interest amounts to twenty to thirty thousand *ke* of barley yearly." A *ke* of barley weighs thirty-three pounds.

Ngarpö recognises that no oppression should be done to the

monasteries or farmers in the increase of the army; and that the necessary funds should be met, as far as possible, from new sources of revenue.

A year later, when I am settled in England, Ringang visits me at our house in Hampshire. He has come again to England to complete his engineering studies, at which he is working very hard, wishing to make the most of this fresh period of training. He says that the long campaign against China has had the good result of making the Tibetans hardier and more self-reliant.

Fourteen years later, during 1935, I spent several months in China, Inner Mongolia and Manchuria, on a private visit. When in Nanking, I called on the three official representatives to China, but the headquarters of the Chinese Government being in Nanking, and many other high Chinese officials being there, they were afraid to return my call. However, a few months later when I was at Peiping,[20] in the Wagon Lits Hotel, they came to me several times for long conversations. We talked, of course, always in Tibetan, and therefore could talk freely, for none of the Chinese, Japanese or Europeans knew the Tibetan language. It was clear that the Tibetan Government had told them to visit me and obtain my opinions on different matters, although I had retired from my work in Tibet more than thirteen years earlier, it was nearly two years since the Dalai Lama had died, and a Regent was in power.

About the army, they say "Tibet has now about twenty thousand trained soldiers. These have each had a three-year period of training. A large number of them have been raised in eastern Tibet, and many are paid by grants of land set aside for them. The Tibetan Government would like to have about one hundred thousand soldiers altogether." They considered that the increase of the army was the chief reason why Tibet had maintained her independence.

No doubt training and equipment are often neglected, for the Tibetans, though good fighters, are not a military race, since they became devout Buddhists several centuries ago. But by degrees the idea grows that they should defend their land and religion by armed force against aggression.

The Tibetans are too good-natured even in the fighting. Palh-

ese tells me, "Formerly, when the Chinese captured our soldiers, they put them to death. Now they keep them and question
them as to how many Tibetan soldiers there are. We hear that
such prisoners are treated well, if they give the required information, but otherwise are put to death. In future, when we capture
Chinese soldiers, I hope we shall treat them in the same way.
Formerly we used simply to send them back to China."

By the beginning of August the desire of some to kill me has
passed off. The reasons for the change, very briefly stated, are
that I have been careful to observe Tibetan customs, and that it is
known I have always done my best to help the Dalai Lama and
the Tibetan Government both in India and Tibet. In fact I have
come into popular favour, and of this there are many signs. One
of these is that towards the end of my stay in Lhasa, Surkang, a
secular official and an authority on Tibetan history, comes for a
final visit. He tells me, "All, who think, are glad you have come,
and many show anxiety now you are going, for they feel that we
are safe from the Chinese while you are here, on account of your
knowledge of Tibetan affairs. As for those who do not think, it
may be that some of them speak differently, but what does that
matter? Our books tell us that some spoke ill even of the Lord
Buddha, when he was on earth."

Only two other incidents, which are of an unusual nature,
might be mentioned.

When Achuk Tsering died, the Government of India sent
Laden La, another Tibetan in Indian employ, as my personal
aide. He tells me that he had heard from the Tibetan Prime
Minister that I have been given a nickname. This is Rakashar.
The Prime Minister tells Laden La, "There was formerly a
Cabinet Minister in the Rakashar family – one of the two oldest
families in central Tibet – who used not to speak much, but
when he did, spoke wisely; he did not laugh often. He was thin
of body; his heart was kind. Everybody feared and respected
him even more than they did the Regent, though he was only a
member of the Cabinet."

Another new experience for me is that I am brought into
personal touch with the Tibetan doctrine of reincarnation. Peo-

ple are saying that in my last life I was a high Tibetan lama who prayed that he might be reborn in a powerful country so as to be able to help Tibet. This became by my *karma* a destined task, left over from that life and bound to be carried through in this one. That explains why I, a Briton in this life, have worked so long for Tibet, and though weak in bodily health, have been preserved during the long, hard winter, contrary to general expectation. The late Enthroned of Ganden – he who was Regent when the British expedition came to Lhasa in 1904 – prayed before he died that he might be reborn, not in Tibet, but in a country where he would be able to help Tibet. "So," I am told, "the people say it has been with you."

Even the Nepalese tell us that everybody thinks so. When we visit Reting monastery, four days' journey north of Lhasa, we find the same belief prevailing there.

A few months after we left Lhasa, Dr. McGovern, a student of Buddhism, went to Lhasa in disguise. His disguise was discovered, his lodging was stoned, and he was treated generally in such a hostile manner that the Tibetan Government had to put guards over the house in which he lodged. He wrote a "thriller" entitled *To Lhasa in Disguise*.

Speaking of him, Ringang, when visiting me in England later, says:

"Dr. McGovern had a hostile reception in Lhasa. But your visit was really more critical. You were the first to go there, and remain a long period, since the visit of Sir Francis Younghusband, who was escorted by an army of two or three thousand soldiers. The monks are intolerant of foreigners, and one never knows what they will do. I thought your long stay in Lhasa was full of risk, but your carefulness in observing our customs and respecting our religious susceptibilities gained you goodwill everywhere, and helped to avert the danger."

Speaking of the belief that I was a Tibetan in my last incarnation, Ringang confirms the story, and adds, "Except yourself, I never heard of any European being connected with Tibet in this manner."

47   Men and Monasteries

Almost every year when I came to Gyangtse the Panchen Lama's agent used to come to see me, and invite me to go and stay at Shigatse as the guest of the Panchen Lama. The agent would bring me a present – to take one instance as a sample – of two boxes of European sweets and twenty bags (fifty pounds in each bag) of Tibetan peas. With the peas we would feed our ponies and those of our clerks. There were, of course, far too many peas, so we gave away the balance to Tibetan friends. For this is the custom of the country; Tibetans pass on to others presents that they do not wish to retain.

Shortly before I came to Lhasa, the Panchen Lama's agent told me a new palatial building had been erected at Shigatse, and would be placed at my disposal. But the Government of India did not permit me to accept this, or any of the Panchen Lama's invitations.

In May of this year at Lhasa I receive yet another invitation from the Panchen Lama. It is worded very cordially, and points out that Tashi Lhünpo is practically on my way back to India. Now that I am making a long visit to Lhasa, it seems to me that I ought to visit the Panchen Lama and his people for a few days on my way back. The Panchen Lama is our oldest friend in Tibet, and on account of his great sanctity his influence is very great. The visit will enable me also to explain our dealings with the Tibetan Government at Lhasa, to promote confidence, and to renew the old friendship. Indeed to refuse the invitation will be a real rebuff. Therefore I point out these considerations to the

Government of India, when asking for their permission to accept the invitation. But the Government of India do not permit the visit.

As regards the relationship between these two highest Lamas, the Dalai Lama and the Panchen Lama, it was noticeable that they themselves appeared to be on good terms, but there was always jealousy between the subordinates on both sides. Whenever the Dalai Lama spoke of the Panchen Lama, to Palhese or to myself, he always spoke in a friendly way, and he was not good at concealing his feelings. He rebuked sternly one of his favourites who was against the Panchen Lama. Many years later, after the Panchen Lama had fled to Mongolia and China, the Dalai Lama tried to facilitate his return to Tibet.

The two seldom met each other. Towering as they did above all others in sanctity, meetings were difficult to arrange. When one was arranged, it was the Panchen Lama, the disciple, who came to meet the Dalai Lama, his spiritual guide.

I take the opportunity here in Lhasa of reminding the Dalai Lama once again how necessary it is to keep on good terms with the Panchen Lama, and to make his Government also do so.

How different are the characters of these two the masterful Dalai Lama and the humble-minded Panchen Lama. The Panchen Lama has a disposition of singular sweetness and charm, and is simply loved by his own people. During the course of their lives both visited Mongolia at different times. There the Panchen Lama had the better name of the two, partly because he was more humble-minded than the Dalai Lama, and his subordinates treated the Mongols more gently than did those in attendance on the Precious Sovereign; though partly also because he was there a longer time and was therefore able to come more thoroughly into touch with the Mongols.

However, if the Dalai Lama's character had been similar to that of the Panchen Lama, he would not have had the success that he did have in restraining the unruly elements in Tibet. From some Lhasan officials in authority I used to hear that in his secular affairs the Panchen Lama had fallen under the controlling influence of three of his agents, one at Kalimpong and two in China. I met all three; all were Tibetans. They were certainly men of ability, vision and push.

The Panchen Lama was criticised also by several of the Mongol leaders for accepting such large religious offerings that many of the inhabitants of Inner Mongolia became impoverished as the result of his lengthy visit.

Our secular guide, Netö, leaves us during June. He is appointed to be the colonel (*depön*) of a battalion in eastern Tibet. He does not like this, for, as he says, "I am now thirty-six years of age, and rather old to start learning military work. I have done a little fighting in eastern Tibet, but have had no military training." However, his religious fervour, perfectly sincere, takes possession as he adds, "If the Dalai Lama told me to go to one of the hells, I would go there gladly." For in Buddhism hells are not forever, and the Dalai Lama will take care of those who obey him.

As his successor, the Dalai Lama has appointed a delightful young member of the Shatra family. Though barely thirty years of age, he has received his share of the family wealth, and lives apart. Accordingly he is known as Shesur, i.e. "Shatra in the Corner." Starting his career as a simple monk in Sera monastery, it was his wish to remain there and work towards the post of Ganden's Enthroned, though he was careful to add, "That would have been far too high for me." His mother supported him in this, but his father, the former Prime Minister, put him into the Government service on the secular side, saying, "Use your brains, do your work thoroughly, and nothing can hold you back."

Though still a young man, he has read deeply into Tibetan literature, and especially the voluminous scriptures. On one occasion I quote to him the lines out of the Ajax of Sophocles, describing the instability of friendship; for an enemy may later on become a friend, and a friend turn into an enemy. Without a moment's hesitation he quotes an old Tibetan saying, which runs as follows:

Even the friend may sometime become a foe;
Even the foe may sometime become a friend;
Remembering this, bear enmity to none.

His occasional flashes of dry humour brighten all conversation with him.

During July the Dalai Lama invites me to take a change of air and scene. We have certainly been a long time in Lhasa, and it seems to be expected of us to make a trip to the country round, for several Tibetan officials, and even the Dalai Lama himself, have been recommending interesting places for me to visit. It is clear also that if we go away for a time, the Tibetan Government may be able more easily to deal with some of their own affairs, as my presence acts as a restraint on them in various ways. We shall also please them by visiting and making presents to different monasteries.

So we talk about it in characteristic Tibetan idiom.

"Precious Protector, if we go to 'Beyond Imagination' (Samye monastery), will that be suitable?"

"It is indeed in the number of the best. Nevertheless, during the sixth and seventh months will not the honourable heat there be very hot? At 'Beyond Imagination' there is much sand. There to me, when age was little, the spirit berry (small-pox) came. So of the heat recollection is good."

"As heat then be come," I reply, "the not going gives pleasure. When the Precious Protector considers in his honourable mind, which, which (repeated thus in Tibetan) places, a little cooler, would be good?"

"Please, Lönchen, there are various places. In my mind Reting and Drikung monasteries are the most pleasing. Yes, they are good, and are level cold-heat" (i.e. temperate in climate).

So I decide to go to Reting, which is some sixty or seventy miles to the north of Lhasa. It is a large and famous monastery; and no European has ever been there.

My conversations with the Dalai Lama are varied, slipping from one subject to another. At this talk we discuss also:

His views as to the future of Tibet in its attitude towards China. These are mentioned in a later chapter.

The restraint of the Chatreng monastery in south-eastern Tibet, which was intending to attack the Chinese, and which I had requested him to restrain. I asked him whether he had had any reply to his letter to the monastery, which is two months' journey from Lhasa.

"Yes," he said, "I received a reply, in which they promise to abstain from fighting. But I cannot trust them to remain quiet for long. Their country is a poor one, and still poorer since the Chinese invaded it. Besides, they have been joined by a number of Chinese bandits, who incite them to take to looting and plunder."

Then the conversation veered round to affairs in the Golok province; I had received news that the Chinese were commencing to invade it. I asked the Dalai Lama whether he had any news of the invasion.

"Yes," he replied, "my agent at Hsining (two months' journey distant in Kansu province) has written to me to that effect. The Chinese, I think, will have difficulty in holding it. The people of Golok have no houses which can be destroyed. They live entirely in tents, and will disappear when the Chinese troops come, but will cut off any small bodies of these that they meet."

The Dalai Lama referred also to the Anglo-Irish dispute, as well as to Gandhi and his influence in India. Like all Tibetans, he wants to know about Gandhi, his influence and his supposed supernatural powers. But he looks on the Irish dispute as more important than Gandhi's opposition to Britain, and hopes that it will be settled as soon as possible.

Finally, His Holiness touched on the ferocity of wild yaks in northern Tibet, one of which in a narrow valley may hold up a large party of travellers.

Shokang, the Prime Minister, is devoted to the Dalai Lama. "The chief necessity for each country," he says, "is to have a ruler who is both strong and just. It does not matter his being severe, provided that he is just. That is why the Dalai Lama's rule is so good for Tibet. If the Dalai Lama 'passed from sorrow,' I might perhaps have to rule Tibet; but ten such as I am would not make up for the loss of the Precious Protector, for he has the twofold power," i.e. the power in both ecclesiastical and secular affairs.

A few weeks afterwards the Prime Minister falls into trouble. The Dalai Lama has passed a decree against him, the second head of the State, for a sum amounting to about two thousand pounds worth of English money, a very large sum for Tibet. The Prime Minister stood surety for a merchant, and the latter defaulted. When told to give his statement on the case, the Prime Minister replied somewhat irritably, and this angered His Holiness. He is ordered to pay the amount by yearly instalments of £160 each, for he is a comparatively poor man. His salary as Prime Minister is only £80 a year, and though, of course, he makes money through the usual routine of presents and in other ways, yet his income is much less than those of the nobility, with whom his social connections lie.

The chief income of Tibetan officials is derived from their landed estates, and some whose work is hardest and their responsibilities the heaviest, have but small estates, while others in easy and subordinate posts have inherited great properties. The Prime Minister is perhaps the most glaring instance of this inequality, his estate being a small one. A movement is at present on foot to transfer estates, or parts thereof, in accordance with the work done by each person. But its chief opponent is the Prime Minister himself; he uses the sentiment, so well known to all who have lived in Asia: "It is not the custom." Power indeed he appreciates, as most Orientals do, but wealth has not sufficient attraction for him to justify an attack on an established custom.

48   The Dalai Lama's Theatre Party

In spite of the rebellion that is coming to a head, the Dalai Lama gives his annual series of theatrical performances. These last for five days. They are part of the spiritual life, and to leave them out would injure the country and people.

It must be explained that there are two kinds of plays in Tibet. One kind, known as *cham,* is performed by the monks of a monastery within their own monastic precincts. Usually a monastery chooses its Tibetan date or dates for the *cham,* and holds to the same date each year. There are numerous subjects for a *cham.* In a previous chapter has been given one of these, namely, "Casting out the Evil of the Old Year."

A *cham* is in effect a lengthy religious service, and it is an act of merit to attend it. At the same time it is an outing, and Tibetans love outings. There are fine dresses to be seen, both of the monk actors and of the spectators, the men as well as the women. And clowns and the like mingle in these religious performances and cause great merriment. One characteristic of the Tibetans, perhaps the most religious race in the world, is that they deem a sacred time and place can also – within limits – be a time and place for mirth. This seems natural in those whose religion is interwoven with every fibre of their cheerful dispositions.

The other kind of play is seen in the dramas that we are now witnessing. The actors wander over the countryside giving their performances. The plays are regarded as secular plays, and have much more freedom of expression than the *cham.* But each has a strong religious flavour, and a pointed moral.

There are several of these theatrical troupes in Tibet. They are composed mostly of farmers, but some are formed from monks, and one at any rate is formed from petty traders. Whether composed of farmers, monks or traders, the troupes come together for this period and give performances in Lhasa and elsewhere. None are allowed to perform in Lhasa until they have done so before the Precious Sovereign.

The name for the actors as well as for the actresses is *Ache Lhamo*, which means "The Elder Sister Goddesses." For the oldest troupe consisted originally of seven sisters, in Tibetan *Pündünpa*. This troupe is still seven in number, but they are all men. Their number is unchanged, and the original name remains, for *pün* means both sister and brother.

Nowadays, except in one company, there are no actresses, the female parts being taken by men and boys. This company does employ actresses, but only in the minor roles. However, in the Jewel Park, this citadel of celibacy, no actresses are allowed to appear.

The opening day is always on the first of the seventh Tibetan month, which this year falls on August 4th. The Precious Sovereign allows the theatrical season to continue in the town of Lhasa only for three days after his own entertainment is finished. It is allowed to continue for some time longer in the parks that border on Lhasa, but the people do not go there to see them as much as they would in Lhasa itself. He does not wish his subjects to spend a lot of time in watching plays. Besides, the great majority of the actors are anxious to return to their homes without undue delay, for their crops will be ready for reaping during September, and many of them will not reach home till then.

At the same time the Dalai Lama wishes these dramas to be maintained. One company that lives in western Tibet, a full month's journey from Lhasa, excused itself from attending last year. The Dalai Lama would not let them off again this year; the people of Lhasa always look forward to seeing them, because their dancing is considered the best in Tibet.

The performance takes place in the outer grounds of the Jewel

Park, just outside the Inner Enclosure. In front of us is a paved square, each of its four sides being thirty to forty yards in length. This forms the stage. On the first day it is uncovered, but on the second day and afterwards a huge sloping tent-roof of Tibetan design covers it.

My mission is invited for all five days. We are given a large tent below, and immediately to the right of, the Dalai Lama's tent, which is screened by a gauze netting from the public gaze. The Jewel Park Palace is a low building, and the Dalai Lama's tent is pitched on its flat roof. Our place is that reserved for the Grand Lama of the Sakya monastery, when he comes; Sakya lies south-west of Shigatse, half-way between it and the Tibet-Nepal frontier. This Lama is the third personage in Tibet, ranking next to the Panchen Lama in order of precedence. The Grand Lamas of Sakya gained the sovereignty over Tibet in A.D. 1270, and held it for seventy-five years. To this is due the high rank of their successors, even at the present day.

In the corresponding position to the left of the Dalai Lama will be pitched to-morrow the tent of the Prime Minister. Neither he, nor any of the officials, ecclesiastical or secular, are invited on this first day. Directly below the Dalai Lama sits his Chief Secretary, on the extreme right of his row. The next two on his left hand are room-stoppers, big men, well over six feet. Next to them are the secretaries. These all sit in the open on the ground. It should perhaps be mentioned that the Chinese Amban was never invited to the theatrical performances.

To the left of the stage is a row of low, whitewashed buildings, in which are fashioned the fresh wooden blocks now being made in the Jewel Park for printing the Buddhist Scriptures. On the flat roofs of these sit two hundred and fifty men of the Dalai Lama's bodyguard. This is composed of picked soldiers, armed with British rifles – of modern, though not quite the latest, design – from the consignment that the British Government gave to Tibet a few years ago. A colonel is in command.

Behind us is the main block of the Palace buildings. On the other two sides are the trees, shrubs and flowers of the Jewel

Park grounds. On the next day and succeeding days the ecclesiastical officials sit on our right; the secular officials on our left. Each side of the stage, except the side in front of us, is lined with spectators.

The actors have their own costumes, but these would not be good enough to show before the Dalai Lama, or indeed before any of the higher officials. There are three or four sets in use today, all of them belonging to the Dalai Lama. As soon as one troupe goes off the stage another comes on, dressed in one of the other sets. For instance, here is a troupe that wears blue masks, with white markings for eyes, nose, mouth, etc. They have short grey smocks, and maroon skirts down which hang white cords ending in large flat tassels. The waistbands are crimson. In their hands are wands two feet long with white cloth at the ends. These wands are known as "the wands that draw good luck." There are six of them, and they represent fishermen. In each of the companies there are two actors with large yellow tam o'shanter hats; these represent kings or chiefs.

In the evening the bodyguard form up behind the stage, bugles and drums sounding. They present arms to the Dalai Lama and then march off accompanied by their band, which has been trained in Western music and drill by the Gurkha regiment at Lansdowne in the western Himalaya. With them are four hundred soldiers of the ordinary Lhasa garrison, some six or seven hundred soldiers altogether. This all makes a lot of noise, but the play does not stop; it goes placidly on.

The play that we are watching tells about the chief disciple of a poet-saint who lived between eight and nine hundred years ago. Towards the end of the play he meets his revered master, who has been meditating for a long time in solitude. At this point the Tibetan Government's presents to the actors are laid on the stage, for the meeting is regarded as a highly auspicious event, and it is therefore well to give the presents now. They are mostly bags of barley grain, the chief cereal food of Tibet.

The proceeding ends with praise of the Dalai Lama, prayers that throughout the world there may be peace, no shortage of water, and good crops everywhere. And for Tibet itself blessings on the Prime Minister and the other Ministers, and on all people, yellow and grey, i.e. priestly and secular.

Here each ecclesiastical and lay official throws on to the stage a white silk scarf with money in it, as a present for the actors. It just rains scarves for half a minute or so, for every one of the numerous lay and clerical officials in Lhasa is bound to attend unless he has obtained special leave of absence; and the rule requires that these scarves must be thrown promptly when the time arrives. The actors do not open them at this time, but gather them up and take them away.

On the third day, as the performance draws to a close, the band suddenly strikes up "God Save the King" as a compliment to us, and the audience shows great interest in seeing us stand up in our tent.

A few days later I give a theatrical entertainment, lasting for three days. I launch it originally for two days, but during the first day I discover that the Dalai Lama would like me to give his favourite troupe, the one that dances so well, a chance of performing. So I have the good dancers on the next day, Saturday; and the others on Monday, this being the recognised order in which these two companies should appear. Each play would take five complete days to act in full, but I limit each to one day. The costumes for the actors and actresses are lent by the Dalai Lama from his own store. He is pleased that I am giving this entertainment.

In one of the plays the king and queen of a country go to worship the god "Great Power and Wealth," and ask his help to obtain a wife for their son. On their way they have to cross a river in a boat. As the boatmen come on the stage, one of them sings out, "I worship the Dalai Lama; I care nothing for the Emperor of China or his father." Giving a vigorous kick, he calls out, "Here is a kick for the Emperor of China." At this sentiment the Tibetan officials among the audience applaud strongly, and the crowd applauds and laughs.

I abstain from detailed descriptions of the plays that were

acted, as they are not necessary to the story, which is lengthening more and more.

At or near the conclusion of each play my presents, sacks of barley, etc., including a silk scarf filled with silver coins, are placed before the actors. The guests and others in the tents, fifty or sixty altogether, throw their presents, wrapped in silk scarves, in the same way that the officials did at the Dalai Lama's theatricals.

49   Rebellion

We have seen in an earlier chapter that during April of this year Drepung Monastery was near to rebelling against the Tibetan Government. By the end of July the storm, that has long been rumbling, draws close. The monks threaten to attack not only Lhasa, but even the Jewel Park, and say that they will seize the Dalai Lama's Chief Secretary. They regard him as the source of their troubles, alleging that he has given to the Dalai Lama advice which has resulted in the banishment of the two treasurers of the Loseling College. When the Chief Secretary is told of this, his only reply is, "What can they do? Let them dance as they will." But the people of Lhasa are nervous, and some of them have commenced again to hide their valuables.

Drepung is trying hard to induce its big brothers Sera and Ganden, to range themselves on its side, but both refuse. Meanwhile the Tibetan Government despatch their hard-riding couriers to summon extra troops to Lhasa from outlying stations. During these preparations we go on quietly with our theatre parties. The troops arrive about the second week in August, some three thousand, more than ample to overpower this monastery, large though it is. They are encamped in tents near Drepung. When riding along the main road, which passes near the monastery, everything seems to be quiet, but the Members of the Cabinet and the Prime Minister are extremely anxious. The former have advised the Dalai Lama to show moderation in punishing the monastery, and have been sorely snubbed by him. The Prime Minister is accordingly afraid to advise moderation, as he would like to do. I hold views somewhat similar to those of the Cabinet Members and the Prime Minister, who therefore entreats me to take his place in giving advice to His Holiness. Naturally I am unwilling to intervene, but the situation is certainly tense. Besides, discussions with the Chinese Government are at present in progress, and they may perhaps result in settling the political status of Tibet.

Accordingly I tell His Holiness that I have always pointed out to my Government how much better Tibet is governed than China is, an argument to show that Tibet is well fitted for autonomy apart from China. Therefore, though I recognise that firm measures are necessary when subjects are defiant, I hope that peace may continue to be maintained in Tibet and Lhasa, so that this argument may still hold good in favour of Tibetan autonomy. He knows well how often China has taken the line that Tibet is unfitted for self-government.

The Dalai Lama accepts my view without demur, but also without enthusiasm. He would not have accepted it from the Prime Minister, any more than he did from his other ministers. He thinks that they are too cautious; he himself has quieted down a good deal, but is still occasionally inclined to impulsive action.

As previously arranged, we leave for Reting on August 24th. About the time of our departure Palhese and Laden La tell me that the authorities of Drepung have asked them to request me to settle the dispute between the Tibetan Government and themselves. That this large monastery, which had at first strongly opposed my suggestion about the army, should so far come round as to desire my arbitration in their affairs, shows that I have stepped up in the favour of the clergy as well as of the laity. It would, however, be wrong for several reasons that the British representative should arbitrate between the Tibetan Government and one of its monasteries, nor have the Tibetan Government as a whole expressed a desire that I should do so.

On September 3rd, the day on which we leave Reting on our return journey, and halt for the night at Pöndo, a written order from the Cabinet reaches the *dzongpön* at this latter place, telling him to seize any Loseling monks who come there. It is apparently thought that they may try to escape by this route to their homes in eastern Tibet, where they mostly belong, and stir up trouble there, seeking Chinese help against the Tibetan Government.

On the following day I receive a message from the Peak Secretary, who has no doubt been told by the Dalai Lama to write to me. It is about Drepung and it asks me not to be anxious; that people may bring me all sorts of stories, true and false; and that the monks of Loseling are expected to submit shortly and acknowledge their guilt. Shesur adds that the roads from Lhasa have all been stopped against them, and the different *dzongs* have been ordered by the Cabinet to capture all that attempt to escape, and to kill those that they cannot capture. The Dalai Lama is clearly experiencing the difficulty of governing a country without ever taking human life; the wonder is that he has been able to abstain in this' as much as he has, for his temper is still a difficulty, and he has now become accustomed to receive unquestioning obedience.

Young Shesur quotes to me a saying of his ancestor, the famous Regent Shatra, who lived some sixty years ago. This was he, who, though but a layman, was made Regent of Tibet in preference to the six high priests, one of whom usually holds the post. He used to say that when a monastery rebels – one perhaps not so large or influential as Drepung – there is no need to fight it, adding, "Shut the monks up in their monastery with their lice, and they will soon find life unendurable." No food to be bought in the neighbouring town or villages; no fresh clothes to be obtained from relations or friends; no visits for bathing purposes to neighbouring streams or ponds; and in the monastery everywhere – lice.

Three days after the message from the Peak Secretary, Palhese receives a letter from the Dalai Lama in the latter's own handwriting, to the following effect:

"As Lönchen Bell is always working for the interests of Tibet, he may be anxious about the affair of Loseling. Please therefore inform him that the monks of Loseling have submitted an impossible petition to me, and I cannot grant it without inviting similarly impossible requests from Sera, Ganden and other monasteries. I intend, therefore, to make a great show of force to frighten these recalcitrants. But the monks of Drepung, in common with all monks, are my disciples. Therefore after frightening them, I shall meet their wishes as far as possible. As you serve Lönchen Bell, you know what is in his mind. Send me, therefore, any advice that he may wish to give me."

I tell Palhese to reply that I am very glad that fighting has been averted, and that I have full confidence in the wisdom of the policy that His Holiness has adopted.

A little later Palhese tells me, "Our Government seem clearly to have gained the upper hand over Drepung. They demand that the ringleaders be given up; it is possible that these will be put to death as a warning to others. The parties sent out in search of these give notice to the villagers, as they pass through. The villagers have to 'peel the mountains' (i.e. examine the mountains very thoroughly) in search of the men. It is their duty to do this work; it is in effect a part of their rent, and if they fail in it, they are liable to be punished by their *dzongpöns*. I think, however, that the ringleaders are still hiding in Drepung, and will later on make a dash for India or Bhutan.

"The Drepung monks, who do not belong to the Loseling College, are regarding the soldiers that are surrounding the monastery in the light of a show. They come out and look at them. If the ringleaders can be got rid of, they will profess innocence. For, as our Tibetan saying runs:

"Out of the hostile country
My mind is now at ease.

"The monastery is probably hiding the rifles which they are believed to possess. For six or seven years ago they gave a letter to say that they had no rifles; so they hardly dare now admit the possession of them. They will either hide them underground below the monastery itself, or underground in the hillside adjoining, so as to be able to obtain possession of them when required."

Two days later we arrive back in Lhasa, and three days after my return I call on the Dalai Lama. We speak of various matters, including former missions from Tibet and Nepal to China, and the present position of the questions at issue between China and Tibet.

Then he himself brings up the rebellion of Drepung Monastery. He says, "I had to show myself the master; otherwise Sera, Ganden and others will all be encouraged to break out when they wish to gain any end of their own. But the affair is now nearing a settlement, and I intend to do as you advise me, namely, to punish the monastery as lightly as possible."

Referring to the letter he wrote some days ago to Palhese, telling the latter to pass the information on to me, the Dalai Lama says:

"Lhasa is the home of all sorts of rumours. I am the one who does the work, and I know what is happening. But the people bring to me – and would bring to you also – a story of what I am doing that is entirely unrecognisable."

That the Dalai Lama is correct about the complete unreliability of rumours in Lhasa is shown by two instances that come to my notice the very next day. Lay officials had told me that monks, whose duty it was to pray for rain, were punished by him if rain did not fall. But I find from the Peak Secretary that he does not punish them, unless they have been negligent in the religious services at which these prayers are offered. I had been told also that the Dalai Lama punishes the *Ache Lhamo* if rain falls during the five days that they act before him. The Peak Secretary informs me that this is not the case. He is one of the Dalai Lama's own secretaries, and thus in the best position to know. Palhese also confirms the Peak Secretary's statement.

It is natural that His Holiness should grow restive under these rumours; as for the outstanding advantages of his position, he takes them for granted. His people are assured of his divine pre-eminence, his power over this life and the next. What a lot he owes to that!

The Tibetan Government's biography refers to the numerous discussions that the Dalai Lama had with me about Tibetan affairs. It says:

"Lönchen Bell, the administrator of Sikkim, being a man of

sincere affection – having no difference between mouth and heart (i.e. being sincere) – towards the Government of Tibet, the great Chief of Buddhas (the Dalai Lama), worked with him concerning many civil and military matters. They enquired and replied to each other in a straightforward manner; they scrutinised and compared minutely, leaving no gaps, and thus brought about benefits in the administration of Tibet. These matters we found in a large number of letters written by the Dalai Lama's own hand."[21]

On September 17th, five days after my return to Lhasa, the Tibetan Government gives a feast to the Tibetan troops in Lhasa to commemorate the subjugation of Drepung monastery. The feast lasts for three days. On the 20th they march through Lhasa, and present arms in front of the Great Temple. Then the troops enter the Temple and worship the famous Buddha there, as well as Palden Lhamo, the guardian goddess of the Tibetan Government. Though, as soldiers, they must take life, they are still good Buddhists. This is said to be the first time that troops carrying arms have ever entered the Temple.

Six years later, when he spent a year with me in England, Palhese gave me the conclusion of the story. "The three or four ringleaders were caught some months afterwards in the mountain-side behind Drepung. They were beaten and expelled from the honourable profession of the clergy. Then they were made over to different officials with iron fetters on their legs and cangues round their necks. One was made over to a Member of the Cabinet, and another to the Dalai Lama's Chief Secretary, the very official that they had threatened to seize. Those receiving them set them to work in the stables, and on similar occupations. Such a man is not imprisoned, but is given a small room in the stables.

"No, he does not run away. He gets his food regularly where he is, and in any case he could not escape, for he would soon be recaptured and suffer heavy punishment. These men were still confined in this way when I left Lhasa in December, 1926, some five years after they were captured. The lesser leaders in this rebellion were merely beaten and turned out of the monastery. Nobody was put to death."

50   End of Our Visit Draws Near

Occasionally the Dalai Lama lays aside the daily round of work. He went three times to Reting monastery, staying twice in the monastery itself and once in the hermitage that nestles among the trees higher up the hillside. In the hermitage he meditated in peaceful seclusion for several months. He had to do the most urgent secular work even when he was there, but at any rate the religious exercises came more to the front. The Dalai Lama has always loved Reting, whose name means "The Uplifted Horn."

During our stay at Reting we visit the private apartments of the Dalai Lama. His sitting-room is large, more than twice as large as any of the private rooms of the Head Lama. At one end of the room is a couch under a yellow silk covering, and along one side are numerous images, bowls of holy water and other religious objects. Windows run down the length of the room, but the cloth that covers them is of the sacred yellow instead of the usual white cloth. Outside the narrow verandah are the curtains of yak hair, of which there must always be two, an upper and a lower, known respectively as the Heaven Curtain and the Earth Curtain.

This private room is entered through the Hall of Audience; the Dalai Lama's throne is on a broad dais that runs the whole length of the hall. Here the Dalai Lama gives audience to laymen who come to receive his blessing.

The dwellings of the monks are of stone below and sun-dried brick above. The roofs are flat; they are made of stone and slate, covered with earth, the whole supported by wooden beams.

A pleasure-house lies below the great monastery, situated in a grove of poplar trees along the bank of the river. It has lately been repaired under the Dalai Lama's order, and it is thought that he will stay here instead of in the monastery when he next visits Reting.

In one of the halls at Reting we see an immense number of sacred books, several thousand volumes, piled up against the walls, each in its massive wooden covers, some plain, but many carved. They are the remnants of those left unburnt after a fire which occurred several hundred years ago. These books are not used. A complete fresh set was made to replace them. I enquire whether it would not have done to replace those that were missing and thus complete the set and use it. But I am told that this would not be right; in such a case fresh sets must be prepared and the old books left unused. It is as though they should be left in peace to enjoy the repose that they have so richly earned after being attacked by this fire.

On my return to Lhasa I tell the Dalai Lama that I shall soon be leaving for India, where I expect to see the Viceroy and the Foreign Secretary; and shortly after that shall go to England on retiring from the service of the Government. But I receive letters from the Precious Sovereign, the Prime Minister, the Cabinet and the Parliament, one from each addressed to the Viceroy, and one from each addressed to me, asking that I may remain in Lhasa, until they receive from the British Government the full reply to their representations. They also ask that, if and when negotiations with the Chinese Government are resumed, I may be the British representative.

In addition to the letters, a deputation from the Parliament calls on me, urging the same requests in person. The deputation consists of three Abbots – one each from Drepung, Sera and Ganden and three Financial Commissioners. I explain to them that during my stay here in Lhasa the British Government have made several requests to the Chinese Government to negotiate, but hitherto without effect. I add that I will let the Dalai Lama know the British Government's reply to their representatives as soon as I receive it. They leave, well pleased with this reply.

Shortly afterwards I receive the reply of the British Govern-

ment to my proposals for a new policy towards Tibet. Every one
of my suggestions has been accepted by the Viceroy and the
British Government. For several years I have struggled to push
through my ideas for the betterment of our relations with Tibet,
but with small success, though I have returned again and again to
the charge. Now all is changed. My ideas have gone through in a
flood; not one has been rejected.

I tell the Dalai Lama the gist of the reply, explaining to him
the outline of the new policy that we are going to adopt, simple
and helpful to Tibet. His pleasure is unbounded. Norbhu, one
of my clerks, says, "All the Tibetans are delighted; you can see it
in their faces."

It is about this time that I show the Inmost One snapshots of
my children. He is interested in the little photographs, so I give
them to him. He is fond of children, as indeed nearly all Tibetans
are.

Now that we are leaving soon, we give a few small extra
presents to our Tibetan friends, having given the bulk of our
presents soon after we arrived, as is the Tibetan custom among
guests. The hosts give their main presents when the guests
depart. Among other things we make a distribution of flower-
seeds to various Tibetans and Tibetan monasteries, because they
are all so fond of flowers. Kündeling is one of those to which we
give; it is the monastery that owns the houses in which my staff
and I are lodged and the land on which these houses stand. But
we cannot give seeds to Drepung, Sera or Ganden, for they are
not allowed to grow flowers.

Such pleasures are regarded as likely to entice them from their
religious duties, which are of exceptional importance, for they
hold an exceptionally high religious position. And they are not
allowed to read books on history, lest they find them too
interesting and are thereby enticed from the reading of their
Buddhist scriptures. Narrow is the gate, and narrow the road
that is marked out for their spiritual life, though, like the followers of Christ, many stray from it.

The Tibetan year is lunar, and has twelve months. To bring it
into line with the solar calendar an extra month must be fre-

quently added. We have an extra month this year, the second seventh; it is ending only now, September the 30th. The fact that the rainfall has been prolonged this year later than usual, and thus improved the out-turn of the crops, is attributed by the Peak Secretary partly to the introduction of this second seventh month. For the seventh month is always reckoned one of the rainy months, and so by putting in a second seventh month you may reckon on prolonging the rainfall.

On the last day of the second seventh month, the Dalai Lama blesses the monks in the lately rebellious Drepung monastery. Truly, as he says, every monk is his disciple. Each is blessed separately. The Dalai Lama stretches out his right arm and lays his right hand on each bowed head. There are probably some seven thousand in residence at this time. To-morrow, the first day of the eighth month (October 1st), he will do the same for each monk in Sera Monastery. Hard work it is, but having done such work from the days of childhood onwards, he is accustomed to it. The monks attend at the Jewel Park Palace early each morning and conduct religious disputations of the kind given by Geshes. These are conducted on the stage where we saw the Dalai Lama's theatre party. Later on, when the Dalai Lama is ready for them, probably at about 9 a.m., they come to him to be blessed.

Another scene. I am to take the Dalai Lama's photograph again; this time it is to be in his own throne-room in the Jewel Park Palace, the first time that anybody has photographed him in the Holy City. When I arrive with Rabden on the day and at the hour appointed, the arrangement of the throne-room is not ready. I watch them arranging it. The throne is built up of two or three wooden pieces; the nine silk scrolls, representing Buddha in the earth-pressing attitude, are already placed on the wall behind and above the throne. In this attitude Buddha is seated with his right hand stretched downwards, the fingers touching the ground. The meaning is that he is keeping down the evil forces who assist Mara, the Tempter, in assailing him just after he has attained to Buddhahood. Below these scrolls red silk brocade covers the wall. The throne is four feet high, a seat without back or arms. It stands on a dais, eighteen inches high, with a low balustrade of beautifully carved woodwork running round it. Hanging down in front of the throne is a cloth of rich white silk, handsomely embroidered in gold, with the crossed vajra. Chrysanthemums, marigolds and other flowers are arranged round the dais. This is the throne that is used on important occasions.

While the room is being arranged, the Dalai Lama comes in to see that the arrangements are made correctly. He is simply and comfortably dressed, as is his custom when not engaged in ceremonies or other public functions. Monk officials and ordinary workmen go about their work, almost jostling against him, while he winds in and out among them, giving an order here, making a slight change there. Workmen clean and polish the boarded floor by sliding over it in their Tibetan boots, with soles of soft yak hide and large woollen flanges attached. Apart from his giving of orders, it would be difficult for a foreigner, who did not know him, to say which is the Dalai Lama among this crowd, so inconspicuously does he move among them.

The scene reminds me of the time in Bhutan, eleven years earlier, when I saw the king of that country walking barefooted in a crowd of Bhutanese, chatting with them, and hardly to be distinguished from the others. A man among his fellows; democracy in feudalism. Whether Divine kings or human kings, there is a simplicity about their everyday lives.

51

"We Two are Men of Like Mind"

The Dalai Lama is taking a little to English food. One of his servants arrives with three or four tomatoes and a few Cape gooseberries, grown in India and known there as *tipari*. The Dalai Lama has sent him to ask me the best way to eat these. The Precious Protector is now forty-five years old and enjoys good health.

At one of the last conversations that I have with the Dalai Lama he says to me, "I want you to write to me from time to time after you go to England. Your letters to me will be opened by nobody but myself; and I ask you to do the same with the letters that I shall write to you."

Tibetans, as we have seen, believe in good and bad luck. People born during an eclipse, itself a bad omen, receive a large share of good luck. Few can be so fortunate as this, but everybody has two lucky days and one unlucky day every week. These all depend on what year out of the cycle of twelve animals he was born in. The Dalai Lama having been born in the Mouse year, his lucky days are Tuesday and Wednesday; his unlucky one is Saturday. On Saturday, therefore, Government work is not carried on in Tibet, the public offices being closed on that day as, in Christian lands, they are closed on Sundays. Palhese's unlucky day is Tuesday, and he is unwilling to commence any important work on a Tuesday.

The two lucky days in each week are termed the life day (*sokza*) and the soul day (*laza*). I choose the life day of the Dalai Lama as our day for departure from Lhasa. The life day of the Inmost One is of universal application; its selection gives great

379

pleasure to the people of Lhasa, and is expected to insure us against illness and accident.

On October 15th, four days before we leave, the Prime Minister pays his farewell call. He is greatly pleased at the reply of the British Government to the requests made by the Government of Tibet, though these requests were indeed modest, such as a friendly nation had every right to expect from India, its neighbour. But for a long time the British Government hung back; and now at last they have been persuaded to take action. So the Prime Minister is delighted. "Now," says he, "I can die happy; it matters not whether I live or die. But if you had returned to India some months ago with Tibet in a dangerous and almost hopeless condition, I should have died in misery."

Towards the end of our time in Lhasa one of the songs of the people is composed about me and sung in the streets, especially on the day of our departure. It runs as follows:

> He who comes from a long distance,
> The guest who has white hair;
> Outwardly he wears foreign dress,
> And shows a stern face;
> Inwardly he helps our religion and our Government.
> We have come to know that he is
> Lönchen Bell.
> May he live long!
> May he be free from illness!
> May he succeed in all his works!
> May he obtain the threefold perfection (grace, glory
> and wealth)!

On October 16th, three days before the mission leaves the Holy City, I pay my farewell visit to the Dalai Lama. It is a sad parting for us both. Kennedy, going in for his farewell visit soon after I come out, notices that the Dalai Lama is markedly depressed.

As the host gives his return presents when the guest leaves, so the Dalai Lama gives me his at this interview. The presents are:

1. A pair of cups of the material called *manohu,* each standing

on a flat dish of the same material. In the Tibetan biography of
the Third Dalai Lama, who took the leading part in converting
Mongolia to Buddhism, it is recorded that the Chinese Emperor
of the Ming dynasty, reigning at that time, sent to the Dalai
Lama many valuable presents, among which *manohu* stones
were included.

2. A jade bowl with ring handles.

3. A jade vessel shaped like a peacock.

4. A small bowl of "fish-eye" jade with handles.

5. A jade vase on a wooden stand.

6. A jade stick, with a crook on the top, for hanging on a
pillar, and for use in the presence of the Emperor of China.

7. Two large blue and white porcelain jars.

8. Two small teapots of Tibetan cloisonné, valued highly in
Tibet, because the art of making it has been lost for more than
two hundred years.

The Dalai Lama tells me that all the above, except the Tibetan
cloisonné teapots, were given by the then Manchu Emperor to
the Fifth Dalai Lama, who visited the Emperor in Peking, two
hundred and sixty-nine years ago. He adds, "I do not wish to
give you a great number of things which would be useless to
you, but rather to give you a few things that are really good."

His Holiness again expresses his pleasure at the reply of the
British Government to the representations of Tibet. His last
words to me are, "My great hope is that you will return to Lhasa
as the British Representative to complete the treaty between
Britain, China and Tibet. We have known each other for a long
time, and in you I have complete confidence, for we two are men
of like mind. I pray continually that you may return to Lhasa."

That the Dalai Lama considered our minds alike is confirmed
by the fact that he has never refused any of my requests, and has
accepted all the opinions that I have given him, and has acted on
them.

During my last few days in Lhasa I exchange farewell visits
with the Ministers, and other leading Tibetans call on me. On
the day of our departure, 19th October, 1921, just as we are
leaving, Tsarong calls at our house informally to say his farewell.

He is not only very pro-British, but is taking a little to European customs, as is shown by his chairs, tables and some of his other furniture, his cutlery and some of his food, his occasional semi-English attire, and now by this "come to see you off" call.

The receptions, guards of honour, etc., on our way out are similar to those on our arrival, with a few added compliments. But there is one notable addition in that the Dalai Lama himself comes out of his seclusion and stands on the roof of a neighbouring house to see us pass down the road, although he is in full view of the crowd of people that throng the roadside to witness our departure. I wave my farewell to him as I pass, and he bows and smiles in return. Such an action on the part of a Dalai Lama is perhaps unprecedented in the annals of Tibet.

After three days the Peak Secretary leaves us. We are now at the foot of the Kampa La, the crossng of which takes us from the Central Province (U) into the Pure Province (Tsang).

Shesur continues with us as far as Gyangtse. From here we are on the easy, familiar track, equipped with our own Government's staging bungalows. So at Gyangtse he and other Tibetan friends give us their farewells. In accordance with Tibetan etiquette, we say to each other, "I must petition you that we may meet again from time to time." And this although they and we know that it is improbable that we shall ever meet again. Shesur says good-bye after all the others. To the above formal words he adds, "Tibet owes much to you; do not forget her!"

Then on to Pari, Chumbi, Gangtok, Kalimpong and Darjeeling. At each place the mountain folk, Tibetans, Sikkimese, Nepalese and Lepchas, come in to say good-bye. In the Chumbi Valley, our last district in Tibetan territory, the Tibetan officer in charge of it and the village headmen come and thank me for preventing an outbreak in Lhasa.

The atmosphere then was indeed electric, and became still more so, when the quarrel broke out between the monks and the soldiery, and when the large monastery rebelled. Had the outbreak occurred, whether or not disastrous to ourselves, it would at any rate have resulted in a serious setback to the interests of Tibet.

Articles have appeared in the Japanese and Manchurian Press. A Japanese paper writes recently, "The prestige of England in Tibet is growing rapidly at the present time, and the Tibetan question is being decided more and more in favour of England."

And now the pleasant trekking on horseback is ended. So by train to Delhi, where I work out with the Indian Foreign Department the details of the new and more friendly policy to be adopted towards Tibet. The chief items in this policy are:

1. Permission to import arms from India up to specified maxima, sufficient only for self-defence and the maintenance of internal order.

2. Help in training Tibetan troops.

3. Help in engaging British mechanics to teach the manufacture of gunpowder and rifles.

4. Help in obtaining good mining prospectors.

5. Help in importing machinery for their mines and their mint.

6. The opening of a school at Gyangtse for Tibetans of the upper middle classes. This to be – as Lönchen Shatra had always insisted – under a British headmaster.

7. And – an object strongly desired by both Tibet and India – the establishment of a telegraph line between Gyangtse and Lhasa, thus putting the Holy City into telegraphic communication with the outer world. From then onwards replies from other countries, which used to take seven days, could be obtained the same day.

The above are all agreed to by the British and Tibetan Governments. Though their national revenue is scanty and ill-adapted to modern needs, the Tibetan Government pay for these services. The object on which they are most keen is the training and equipment of the army which they are now increasing and improving.

My aim was that Tibet should enjoy internal autonomy, free to live her own life, and in her freedom the best possible barrier for the northern frontier of India.

The only disagreement between the Foreign Secretary and myself at this stage is in the selection of the expert who will prospect for minerals. He wants to send the head of the Indian Geological Department, an elderly officer approaching retirement. This officer seems to me to have already expressed opinions adverse to Tibetan mining prospects. Also he has said that he wants to explore a range of mountains in Tibet, and is evidently more keen on that than on examining mines. Accordingly I advocate sending a younger man with an open mind, keen to discover minerals, and to search far and wide for them. But the Foreign Secretary insists on his choice. The elderly officer's report, however, is submitted only after long delay, and is perfunctory. No serious attempt is made to discover new mines, though the Dalai Lama is keen on their discovery. He needs fresh revenue to pay for the new army, and for other expenses in improving the administration of his country. Some twenty years later, China seems to have discovered a number of mines in Tibet, and to have seized them and the districts that contain them, mapping these districts as part of China. Had a younger man, trained to that work, been employed, he and his assistants might well have discovered those mines. The Tibetan Government could have occupied them, and their seizure by the Chinese have been prevented.

My mission ended, I left for England, which had become a half-forgotten country. The Viceroy wrote officially to the Dalai Lama thanking him and the Tibetan Government for their friendly treatment of me. In his reply, over his large red square official seal, the Dalai Lama expressed great pleasure at the Viceroy's letter, and added, "As Lönchen Bell, whom Your Excellency sent to Tibet as your agent, possesses great experience of the duties of both the British and Tibetan Governments, and is very wise, all the people of Tibet and myself have become of one mind, and the British and Tibetans have become one family."

It is pleasant to be able to record that the Government of India gave Palhese the title of "Dewan Bahadur." This was the highest Indian honour next to that of Raja. Palhese told me that he did not want to be made a Raja, as nearly all Rajas are wealthy, and he was not. He was worthy of either title.

Part Six
Foreign Affairs

52

Mongolia, Nepal, Russia, Japan

Isolated though Tibet is, the Dalai Lama has in this year, 1921, a somewhat wide range of political relationships. Mongolia. Nepal, Russia, Japan, China and Britain are all in his thoughts, it will be convenient, therefore, to deal briefly with these countries, and more especially with the Dalai Lama's outlook on them.

How does the solitary figure in the Jewel Park form his opinions on these nations, some of them far distant? It is not so difficult as it may seem. With three of them – China, Mongolia and Nepal – Tibet has held political dealings for hundreds of years. With Russia there has been a slight contact since the latter's annexation of the territory of the Buriat Mongols some two hundred and fifty years ago; and this contact has become stronger since Russia's treaty with Outer Mongolian in 1912.

As regards Japan, some information is gained from Tibetans who have stayed there, but still more from the numerous Japanese in China as well as from Japanese who live or visit in Calcutta, for Tibetans make long visits to both China and Calcutta. Occasionally, Japanese penetrate into Tibet; one of them was employed by the Tibetan Government in the training of troops. We have one now by name Tada, living and studying in Sera monastery for the last eight years. He is studying hard, and comparing the Buddhist scriptures of Tibet with the Buddhist scriptures of Japan. He has shown no outward sign of political activity, but Japanese as a rule, with their patriotic feelings so firmly embedded, find it difficult to abstain from politics. He can, of course, easily send letters to Calcutta through Tibetan traders, if he is so disposed, and thence send news to the

The Dalai Lama's annual state procession to the Potala, 4th February, 1921.

Japanese Government. In any case, Tibetans will like to hear what he says about the Japanese who have more or less the same religion as themselves, and are extremely powerful, and may help them against China.

As regards Britain, the events since 1903 have taught the Dalai Lama a great deal. He studies the English newspapers published in India, and has himself travelled in India on pilgrimage, visiting sites connected with Buddhism. On his pilgrimage he receives many people, and no doubt asks many questions. For holding the twofold power, the religious and the secular, he must do this.

To me also he puts innumerable questions, both as to facts and my opinions on the facts. In whatever way his own opinion may be formed, it goes through. None can openly question it; none can oppose it.

How does the Dalai Lama react to affairs in Mongolia? We have seen that in his third incarnation he laid the foundations of their present religion, and he still holds the spiritual sovereignty over all Mongolia. The present Grand Lama of Mongolia, the secular ruler of that country, is a Tibetan, born in the village lying at the foot of the Potala. There are many other strong bonds between the Dalai Lama and Mongolia. Besides receiving a large amount of religious offerings from it, many hundreds of Mongol monks serve in the leading monasteries near Lhasa. The agent of his bank in Mongolia serves as a regular means of communication; every month or two he writes to Shokang, the present Prime Minister of Tibet.

During the Conference between Britain, China and Tibet, held at Simla in 1913-14, it was stated that Tibet and Mongolia, through the agency of Dorjieff, had signed a treaty of alliance. Russia claimed that such a treaty had been made. As Mongolia had by that time come more and more under Russian control, the British Government felt that such a treaty would seriously endanger British and Indian interests. The Dalai Lama was said to have given Dorjieff a letter which authorised him to conclude a treaty.

But the Prime Minister and the Tibetan Government denied

that the Dalai Lama's letter gave Dorjieff any such authority, asserting that the letter was of a general nature, asking Dorjieff merely to work for the benefit of the Buddhist religion.

"It is the custom of us Tibetans," the Prime Minister added, "to write to everybody asking for help; for instance, in the letters written to you yourself we frequently made requests similar to that which the Precious Protector made to the Abbot of Metaphysics (Dorjieff). The draft of the letter cannot be traced now, and it is feared that it was destroyed when the Turquoise Roof house was burnt down, as the Lord Chamberlain at that time belonged to the Turquoise Roof family, and all the records regarding the tour of the Dalai Lama in Mongolia and China were in his charge."

This year, being in Lhasa, I see clearly the evidence of this fire.

As a matter of fact, Tibetans and Mongols are so closely related by race that when, so often happens, a Tibetan is wearing a Mongol style of dress, it is difficult to tell the two apart. They are bound together by the same religion. There is little, if any, need for a treaty between the two; their relations are already as close as long distance allows. But Lhasa is so far from Mongolia that neither can render much assistance to the other.

Mongols have indeed invaded Tibet from time to time, but these contests were of the same kind as sometimes occur between the tribes of Tibet itself. The Mongols are predominantly of Tsongkapa's reformed sect, the Yellow Hats; and their incursions into Tibet in former times were to help these against the pre-reformation Red Hats.

As for the Dalai Lama, he has no policy towards Mongolia, but just simple friendship. The people are a branch, though a distant one, of his spiritual flock. They have great faith in him, and – be it admitted – bring him copious offerings.[22]

Very different are the Dalai Lama's feelings towards Nepal, which lies on his southern frontier, close to the inhabited districts of south-central Tibet, and not far from Lhasa. The rulers of Nepal are of a different religion to the Tibetans, and this lays the groundwork of the hostility that prevails between the two races. In the old days the Nepalese were under the rule of

Buddhist kings. Indeed, Tibet obtained her Buddhism a good deal from Nepal. This country has always had a predominantly Mongoloid, rather than Indian population. It has thus always formed a suitable channel of communication between India and Tibet.

The State of Gorkha was one among several petty kingdoms that made up the present territory of Nepal during the first half of the eighteenth century. In 1769 this warlike State gained the ascendancy throughout Nepal. In 1791 the Gurkhas invaded Tibet and occupied Shigatse. The Manchu Government despatched an army composed partly of Chinese and partly of Tibetans, which marched through Tibet in the heart of winter, defeated the Gurkhas in several engagements during the spring of 1792, and finally dictated terms of peace within a few miles of their capital. But China found this warlike nation too far away to hold down by force; it remained a constant thorn in the side of Tibet.

In 1855 hostilities broke out again between Nepal and Tibet, and in the following year a treaty was made between the two which gave the Nepalese great advantages. The gist of this treaty was that Tibet paid to Nepal ten thousand rupees yearly, and the Nepalese gained also the right of living in Tibet without paying duties or taxes of any kind, even though such taxes were paid by the Tibetans among whom they lived. They gained also rights of extra-territoriality, Nepalese magistrates trying Nepalese subjects in Tibet for all offences, adjudicating themselves on all disputes between Nepalese, and deciding jointly with Tibetan magistrates those questions in which the interests of both Tibetans and Nepalese were involved. In return Nepal undertook to come to the help of Tibet, if the latter were invaded.

This is a truly advantageous position which Napel is determined to retain. But when Tibet was invaded, first by British forces in 1904, and a few years later by Chinese troops, Nepal furnished no military help whatever. Partly for this reason, and partly from numerous irritating incidents that have occurred from time to time, the Tibetans feel an intense hatred towards the Nepalese. The mutual relations have been still further embittered by the Nepalese agent's discourtesy towards the Dalai Lama himself. When passing His Holiness in the street one day, he did not dismount from his pony, and thus, according to Oriental standards, was guilty of unpardonable rudeness.

The Nepalese Government had a dispute with the Tibetan Government as to how the mutual frontier runs in an important district near Katmandu, the capital of Nepal. They wrote to the Tibetan Cabinet that unless the matter was settled quickly they would send an army against Tibet. The Dalai Lama ordered the Cabinet to reply, promising that a British officer should be appointed to arbitrate. to this the Nepalese Government replied to the following effect:

"We are deeply pained at your suggestion; we are good friends and can adjust our differences without reference to outsiders."

The Dalai Lama was my authority for this. The suggestion that he made was a reasonable one, for Nepal is a very old ally of the British Government, and Tibet until comparatively recent years was an enemy. By his resourcefulness, and his reliance on the fairness of the British attitude, he averted this danger from Tibet.

The Dalai Lama has taken to dealing direct with the Prime Minister of Nepal instead of letting his Cabinet deal with their agent at Lhasa; he finds the Prime Minister a great deal fairer.

Such is the Tibetan case against Nepal. Nepal has no doubt her own side to the disputes, and in any case has always proved herself a good friend to the British, rendering us invaluable help in military matters and in other ways. During the first World War she sent over two hundred thousand soldiers, some twenty per cent. of the adult males between the ages of eighteen and fifty. This was indeed a wonderful contribution from an ally living in the safety of the great Himalayan range, and far away from the lands where the war was being fought.[23]

The Dalai Lama thinks continually of Russia. In common with his subjects, he feels that Tibetans certainly have affinity with the Siberian Russians, for these latter bear a considerable resemblance to the Mongols and have indeed often inter-married with them. Until the time of the first World War he used to look on Russia as not only the most powerful nation in the world, but also as more favourable to Buddhism than any other non-Buddhist nation. The Tsar had many Buddhist subjects, namely, Buriats in Siberia; Torgots widespread in Mongolia, Sinkiang and European Russia; and other Buddhists as well. The members of these Mongol tribes could be found in the three great monasteries round Lhasa, and they all recognise the Precious Protector as their spiritual ruler. Certainly the Emperor of all the Russias has written him many friendly letters, more warm and friendly than those he has received from the Ruler of the scattered British Empire.

If at the time of the British invasion of Tibet in the Wood Dragon year (1904) the Chinese had already deposed their Manchu Emperor and turned China into a republic, the Dalai Lama would have fled to Russia and not to China. For the connection between China and Tibet was originated by the Manchu dynasty, supposedly Buddhist, and came logically to an end with the extinction of that dynasty. Even when he was in China, he hoped for Russian assistance, but the assistance was not given. He felt that Dorjieff had exaggerated Russia's desire to help him.

After the Anglo-Russian Convention in 1907 he could understand that no help would come from Russia.

But now. Was there ever such a change, so great a disaster? Under the rule of the Balchebuks (Bolshevists) this nation, at one time Tibet's greatest hope, has now turned completely round and become her greatest menace. So it is now in this year of the Iron Bird, (1921). These Balchebuks, he feels, are without law and without custom; and, worst of all, many among them have abandoned their religion, and are setting their minds on destroying the religion of other nations also. Outer Mongolia, already in their grip, is suffering terribly, so his own agent and the commercial agents of his subjects tell him. They have taken all the gold in Outer Mongolia and sent it to Russia. And worst of all, they are interfering with Mongolia's holy religion.[24]

Of Japan, too, he thinks often. When he was young in this present incarnation, it seemed a small country, not to be much considered. But since then the Japanese defeated China thoroughly in the war over Korea (1894). They even tripped up great Russia at the extremity of her vast kingdom. They are a Buddhist nation, more so than the Chinese who are essentially materialistic.

Besides, they are helping Mongolia against the Balchebuks. They have recently sent many rifles and machine-guns into Mongolia; a machine-gun, a few rifles, and some bombs have been brought across the Northern Plains to Lhasa. They have been tested here, and are said to be serviceable and good. Again and again the Tibetan Government have tried to induce the Government of India to allow them to import arms and ammunition through India, but the latter never gave permission. It professes friendship, but does very little to help. Tsarong tells him he can arrange to bring the barrels of these Japanese rifles on camels, twenty to thirty on each camel, and manufacture the stocks for the rifles from walnut wood in Tibet. And he can engage Japanese instructors to train his army. If the British continue to hold back, he cannot wait for ever.

The Japanese are also clever in the arts of peace. They manufacture many kinds of articles; they make them well and cheaply. Fellow Buddhists and clever in war and peace, they may help Tibet against the Chinese oppressor. But Japan is far, far away, and the whole bulk of The Black Expanse (China with her people in their black clothes) comes in between.

Thus his thoughts turn often to Japan. He continually asks me for news of Sino-Japanese relations. I can see the pleasure that lights up his face when he hears that Japan has put pressure on China by military measures or otherwise, hoping that this, for some time at any rate, will prevent China from attacking Tibet.[25]

In 1922, according to the Tibetan biography, a prophecy was given out which said, "This is the time for the Lower Horpas (Japan) to rise to the position of a Great Power." The prophet was a Geshe in the Chumbi Valley, a real saint, revered and beloved by all. "And about this time," we are told, "there were rumours in Tibet that Japan was making preparation to attack some foreign countries."

The Dalai Lama did not wish Tibet to join the League of Nations. He seems to have felt somewhat as follows: "The League does much good work in the promotion of material objects, but the chief aims of Tibet are the maintenance of her religion and the independence of her country. We should have to make the League understand that we are an independent nation; that China has claimed suzerainty over us, but we have never admitted this; that in 1912 we fought against the Chinese and drove them all out, the Amban and his soldiers; and since then we have governed the larger part of our own country.

"If Tibet joins the League, she must be friendly with the other nations that belong to it. Some of them may wish to send representatives to Tibet; the travellers of other nations may wish to penetrate our country. These representatives and travellers may press inconvenient questions on myself and the Tibetan Government. Our customs are often different from those of Europe and America, and we do not wish to change them. Perhaps Christian missionaries may come to Tibet, and in trying to spread Christianity may speak against our religion. We could not tolerate that.

"If the Chinese should threaten to invade Tibet, would the League of Nations help Tibet? Would it, for example, say, 'This is a domestic concern of you two; we cannot intervene.' Presumably the League would not say this, for by admitting Tibet to the League of Nations the latter would recognise her as an independent State, not as a vassal of China. But the remoteness of the Tibetan frontiers from those of most other countries, and the difficulty of bringing troops such a long way, and through a land of such geographical difficulties as is Tibet, might make them refuse to send military help. Whether pressure of any other kind could be brought to bear on China, if she made an attack on Tibet, is doubtful. China is changing so much that we do not know what will be the character of her Government during future years."

Tibetans call the League of Nations "The Assembly in Europe." Although Asiatic States belong to it, Tibetans look on it as governed by European ideas.

As regards general world affairs, the Dalai Lama's chief interest was as to how they affected his own country. For instance, in the first World War, 1914-18, he was on the side of Britain, for this was the nation that could help him, and though slow-moving, seemed inclined to do so by degrees. Germany's motives were a matter of doubt, and in any case she was too far away to help him. But he disapproved of what seemed to him the absurd sum demanded from Germany as reparation. The wealth of the Great Powers was, of course, beyond his range of knowledge.

His travels, though limited, increased his breadth of outlook. The keenness of his mind enabled him to gain a considerable knowledge of world affairs, in spite of the isolation of his country.

53   China

China is determined to seize Tibet if she can. Tibet is a poor country, and the two races are related to each other very little, less than British to Italians. The Tibetans are related to the peoples of the steppes and deserts farther to the north. According to her own records, China claims to have exercised a measure of control, on and off, since A.D. 1720; before that time Tibet was clearly independent.

W. W. Rockhill, to whose scholarly work I have already referred, was for some years American Minister to China. He dealt with the question of Tibetan independence of China, and obtained his information for the most part from Chinese sources. As a result of his enquiries, he came to the conclusion that the Fifth Dalai Lama, when visiting Peking in A.D. 1652, came there as an independent monarch, being at that time neither under China nor under any other nation.

Britain and the United States, and probably most of the European nations, regard Tibet as being under Chinese rule. No doubt this is a convenient arrangement for them, as they have thus only one authority to deal with. Besides, we are always being told about the vast potentialities of trade with China. To my recollection we were told this fifty years ago, but during those fifty years no such vast development has materialised; the potentialities are still no more than potentialities. However, the foreign nations wish to gain a good share of this trade, and to that end try to please China. But it is an outrage that they should sell Tibet in order to increase their own commercial profits in China.

For many years China claimed Tibet as a part of the Chinese Empire on the ground that Tibetans are one of the Five Races who compose that empire, the others being Chinese, Manchus, Mongols and Mahomedans. But later on Chiang Kaishek, realising perhaps that the Atlantic Charter will open the door for Tibetan independence, appears to have shifted his ground and to take the line that Tibetans and Chinese are of the same race. As pointed out above, they are different race; it should also be pointed out that the two races differ strongly in many qualities which have their roots deep down in the characters of the two nations. Of these fundamental differences, four examples will perhaps suffice.

Firstly, the Tibetans are deeply religious; they have fought for their religion and it has been a strong bond of unity for the whole race. The Chinese have never fought for religion nor been united by it; they have adopted forms of philosophy, but very little religion.

The Tibetan Government is truthful. It can be slow, obstinate and secretive in dealing with foreigners, but it has a strong regard for the truth. But the Chinese authorities from time to time made statements which were deliberately untrue. For instance, when the Dalai Lama was in exile in India during 1910 to 1912, the Chinese Amban violated the Trade Regulations of 1908 by forbidding the Panchen Lama and his officials to communicate with the British Trade Agent at Gyangtse. The Chinese denied that this had been done, but we obtained a photograph of the prohibitory order, after which the denials ceased. Many years after the Younghusband expedition had returned to India, reports were frequently issued that a fresh British army had invaded Tibet; every one of these reports was completely untrue.

The Chinese are far more cruel than the Tibetans are. When they tried to conquer areas in Tibet, they used to put to death what prisoners of war they captured, although the only offence of these was fighting in defence of their homeland. The Tibetans, when they captured Chinese prisoners of war, used simply to send them back to China.

The Chinese treat the granting of a favour merely as a step

towards asking for another. So it was in their dealings with Tibet, as the Dalai Lama used to point out; so it is in their war against Japan. They had full notice that this war was coming. Their population is more than four times as numerous as that of Japan, and they might have done much more to help themselves. The help that the Chinese Government has received from the United Nations it has not only used as a stepping-stone for obtaining further assistance, it has utilised it also in fighting its own people to keep itself in power. It fears the strength of the Chinese Communists in northern China, and seems accordingly to have posted several hundred thousand of its troops in the north, where they hold the Communists in check but do little, if anything, to fight the Japanese.

The Tibetans do not treat favours in this way. They have a national memory of things for which they are grateful, and of things that they cannot forgive. The kind treatment of the Dalai Lama during his exile in India established a strong bond of friendship between Britain and Tibet. The memory of Chao Erhfeng's ruthless invasion in eastern Tibet, his destruction of the monasteries and killing of monks, has established a memory of bitterness that is still alive in Tibet.

One would have expected higher standards in truth, mercy and gratitude from the governing authorities of a nation that boasts of its "five thousand years of culture."

Many other examples of the differences dividing these two nations could be given, some of which have already been inserted in these pages. For instance, the status of women in Tibet, is higher than in China; the kinder treatment of animals; and the more orderly government. Of course the Chinese on their side have many national qualities in which they are superior to the Tibetans. For instance, the Chinese mind is quicker, more ingenious and more versatile; but these differences emphasise still further that the two nations are distinct. Emphatically we have here two separate and distinct nations.

China herself during recent times has claimed a jurisdiction over Tibet far greater than that of suzerainty. During the early years of this century Yuan Shihkai, then the Head of China,

speaking to Sir John Jordan, British Minister to China, disclaimed all idea of treating Tibet as provinces of China. Yet
Wang Chingwei – the Head of the Executive in China under
Chiang Kaishek, and now Japan's puppet ruler of China – at an
interview which he gave me in 1935, told me that the different
parts of Tibet are simply provinces of China. Other Chinese
leaders have made the same claim. On the other hand, the Dalai
Lama and his Ministers always maintained that Tibet was entirely independent of China.

The Chinese Government, having been long accustomed to
Europeans and their points of view, write in their records that
Tibet is a part of China. They show it in their maps as included
in China. The Tibetan Government, having had hardly any
contact with Europeans and being unable to speak or write any
European language, have published no records. Maps they cannot make.

After the Sixth Dalai Lama had been put to death, the great
Manchu Emperor Kang Hsi tried to put in another Dalai Lama
chosen by the Chinese. The Tibetans had already discovered, as
they believed, the true Incarnation in Litang in south-eastern
Tibet. For had not the Sixth Dalai Lama written thus in one of
his verses?

> It is not far that I shall roam;
> Lend me your wings, white crane!
> I go no farther than Litang,
> And thence return again.

They refused to recognise the Chinese nominee, and nearly all
the Mongol tribes were in favour of the Tibetan choice. Kang
Hsi feared a Mongol-Tibetan combination against China, and
despatched an army into Tibet to enforce acceptance of his
choice. But this army was defeated by the Tibetans and Mongols. Thereupon he abandoned his own nominee and adopted
the boy recognised by the Tibetans. He then despatched another
army to enthrone this boy, and the Tibetans helped the Chinese
troops on their way. There was no conquest of Tibet here.

However, in 1750 the Emperor Chienlung despatched

another army and restored Chinese ascendency, which had been brought to a low ebb during the intervening years. Later on, when the Gurkhas invaded Tibet, the Chinese despatched an army, composed of Chinese, Mongols and some Tibetans, which defeated and expelled them. To cut short these episodes that favour one side or the other, it seems that since 1720 China had more power in Tibet than the Dalai Lama and other Tibetans admit, but a great deal less than she herself claims. The Tibetan claim is nearer to the truth. But China can make its case known to the world; Tibet cannot do so. And the world judges accordingly, after hearing the evidence on one side only.

What, then, are the main points of the Tibetan case? The Dalai Lama and his Ministers show me clearly that Tibet, hidden away in the heart of Asia, does not think along European lines. They maintain that the Dalai Lama is the spiritual guide and the Manchu Emperor his lay supporter. All who are well acquainted with India and other Oriental countries know what this relationship involves. It is the duty of the layman to help a monk in all ways possible, but the monk does not on that account become the layman's servant. Whatever help China may have rendered to Tibet was rendered in that capacity and does not in any sense put Tibet under China. "You will find no treaty," they used to continue, "by which Tibet recognises that China is her overlord."

"The Dalai Lama," I am told, "has received his secular sovereignty over Tibet from a powerful Mongol chieftain, and not from China. Tibet has a separate Mint and coinage of its own, and its own munition factories. If Tibet had been under China, the latter would have sent soldiers to defend her own dependency whenever foreign nations attacked it. The war against Kashmir, the war against Nepal in 1855, the wars against Britain in 1888 and 1904, and the ancient wars between Tibet and Bhutan, were all fought and settled by the Tibetans themselves without any assistance from China. Therefore, Tibet says to China, 'Even if you should consider that we were in some measure subordinate to you, yet by failing to give us assistance in defending our country on so many occasions, you have failed to keep your part of the bargain. We will not keep ours.'

"Again, Tibet pays no tribute or taxes to China. The two countries used to exchange complimentary presents and letters." In 1921, referring to these letters and presents, the Dalai Lama tells me that they were exchanged with the Chinese Government by Nepal as well as by Tibet. "Tibet," he says, "used formerly to send these to Peking once in every three years. They are known as Tenche (a word meaning 'gifts'). Tibet has not sent them for about twelve years; Nepal not for sixteen years."

Regarding these missions, I am told that they received free transport for themselves and their belongings all the way through China to Peking. Consequently they used to carry other articles also with them for trading on the way. In Peking they received valuable return presents from the Chinese Government. The Tibetans, in fact, regarded the missions as profitable trading expeditions.

"The reason why the exchange of presents was abandoned," continues the Dalai Lama, "was because the connection with China was the connection of the Dalai Lama with the Manchu Emperor. The Manchus were considered as Buddhists; the Chinese were not. When the Chinese revolution broke out in 1911, China deposed the Manchu Emperor. There was then no longer that connection between the two. The connecting link was broken, and Tibet is now completely separate from China." Mongolian leaders have advanced similar arguments as regards the connection between China and Mongolia.

On another day he tells me his views as to the future of Tibet. He says, "I would like to have Tibet entirely independent of China, and to consult the British Government whenever necessity arises. The British Government, in the Simla Convention, having decided that there should be a Chinese Amban in Lhasa with an escort of three hundred soldiers, I have not ventured to represent the matter to them again. But I am opposed to having an Amban in Lhasa. When the Chinese Government first sent an Amban with the Chinese soldiers to Lhasa, they said that the soldiers were a bodyguard for the Dalai Lama of that period, namely the Seventh. Gradually the escort was increased in size, and was made the escort of the Amban, not of the Dalai Lama. And, later on, a second Amban was introduced.

"By myself I can control any disaffected elements in Tibet, and hold the country together. But if an Amban comes, those who are dissatisfied will turn to him, and he will be able to foment opposition to the Tibetan Government and myself. If an Amban must come, I want to have a British Representative also at Lhasa. But until an Amban comes, it is sufficient that a British Representative should visit Lhasa occasionally as necessity arises.

"The Chinese will make every effort to increase the number of their soldiers in Lhasa, by sending up a fresh escort to relieve the old one, and then not taking the old escort away; and by whatever other means they can devise. If the Chinese Amban is to have an escort, it should be furnished by Tibetan, not Chinese, soldiers. And the escort should be a good deal less than three hundred, the number fixed by the Simla Convention."

We Europeans regard the great Chinese people as patient and kindly. We know the wide culture in the educated classes; we know the good work of the Chinese peasant, and the efficiency of the Chinese mercantile community and the Chinese manual worker. But the great majority of European men and women who live in China live in large communities of their own; they have no good knowledge of the Chinese language; their intercourse is more with their own people than with the Chinese, and is still less with those Chinese in the vast rural areas, who are influenced little, if at all, by Western ideas. Of course, Christian missionaries live in rural areas and speak Chinese. But the crucial point is that only a very few Europeans know the Chinese in their relationship to Tibetans or Mongols; and these, if they live in China, are often afraid – as they themselves have told me – to speak out their views, lest the Chinese take revenge upon them.

The Chinese treated the Tibetans with haughtiness and discourtesy, even though they had lost most of their power in Tibet. Chinese officials stationed there, especially during my earlier years in that country, used to take Tibetan mistresses in place of the wives they had left in their own land. From these mistresses they learnt to speak the Tibetan language. But they would never speak it in public, for they looked on the Tibetans as savages, and their language therefore as degrading.

Mr. Spencer Chapman was at Lhasa with the Gould mission in 1936-37, three years after the Dalai Lama's death. In his interesting book, *Lhasa: The Holy City,*[26] he relates how the Chinese officials in Lhasa arrived at the Potala when a religious drama was in progress. They stopped the performance by walking to their seats right across the stage, a typical proceeding which Chapman describes as "a singular lack of courtesy."

The Mongols and Tibetans do not receive from the Chinese the same treatment that Europeans and Americans do. Indeed the Chinese treatment of the countries which she claims as dependencies, Tibet, Mongolia and Chinese Turkistan (Sinkiang), has been very harsh.

We have seen how the Dalai Lama and the Tibetan Government and many of the Tibetan people regarded the Chinese during my time in Tibet; and how they liked the Japanese, while disliking the Chinese.

The Mongols also for the most part dislike the Chinese, when brought into close contact with them. The Chinese ridicule their religion. Besides, they have expelled the Mongols of Inner Mongolia from a large area of their land by sending soldiers to seize it, and these make it over to Chinese peasants and burn the Mongol tents, unless the Mongols turn out quickly. When I was in Peking, Manchuria and Inner Mongolia in 1935, I used to meet and hear about Mongols of various tribes and classes. Among others, I became acquainted with De Wang, the most influential chief in Inner Mongolia. And his right-hand man, Tsen Bayar, known to the Chinese by his Chinese name, Pau Yueh-ching, used often to come to see me. He tells me, "The Chinese treat the Mongols as wild animals. They have sent up thieves and robbers who steal the Mongols' land. They are doing the same in Tibet. They work for their own ends, not for the benefit of Mongols or Tibetans, and both Mongols and Tibetans are becoming aware of this.

"Tibetans, Mongols and Turkis should establish independent

States, which should work in close relationship with each other. We shall have to rely on the Japanese to help us against the Chinese. They are far from desirable, but the Soviet Russians are impossible."

I usually found that the Japanese were praised most highly by nations living far away from them, and less so by those who had come under their administration. But even when governed by them, most Mongols seemed to prefer them to the Chinese. They looked on the Japanese as co-religionists. They received more help from them – schools, military training, etc. – than they did from the Chinese. They found them more powerful and efficient; kinder, more humane.

A young prince of Astrakhan – of the Torgot tribe of Mongols – spoke to me as follows:

"Before the Chinese annexed Sinkiang, about one hundred and ninety years ago, part was under the rule of the Chungkars (a Mongol tribe); the remainder under the rule of the Turkis. In the Chungkar region were also Oelots, Buriats and Barkas (Mongol tribes).

"During the hundred and ninety years of their rule the Chinese have never done one good thing for Sinkiang. The British have ruled India for the same period, and during it have built railways, roads and hospitals, have preserved the forests, promoted education and sanitation, and have made numerous other improvements. But in Sinkiang the Chinese Government have done nothing but send officials there, who themselves do nothing but fill their own pockets."

Members of European races, other than British, travelling in Sinkiang, have often received from the people there reports on similar lines.

So harshly have the Chinese exploited these three large countries, embracing an area thinly inhabited but in the agregate more than double the area of China proper, that all three wish to seek their destinies apart from Chinese overlordship, if some neighbouring Power would treat them with reasonable understanding and sympathy. Indeed all three – Mongol, Tibetan and Turki – are doing so already. I predicted this, as regards Tibet and

Mongolia, in my *Tibet, Past and Present,* published in 1924.

Tibetans, in personal relationship with educated Chinese, are apt to suffer from an inferiority complex, and the Chinese take full advantage of this. However, the Dalai Lama did not suffer from such a complex, at any rate in his own country. When he made his final return to Tibet after his second exile, he removed all Chinese influence from that part of Tibet which he was able to hold against China. He had replied firmly to Yuan Shihkai, expressing his determination to rule Tibet himself, and over the area of Tibet which he held – the larger part – he carried this out to the letter. Chinese soldiers and Chinese officals were barred from entering this portion of Tibet.

Put briefly, we may say that Outer Tibet entirely, and Inner Tibet partially, gained independence from China during the reign of the Thirteenth Dalai Lama.[27]

Part Seven
Later Years

It is not possible to write so intimately about the Dalai Lama's life and work after my retirement in 1921. The India Office seemed very nervous about my corresponding with any Tibetans; they told me they were afraid that my influence would overshadow that of my successor. Their attitude evidently became clear to the Dalai Lama also, for the correspondence between His Holiness and myself became fitful, and did not deal with matters of importance. He and his Government could not afford to displease the British Government or the Government of India.

Major (later Lt.-Col.) F. M. Bailey succeeded me. He had been a military officer in Younghusband's expedition to Lhasa, and subsequently was British Trade Agent at Gyangtse. He had distinguished himself by carrying out adventurous work for the Government in Russian Turkistan during the early days of the Soviet Government.

The telegraph line from India to Tibet, made during the British military expedition in 1904, ended at Gyangtse. I advised the Dalai Lama to ask the Government of India to extend the line to Lhasa. He readily welcomed my suggestion, for he, too, was keen that the line should be extended. But while the Government of India were considering my recommendations in this respect, the World War of 1914-18 broke out and blocked the way, for all our resources were of necessity employed in it.

After the war was over I brought up the matter again and during 1920 the line was surveyed, and during 1922, a few months after I had left Tibet, the construction was completed.

His Holiness the Thirteenth Dalai Lama.

Formerly it had taken Lhasa seven days at the least to receive a reply from India; thereafter the reply could be received the same day. The Government of India was pleased; the Dalai Lama was delighted.

The first telegram over the new line from the Tibetan Government was sent, I think, to the Viceroy of India, and the first cable to me. I had retired some eight months earlier; it reached me at the little town of Banff in Scotland. It said, "Telegraph completed Lhasa, due entirely your help. We offer greetings, best wishes your health."

The line was built by Mr. W. H. King, and maintained by Mr. Rosemeyer. The latter visited Lhasa seven times, and always found the Dalai Lama helpful. Once when Rosemeyer was short of workmen in Lhasa, His Holiness sent him six soldiers to work on the telegraph line.

Between two and three years after I left, Lt.-Col. Bailey made a brief visit to Lhasa. The Tibetan biography records his visit as follows:

"The Political Officer in Sikkim, Bailey Sahib, arrived in Lhasa. A Peak Secretary, named Lobsang Jamyang, was instructed to meet him at the place of reception with a silver pot of tea, five layers of bread, and the best kind of ceremonial scarf. Afterwards he came to see the Dalai Lama in the camp of the Bodyguard."

During the following year a breach occurred between the Dalai and Panchen Lamas. The latter fled to China, avoiding India, thus losing touch with the British connection. The result was highly injurious to Tibet. The reason given by the British authorities for taking no steps to prevent the flight was apparently that it was not possible for them to interfere with the internal administration of Tibet. In a letter which the Panchen Lama wrote to Mr. Macdonald some years later, he mentioned that this was the reason given to him. But it is not in the least necessary to interfere with the internal administration of Tibet. The Dalai and Panchen Lamas can easily ascertain the British Political Officer's private opinion, and if they think it is "sound from the root," as their saying is, they are always ready to seize on it and adopt it.

Wandering about in China, Manchuria and Mongolia, the Panchen Lama never returned to his own country. He died in November, 1937, four years after the Dalai Lama's death, in the part of Tibet that was under Chinese control.

The Panchen Lama's absence injured Tibet grievously in several ways. Tashi Lhünpo is, after Lhasa, the chief spiritual centre of this religious land. Further, during all his years in China, the Chinese Government paid the Panchen Lama and his officers large sums of money, so as to attach them all to their side during their struggle with the Tibetan Government at Lhasa. They used him to promote disaffection in Tibet, and thereby to increase their chance of obtaining control over that country. It became a very difficult problem for the Tibetan Government to deal with these insidious attacks, especially after the Dalai Lama's death had removed Tibet's strong Ruler.

In spite of the Panchen Lama's flight the Dalai Lama remained friendly, or half-friendly, towards him. Several years later, when in China, the Panchen Lama met a Chinese representative of the Dalai Lama. This representative told the Panchen Lama that the Dalai Lama was ready to invite him back to Tibet and restore all his privileges. The Panchen Lama accordingly sent two representatives to Lhasa. His Holiness received them favourably, but told them that it would be necessary to take the opinion of the Parliament in Lhasa. Unfortunately two of the most influential members of this body were hostile to the Panchen Lama and dominated the meeting, nobody else daring to speak. So the Parliament gave an unfavourable reply. This greatly annoyed the Dalai Lama, for it complicated the matter further. This event happened not long before the Dalai Lama's death, when he was not as strong in health or will power as formerly.

In August, 1933, the Dalai Lama sent for Dewan Bahadur Palhese and gave him a private interview. I was coming out from England on a visit to Tibet, and Palhese intended to start soon to meet me in Darjeeling. After speaking to him about my visit, the

Dalai Lama spoke to Palhese about the Panchen Lama. He said, "When I went to China, the Emperor was ruling and there was peace in China; but I fear that the Panchen Lama must have been put to great trouble by the disorder prevailing in China during recent years."

However, the Inmost One objected when the Chinese Government, trying to make trouble between the two Grand Lamas, gave to the Panchen Lama a title, calling him "Complete Lord of the Religion of the Conqueror" (i.e. the Buddhist religion). But the Chinese Government refused to alter it.

The Inmost One used to instruct his representatives in China from time to time to observe especially what relations the Panchen Lama had with the Soviet Government in Outer Mongolia, which is the largest part of Mongolia and is under Soviet control. For the Panchen Lama had an agent in Urga, the capital of Outer Mongolia; and the Tibetan Government believed that this agent was in close touch with the Soviets, though the latter were the enemies of all religions, including the Buddhist religion.

During 1933 and 1934, twelve years after my retirement from Government service, I visited Tibet and the Indo-Tibetan borderland on a private visit. During 1935 I went to China and Inner Mongolia. The Panchen Lama wrote to me two or three times, and sent telegrams to all his chief agents in Kalimpong and in China to come and see me and get me to use my influence to bring about a compromise between the Tibetan Government and himself. One such letter asked me (*a*) to promote still further the friendly relationship between Britain and Tibet; (*b*) to help in restoring harmony between "The Conquerors, Father and Son" (i.e. the Dalai and Panchen Lamas); (*c*) to advise Tsa Serkang (his agent in Kalimpong) on the points on which he may consult me, and give deep and firm assistance.

The Panchen Lama had then been a long time in China, and the Chinese had encouraged him to enlarge his demands in the hope of increasing the friction between the Tibetan Government and himself. He demanded the right to maintain an army of his own, as is done by Ruling Princes in India. He had also various other claims, one of which was that the number of districts under his jurisdiction in Tibet should be increased, including some important ones near his own monastery, Tashi Lhünpo.

In 1934, with Lt.-Col. Harnett, I visited Tashi Lhünpo. We went over the great monastery, which, in the absence of the Panchen Lama, seemed weary and mournful; Shigatse, the town half a mile away, where we stayed for a week, was like a city of the dead. We saw the Panchen Lama's palaces. In "The Palace of the Western Paradise" was a small Hall of Audience, a large library, and many other rooms, large and small. In this Hall of Audience he received his officials and blessed them, and blessed other groups of people. Above his throne was the usual canopy of silk; on the left front was "The Fire of Religion." Further to the left was a glass-fronted cabinet with images. Behind the throne were the sacred pictures, painted on Tibetan parchment, with silk surrounds. It was pathetic to see, over the seat of the throne, one of his gowns ready to wear when he next came in and sat down there. He had not been in Tashi Lhünpo for ten years, and, as it turned out, never came back to Tibet.

By the other chief palace a flood was raging. The river had overflowed and was rushing by, threatening to sweep part of it away. The monks of Tashi Lhünpo turned out in full force. They drew up their long robes, and waded through the cold water that surged down the roadway and rose above their knees. In the palace, flooded outside and very wet inside – so different from their comfortable temple in Tashi Lhünpo – they held a service for stopping the flood. Certainly from that hour the water went down, as everbody had placidly assumed that it would do. So it may be claimed that some of the great Panchen Lama's spiritual power still remained there.

One day the Panchen Lama's Chief Secretary, after being treated by Harnett for ear trouble, came to my tent. He said, "The Dalai Lama passed to the Honourable Field last year, and the Panchen Lama is still in China. Neither of the two Great Religious Supports is with us. Tibet is in black darkness."

In 1929 or 1930 Palhese heard of a prophecy which stated that the Panchen Lama would return to Tibet either in the Dog year or in the Pig year, that is to say, between February, 1934, and

Februrary, 1936; and that if he did not return then, it would be difficult for him to return at all, meaning that he would die quickly. I heard this prophecy in December, 1933, soon after I had come from England to the Tibetan frontier. And, sure enough, the Panchen Lama died on 1st September, 1937. He was then in eastern Tibet, the portion under Chinese control, far away from both Lhasa and Tashi Lhünpo. The day before he died, an accident caused much consternation in Lhasa. While the image of Palden Lhamo was being carried round the Great Temple, the bearer slipped and fell, though the image itself was saved from falling on the ground. It was said that some calamity must follow, a serious epidemic or some other such disaster, or – the death of the Panchen Lama.

55 The Dalai Lama Turns Towards China

By 1925 the Dalai Lama was turning strongly away from Britain towards China. During the same year he appointed an official named Lungshar as Commander-in-Chief of the Tibetan army. Lungshar was markedly anti-British. Our old friend, Tsarong, the former Commander-in-Chief, who was always very pro-British, lost most of his power, and was subsequently degraded. In 1926 the English school at Gyangtse was closed. At this time also the British political authorities in Tibet started to establish a motor mail service between Pari and Gyangtse in order to quicken the mails, but the Tibetan Government forbade it. The Russian Press published exultant reports of "the crash of British influence in Tibet." There can be no doubt that a great deal of the British influence was lost. In the following year the Dalai Lama was showing signs of unwillingness to invite the British Representative to Lhasa. The position was greatly changed from that time, five years earlier, when the Dalai Lama wrote, "The British and Tibetans have become one family." During those years there was a manifest tendency for the two leaders of Tibet, the Dalai Lama and Panchen Lama, to turn to China.

In 1927 a party of Mongols came to Lhasa. They were clearly agents of the Soviet. They distributed a great deal of money and took a large number of photographs. They gave out that the Russians would help Tibet with guns and with men. "The British," they said, "send only guns, but we will send men also." They remained in Lhasa from the spring of 1927 to December of the same year.

In the following year another Soviet agent arrived in Lhasa and remained for more than a year. He lived there openly in expensive style; he was believed to be on terms of intimacy with high Tibetan officials, and to have been received by the Dalai Lama himself.

Tibetans, even of the poorer classes, have not hitherto favoured Bolshevism. They go by the Tibetan proverb:

> The master must have subjects;
> The subjects must have a master.

Their general opinion on this subject was:

"People are not born equal, but go up and down the scale according to their good deeds or evil deeds in previous lives. As for us Tibetans, what we want is a class of officials and landed proprietors who will give us straight justice. Later on, if Russian or Chinese communists come to Tibet, some of the people may favour Balchubuk ideas, but it is not likely that many will, because most of them know how greatly the Balchebuks interfered with religion, and how they behaved like wild animals, killing those that did not agree with them. Those who are better educated know also that the Balchebuks always pretend to a country that they are coming to help it and will not interfere with religion, but that is mere head-turning (i.e. deceit), and they never keep their promises."

During the presence of this Soviet mission in Lhasa, a letter from the Dalai Lama to me was stopped on its way. The officer who stopped it explained that he thought it might contain some reference to that mission, and asked the Indian Foreign Department for leave to open it. The question being referred to the India Office in London, the latter asked me whether I had any objection to it being opened. I was, however, unable to agree, more especially as I had given my promise to the Dalai Lama that nobody but myself should open his letters to me. The letter was then forwarded to me, reaching me twenty-two days after another letter, written by the Dalai Lama on the same date, arrived for Palhese, who was with me in England. As soon as the letter reached me I was able to assure the India Office that it had nothing to do with the Soviet mission. This was the letter:

"Reason for writing. I have received your letter with a silk scarf of the *ashe* quality dated the fifteenth day of the second month of the Fire Hare year. You write that Dewan Bahadur Palhese has reached you. You add that when Dewan Bahadur Palhese returns, you will write to me a detailed letter explaining different matters clearly, and you ask me to bear this in mind. This letter is despatched by me on the second eleventh day of the fourth month of the Fire Hare year, an auspicious date, supported by a silk scarf of the *ashe* quality."

In all probability the Dalai Lama came to hear of the stoppage – for he had a wonderful system of obtaining information – and this rendered him still more nervous about writing to me. On my side also I held back from writing to him, as the India Office was so much against it. I thought, then, and think still, that their attitude was wrong. The friendship between the Dalai Lama and myself would not have harmed Britain or Tibet; on the contrary, it would, in some small degree at any rate, have helped them both.

In 1930 a Tibetan official, with the high rank of Dzasa, who resided in Peking, arrived in Lhasa. He was accompanied by Liu Manchin, a girl of about twenty-three years of age, born of a Chinese father and a Tibetan mother. They were sent by the Nanking Government with a letter to the Dalai Lama. The Dalai Lama sent officials to go out and welcome them in accordance with the Tibetan customs observed in dealing with honoured guests. They were warmly welcomed and entertained. The letter contained proposals from the Chinese Government for establishing friendly relations between China and Tibet. His Holiness received Liu Manchin, as well as the Dzasa, in audience, and sent a reply by them. They expressed themselves as well pleased with the result of their visit.

Laden La, who was in Lhasa at the time, was struck by the increase in Chinese influence. In a letter to me he wrote, "The Dalai Lama said to me, 'I had to suffer a great deal after Lönchen Bell's departure.' He regards me as the last of your remnants; he talks to me quite frankly."

In 1931 another Chinese representative was on his way to Lhasa, but died a short distance from the capital. His body was brought to Lhasa, and the Dalai Lama himself is said to have performed the funeral ceremony.

Though he was strengthening his hold upon China, and the link with Britain had weakened, the Precious Sovereign was careful not to let Britain go altogether. In his political testament he writes that Tibet should maintain "firm friendship" with India and China, because each "has a large army."

A young favourite of the Dalai Lama, a lad of singular personal charm, was coming into influence and power as the years passed. When he was ordained as a monk, the Dalai Lama himself gave him his religious name, Tupten Künpel, which means "Doctrines of Buddha, All, Increase." That is to say, "He who spreads the doctrines of Buddha in all directions." For general use his name was Künpel La, La being an honorific affix. By 1930 he had become, after the Dalai Lama, the most powerful man in Tibet. He held the charge over the Precious Sovereign's property, and had himself accumulated considerable wealth. His power was on both the civil and the military side. All orders of the Dalai Lama were carried out through him; he knew every action that the Inmost One took. To him I am indebted for some of my information on Tibetan affairs after my departure.

Four years after the Dalai Lama's death, the Rev. Tharchin, of the Church of Scotland – a member of the Lepcha race – wrote to me from Kalimpong, where he had made friends with Künpel La. In his quaint English he wrote, "I came to know all about Künpel La and he is really wonderful man. I think he had the most experience of the Dalai Lama, and a clever man. His age is thirty-three. He says the Dalai Lama was very very friend of yours and always talked about you. He knows all about the private affairs of the Dalai Lama and all the confidence. During Dalai Lama's time he was called 'The Keys of the Dalai Lama,' and it was true."

Lt.-Col. Weir held the Political Officer's post from 1928 to about 1933, visiting Lhasa in 1930 and in 1932, for two or three months each time. His genial, kindly disposition helped him to establish relations of personal friendliness with the Tibetans, especially as he aided them in their troubles with the Chinese. The Tibetan Government's biography records one of his visits. And Dorje Pamo, the holiest lady in Tibet, regarded him as a real friend.

Mrs. Weir was the first Englishwoman to visit Lhasa. The Government of India had not permitted Mrs. Bailey to come with her husband, who made a short visit in 1924. Mrs. Weir had a conversation with the Dalai Lama. Wishing to make him appreciate the achievements of her sex, she told him how Amy Johnson had flown from England to Australia at such speed that she held the record for men as well as for women. The Dalai Lama pondered over the story a few seconds, and then remarked, with some surprise, "And why was she in a hurry?" Typical indeed of timeless Tibet, which sees no merit in a "record" as such.

Lt.-Col. Weir was succeeded by Mr. Williamson of the Indian Civil Service, who visited Lhasa from August to October, 1933. He was still holding the post when the Dalai Lama died in December, 1933. Unfortunately he himself died in Lhasa in 1935.

The Dalai Lama's friendship with me continued to the end of his life. It is unnecessary to give more instances of this friendship; many – perhaps too many – have already slipped into this narrative. They do, however, show two things. Firstly, that in this country where Europeans used to be strongly distrusted and disliked, it is possible for him to enjoy real friendship with the Tibetans. Secondly, that the Dalai Lama was cautious in making friends, but once made, was firm in friendship. Most Tibetans are like that, and with him this characteristic was very strongly marked.

The Panchen Lama was equally firm in friendship. Till his death in 1937 he seemed to repose especial confidence in Sir Frederick O'Connor and myself, though I had not met him since 1906, and Sir Frederick not for very many years. Indeed, the extent to which O'Connor gained the goodwill and confidence of the Tibetans after working a few years among them was a triumph of personality. His friendship with the Panchen Lama's people was especially strong. But, as far as I am aware, he did not come into contact with the Dalai Lama.

David Macdonald did wonderful work at Yatung and Gyangtse as an agent subordinate to the British Representative. In June, 1929, several years after his retirement, the Tibetan Prime Minister wrote to him, "During the time that you were in Tibet relations between the British and the Tibetans were very friendly." And when I returned to Tibet on a private visit in 1934, I could see how beloved he still was, though it was some ten years since I had retired. As long as the Dalai Lama lived, he exchanged letters with Macdonald.

In 1925, shortly before Palhese started on his journey to come and stay with me in England, the Dalai Lama ordered the Cabinet to give him a passport, written, of course, in Tibetan. It was worded as follows:

"We have received a letter from Sir Charles Bell, the former Lönchen and Administrator in Sikkim, asking us to send Dewan Bahadur Palhese Sönam Wangyal. Sir Charles Bell brought about the former friendship between the British and Tibetan Governments, making the Tibetan Government like the son or the brother of the British Government. Therefore we grant the request of Dewan Bahadur Palhese Sönam Wangyal to go for a time to Sir Charles Bell in England. This is the passport for him to go and serve zealously."

In due course Palhese, now a Dewan Bahadur, arrived in our Berkshire village. He brought a letter and presents to me from the Inmost One. The presents included a pair of beautiful blue and white porcelain vases of the Chienlung period, used as flower vases. On each a design of two dragons facing each other, and clouds. Also a pair of old cloisonné flower vases with black backgrounds and designs of apricot blossom. In each of these vases was a handful of dried pieces of sweet potato. To present any vessel without something in it is liable to bring bad fortune to the recipient. A sweet potato is of especially good omen, for the Tibetan name for it is *troma*. As words standing alone, *tro* means "wheat," and *ma* means "mother." "The mother of wheat," a highly auspicious combination.

When I replied to the Dalai Lama's letter, I showed Palhese my collection of ceremonial scarves, that he might select one for covering the letter inside its envelope. The Dewan Bahadur chose a good scarf, but not one of the very largest. He said, "We use a smaller scarf for this than we use in a personal interview. It is but an envelope."

Palhese and I had a very pleasant year together. He saw something of rural life in England, visited London, and, through the kindness of the Hon. Mary Scott, saw a little of the Scottish lowlands and highlands. He liked the cold of winter best; the warm days of summer not so well. But he missed the long Tibetan sunshine, cold and crystal clear.

As he did not speak or write English, friends on the Indo-Tibetan frontier had arranged a young companion for him. Lobsang both spoke and wrote English, and treated Palhese as a dutiful son treats his father – a delightful picture. I had taken a suite of rooms in a little house for them, close to our own house. They had the Tibetan fondness for children in full measure, so much so that when they left, the landlady and her two children were in such a flood of tears that it seemed doubtful whether I should be able to get my Tibetan friends away in time to catch the train.

56   Occupations in Old Age

The Dalai Lama had re-entered the world for his Thirteenth Incarnation during the year of the Fire Mouse (1876). Before 1930 he had grown old.

As a race the Tibetans are robust and tough, inured to general hardships and to intense cold. He was inured to heat as well, having been born in one of the provinces south-east of Lhasa, named Takpo, which has a period of real hot weather each year. But he had always overworked and overstrained at the heavy task of ruling Tibet both on the spiritual and the secular side, and his quick temper must have strained him still further. Besides, he had suffered two hard exiles. Laden La saw him in Lhasa in 1930. He had lost two of his front teeth, his eyesight was impaired, and he seemed old beyond his years.

To Künpel La, his young favourite, who was then in very close attendance on him, I am indebted for a description of an ordinary day during the last few years of the Dalai Lama's life. He rose between six and seven, drank three cups of tea, and went for a walk. From seven o'clock he spent an hour in prayer. After this he issued orders and wrote letters until about ten. Then he washed his face and hands; but if he had to go on a long journey he washed earlier.

Next he performed the *Sungtor* ceremony for half an hour, in this ceremony there is an offering of cakes, made of rice, barley flour or wheat, shaped like a cone, and mixed with butter into a firm consistency. The cakes are offered to deities, saints and evil spirits, to avert dangers to the living, and to succour the dead who are being punished with tortures for their past sins. It also guards against drought, famine and epidemics of disease. It is essential that after the ceremony the cake offered shall be burnt or cast away.

Breakfast followed. From twelve till two he attended to State business. He then left Clear Eye Palace and went to the Jewel Park Palace, the two being close to each other. Here he went through each of the forty rooms and lighted about five butter lamps on the altar of each. If any room was not clean, he ordered the attendants to clean it.

About four or five in the afternoon he would stroll in the garden. Dinner followed. Breakfast and dinner were much the same as when I was in Lhasa. But he rose later than in his earlier years, breakfasted later and omitted lunch.

Then an evening walk, after which he dictated letters and did other work for three hours, ending at ten o'clock. As he read the letters dictated by him and dated them, he uttered prayers all the time. There was no signature; His Holiness dated each letter, and the favourite – in this case Künpel La – affixed the appropriate seal in his presence.

That finished, the Dalai Lama wrote his orders with chalk on wooden slates and sent them to the Prime Minister, the Members of the Cabinet, the Ecclesiastical Court, the Financial Commissioners and the heads of other departments. They wrote their replies on these wooden slates and returned them. The idea in having the slates sent back to him with their replies was that they should not keep his writings.

Supper followed, consisting of soup and meat, but no vegetables. Soon afterwards he entered his bedroom and took a cupful of curds and whey. Then he went to bed. The hours of work were less and the hours of sleep more than when I was in Lhasa.

When in the garden, he gave directions to the gardeners how to plant the flowers, what kinds of flowers he liked best, how to dig the ground, and so on. Gardening was his chief hobby. And he was very fond of dogs. It will be noticed that his tastes in these respects changed very little from the time when I first met him till his death twenty-five years later.

During his last years he had a few motor cars, and sometimes he would motor out some distance and take a walk in that place, for walking was his chief exercise. He had a tall bearded Indian as chauffeur, and would occasionally take one of his favourites with him. None but the Indian was allowed to drive the Dalai Lama's own special car, and no one else was allowed to use it. Motor roads had been constructed to Drepung and Sera monasteries; the former four and a half miles west of Lhasa, and the latter between two and three miles north of Lhasa.

The Dalai Lama favoured modern ideas when, after enquiry and due consideration, he thought they were likely to help Tibet. But he declined to be rushed, and he liked, if possible, to carry his people with him. As regards aeroplanes, he never flew in one, but he took great interest in them. Probably he disliked their growing power, fearing that in the future they would be able to invade even his large and lofty dominion.

Before his death he was arranging for an installation of wireless at Lhasa, but he passed away before this was accomplished.

Sometimes when he returned home from a drive or walk he played the game known as *Shata*, a Mongolian version of chess, the pieces representing a king, a queen, a camel, an elephant, a horse, a horse-drawn cart, etc. He would play this with his personal attendants, or with some Mongols who happened to come to the Palace. Three or four of these lived in the Jewel Park grounds; the Dalai Lama gave them their board and lodging, and they did wood-carving of various kinds.

Another sidelight on the Dalai Lama's daily life during his last few years comes from a Tibetan who was in my employ when I was on Government service in Tibet, and when I returned there in 1934 on a private visit. He went to Lhasa about 1924 and joined the Dalai Lama's bodyguard. He told me:

"I had three soldiers under me, and it was my duty to accompany the Dalai Lama from the Jewel Park Palace to Clear Eye Palace every evening at about seven o'clock. He used to go to bed between ten and eleven, but rose for a short time every night to perform religious devotions.

"I saw the Dalai Lama daily for several years. At about five in the afternoon he would take a stroll in the grounds. Occasionally he would send for me to walk with him. He used to put one

hand on my shoulder and talk about various matters. For instance, where I was born and where I had lived, and what my
family had consisted of; how the soldiers of the bodyguard were
working, and whether they had regular training together.

"He was fond of gardening and planted seedlings in the
grounds with his own hands. And he used to visit his animals.

"I went on escort duty with the Dalai Lama to Ganden
monastery (twenty-seven miles from Lhasa). This was eight
years ago. (The Dalai Lama was then just fifty years old.) Part of
the way he rode a mule of the Kongpo breed and went at a slow
amble; part of the way he was carried in his palanquin. He was
fond of mules from Kongpo. This is a province a little east of
Lhasa; the mules are small and steady, often light-brown with a
dark line along the back. Such a mule Tibetans consider especially reliable. His escort of ten men from the bodyguard was
commanded by a colonel."

A few years after I left, thhe Inmost One cut his hours of
work down a little and made over some of the less important
matters to his subordinates, chiefly to his favourite. But even
these were expected to consult with the Precious Protector
before they gave the final decision. By 1931 he contemplated
giving up not only his temporal power, but his ecclesiastical
authority as well. He felt that he should spend the short remainder of his thirteenth Incarnation in religious exercises, in spiritual
devotion.

However, he could not bring himself to give up the work, and
in some ways even increased his control. For instance, when a
post was vacant, and the Cabinet forwarded through the Prime
Minister the names of two or three persons whom they considered suitable, but not the name he wished, he would often
insert the name of his choice. He did not follow his previous
practice and refer the list back for fresh names. He even increased the rents payable to the Government by the nobility and
other landed proprietors, thus attacking that citadel of privilege
which he had feared to attack when increasing and improving the
army in 1921.

To the end of his life his control over the administration
remaind firm and complete.

57   His Political Testament

During 1931 the Nechung Oracle let it be known that the Dalai Lama was ill, and likely to depart soon to the Honourable Field. Consequently he advised the Tibetan Government to offer prayers to him to remain in this life. The Cabinet did so.

The Dalai Lama made his reply to their prayers in a book of nine small pages which he wrote with his own hand, it being of so great importance. This is the only book of which it can be said with absolute certainty that it was written by a Dalai Lama. A remarkable book indeed.

The book was printed on the usual Tibetan wooden blocks. The blocks were made in Lhasa; and, later on, the Chief Minister of the subordinate Government at Tashi Lhünpo had fresh printing blocks made there.

Nine or ten months after the Dalai Lama's death the Chief Prophet of the great Samye monastery gave me his printed copy of this testament. Himself a most devoted admirer of the Dalai Lama, he knew – as most Tibetans did – the close friendship that united the Dalai Lama and myself. When giving me the book, he said, "Your mind is seen in it," referring to the advice that I gave to the Inmost One during our long conversations with each other.

In conversation, Tibetans term this little book the Precious Protector's *Kachem;* i.e. his Last Testament. In it he justifies his rule, reprimands his subjects, and instructs them how to conduct themselves. It contains a large amount of political matter, and might therefore also be termed his Political Testament.

"Water Monkey Year.[28] In consequence of the prophecy of

the Nechung Oracle, all the people of Tibet, the Yellow and the Grey, offered prayers to the Precious Protector to remain for a long time in this life. The essence of that petition and the Precious Protector's reply to it are printed here together in this book. The reply, like a precious medicine, restores the fat which had become rotten, and enables all to see at once the dark places. It is the fresh nectar of the gods."

The essence of the above petition is given here:

"We, the Prime Minister, the Members of the Cabinet, the ecclesiastical and civil officials, in consequence of the Nechung Oracle's prophecy, have jointly made earnest supplication to the Precious Protector to remain long in this life. We have done this in accordance with the discourses of the Lord Buddha. We have all made these prayers in accordance with our different ranks and duties, and we have made them to the best of our ability. Please do not be angry with us; this is the prayer of us all, the Yellow and the Grey."

The reply of the Dalai Lama then begins thus:

"I was not identified in accordance with the previous custom of the golden urn. It was judged unnecessary, for from the prophecies and divinations it was clear that I was the true Incarnation. And so I was enthroned. In accordance with the old custom, a Regent was appointed for a time. This was the *Hutuktu;*[29] also the Head Lama of the Purchok Monastery, a learned and saintly man. I joined the monkhood. I became a novice. I read several books, for instance *The Great Centre,*[30] and numerous books on theological disputation, and the long succession of exoteric and esoteric discourses by the Lord Buddha with meanings as vast as the ocean. I was invested by my instructors with spiritual power.[31] I worked very hard every day without cessation, to the utmost of my powers, and thus attained a moderate amount of knowledge and ability.

"When I arrived at the age of eighteen, in accordance with the former custom, I had come to the time at which I should carry on the secular and the spiritual administration of the country. Though I had not hitherto exercised the religious or secular control, and though I was lacking in skill and resource, yet the whole of Tibet, both supreme beings and human beings, requested me to take up the power. The great Manchu Emperor, appointed by Heaven, gave me a similar order, which I placed on my head. I took up the spiritual and secular administration. From that time forward there was no leisure for me, no time for pleasure. Day and night I had to ponder anxiously over problems of Church and State, in order to decide how each might prosper best. I had to consider the welfare of the peasantry, how best to remove their sorrows; how to open the three doors of promptitude, impartiality, and the removal of injuries.

"In the Wood Dragon year[32] there arrived a great army of soldiers under the British Government. Had I considered my own comfort, I could have come to an amicable settlement with them. But if our country had thereby suffered afterwards, it would have been like the rubbing out of a footprint. Formerly, the Great Fifth Dalai Lama and the Manchu Emperor had made an agreement to help each other in the way that a monk and a layman help each other. So although it entailed hardship on me, I paid no attention to that, but went over northern Tibet, through China and Mongolia, to the great capital, Golden Peking. The Sovereigns, mother and son,[33] treated me well beyond measure. But shortly afterwards the mother and the son both died, one after the other.

"After this, the Emperor Shontong was enthroned, and to him I represented fully the facts of our case. Keeping the whole case of Tibet in my mind, I returned, but the Amban in Tibet representing matters falsely, Chinese officers and soldiers arrived in Lhasa, and seized the power over the administration of Tibet. Then I, the King, and with me my Ministers and other governmental officers, came to the holy land of India, paying no attention to the hardships of the journey. We arrived in good health, and through the British Government we represented matters fully to the Government of China.

"Religious services were held on behalf of the Faith and the secular side of State affairs. These ensured the full ripening of the evil deeds of the Chinese, and in consequence, internal commotion broke out in China, and the time was changed.[34] The Chinese troops in Tibet had none to help them; they became stagnant like a pond, and therefore, bit by bit, we were able to expel them from the country. As for myself, I came back to Tibet, the land that I have to protect, the field of religion. From that year, the year of the Water Bull,[35] to this present Water Monkey year, this land of Tibet has become completely happy and prosperous; it is like a land made new. All the people are at ease and happy.

"This is clearly evident from the records in the State archives. You all, supreme beings and human beings, are aware of these facts. I have written these matters briefly, for if I were to explain them in detail, a very long letter would be required. I have been very merciful in all things. Consider this and understand it, all ye people! Do not make your desires great. Make them small! Understand that what has been done is excellent! If the work that has been performed is of advantage to Tibet, harmonise your minds with it, and know that your desires have been fulfilled. I do not say that I have performed all this. I do not recount these matters in any hope that people will say that the Dalai Lama has done this work; of that my hope is less than a single seed of sesame.

"Having regard to my present age, it were better that I should lay down the ecclesiastical and temporal power, and devote the short remainder of this life to religious devotion. My future lives are many, and I would like to devote myself entirely to spiritual concerns. But by reason of the Guardian Deities inside my body and my Root Lama, people come to me to hear religion, they come to me to decide their disputes, and their hope lies deep in their hearts that I will not give up the secular administration.[36] So far I have done my work to the best of my ability, but I am nearly fifty-eight years old, when it will become difficult to carry on the ecclesiastical and secular work any longer. This is understood by all, is it not.[37]

"The Government of India is near to us and has a large army.

The Government of China also has a large army. We should therefore maintain firm friendship with these two; both are powerful.

"There are one or two small countries over there that show hostility towards us.[38] In order to prevail against them, you must enlist in the army young, vigorous men, and you must give military training of such a kind as will benefit afterwards.

"Besides, the present is the time of the Five Kinds of Degeneration[39] in all countries. In the worst class is the manner of working among the red people.[40] They do not allow search to be made for the new Incarnation of the Grand Lama of Urga. They have seized and taken away all the sacred objects from the monasteries. They have made monks to work as soldiers. They have broken religion, so that not even the name of it remains. Have you heard of all these things that have happened at Urga? And they are still continuing. It may happen that here in the centre of Tibet the Religion and the secular administration may be attacked both from the outside and from the inside.[41] Unless we can guard our own country, it will now happen that the Dalai and Panchen Lamas, the Father and the Son, the Holders of the Faith, the glorious Rebirths, will be broken down and left without a name. As regards the monasteries and the monks and nuns, their lands and other properties will be destroyed. The administrative customs of the Three Religious Kings[42] will be weakened. The officers of the State, ecclesiastical and secular, will find their lands seized and their other property confiscated, and they themselves made to serve their enemies, or wander about the country as beggars do. All beings will be sunk in great hardship and in overpowering fear; the days and the nights will drag on slowly in suffering.

"Do not be traitors to Church and State by working for another country against your own. Tibet is happy, and in comfort now; the matter rests in your own hands. All civil and military matters should be organised with knowledge; act in harmony with each other; do not pretend that you can do what you cannot do. The improvement of the secular administration depends on your ecclesiastical and secular officials. High officials, low officials, and peasants must all act in harmony to bring happiness to Tibet: one person alone cannot lift a heavy carpet; several must unite to do so.

"What is to be done and what to be omitted, consider that, and do all your work without harbouring doubt, in the manner desired by the Teacher,[43] who knows everything as though it lay before his eyes. Work in that spirit and all will turn out well. Those who work zealously like that on the religious and secular side in accordance with my will, not those who show obedience before my face, but plan evil behind my back, those I will take under my protection, both in this life and the next. All will see that the Protectors of the Religion help those who walk in The Way. Those who break away from law and custom and follow an evil road, these the Protectors will certainly punish. Those who regard only their own interests, who help only those who please them and do not help others, those who, as at present, are untrustworthy, and do not exert themselves to work well, the aims of these will not be fulfilled, and all will see it. Then these may say, 'What ought we to do now?' and many repent of their former actions, but there will be no advantage therefrom. You will all see that, as long as I live, Tibet will remain happy and prosperous, as indeed it is at present.

"Whatever troubles befall the people, I shall see, and I shall hold religious services for them in the future, as I have done in the past.

"Now, I have given you clear instructions. There is no need for me to continue it further. The most important need for the welfare of the inside[44] is that you should repent of your wrong actions in the past and ponder carefully and always on my instructions in the future.

"If you are able to do this, I for my part will carry on the religious and civil administration to the best of my ability, so that good may result both now and in the future. I will keep in my mind the names and the purposes of all you ecclesiastical and secular officials. As for all the subjects, I will arrange that for the space of several hundreds of years they shall remain happy and prosperous as at present, and be free from great suffering. Be all of one mind, and work with zeal to the best of your ability, as in the olden days. That in itself will constitute a religious service; there is no need for you to perform any other religious services.

"The above are my instructions in answer to your representations. It is of great importance that, day and night, in your four actions,[45] you should deliberate carefully on what I have written, and that without error you should reject what is evil, and follow what is good."

Such was the letter that the Dalai Lama wrote to his people, both supreme beings and human beings, and especially to those to whom he, "The Great Owner," had entrusted the ecclesiastical as well as the secular government.

Part Eight
Changing the Body

In November, 1933, the Dalai Lama summoned one of the Nepalese photographers-in Lhasa to take his photograph. This alarmed the people of Lhasa, who took it as a sign that he intended to die soon. Towards the end of November I arrived from England, at Kalimpong, hoping to go to Tibet the following May as soon as the passes over the mountain ranges were open. On December 19th my wife and daughter and I were having tea with David Macdonald and his family in the little hotel that his daughter, Mrs. Perry, was running there.

Suddenly the blow fell. A note from Tharchin was handed to Macdonald. It told him that Tharchin had heard a report that the Dalai Lama had gone to the Honourable Field, or in other words, had passed out of his thirteenth Incarnation.

A Chinese newspaper declared the story to be a hoax. The Dalai Lama, it said, was going towards eastern Tibet for the purpose of making war. But the Tibetan report was true; the Chinese statement was entirely devoid of foundation, as Chinese statements about Tibet often are.

I sent a telegram of condolence to the Prime Minister and another to the Cabinet. In their replies they said they were "holding services with religious offerings and prayers for a speedy Reincarnation." In their reply the Cabinet added, "Conducting all foreign and internal affairs as before." Prayers for a speedy Reincarnation were naturally of the first importance.

Now rumours began in Tibet as to the cause of the illness and its nature. The traders coming down from Tibet with their strings of mules carrying the yearly supply of wool, yak tails,

The fourteenth Dalai Lama in 1950, aged 15, on the throne of his predecessor.

skins and other products, brought their own stories with them.

It appeared that the Precious Protector had gone to the Field on the last day of the tenth Tibetan month, corresponding with the middle of December. The day of the week was Sunday. According to Tibetan ideas, if a man dies on a Sunday or a Tuesday, it is an evil omen. People say, "He died on a stormy day." The family may expect much sickness and other calamities.

As the Dalai Lama has no family, it seemed to many Tibetans that this passing away on a Sunday portended evil to the Government of Tibet, and through the Government to the whole country.

All reports agreed that the Precious Protector's illness had been short.

Among stories that were then being passed from mouth to mouth, the following might be related. At the end of February, 1934, Palhese, coming for his daily talk, asked me with suppressed eagerness, "Has Rai Bahadur Norbhu told you about recent happenings in Lhasa concerning the passing of the Precious Protector to the Field?"

"He has told me about the medium of the Nechung Oracle giving the Precious Protector medicine which injured him."

Says Palhese, "It is about the medicine that I wish to speak. It was given at the instigation of a tulku from Nyarong (a province in eastern Tibet), who has been reborn as a devil. It did indeed do injury; in fact, it made the Precious Protector an 'Is Not.'

"At the time when the Tengyeling Regent was ruling, this tulku held religious services to promote the interests of Tengyeling and destroy the Precious Sovereign. The tulku was arrested, put in prison, and given many severe floggings with the usual leather thongs on his bare skin, so that his flesh hung in strips after each flogging. But he was a Lama of great learning and ability, and he used to meditate on 'the void.'[46] So it was noticed that during each flogging, severe though it was, he uttered no exclamation of pain, not even the smallest sound. And what was still more remarkable, by the next day his flesh had entirely healed.

"At length, however, angry at this treatment, the Nyarong tulku asked the warder in charge of him for a small knife to cut a lump out of his boot. The warder gave it. When the lama went to pay a call of nature, he used the opportunity to cut his throat. The warder rushed up to seize him, so the lama jumped out of the window of his cell, which was two floors above the ground. The fall killed him.

"Passing from life thus, in anger at the treatment he had received, he reincarnated as a devil, and being of great learning and ability, as a powerful devil. So a high lama of eastern Tibet was engaged to catch the tulku's mind, put it in the ground, and build a *chöten* over it. This was done; the *chöten* was strongly built, and the necessary articles – religious books and the like – were placed inside it. But a day or two afterwards a great vertical crack was seen in the *chöten*. There had been no earthquake or thunderstorm, and it was clear that the devil was one of great power, and so the mind was able to crack the *chöten* and escape through it.

"Later on, it was noticed that the prophecies issuing through the prophet of the Nechung Oracle were wrong and harmful. At the time of the British military expedition to Lhasa in the Wood Dragon year, he gave out that the Tibetan Government should send soldiers against the British, but that the soldiers should not fire their rifles; this was what happened at Guru.[47] This and other evil counsels were not the true utterances of the Oracle, but were put into the mind of the prophet by this evil. And it was this devil who instigated the prophet to give this deadly medicine. There are in Tibet those who can see and recognise deities and devils, and these recognised the devil by their own methods, while the high lamas did so by their power of divination.

"That prophet had been dismissed after the British expedition, but two or three years ago the Precious Protector reinstated him, allowing the deity to come again inside him."

This is the only instance which I heard that a tulku had been reborn as a devil.

The Tibetan Government's biography maintains the Tibetan

Buddhist's faith that a Dalai Lama need not die, unless he wishes to do so. It refers to his prophecy in his political testament, "I am nearly fifty-eight years old, when it will become difficult to carry on the work any longer." It expatiates on the sinfulness of the people. "Our Dalai Lama tried his utmost to improve the religion. But the evil time showed its real colours. Most of the monks and laymen indulged in sinful actions without being compelled by anybody to do so; they avoided virtuous actions like grass of no value. So groups of evil fruits burst out one after another.

"The Inmost One told them, 'If you continue to regard brass as gold, a great accident will happen soon. You may feel regret, but it will be too late." In fact, he passed through death to make people repent of their sins.

Most of the reports in currency at this time said that the Dalai Lama had departed to the Field in anger, because Künpel La often thwarted his purposes. Some said that the Precious Protector wanted to bring back the Panchen Lama, and to restore to the latter the property and power that he used to possess; and that Künpel La had thwarted him in this also by contending that a question of that kind ought first to be referred to the Parliament. On being so referred, Künpel La – according to popular report – stirred up opposition in the Parliament, so that the latter gave an unfavourable reply, and the Dalai Lama seemed to "wipe his dirty hand on the Parliament's sleeve," as the Tibetan saying is. "This," I used to be told, "was one of the matters that greatly annoyed the Precious Protector and hastened his death."

Many people were also saying, "The Precious Protector would say to Künpel La, "Issue such and such orders; that will be best, don't you think?" And Künpel La would object and suggest another course. Weak in body and weary in mind, the Presence would say, "Have it your own way," but feel sore displeasure in his mind; though like a true Lama he would conceal his feelings. Also Künpel La would issue his own orders, saying that they were the Precious Protector's orders. The latter found him out and that, too, made him angry; the anger entered into him, but did not issue from his mouth. People therefore asserted that Künpel La was responsible for the Presence departing to the Field.

Said Palhese, "I do not think we shall know what the Precious Protector's illness was till we go to Tibet. The traders who come to Kalimpong have not much opportunity of learning the truth in such a matter."

And so it was. Some seven months after the Dalai Lama's passing, Harnett and I were staying in the large country house named Penjor Lhünpo, two miles outside Gyangtse. This house belonged to Palhese's cousin, the head of the family, and he invited me with my party to stay there as long and as often as I wished. The Penjor Lhünpo estate is one of several, large and small, which belong to the Palha family.

At this house Palhese brought to me the son of the steward of the Penjor Lhünpo estate, for the lad had been working in close contact with the Dalai Lama during the last two years of the latter's life, being an apprentice under the principal clerk. He was a quiet, intelligent young man. Among other duties he had to fetch books for the Inmost One, who would sometimes also call him up and dictate to him instructions, messages, etc., the young man writing the words in chalk on wooden tablets, the thin narrow boards that Tibetans use for this purpose. His living quarters were usually in the Clear Eye Palace, where these events happened.

The clerk's account of the last illness was as follows:

"On the 28th of the tenth Tibetan month (November-December) the Precious Protector worked as usual. He was a little unwell with a cough, but not at all severe. Before this date there appeared nothing wrong with the Presence except this slight cough. Apart from that he had no cold, no blowing of the nose.

"On the 29th, whereas he would usually write letters without stopping, he wrote none. First, he sat in his chair, and then lay down on his couch. I should mention that he spent most of each day and night in this room, working, eating and sleeping in it.

The room was about 22 by 16 feet and 8 feet high. He always drank two bowls of soup when he went to bed; on this day he drank nothing. And he passed no urine before retiring.

"Seeing him ill, Künpel La summoned us servants between ten and eleven o'clock that night, to rise from our beds and come at once to the vicinity of the Precious Protector's room. We lived in Clear Eye Palace, in which his room was. We came at once. The Precious Protector was then lying down in his room. We were sent to call the Chief Secretary, the Treasurer and Kezang, the tulku who comes to the Jewel Park Palace from time to time. We were sent to call them from the Jewel Park Palace to the Clear Eye Palace. They came and entered the Precious Protector's room.

"At about 11 p.m. the Precious Protector ordered the medium of the Oracle of Nechung, whom Künpel La had hastily summoned, to worship the goddess, named Palhajok, whose image is in the Temple in Lhasa. The medium had come at once in a great hurry; he had not even stopped to put on his robes before coming.

"The same night, between 1 and 2 a.m., the medium gave the Precious Protector some medicine in the form of a powder. When the medium came out, Champa La, the Presence's regular doctor, said to the medium, 'You have made a mistake in the medicine' (*Men di norra nangzha*). So soon after this the medium gave the Presence another powder in accordance with what Champa La prescribed. During all this time the Presence uttered no word.

"On the 30th the Precious Protector stayed the whole day in bed. He neither ate nor drank anything, and his tongue was very dry. In the evening, at half-past seven, he went to the Honourable Field.

"The second dose of medicine was given about one hour after the first. After both doses had been given, between 2 and 3 a.m. on this morning of the 30th, the *Tisur* came and asked the Presence not to retire to the Honourable Field.

"In Lhasa there is a widespread report that the Precious Protector departed to the Honourable Field in anger, because

Künpel La disobeyed his orders in several instances. In that there is no truth. Künpel La always carried out the Precious Protector's orders.

"The illness of the Presence was strong enough on the 29th to prevent him from writing letters, but he said at that time that he felt only a little indisposed. His illness appeared to be really serious from nine o'clock in the evening of the 29th, and he passed away the following evening at half-past seven."

When we were in Lhasa in 1921, Kennedy, from such reports as reached him, thought that the Dalai Lama's heart was weak. In 1934, Harnett, from what I told him, thought that the symptoms of the Dalai Lama's last illness perhaps indicated uraemia or pneumonia, aggravated by the giving of wrong medicine. In his advanced years and growing weakness he may well have caught a chill, going backwards and forwards at night between Clear Eye Palace and Jewel Park Palace. The season at this time was mid-December.

It would be equally true to say of this selfless ruler that he died of overwork in the service of his country. The overstrain of this was aggravated by his quick temper, checked more and more from bursting out as he grew older; but the strain was always there. And he had suffered those two hard periods of exile, hard for the body and hard for the mind.

59   Opinions on His Rule

Thus the Thirteenth Dalai Lama passed to the Honourable Field. Within a few months of his death he came to be called "The Great Thirteenth," equal to, if not greater than, him whom men had always called "The Great Fifth."

During his life Tibetan opinion was divided regarding his administration. The great Tashi Lhünpo Monastery, focusing the ideas of the Panchen Lama's party, was against him. So was that portion of the Tsang province which lies under its shadow, as well as the supporters of the Tengyeling Monastery, and the greater part of Drepung Monastery. A number of those living outside the boundaries of his secular rule, for instance in Bhutan and Sikkim, were glad to show their independence by criticism. This antagonism came from the educated classes; to the peasants he was above criticism, just the Precious Protector, the Inmost One.

In order to strengthen Tibet internally and externally he found it necessary to impose fresh taxation, and no country dislikes increased taxes more than Tibet does.

The commonest criticism was that he should have confined himself to the purity of the spiritual rule, and appointed a Regent to hold the dirty reins of the worldly government. Neither from Asiatic or European did I ever hear the smallest whisper against his moral character. Still, Kazi Dawa Samdrup, a learned Bhutanese, was one of several who expressed the opinion that by taking up the secular rule the Dalai Lama became more earthly, and when he went to the Honourable Field, would have to work hard to regain his previous spiritual position.

However, from Lhasa eastwards, comprising more than three-fourths of the Tibetan population, as well as a large proportion of the remainder, his secular rule was highly appreciated. They were grateful for his reduction of bribery and oppression, for his promptitude in the despatch of business, and the strength of his government. The Dalai Lama realised in large measure his own ideal, "to open the three doors of promptitude, impartiality, and the removal of injuries."

But the chief appreciation came after the Dalai Lama's death. It was strong and almost universal, and still continues several years later. Tibetans realise what he did for their fatherland.

Three or four years after the Dalai Lama's death, most of those who had privately thought him too stern, because he had degraded so many officials, were changing their minds. Now they were saying, "The Precious Protector's discipline over the officials made the subjects happy. The high officials are now not held in check; they try only to gain wealth for themselves."

The traders were saying, "We were far more free to trade when the Precious Protector was in life. Now the officials are trading themselves, and taking business from us. An Indian trader is trading in various parts of Tibet, where he has no permission to go, either by the treaties or otherwise, and injuring our trade."

The army was being neglected and was not paid regularly. The former trained officers left and untrained officers took their places.

The people were all praising the Precious Sovereign, saying, "He was a real Incarnation of Chenrezig. Now we have lost the Great Compassionate One. The glory of Tibet has disappeared. We are people of dry (bad) fortune. Shall we ever have another like him?" It is difficult to picture the depth of the sorrow into which they were plunged by his withdrawal, faced, as they were, by the dark period that must intervene before he returned to earth again. Old men and women wept at his tomb, crying, "Oh! Gem that grants every wish, come quickly and hold us under your protection."

Some may ask how the Dalai Lama's rule compared with that

of rulers in European or American countries. But such a comparison would not be fair, unless applied to the Europe of several hundred years ago, when it was still in the same stage of feudal development that Tibet is in at the present day. Certain it is that Tibetans would not be happy if they were governed as people are in England; and it is probable that they are on the whole happier than are people in Europe or America under their own governments. Great changes will come in time; but unless they come slowly, when the people are ready to assimilate them, they will cause great unhappiness. Meanwhile, the general administration in Tibet is more orderly than the administration in China; the Tibetan standard of living is higher than the standard in China or India; and the status of women in Tibet is higher than their status in either of those two large countries.

Was the Dalai Lama on the whole a good ruler? We may safely say that he was, on the spiritual as well as the secular side. As for the former, he had studied the complicated structure of Tibetan Buddhism with exceptional energy when a boy, and had become exceptionally learned in it. He improved the standard of the monks, made them keep up their studies, checked greed, laziness and bribery among them, and diminished their interference in politics. He took care of the innumerable religious buildings as far as possible. On the whole it must certainly be said that he increased the spirituality of Tibetan Buddhism.

On the secular side he improved law and order, increased his own contact with his people, introduced more merciful standards into the administration of justice and, as stated above, lessened monastic domination in secular affairs. In the hope of preventing Chinese invasions he built up an army in the face of opposition from the monasteries; prior to his rule there was practically no army at all. In view of the extreme stringency of Tibetan finance, the intense monastic opposition and other difficulties, he could have gone no farther than he did.

During his reign the Dalai Lama abolished Chinese domination entirely throughout the large part of Tibet governed by him, excluding Chinese officials and soldiers. That portion of Tibet became a completely independent kingdom, and remained independent during the last twenty years of his life.

60 The Return

After the Dalai Lama's departure to the Honourable Field, Künpel La exercised power for a brief period, but was then arrested and imprisoned. He was tried by the now powerful Parliament. The main charge against him was that he had failed to report the illness of the Precious Protector to the Cabinet, and would not let the Members of the Cabinet see His Holiness. His defence was that the Precious Protector had told him to act as he did.

But he had many enemies; his position as the Dalai Lama's chief favourite rendered that inevitable. He was found guilty; the wealth which he had amassed during his years of power was confiscated, and he himself was banished to a monastery in the province of Kongpo, about one week's journey to the east of Lhasa.

Then a surprising change occurred. Being endowed with a disposition of singular charm and other attractive qualities, he was so greatly liked by the monks that in the course of time they made him, their prisoner, the head of the monastery. This enabled him to escape through Bhutan to British India and settle at Kalimpong. Having now secured his personal safety, he applied to the Tibetan Government to permit him to return to Tibet and live in safety there, but this request was naturally refused. So he who had gained and lost between two and three hundred thousand rupees (£20,000), and had exercised extensive powers over Tibet, was reduced to working in Kalimpong as the manager of a warehouse where Tibetan wool was stored on its way to India.

After Künpel La's arrival in Kalimpong, Chinese officers tried to persuade him to come to China, saying that he would be paid a salary there. They desired to use him against Tibet as a discontented element; as the Chinese Government had done in the case of the Panchen Lama and the officers who accompanied the latter to China. Things were happening just as the Dalai Lama had predicted, when he had said that the Chinese would try to foment internal discord among the Tibetan people, in order to make it easier for China to dominate Tibet. But Künpel La stood firm against the temptation.

A few days after the Dalai Lama's death public mourning commenced. While this was in force, men and women abstained from wearing new clothes. Men took the long ear-ring out of the left ear, the ear-ring that denotes an official position. Women removed their ornaments, the head-dress, the charm box (*kau*) that is worn on the breast, and so on. Theatricals were forbidden, and dancing by either sex, and singing also even while working. Old clothes of any colour were permitted; there is no rule among Tibetans to wear black, as Westerners do, or white, as Chinese do.

The house-roofs in Lhasa are flat; everybody lighted a line of lamps on his roof. Of the chief lamas, the biography compiled by the Tibetan Government tells us, "We performed sacrificial ceremony before his precious body continually. We composed a poem asking him to reincarnate soon, and distributed it in the monasteries with perfect presentation."

The body was embalmed and treated at intervals with salt. Not only lamas and Government officials, but many members of the public came before it and offered sacrifices "with tears in their eyes and grief in their minds, and all cried out asking him to return very soon in his new Incarnation." So says the biography, which gives a long account of what happened at this time.

Mourning for deceased persons lasts ordinarily for seven weeks. In the Dalai Lama's case the period of public mourning was reduced to three weeks, and that for a curious reason. This quick termination of the mourning was an omen in favour of the new Incarnation coming quickly.

In a letter to me the Panchen Lama wrote:

"The passing of the Dalai Lama has caused great grief to all beings, and especially to me whose sole place of trust he was. He was my holy Lama, his knowledge and capacity were beyond my power of description, but now he has gone. I am making offerings in the monasteries of China and Mongolia that the new Incarnation may come quickly with the face of the white moon. For this reason I have sent my monk officer of the fourth rank, Serkang, and a lay official, to make offerings of butter-lamps on the altars of monasteries, and gifts of tea to the monks.

"In addition, I have given these, my officers, detailed instructions as to all the matters that they should represent to you. Please confer benefit on our Church and State by discussing matters frankly and intimately with them. Please help on the spirit of harmony and love in all countries, not forgetting the manner in which you worked before.

"I hope to return to Tibet at no distant date. When I do, I want to meet you again face to face, and not merely thus in letters."

The more I heard about the relations between the two Grand Lamas the more convinced I was that, though there was a measure of suspicion between them, it was far more intense between their respective groups of followers.

Chinese officials, under a high-ranking chief, General Huang Musung, came to Lhasa to attend the funeral ceremonies. Having thus gained a foothold in Lhasa, they endeavoured to bring Tibet under Chinese rule. I was on a private visit to Tibet while their mission – for such it was – was still there. The Tibetan Government kept writing me to advise them. They did not tell me how things stood, but just asked in a general way for advice. I tendered certain advice, and soon afterwards Huang Musung and his chief assistants left with their purpose unfulfilled. The Tibetan Parliament took a firm stand against the Chinese mission. The sequel came next year, when I was in Peiping and visited Inner Mongolia. Prince De Wang, the leading Chief in Inner Mongolia, informed me with a hearty laugh that Huang Musung had written to them that I was a very dangerous man, and they should have nothing to do with me. De Wang, too, and other leading Mongols wanted me to advise them on their affairs. But I could not agree to that, as the Chinese Government had allowed me to cross the strip of China between Peiping and Mongolia only on condition that I would not give advice. When I informed De Wang of this, he and the Mongols with him laughed again.

Two months after the Dalai Lama's death the Parliament appointed the Head Lama of Reting Monastery to be the Regent of Tibet. The latter was only twenty-three years old, but the Dalai Lama had asked him to take the post, and so the Parliament chose him.

"Then," says the Tibetan biography, referring to the late Dalai Lama, "an important meeting was held by lamas and officers to confer about the construction of his monument, as this great Thirteenth Dalai Lama resembled the Fifth and the Seventh Dalai Lama in action and fame. Especially he did great work for the public, and improved the administration, which fared so well under him."

It is the custom for each Dalai Lama to collect the materials for his own tomb. The Thirteenth having lived longer than nearly all the others, and having ruled longer than any, had made a great accumulation. The Tibetan biography says:

"His present treasure-house was full of gold, silver, silk and jewels that seemed inexhaustible and like a treasure of Heaven. Also there was a large collection of subscriptions raised from the public. So all the officers agreed unanimously to build his monument with gold, and of the same size as that of the Fifth Dalai Lama. Then the construction work began and was in progress with untiring exertion, and not long afterwards the monument was completed. It was a cubit higher than that of the Fifth Dalai Lama, and covered with precious stones and various decorations."

On the summit of the Potala are golden pagoda-like shrines covering the tombs wherein are embalmed the mortal remains of former Dalai Lamas. The late Dalai Lama's tomb is on the northern face (i.e. furthest from the main road). Mr. Spencer

Chapman, who was in Lhasa in 1937, tells us,[48] "The framework is of solid silver; it is covered with exquisitely worked gold leaf, embellished with gifts of onyx snuff-boxes, strings of amber and pearls, turquoise head ornaments and charm-boxes, pieces of lapis lazuli, amethyst, coral and other semi-precious stones. Around the foot of the shrine are shelves whereon are displayed more precious presents: gifts from the rich monasteries of Mongolia and China, and from the ancient and noble families of Lhasa. Here are chalice-like golden vessels, heavy silver bowls and butter-lamps, marvellous examples of cloisonné, rare porcelains and vases, meticulously wrought metal work, and curiously fashioned china plants in glass cases. Against one wall are images of different Buddhas, and holy books set in carved alcoves, and in front of the tomb are immense silver butter-lamps always burning to the memory of the saintly ruler."

The Dalai Lama's pet animals were kept in the Jewel Park just as he had left them; stags, pheasants, bar-headed geese, Brahmany ducks, the fierce black Tibetan mastiffs, and so on. All seemed to be awaiting the Great Owner's return. In the Jewel Park Palace the rooms were kept clean; his religious implements, prayer-wheel, bell and vajra, stood ready on the little table; his teacup, too, and a bowl of fruit, as though he might come back at any moment.

Tibet felt as though orphaned. One of the glorious Rebirths had gone to the Field; the other was absent far away in China. On the worldly side she was sadly weakened by the passing of the Precious Sovereign, for who else could hold the Land of Snow against foreign aggression and internal commotion?

Tibetans are fervent in prayer, for they believe whole-heartedly in its efficacy. Nine months after the Dalai Lama's death, I was on a private visit to the monastery named "Beyond Imagination" (Samye), the first large monastery to be built in Tibet. Dewan Bahadur Palhese was with me. The Chief Prophet of Samye – Tibetans call him the Abbot Prophet – was in charge of the monastery and was one of the few whose duty it is, by prophecy and otherwise, to help in discovering the new Reincarnation.

He was showing Palhese and myself round the main temple, which houses the great statue of the Buddha. Notices, written on paper, were affixed to the pillars inside the temple and to the statue asking all to pray for a speedy Reincarnation. The Abbot Prophet took Palhese and myself up to the high altar, where we stood talking about the late Dalai Lama. The Abbot Prophet made three prostrations before the altar, and Palhese, in sorrowful remembrance of the time that was past, followed his example.

Whispering to me, "Dewan is in tears," the Abbot Prophet went to a stand at the side of the altar and picked up a small jar of holy water. He took some himself, and poured some into my hands. Then he drew me behind the high altar and up a short wooden ladder leading to a small platform between the altar and the great Buddha. We stood alone together in this holy of holies, almost touching the knees of the image towering above us. He stood praying silently for two or three minutes, with his hands raised, palm to palm, in front of his forehead. Then he turned to me and said, "Will you also pray in accordance with the custom of your religion?" So for the welfare of Tibet we prayed; he in his religion, I in mine. Meanwhile the monks, who were going round with us, stood below with bowed heads, silent, motionless.

On the following day I visited the main temple a second time. On account of its age it differs greatly from the ordinary Tibetan temple, and there is consequently much to see in it. The Abbot Prophet, hearing I was there, came from his house and conducted me again to the holy of holies, and we prayed as before. There could be no real happiness till the Dalai Lama came back. In the interval, lamas and people prayed for his return.

The search for the new Incarnation continued always. In the summer of 1935 the Regent visited "The Victorious Wheel of Religion," that prophetic lake where the Dalai Lama's soul resides. In it he saw the letters *Ah Ka Ma*. Most people took *Ah* as referring to the Tibetan province of Amdo in north-eastern Tibet, near the Koko Nor Lake and the border of China. This is the province in which was born the great Reformer, Tsongkapa, the founder of the Yellow Hat sect. As to the meaning of *Ka* and *Ma*, there was no settled opinion. The Regent saw also a three-storied monastery with a gilded roof and turquoise tiles; a twisting road which led east of the monastery to a bare hillock, and opposite the hillock a small house with eaves of an unfamiliar type.

There were other signs that the Rebirth would take place in the north-east. The Tibetan biography tells us that when the Dalai Lama's body was embalmed, "The face was turned towards the south. The people kept coming to pay their homage. One day when we opened the box to put in fresh salt, we found the precious body with the face turned towards the north-east. We were astonished, and we and all the attendants who were there are eye-witnesses of this. And we saw many rainbows and clouds going towards the north-east. This must be a sign that the coming Incarnation will be born in the same direction."

The other search-parties having been unsuccessful, three more were despatched, one to the north-east, one to the east and one to the south-east.

I was fortunate enough to receive from Sir Basil Gould, who was at the time in Lhasa and elsewhere in central Tibet, his account of the expedition to the north-east. To this expedition the Chief Prophet of Samye, when in a trance, gave his breastplate. The party took with it also articles that had belonged to the late Dalai Lama, and exact copies of these articles.

When the party arrived at Jyekundo in eastern Tibet, one of the many districts annexed by the Chinese during their invasion, they met the Panchen Lama, who gave the names of three young boys, one of whom might well be the new Incarnation. Pursuing their way, they found the first of these was dead, and the second, when shown the articles belonging to the late Dalai Lama, ran away crying.

On approaching the house of the third, Kyitsang, the tulku in charge of the party, found that the scenery coincided with the description which the Regent had given of his vision in the lake. He made one of his subordinates, an ecclesiastical official, named Lobsang, take the rôle of head of the party, while he disguised himself as a servant. With Lobsang's monk-servant he entered the ante-room which served as a kitchen. Here he found the small boy playing. The boy went to Kyitsang at once and said, "Lama, Lama." With the party was a monk of Amdo, who had learnt the Lhasan dialect of the Tibetan language, for the people of Amdo do not understand the dialect of Lhasa. "Who is this?" said the interpreter monk, pointing to the ecclesiastical official. The boy replied, "Tsetrung," the general Tibetan word for such an official. Being questioned further, the boy mentioned the monastery from which Lobsang's monk-servant came.

A few days later he was shown the articles. In each case, so it was claimed, he chose the right one. He picked up the wrong walking-stick at first, examined it, shook his head, and dropped it. Then he picked up the right one, and would not let it go. On his body were found three of the physical marks that are seen on Incarnations of Chenrezig.

Kyitsang was sure that he was the young Dalai Lama, and reported accordingly to the Tibetan Government in Lhasa. About mid-summer of 1938 the latter replied instructing him to bring the boy to Lhasa for further test. The Tibetan Government were sure that he was the Dalai Lama, but they knew that if they declared him to be the Dalai Lama, the Chinese Government would insist on sending a large body of Chinese troops with him as an escort. The troops would come to Lhasa and refuse to go back.

But Kyitsang found it extremely difficult to carry out his Government's order. The Chinese Governor said he would not permit the little boy to depart unless he were declared to be the Dalai Lama. This demand was withdrawn in return for a payment of a hundred thousand Chinese dollars (£7,500), which Kyitsang managed to raise. On the arrival of the party at Künbum, the large monastery there refused to let the boy go on, unless he were immediately declared to be the Dalai Lama. The Governor also put in a demand for a further instalment of blackmail, this time amounting to three hundred and thirty thousand dollars (£25,000). The Governor explained that one hundred thousand of this new demand was for his Government officials, a similar amount for the local commander in chief, the same amount also for the Künbum Monastery, twenty thousand for the escort he would send, and ten thousand for himself.

These sums were far beyond any means at Kyitsang's disposal. But after negotiations lasting a full year, he was able to arrange for a further payment of three hundred thousand dollars through a party of rich Mahomedan merchants, who were going to Lhasa and India, and would provide the escort. They were to be repaid by the Tibetan Government at an advantageous rate of exchange in Lhasa or India.

The Chinese Government at headquarters contributed fifty-five thousand dollars for the search and the journey back, so that the blackmail may be said to have been reduced by that comparatively small amount. And the Chinese could hardly pretend any more that a large escort of Chinese soldiers was necessary. Twenty men only were sent. The Mahomedans in that part of China are virile people; this band of them would have little to fear from brigands.

After these protracted delays, the party started on the long journey back to Lhasa. When the Tibetan Government heard that they were inside the portion of Tibet under their administration, a meeting was held at the Potala and the boy was declared the true Incarnation. In September, 1939, the party reached the vicinity of Nagchuka, ten days' journey short of Lhasa, where they were met by one of the members of the Cabinet with a number of officials, and the sedan-chair of the Dalai Lama. Here the young boy was conducted to a temporary throne in an elaborate camp. The Cabinet Minister prostrated himself three times before him, and handed him a letter from the Regent, acknowledging him as the Dalai Lama. The Tibetan Government had kept their secret successfully.

The new Incarnation was born in June, 1935, one and a half years after the thirteenth had gone to the Field. His parents were Tibetan, not Chinese; his name was Lhamo Dondrup. In the Temple in Lhasa he was ordained a monk, and received a name meaning "The Holy One, The Gentle Glory, Powerful in Speech, Pure in Mind, of Divine Wisdom, Holding the Faith, Ocean-Wide."

At the Tibetan New Year, in February; 1940, the enthronement ceremony took place in the Potala. The Tibetan Government allowed a Chinese envoy, Mr. Wu Chunghsin, to come to
Lhasa for the ceremony, and the British Representative was also
admitted. The report was issued in the Chinese Press that Mr.
Wu had escorted the Dalai Lama to his throne and announced
his installation, that the Dalai Lama had returned thanks, and
prostrated himself in token of his gratitude. Every one of these
Chinese claims was false. Mr. Wu was merely a passive specta-
tor. He did no more than present a ceremonial scarf, as was done
by others, including the British Representative. But the Chinese
have the ear of the world, and can later refer to their Press
records and present an account of historical events that is wholly
untrue. Tibet has no newspapers, either in English or Tibetan,
and has therefore no means of exposing these falsehoods.

Everyone noticed the quiet dignity of the young Dalai Lama,
now four and a half years old. While taking great interest in the
enthronement ceremony, he never fidgeted, and seemed always
to do the right thing in a perfectly natural manner.

The enthronement ceremony was repeated several times. All
recognised the young boy as the genuine Reincarnation.
Throughout Tibet there was rejoicing. That feeling of orphan-
hood was removed. The Great Thirteenth had come back to his
own.

Notes

1. The accent is on the first a. The name is from Sanskrit, and means "The Abode of Snow."
2. The people call themselves "Gorkhali," but the spelling "Gurkha" is so well known that it seems best to retain it.
3. The title Lönchen means "Great Minister" and was the title of the Prime Minister of Tibet. It was in effect no compliment to me; I had arranged it myself. It is important for a country dealing with Tibet that its diplomatic representative should hold a good rank; during the first diplomatic meetings between British and Tibetans there had been too many instances in which British officers of high rank had met in solemn conclave with Tibetan or Chinese officials of low position and devoid of power. Accordingly I placed myself on an equality with Tibet's Prime Ministers, of whom there were then three, but shortly afterwards only one. As I had come to be on very friendly terms, the Tibetan Government granted this readily. It was better for my country and myself; and for my successors, who of course inherited the title.
4. See 'Hinduism and Buddhism' by Sir Charles Eliot, vol. iii, pp. 347-371 (London, Edward Arnold, 1921).
5. See 'The Dalai Lamas of Lhasa,' pp. 8 and 9 by W.W. Rockhill, formerly American Minister to China (Oriental Printing Offices, late E.J. Brill, Leyden, 1910).
6. 'The Dalai Lamas of Lhasa' by W.W. Rockhill, p. 34. Reprinted from the T'oung Pao, Series III, vol. i, no. 1.
7. For a fuller description of these missionaries see my 'Religion of Tibet' (Oxford University Press, 1931).

8. For a fuller account of this expedition see my 'Tibet Past and Present' (Oxford University Press, 1924), pp. 59-72.

9. In Chapter Six.

10. The treaty of 1890 recognized Sikkim as a British Protectorate and defined its boundary with Tibet. By the treaty of 1906 Great Britain recognized Tibet as a part of the Chinese Empire, and made the various arrangements with China about Tibet independently of Tibet herself. China recognized the Lhasa treaty of 1904.

11. 'Tents in Mongolia' by Haslund (Kegan Paul, 1934).

12. For my suggestions regarding British policy towards Tibet see my 'Tibet Past and Present' (Oxford University Press, 1924), pp. 190-195.

13. For a fuller description of Tibetan tea, see my 'People of Tibet' (Oxford University Press, 1920), pp. 235-240.

14. Tibetan nobles and officials are graded in seven different ranks.

15. 'Hinduism and Buddhism,' vol. i, p. 22, by Eliot (Arnold 1921).

16. The meaning of the name "Lhasa."

17. The Image of Buddha in the Great Temple at Lhasa, the one brought there by a Princess from China.

18. Oxford University Press, 1924.

19. Gyal rab Säl we me long p. 128. These Tibetan books are mostly printed from thick wooden blocks, with the Tibetan letters incised on them in reverse. I sent the Dalai Lama the titles of a large number of books which seemed to me of particular interest, and he had fresh copies specially printed for me, all beautifully clear, no smudging. This 'Clear Mirror of the Line of Kings' was among them.

20. Peking was named Peiping in 1928.

21. Tibetan Government's biography of the Thirteenth Dalai Lama, vol. ii, p. 305.

22. For a fuller account of the relations between Tibet and Mongolia, see my 'Tibet Past and Present,' pp. 224-230.

23. For a fuller account of the relations between Tibet and Nepal see 'Tibet Past and Present,' pp. 231-243.

24. For a fuller account of relations between Russia and Tibet, see 'Tibet Past and Present,' pp. 222, 223.
25. For a fuller account of relations between Japan and Tibet, see 'Tibet Past and Present,' pp. 220-222.
26. Published by Chatto & Windus, London, 1938.
27. For a fuller account of the relations between China and Tibet, see 'Tibet Past and Present,' pp. 208-219.
28. February 1932 to February 1933.
29. A Hutuktu is a very high Lama; there are only a few of them.
30. A book on Metaphysics, in five volumes.
31. They placed images, holy books, etc. on the Dalai Lama's head, for even a Dalai Lama cannot give power until he first empowered himself.
32. 1904.
33. The Dowager Empress and the Manchu Emperor.
34. The Chinese Revolution broke out and the Emperor was dethroned.
35. 1913.
36. The Dalai Lama was the Ruler of Tibet. Therefore, as is the Tibetan custom, he first explained the events of his life, his different actions and his reasons for them, before explaining what course should be followed in the future.
37. Tibetans regard this as a prophecy, for the Dalai Lama died when fifty-eight years old (Tibetan reckoning).
38. This refers mainly to Nepal, and in a lesser degree to Bhutan, for occasionally there was a disagreement with her also. In such cases it is not the Tibetan custom to mention names, but an indication of this kind is given.
39. War calamities of nature, shortening of the period of a human life, etc.
40. The U.S.S.R.
41. As actually happened after the Dalai Lama's death, when Lungshar and his band tried to seize the Regent and Ministers.
42. Srong. tsen gam. po (Straight Strong Deep), Tri. song. de. tsen and Ralpachan, who reigned during the period A.D. 600-900.

43. Padma Sambhava.
44. Tibet.
45. Walking, standing, sitting, sleeping.
46. A highly complicated system of metaphysics.
47. The place, about twenty-eight miles beyond Pari, where fighting first broke out between the Indian and Tibetan troops.
48. 'Royal Geographical Journal' for June 1938, pp. 500-501.

Index

Publisher's Acknowledgement

The publishers wish to thank the late Mr. Ted Bilger of Queensland, Australia, and the Tibetan and Hindu Dharma Trust that he established for their kind help in financing the production of this book.